D0206569

Map
of
Metropolitan
Montreal

N

Des-Mile-Iles River

Mirabel
International
Airport

Ile
Bizard

Roxboro

St-

Dollard-des-Or

Pierrefonds

Kirkland

Beaconsfield

Ste-Anne
de-Bellevue

Vaudreuil

Dorion

Ile
Perrot

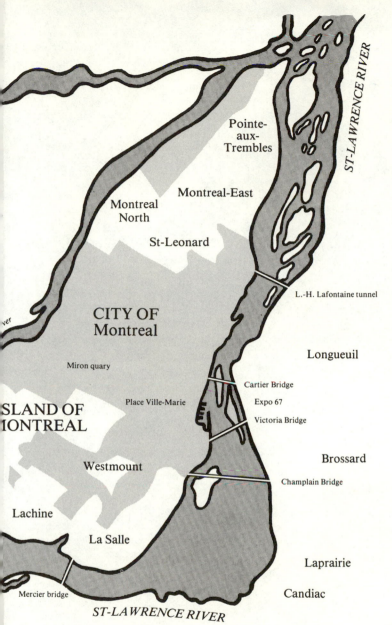

Pointe-
aux-
Trembles

Montreal-East

Montreal
North

St-Leonard

**CITY OF
Montreal**

Miron quary

Place Ville-Marie

**SLAND OF
1ONTREAL**

Westmount

Lachine

La Salle

Mercier bridge

ST-LAWRENCE RIVER

uguay

SOUTH SHORE

ST-LAWRENCE RIVER

L.-H. Lafontaine tunnel

Longueuil

Cartier Bridge

Expo 67

Victoria Bridge

Brossard

Champlain Bridge

Laprairie

Candiac

Chambly

Delson

ver

City for Sale

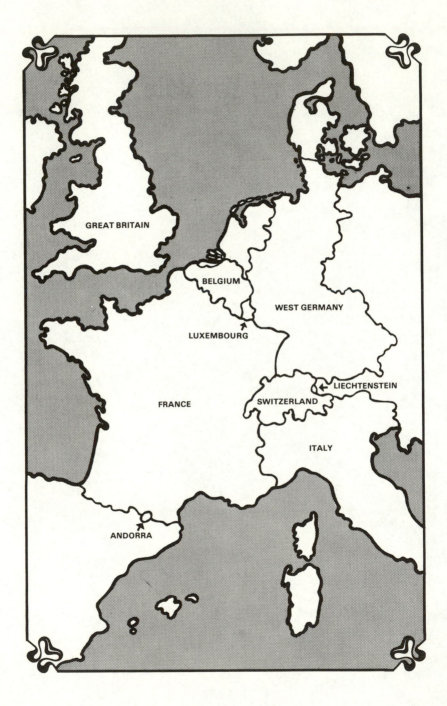

Henry Aubin

City for Sale

éditions l'ÉTINCELLE,
Montréal,
in association with
James Lorimer & Company, Publishers
Toronto

Éditions l'Étincelle:
Louise Cardinal, Robert Davies, Suzanne Ethier, Madeleine Hébert,
Danielle Lareau, Ginette Loranger, Marlyse Piccand, Marie-Noël Pichelin

---

This book is co-published with James Lorimer & Company, Publishers, Toronto

The French version of this book entitled: **Les Vrais propriétaires de Montréal**
was published in 1977 by Éditions l'Étincelle. The same book was released
in Europe under the title: **La Nouvelle Conquête de l'Amérique.**

Distributed by:
In Quebec:
Messageries Prologue
1651 rue Saint-Denis
Montréal, Québec

In the rest of Canada:
James Lorimer & Company, Publishers
Egerton Ryerson Memorial Building
35 Britain Street
Toronto, Ontario

To
Robert Arnold Aubin
1900-1976

Contents

Introduction   *11*

Chapter 1
The Liechtenstein Pipeline   21

Chapter 2
«La Fuga»   43

Chapter 3
A Cluster of Giants   63

Chapter 4
A Colonial Heritage   101

Chapter 5
The House of Rothschild   129

Chapter 6
«Das Mekka»   157

Chapter 7
Canada: The Surrogate Congo   179

Chapter 8
The Agnellis:
Laying the Groundwork for Transformation   223

Chapter 9
French Building Blocks   239

Chapter 10
Whisky à Gogo:
Bronfman Development   263

Chapter 11
The Vatican Realm   291

Chapter 12
Yankee Peril   313

Chapter 13
The South Shore's Suburban Jungle   323

Chapter 14
The Vested Interests in Energy Waste   345

Chapter 15
Bonds:
Europe expands its hegemony   369

Chapter 16
Conclusion   383

Index   391

Introduction

ONE AFTERNOON IN LATE 1974 the city editor at the Montreal Gazette, where I was a reporter, called me into his office. We were supposed to discuss upcoming investigative work. He looked up at me as I walked in and said, "Well, what would you like to do?"

It was the question which almost every reporter dreams of being asked someday. The ultimate ticket. No other assignments, no drudgery of writing stories about subjects thought up by others. Simply the freedom to pursue your own interests.

"I don't know," I said.

He burst out laughing. "I'm surprised at you," he said.

So was I. But now that the question had actually been asked, it was worth mulling over. The city editor, Jim Peters, was presenting me with an opportunity to choose almost any subject for investigation. What would interest readers most?

"How about the oil industry?" Peters suggested. It was true, everyone was talking about the energy cartel and rising prices. As a corporate investigative reporter, I knew enough about the industry to know it would take a lot of time, probably too much time, to trace its inner-workings. After all, seven of the world's ten largest industrial corporations, according to the latest ratings of Fortune magazine, are oil companies, and they aren't famous for letting people poke through their filing cabinets. Besides, I'd just finished an 11-week probe of another industry and shuddered at the thought of another long period of research. Other reporters in the office, saddled with routine daily articles, look at you cross-eyed because they think you're not pulling your oar, or so you imagine. Your wife and kids look at you like a stranger because you're never home.

"Everyone's looking at the oil industry," I said, seizing on that as an excuse. "We could find some new stuff on it but the public is already pretty familiar with the overall problems."

What, I asked myself, affected Montrealers the most? After a day, the answer appeared ridiculously self-evident: Montreal itself, the whole urban environment we move in and the forces behind its transformation.

Montreal is, after all, a city, which has gone through sweeping, almost revolutionary change since the early 1960s.

Within the last 15 or 20 years it has emerged from being a graceful, slow-paced hub of the Canadian economy to a slick boomtown for the branch offices of multinational corporations and a prime consumer of the way of life they offer. It had been known for its distinctive buoyancy and elegant simplicity — a character which found expression in its celebrated graystone architecture, plain and fancy at the same time. It still was one of the most remarkably original and vibrant cities of the world, with two cultures living side by side in the heart of an otherwise largely linguistically monotonous continent; as the tourist brochures always repeated, the French-speaking world's second largest city after Paris. And yet, not two decades later, it had gained the anonymous, "this-could-be-anywhere" stamp of development. As with so many other cities around North America and in the industrialized world as a whole, entire neighborhoods had been levelled by the wrecker's ball to make room for a *déjà vu* landscape of highways, parking lots and the "glass box" or "concrete slab" form of high-rise.

Montreal had changed from a city that most people around the world had barely heard of to a budding cosmopolis. Indeed, its mayor, fresh on the heels of the city's successes with the Expo '67 world's fair and the 1976 summer Olympic Games, had gone so far as to predict it would become "the number one city of the world." And super-developer (Place Ville Marie) William Zeckendorf Sr., of New York, hailed it shortly before his death in 1976 as the potential "Rome of the 21st century," standing at the gateway of a vast resource-rich land in a resource-poor world.

Today, the Montreal area population is 2.8 million. Montreal is one of the ten most populous metropoli in North America — bigger, for example, than Boston, St. Louis, Baltimore, or Cleveland.

Who is mostly behind the massive transformation of Montreal? Who makes the key decisions? Whom, really, is City Hall servicing? Mayor Jean Drapeau, while he may appear a master of "la politique de grandeur" to many Montrealers, is, from a global perspective, but an engaging little catalyst making business for his city, an usher rolling out the long red carpet. The question was for whom is he rolling it out?

I didn't know, aside from a few of the more obvious examples. For that matter, none of the other reporters who covered the city knew either. None of the urban affairs specialists at the universities knew. And, as I later discovered, virtually none of the businessmen — even those few who would talk — knew anything outside of their own little corner of activity. As a member at one of urban Canada's main architectural firms —the designer of many of the largest and most controversial skyscrapers — once remarked at a party, "Hell, I don't know who I work for, who's behind those buildings we design — I mean, who ultimately owns the company that may be our client. It doesn't occur to you to ask. If you got curious about that kind of thing you wouldn't get many clients. It's none of your business. You just do what they want."

In other words, practically everyone is in the dark. This state of affairs, of course, holds true not only for Montreal but for most other major cities in the industrialized world. I often run into people who *think* they know who owns their cities — but after a few names they run out of ideas, and they generally can give only a sketchy description of the activities of those whose names they do know.

Not long ago a poignant article appeared in North America's most astute media review, the Columbia Journalism Review.[1] Written by an ex-reporter named Jane Holtz Kay, it criticized the mass media for consistently overlooking the obvious. Her comments were aimed at a U.S. rather than Canadian audience, but they are relevant to anyone living in "manhattanized" Montreal or any other modern city:

> "It is ironic, even Kafka-esque, that journalists — boxed in by four walls, floor, and ceiling of the environment, as all humankind is boxed — deal so poorly with the subject of urban design and personal space ... Yet even in this hour of urban and environmental awareness, the press dallies with design as a luxury, an art, perhaps a hobby for "Leisure and Culture," not as the mold for our lives as it is ..."

"Why do we need so many cars — we now have 90 million-plus of them — except to reach the housing sprawl built since World War II? Would our drinking water be as polluted as it is if tract housing had not been haphazardly constructed around our sources of water?... Newspapers give us the events after the fact — revolts and pollution, or the loss of farm land or rising energy costs — but they seem less interested in a basic cause: the way we handle the built world."

"We have no figures to tell us how the urbanite reacts to the adamant geometry of the glass box or how the bleakness of our Main Streets, studded now with parking lots, hits small-town and rural folk. Who can doubt, though, that our architecture of the slick, boring high-rise, the empty plaza, the desolate shopping mall in the suburbs — all those structures that forbid human congress — contributes to the poverty of public life?"

These were things I had in mind when I finally went back to the city editor and proposed we track down the identity of the shapers of our city. No one anywhere had ever done quite the same kind of urban probe, though I was later to come across several precursor studies which had evolved along somewhat different lines.*

"How long will all this take?" the city editor asked.

"Oh," I said, having selected the subject with an eye to its anticipated brevity, "two months, maybe three."

Well, for a short and sweet study I should have stuck with the oil industry. There's already enough written on it to put one quickly on the track. The "two or three" month look at the forces behind Montreal's transformation turned into what may well be one of the longest projects ever undertaken by any newspaper anywhere, a most unwelcome distinction: it took over a year and a half.

---

* One of the best is Donald Gutstein's *Vancouver Ltd.,* published in 1975 and already a landmark work in fact-filled advocacy urban writing. It explores the power structure behind Vancouver's development (James Lorimer & Co., Toronto). Another advocacy analysis, *Politics of Land,* was produced in 1973 by a Ralph Nader study group headed by Robert Ç. Fellmeth; it examines California on a statewide basis, treating rural and urban land alike (Grossman Publishers, New York). Both books start with a look at ownership, then move on to analysis of the politics and mechanics of development and the role of the citizen's groups. The only remotely comparable probe I've seen in newspapers was in the London Evening News of Oct. 3, 1972. It was a feisty but sketchy *tour d'horizon* entitled, "So who own London?" by Keith Blogg and Paul Smith.

So before going any further let me thank the Montreal Gazette, a division of Canada's largest communications company, Southam Press Ltd., for its tolerance in underwriting the study and then in publishing a large part of it. Research included visits to six countries, interviews with more than 400 persons and hundreds of hours' study of municipal property records and also provincial and federal corporate registration reports. The findings first ran as an unusually long series of articles between Dec. 4 and 20, 1976. Thanks to a company (temporarily) on the opposite end of the scale, Editions l'Etincelle, this book is a much expanded, updated outgrowth of that series.

Ironically, though I turned my back on the oil industry before starting, that's exactly what I ended up exploring – like a round-the-world traveller who leaves by his front door but returns by the back door. The intimate relationship between energy interests and urban development interests, stumbled across towards the end of the research, is the subject of Chapter 14.

I had expected to write about a very different collection of people than those I eventually found. I had naively assumed that indigenous interests – wealthy Montrealers – basically owned the city, with foreigners through their investments being on the periphery of power. The planned thrust of the study was to document what these local VIPs owned and then to profile them. Also, I thought it would be enough to limit the probe to property ownership.

To begin to understand the true influence of those who are molding the city, however, it was necessary to go well beyond the ownership of real estate *per se*. This book looks at such other pieces of the urban puzzle as ownership of major development companies, public works contractors, building supply manufacturers and moneylending institutions. It is the interrelationships between these and other sectors which produce power. And most of this power turned out to be held from afar, not locally.

This, then, is a story about the private forces behind the urban transformation of Montreal. Unique though the situation may be in this social and business capital of French Canada, the story is really about many, perhaps most, cities in the West. Many of the interests active in levelling neighborhoods and building forests of high-rises in Montreal are, as will be shown, the same interests active in scores of other major cities — whether it be Calgary, New York, Los Angeles, Atlanta, Paris, Brussels, Rome, Casablanca, Melbourne or Johannesburg. They include the biggest interests in the world, bigger even than the oil companies, which in many cases they own.

This book does not, I should note, set out to establish all the intricate interactions between this world of private enterprise and that of government, a subject which would deserve a book in itself. Nor does it seek to explore the innumerable second- and third-tier domestic interests contributing to Montreal's development; it is concerned primarily with those *dominant* forces which set the direction and tone for development here.

Which particular corporation owned by which particular holding company controlled by which particular tycoon ultimately owns the high-rise on your block, is unimportant in the long run. In the fast-moving world of real estate, the details could change next week. What is important is the patterns which emerge.

This story, if you will, is also a partial X-ray of how power over a city works. It is a case history of what goes on beyond the parochial world of City Hall which helps cause so much of what sociologists and psychologists call "urban alienation."

In Montreal's case, the bulk of the influence over urban growth happens to come from outside French Canada, even outside Canada. Much of what the local radicals call with awe the "local power structure" is, in fact, little more than a collection of local yokels acting as agents and intermediaries for these much larger global interests.

Peter C. Newman described it tersely: "The most influential men in most Canadian cities and towns no longer belong to local power clusters. Instead, they are the smooth ambassadors of large multinational or transnational corporations. Careers are made in companies, not communities. The equations of power are changing."[2]

Montreal's combination of local passivity and foreign strength finds counterparts — in varying ratios — throughout urban Canada. Donald Gutstein in his 1975 book *Vancouver Ltd.*

says of the situation on the other side of the country: "Foreigners are reluctant to reveal their interests, for if the extent to which British Columbia is already foreign-owned was made public, there would be a massive outcry and pressure for restrictive legislation. This action would be bad for the real estate industry — it would mean lower prices — so (it) is very careful to mask foreign owners."[3] In metropolitan Toronto, foreigners had made enough real estate inroads by 1973 for the Ontario government to pass legislation slapping a 20 per cent tax on land sales to foreigners. This simply had the effect of sending foreigners to other, more speculatively under-developed Canadian cities, notably Calgary and Montreal, and to the U.S. When in May, 1976 the Quebec provincial government, then under the Liberals, proposed an even more prohibitive 33 per cent tax on land sales to non-residents of Canada, the real estate lobby easily scuttled the proposal which would have drastically affected Montreal and other urban areas around the province. Interestingly, later events revealed that the Liberals had naively proposed the measure without any real idea of how extensive foreign ownership was in Quebec — or how strong was the potential political dimension of that foreign presence. The haste with which the Liberals withdrew this pressure speaks for itself.

In many other countries undergoing the same "urban alienation" the particular circumstances are often different. In Canada the forces of transformation often happen to be foreign, but this is not so everywhere. Though it is difficult to make global generalizations because of the dearth of this kind of research elsewhere, what published accounts exist of such U.S. and U.K. cities as New York, Los Angeles, and London suggest that indigenous interests have spearheaded transformation there. Thus, the polarities of conflicting interests are not quite so clearly defined as in Canada. The question of nationality aside, however, often the result is much the same. It is outsiders — faceless individual or institutional investors, multinational corporations or, as in the case of Robert Moses, the behind-the-scenes master of New York's development, unaccountable and unelected individuals — with few ties to the community and still less public awareness who do much of the changing and who profit by it.

Perhaps the most important story told here is about one community's loss of control over the form and character of its own growth.

I want to thank all my colleagues at the Gazette, in particular several whose individual help was enormous. At the start, of course, there was Peters, much missed after he left Montreal several months after the project got underway. I am also immensely grateful to Kendal Windeyer, a constant source of insight and, in effect, the *eminence grise* of this search for *eminences grises,* and to Robert Neal, who gave sympathetic interest and help at a most critical point. To Agnes McFarlane, Margaret Coonan, Suzanne Matthews and others of the library staff, who were able to produce abundant information on some of the most obscure subjects almost instantaneously, I wish to express amazement and appreciation. Many others at the paper took time out to contribute in useful ways; I wish to thank Edgar Andrew Collard, Tim Creery, Mike Dugas, Ken Ernhofer, Bill Fox, Donna Gabeline, Karl Gerhard, Doug Gilbert, Alan Gray, Nancy Guillemette, Mark Farrell, Mark Harrison, René Laurent, Ross Munro, Dave Pinto, Rosemary Rees, Fred Rose, Lise Simard and, mother of us all, Millie Thompson.

Reporters in other cities and countries were also invaluable sources of insight and advice, among them Pierre Beaudeux, John Brennan, David Brewerton, Peter Calamai, Mauro Calamandrei, Bruce Kinlock, Ian Urquhart and, at *Last Post* magazine, Drummond Burgess and Nick auf der Maur.

I am also most grateful to Prof. Jeanne Wolfe and graduate student Joanabbey Sack of McGill University's school of urban planning for their insights on the course of suburban development; and to Ernest Virgint, doing graduate work at McMaster University, for his views on the historical role of the Rothschilds. Of course, I would also like to thank scores of sources in the worlds of business and government, here and abroad, who gave me their time and patience but who would just as soon not be named.

A warm and profound sense of indebtedness goes to those at L'Etincelle who gave so much of themselves to the actual preparation of this book. Without Arabelle, Louise Cardinal, Michèle Mailhot, Jacques Maltais and Marie-Noël Pichelin, who often worked up to 20 hours a day for weeks on end to meet deadlines, the book would never have made it into port.

I feel especially grateful to two friends at L'Etincelle: Denyse Demers-Beaudry, for her energetic editing and attention to the details on which the strength, such as it is, of the book rests; and Robert Davies, publisher, who showed confidence in continuing with this project when no one else, save my wife did, and provided me with every bit of help a writer could ask for, and more.

In quite another category of gratitude is my wife, Penny. But how does one even begin to describe what one owes a muse? It is perhaps something best left to oneself to celebrate than to try to explain.

INTRODUCTION

1 "Architecture and Design — Who Cares?," by Jane Holtz Kay in Columbia Journalism Review, July-August 1975, pp. 30-31.
2 *The Canadian Establishment*, Vol. I, by Peter C. Newman, Toronto: McClelland and Stewart Ltd., 1975, p. 389.
3 *Vancouver Ltd.*, by Donald Gutstein, Toronto: James Lorimer & Co., 1975, p. 58.

Chapter 1
The Liechtenstein Pipeline

AT THE END OF A QUIET STREET in the Alpine town of Schaan in Liechtenstein is a large stucco house with lace-curtained windows. It is the only house on the street showing no street number. But the mailman says it is Kirchstrasse, 236.

It is here at 236 Kirchstrasse on the outskirts of a quiet little town in the centre of Europe that the search for major Montreal landownership begins.

This address more than any other appears in official records as the place of ownership for major high-rise apartment buildings in the City of Montreal.

These property records[1] show 113 privately-owned apartment buildings each evaluated at $1 million or more (with market value far higher) in the municipality of Montreal. Foreigners own an estimated 60 to 75 per cent of these buildings. Fifteen of them list their ownership as being in Liechtenstein. Of these, six are listed at 236 Kirchstrasse.

This neat, upper-middle-class home at the foot of a mountain serves a useful function. It is a combination tax shelter and money laundry, washing out the identity of the owner, and a haven for dummy companies, providing a curtain behind which people investing in Montreal property may hide.

Property records show at least a dozen different addresses around Liechtenstein, including 236 Kirchstrasse, for owners of:

• At least 33 apartment buildings of all sizes in municipalities in the central part of Montreal Island including Montreal itself, Ville Saint-Laurent, Town of Mount Royal and Westmount.

• A peppering of office buildings, commercial properties and vast tracts of vacant land all over the metropolitan area ranging from quaint Old Montreal to the prosperous suburbs of the West Island to the sprawling subdivisions of the South Shore.

Since the beginning of the 1970's foreign investors have poured literally billions of dollars worth of investments into Montreal-area real estate. Only a fraction of this has come through the Liechtenstein pipeline, but its users are typical of the anonymous, unaccountable investors who have been largely determining the transformation of the Montreal area in recent years.

Since the election of the Parti Québécois on Nov. 15, 1976, Liechtenstein money committed prior to the election is still having an impact. Thus in the spring of 1977, for example, a Montreal-based company called Les Constructions Promirad Inc. began work on residential development on a massive, 25 square kilometre site near Mirabel Airport in and around the municipality of Wentworth. The company is 50 per cent owned by a Liechtenstein firm, Fiducan Trust.

Some Liechtenstein companies arrived here well over a decade before — buying up suburban terrain and then just sitting on it, waiting for it to appreciate before developing it or simply selling it off at speculative prices.

Others, like Feru Investments Ltd., have helped spur the flood of recent foreign money. After 10 months' wrangling with the newly formed federal Foreign Investment Review Agency, Feru in 1975 became the first foreign-owned company to obtain agency permission to buy a chunk of real estate anywhere in Canada.

The coveted prize in this historical footnote is one of Westmount's largest office buildings, the nine-storey cube at 245 Victoria Ave., a stone's throw from Canadian Pacific's Westmount railroad station.

Incidentally, Westmount's biggest apartment building is also in Liechtenstein hands — the "4300" on de Maisonneuve Blvd., home to company presidents, diplomats, politicians and judges. The manager says the owners could take the controversial step of forcing conversion of its 320 units to condominiums if there is difficulty raising rents — which in 1977 ranged from $360 a month for an "efficiency" apartment to $2,000 for a penthouse flat. Well-off though they are, tenants of a record 58 units took complaints over rental increases and deteriorating maintenance in 1976 to the Quebec Rent Control Board.

The building is owned by Tipmobil Anstalt, a company at an unlisted address in Schaan. Typical of the secrecy surrounding such firms, the building's manager, Mme. Madeleine Dussault, says she has no idea who owns that company.

"Twice a year a man comes from Switzerland — from Lugano. He doesn't want to be known. He never meets with anyone except myself," says Mme Dussault, who heads a staff of 30.

"He may not be the owner. I think he's just an administrator. I don't know who the owner is. They want us to know as little as possible. They don't want to be disturbed with our problems."

There is nothing unusual in that. A Canadian who is a member of the board of directors of Feru — a man who successfully helped fight for Feru's trailblazing application to the investment review agency — says he has "no idea" of who he was fighting for.

So impenetrable is the secrecy surrounding these companies that even the man who lives at 236 Kirchstrasse — himself a president and director of many of the dummy companies that call his house their home — says he does not know who owns them.

"I have no reason to be curious," he says.

His name is Josef Hilti. Seventy-one years old, he is one of six sons of a butcher. They have come a long way: the brothers today form one of the leading industrial-financial families in the loose economic unit of Liechtenstein and neighboring Switzerland.

Hilti retired in 1971 as manager and director of Liechtenstein's oldest and largest bank, Liechtensteinische Landesbank, which through its network of correspondents makes transactions with all continents (its correspondent in Canada is the Royal Bank). His retirement leaves him, he acknowledges, plenty of time to mind the affairs of the hundreds of companies whose only physical presence in Liechtenstein are manila folders in his second-floor filing cabinet and cards in the national registry office located a few miles down the valley in Vaduz, the capital.

A solemn, balding man who declined to be photographed, Hilti appeared surprised to see a reporter from Canada and annoyed at his young wife after she ushered me out of the rain and into his living room one morning while he was finishing his coffee.

"I did not even know these companies do business in Montreal," he said, throwing up his hands.

The Palais de Justice in Montreal is 6,500 kilometres from Hilti's home. In a hearing room on the 11th floor of the Palais de Justice it was standing room only.[2]

The crowd was not composed of the usual, down-at-the-heels and angry type of person protesting about being "exploited." This was a new and increasingly common breed of complainer: the upper middle class. Many of the protesters were middle-aged couples, the men wearing $300 suits, the ladies draped in furs. They looked like they stepped from a Holt Renfrew ad, and it was top-of-the-hill all the way.

In all, people from 48 different apartments were present. They came from two buildings just below the crest of Westmount Mountain: the building called "The Boulevard" at 4840 Côte St. Luc Rd. and "Westmount Towers" just two doors down at 4900 Côte St. Luc, both at the eastern fringe of Notre-Dame-de-Grâce.

Both buildings are owned by companies registered at 236 Kirchstrasse, Schaan, Liechtenstein. One company is called Trading Fund Establishment, the other, Oceanic Investments Establishment. Both companies bought the buildings in July, 1973, from a Montreal construction family, the Deckelbaums.

One by one, tenants from 13 of "The Boulevard's" apartments, often appearing slightly embarrassed to be speaking of such things, testified before Rental Board Administrator Gérard Lebeuf. They told of the building management's proposal to increase rents well in excess of the inflationary rate.

The highest proposed increase involved the case of Mme. France Émard, before the board for the second straight year. The year before management had asked for a 44 per cent raise, but in January, 1975, the board had ruled that this was excessive and knocked the raise all the way down to 8 per cent. Management, however, was not easily discouraged: Mme. Émard was now back before the board complaining that her rent, now

The Gazette (Michael Dugas)

The Boulevard *(left) and* Westmount Towers *(right), two apartment buildings on Côte St. Luc road near Victoria Avenue, were bought by Liechtenstein companies in 1973. The building between them, the* Montebello, *was sold by a Swiss engineer named Gian Carlo Tozzi in 1975 to a company registered in Panama.*

at $157 for a one-and-a-half room apartment, was being raised to $210; plus she was being asked to pay the water tax. With water tax averaging about 8 per cent of rent, this worked out to the same proposed overall increase as the last time around — 44 per cent.

The proposed increases for all the tenants present ranged between 24 and 44 per cent. Management representatives testified the increases were necessitated by rising costs, particularly fuel oil and taxes.

One gray-haired tenant was not embarrassed at all to be speaking of his financial pinch.

He had an eloquent courtroom manner and, indeed, he turned out to be a lawyer — E. Michael Berger, Q.C., of the firm Berger & Bierbrier.

Not only did he object to paying $495 for a six-room apartment, he said, but as a seven-year resident of "The Boulevard" he could bear witness that since ownership had changed three years before "there has been a debasement of lifestyle, a debasement of accommodation." He cited a lack of painting and other maintenance and the loss of a 24-hour doorman for security.

His voice rising, Berger said, "The general policy (at "The Boulevard") now — and I make this a direct accusation made in the presence of a representative of the proprietor — is to collect as much as you can and spend as little as you can.

"I'd like to know," Berger continued, "who the owner is."

No answer came from André Auclair, a representative of the building's management.

"I would like to know," Berger insisted, "who the owner of my building is."

Auclair, a short, wiry man in white shoes and a flashy check suit, said, "Trading Fund Establishment."

"And just who," said Berger, hands on hips, "is Trading Fund Establishment?"

Auclair whispered, "I don't know."

Berger pursued the matter, but the government administrator interrupted. The matter, he said, was "not relevant" to the inquiry.

To many, however, ownership is relevant.

As Berger puts it, debating policy with managers instead of owners is "just shadow boxing, chasing shadows — you're not dealing with real authority."

Managers are hired hands. They may, like André Auclair or Madeleine Dussault, be visible to the public and make day-to-day decisions. But they do not make the policy directives which they must obey — or be fired.

Who makes the policy and the profits? Who is accountable for the transformation of Montreal? This transformation, of course, goes much deeper than changing conditions at "The Boulevard" or hundreds of other apartment buildings around town. The transformation extends to almost all the 'built world' around us which defines what we do and where we do it. It extends to highways, office buildings, industrial properties, shopping centres and housing developments. It includes speculation, construction, demolition, land banking, real estate financing and construction material manufacturing.

Innumerable sectors are involved in this process and each sector, whether it be land ownership *per se* or construction, contains innumerable components — probably to a greater degree than any other major city in Canada. In short, those behind Montreal's development are, to use the urbanologists' expression, highly fragmentized.

But it is not quite the chaos it seems. To look at all the names of companies involved it might appear that Montreal's transformation is the work of a swarm of thousands of interests each buzzing their own separate way.

In fact, however, interests which may at first seem to be small isolated gnats — like 236 Kirchstrasse — turn out to be related to other interests in totally different spheres of the transformation process. And this is what power is all about.

One of the most insightful books on this subject is Anthony Sampson's "The New Anatomy of Britain." It is about how power works in the U.K., but Sampson reaches a general conclusion which could apply equally well to my own inquiry in Montreal.

"Any quest for the sources of power," he says, "must be a frustrating journey; the politician, the journalist or the ordinary citizen who sets out to discover the caves of decision-making finds himself led through a maze which turns out to have no centre . . ."

"Power," says Sampson, "depends on a confederation of interests which rarely work together." The "different spheres of institutions and interest-groups connect up with each other and sometimes overlap, but they have no decisive centre.

"It is in linking one sphere to another that the capacity to influence events lies."[3]

And it is from these links between different spheres at work in Montreal's transformation that a framework for power and influence may be assembled. That microcosm of a place called Liechtenstein is as good a place as any to begin to see how it works.

"*Ja*, I am the president of that company," Hilti acknowledged after checking his files for one of the companies on my list, Trading Fund Establishment. "Ja, I am on the board of directors.

"But that is all I know. I do not know the owners.

"I just mail letters for them. I just walk to the post box."

Hilti's role is not quite so pedestrian as he would have us believe, but he is still only a cog in a much wider mechanism . . .

Michael Dugas

The Quebec arm of Hilti A.G.

. . . another 22 kilometres west of the Palais de Justice, the Trans-Canada Highway slices through the suburb of Pointe Claire. Just a few yards from the roar of the six lanes of traffic there is a nondescript one-storey industrial office and warehouse.

It is the branch office of a major Liechtenstein company. Indeed, it is no dummy company but an authentic, productive corporation. Its head office as well as its mailing address are in Schaan. It happens to be the largest employer in that 62-square mile principality, employing 1,200 workers out of a total population of 22,000.

It may jar with Liechtenstein's image as a rustic little hinterland whose contributions to the world amount to postage stamps and souvenir cowbells, but this is a multinational corporation with operations in 65 countries at last count.

The company calculates it is the world's No. 1 manufacturer of an inconspicuous but crucial component of modern construction techniques called the "fastening." Fastenings are the metal bindings which are shot into the concrete and steel of tall buildings and dams to hold them together. They are as essential to large-scale construction around Quebec as nails or screws are to building a bookcase on a basement workbench. To shoot these fastenings into concrete and steel, special power tools are needed; and these too are made by this company.

So, just as 236 Kirchstrasse is a leader in one small aspect of the transformation of Montreal, another Liechtenstein interest is a leader in a very different aspect.

The company is called Hilti Aktiengesellschaft,* and it is owned by the brothers of Josef Hilti, the man who lives at 236 Kirchstrasse. While Josef was building up Landesbank, his brothers were building up this and several other industrial companies.

Again and again in tracing back the diverse participants in Montreal development one finds connections between them — whether they be via bloodlines, intertwined investments, interlocking directorates or banking, legal or advisory functions.

---

* The word "Aktiengesellschaft." German for corporation, will be abbreviated "A.G." throughout the rest of the book. Similarly, the term "société anonyme," the corporate term which commonly follows the name of French companies, will be abbreviated "S.A".

In fact, while not much can be known of what other kinds of businesses flow through 236 Kirchstrasse it is clear that the residents of that house serve as more than just passive conduits for Montreal affairs.

There is a third resident of 236 Kirchstrasse.

Herr and Frau Hilti occupy the spacious upper storeys of that gabled house, but on the first floor — with a separate entrance — lives a bachelor.

The shades were drawn on all the first floor windows when I visited the house, and no one answered the bell. Next to the doorbell was a card, wet from the rain, which read:

Ernesto Fabio Beck
Consulente legale
Studio legale e commerciale

Who was Beck? Just a legal consultant, as the card indicated, who by chance happened to share this house? It was somewhat curious that, here in a place where everyone spoke German, his card should be written in Italian. But then a lot of things about Liechtenstein were curious.

However, Italy, it turns out, is a large piece of the Kirchstrasse puzzle.

When Hilti later found me in his living room and appeared to be seeking polite ways to get me out, he recommended that I talk to his neighbor downstairs. "I know nothing about these companies, but I am sure Mr. Beck would be able to help. He is the fiduciary for the companies you ask about."

When I mentioned that Beck appeared to be absent, Frau Hilti earned a second round of scowls from her husband. She volunteered that Beck would be out of town for weeks. Frau Hilti, a handsome woman considerably younger than her husband, added that Beck had left about a month ago for Lugano, a city 100 miles south across the Alps just on the Swiss side of the border with Italy. He spends much of the year there on business, she said.

I had no intention of going to Lugano. But out of curiosity I asked where I could reach him. Almost eagerly, Hilti walked into his den, typed a name and phone number out on a scrap of paper and handed it to me.

There are 473 banks in Switzerland, at last count, and the name on the paper was that of one of the smaller ones among

236 Kirchstrasse.

them: Soginvest Banca S.A. But few have generated more controversy in Montreal in recent years. The connection of Soginvest with Kirchstrasse opened a whole new dimension to the activities of this mechanism.

In a telephone interview I asked Soginvest manager Claudio Casellini, "Hilti, Beck and you all work together?"

He paused. "You can say that," he said.

"Mr. Beck is our legal advisor in Liechtenstein. We sort of work with him in the formation of these companies." He estimated there were "eight or nine" such companies, including Trading Fund.

Soginvest Bank achieved a name for itself in Montreal because it has an affiliate company there called Valorinvest (Canada) Ltd. It was this company that made headlines in the Montreal press in 1975 through its agreement with the Gray Nuns to buy their Motherhouse in the heart of downtown Montreal, knock it down, develop the surrounding private park and build a multi-tower, office-residential-hotel complex. The project, which would have dominated the neighborhood, would have been one of the largest of its kind in the city. Three of the towers would have been over 40 floors high. The complex would have stretched out over the entire block surrounded by Dorchester Blvd. and Guy, Ste. Catherine and St. Mathieu Sts. Such groups as Heritage Canada, Société d'Architecture de Montréal, Save Montreal and Corporation des Urbanistes protested; the provincial government's cultural affairs department eventually declared the site of such historical importance that there could be no demolition.

But Valorinvest's influence in the city remains significant.

In addition to its bold plan for high-rise development, Valorinvest also has extensive activity as a real estate *management* company. That is, it takes care of about 20 properties which are owned by other companies in both the Montreal and Quebec City areas, according to Valorinvest's executive vice president, Eric Hahto. These include, he says, residential and commercial properties as well as a hotel, which he declined to identify. The total value of the properties administered by Valorinvest "is in the ballpark of $50 million," he says.

Of these 20 properties, at least four are high-rise apartment buildings owned by companies registered at 236 Kirchstrasse. These include "The Boulevard" and "Westmount Towers." Indeed, André Auclair, who defended the buildings against tenants' complaints before the rental board, is Valorinvest's comptroller. The firm also manages "The Carillon" at 2255 St. Mathieu St. and "The Maricourt" at 1530 McGregor St.

The company's preference for luxury apartment buildings extends to Quebec City, where it owns "Le Samuel de Champlain," at 350 Chemin Ste. Foy, among others. Here, too, it is getting flack from tenants. Says one such tenant Col. Anthony J. Scotti, a retired Canadian army Provost Marshall: "Services have deteriorated and rents are going sky high. They are just here to bleed us white."

Asked to comment on such complaints on service, Valorinvest's executive vice president, Hahto, says: "They should complain to the super. These are the same people who give the super $100 at Christmas time. If they don't like the job he's doing, don't give him $100."

One thing is clear, though. Even if a tenant *wants* to tip each and every member of the building's staff, he won't have as *many* people to tip. At "Westmount Towers," for example, Valorinvest representatives concede that the number of employees is down from eleven to nine. (One of the casualties is round-the-clock security: on the early morning shift the door-man frequently has to leave his post to double as "car jockey," parking cars.)

Soginvest Bank is intimately involved in the financing of these buildings. Records on file at the Montreal registry office, for example, show that Soginvest helped Trading Fund Establishment meet the $1,150,000 price for "The Boulevard" in 1973 by lending it $300,000 at a 9.5 per cent interest rate.

Such links hold potential advantages when Valorinvest goes before the rental board to justify its proposed rent increases on grounds of high costs. "The Boulevard" can thus count the 9.5 per cent interest on Soginvest's loan to Trading Fund as part of its onerous "costs" — even though this sum which shows up as costs on the books of one company also shows up, unbeknownst to the rental board, as income on the accounts of a closely related company. By such methods of "all in the family" financing, a network of related interests can try to persuade a government agency that the ostensibly high costs of owning a Montreal building justify large rent increases.

Based on what Soginvest's Casellini says, a common practice seems to be this: Valorinvest often manages buildings for owners who are clients of Soginvest Bank but who sometimes register their companies — legal fictions — via Liechtenstein.

Casellini, who in addition to being Soginvest's manager is a Valorinvest vice president, said these clients — that is, owners of buildings like "The Boulevard" — are typically Italian or German, but he declined to give names. Besides Canada, there were also property investments in the U.S., Brazil and Italy.

I asked Casellini, "Why are your clients going through Liechtenstein — for taxes or secrecy?"

"Both," he replied.

"What are you afraid of in being so secretive?"

"We are afraid of nothing."

"Then why can't the owners of these companies be made public?"

"Why should they be made public? It is their business."

That may not satisfy tenants like Mr. Berger.

But recently he and most other plaintiffs from "The Boulevard" got some good news.

The far-flung presence of Liechtenstein investment in Montreal.

Almost every municipality in metropolitan Montreal has some portion of its land owned by Liechtenstein companies.

On the West Island, Tuxana A.G. is co-owner of 85 vacant lots in Dollard des Ormeaux, 27 of them on a street named Charade Place. The same firm owns land in Pierrefonds.

York Establishment and Conin Establishment between them hold about 66 hectares in Ville St. Laurent's Bois Franc area.

In Dorval, Arbafin Anstalt owns property evaluated at $1.2 million in an industrial park at 2121 Trans Canada Highway.

In the East End, Geneva Investment Establishment owns about 16 hectares near Gouin Blvd.

And on the South Shore, Pindar A.G. owns 52 vacant hectares in Brossard.

Apart from that sampling culled from property records, there are more important holdings including some in Old Montreal, downtown and Montreal North.

There are more holdings linked to Liechenstein than can be found in property records, however, because it is common for firms incorporated in Canada to be controlled by holding companies registered abroad.

So these statistics on Liechenstein interests active in Montreal are, if anything, conservative.

Of seven apartment buildings which were bought by firms giving their address as 236 Kirchstrasse, six are evaluated at over $1 million.

Evaluation figures show the total value of both land and building as assessed by municipal tax authorities. As a rule, market value is considerably higher:

4840 Cote St. Luc Rd., *The Boulevard*	$1,142,900
4900 Cote St. Luc Rd., *Westmount Towers*	$2,894,000
1460 McGregor Ave., *The Redpath*	$1,493,000
1530 McGregor Ave., *The Maricourt*	$2,604,000
1700 McGregor Ave.	$800,000
2255 St. Matthew St., *Le Carillon*	$1,548,000
1800-08 Sherbrooke St. W., *Chelsea House*	$1,373,000

The *Redpath* on McGregor Ave. illustrates the speculative side of such ownership. The Kirchstrasse firm which bought the high-rise in 1973 sold it in 1976 to a firm called Scarteen Management Corp. Ltd. for an undisclosed price.

Other companies based in Liechtenstein own the following 30 apartment buildings in the municipality of Montreal, according to evaluation records of December 1976:

7374 Chambord St.	$52,500
360 Charon St.	$54,000
1010-30 Cherrier St., *Le Cherrier*	$2,179,000
3488 Cote des Neiges Rd. *Ramesay House*	$4,006,000
3555 Cote des Neiges Rd., *The Regency*	$7,043,000
3435 Drummond St., *Drummond Plaza*	$1,428,000
5685 Gatineau Ave.	$122,000
1230 McGregor Ave.	$1,710,000
1545 McGregor Ave., *Embassy Row*	$2,637,000
1550 McGregor Ave., *Gregor House*	$3,422,000
1430-32 Mountain St., *St. Andrew's Towers*	$3,205,000
3500 Mountain St. *Le Crillon*	$912,000
3510 Mountain St., *Le Chambord*	$742,000
8045 de Normanville St.	$346,000
7935 de Normanville St.	$346,600
7955 de Normanville St.	$346,650
7975 de Normanville St.	$346,750
7995 de Normanville St.	$346,950
8005 de Normanville St.	$347,050
8025 de Normanville St.	$347,500
1101 Rachel St. E., *Parc Lafontaine*	$1,708,400
3455 Redpath Cr., *Redpath Manor*	$595,000
3335 Ridgewood Ave.	$158,000
2185 St. Joseph St. E.	$45,000
5710 de Salaberry Ave.	$233,200
3325 Van Horne St.	$119,500
5161-75 Walkley St., *Walkley Manor*	$162,200
1790 de Salaberry Ave.	$196,050
1800 de Salaberry Ave.	$195,100
5650 17th Ave., Rosemount	$170,000

In other municipalities, Liechtenstein companies own such buildings as: 5650 17th Ave., Rosemount; 1009 Laird Blvd. *(The Connaught)* in Town of Mount Royal; 4300 de Maisonneuve Blvd., Westmount, and 990 Cote Vertu and 239 Deguire Blvd., both in St. Laurent.

A refresher on measure.

A hectare is almost two and a half times the size of an acre. There are 100 hectares to a square kilometre. And there are almost 2.6 square kilometres to the square mile.

A playing field in the Canadian Football League is about six-tenths of a hectare (or one and a half acres).

The island of Montréal comprises about 45,900 hectares, or 459 square kilometres (or approximately 114,800 acres or 179 square miles).

Some of the better known parks around town are Lafontaine Park at 40 hectares (or 102 acres) and Mount Royal Park at 212 hectares (or 530 acres).

Rental Board Administrator Lebeuf, announcing his decisions several months after the hearing, found that Valorinvest's proposed rent increases were generally unjustified by the building's rising costs. He rolled back the increases to levels more in line with the eight to 10 per cent increases which the board typically finds justified.

Berger himself had his proposed increase slashed from 24 per cent to 9.3 per cent.

Then came the bad news.

Valorinvest sent him a letter saying that when his present lease expired, it would offer him a new one. The proposed rent increase on the coming lease?

Twenty-four per cent — again.

The trail from Hilti's house in Liechtenstein may, as we have seen, lead to a fairly obscure Swiss bank. But this is not to suggest that it is only the more modest, fringe elements of global finance which make use of the Liechtenstein pipeline for their Montreal affairs. Liechtenstein also provides a popular conduit for the international investment establishment.

For example, in the case of the biggest apartment building mentioned so far, "The 4300" owned by Tipmobil Anstalt at an unlisted Schaan address, the go-between bank is none other than one of Switzerland's Big Three banks, the Swiss Credit Bank (Crédit Suisse). It stands close to the very epicentre of the international financial community. And over in suburban Dorval we encounter a firm called Dongof Anstalt which owns 21 acres of vacant land near Guthrie St.; Dongof's affairs are at least partly handled by a subsidiary of another of the Big Three, Swiss Bank Corp. (Société de Banque Suisse).

Why, one may well ask, is Liechtenstein so popular with so many elements of the investment world? Or, more pertinently, why is it necessary? Why should people interested in anonymity and low taxes not be satisfied with Switzerland, which is famous for both? And, why do the Swiss themselves go to Liechtenstein?

The answer is quite simple: what Switzerland is to the rest of the world in the way of providing a haven for unaccountability and tax evasion, Liechtenstein is to Switzerland. Swiss bankers may have a reputation for solemn silence about clients. But compared to what goes on across the Rhine in Liechtenstein, they can be positively garrulous.

The picture-postcard town of Schaan has an "away-from-it-all" charm, but not only for tourists. Those with money to hide or taxes to avoid are also drawn to its even more picturesque banking and business laws.

If quaint little Liechtenstein could be called a "never-never land," the two "nevers" would be:

• Never bend in the face of international pressure, as have the Swiss on occasion, in giving out information on clients when criminal activity, including tax fraud, is suspected. In Switzerland tax fraud is a criminal offense and may be pursued by authorities; but tax evasion — the failure to pay or declare taxes — is not criminal at all, unlike in North America.

• Never ask questions of clients so that, even if your arm is twisted or if you are wined and dined by an inquirer, you will have no information to give. Louis Burke, Canada's trade commissioner to both Switzerland and Liechtenstein, with headquarters in the former, recalls a trip to Vaduz to get some background on a Liechtenstein firm seeking to begin operations in Canada outside the real estate field: "I spent a whole week there taking bankers out to dinner, lawyers out to dinner, the whole works, and I never got a thing."

Burke sums up the difference: "The Swiss are under considerable international pressure to give out information. But in Liechtenstein you do not get any information.

"There's really no human way of knowing what's going on there."

As a booming centre for the shy and the sly with money on their hands, Liechtenstein is — despite the jet age — somewhat secluded. If you headed there lugging a cash-filled suitcase, the closest you could get by air is Zurich. There you'd have to board a train for a winding two-hour ride through scenic mountain passes before finally transferring to a bus for the last leg across the Rhine.

But the most inconvenient part of such an itinerary is that customs officials back in Zurich would probably long since have relieved you of most of your cash: Switzerland now has a $8,000 limit on currency imports.

Fortunately, however, corporate laws in Liechtenstein, more sophisticated than its transport, circumvent such roadblocks. To set up a company to launder your money and free it from taxes back home, Liechtenstein provides mail-order service.

Some people may fear that if their letters were ever intercepted and seen by the wrong people there could be problems. But not to worry. As the vice-president of Hilti's old bank remarks, "Even by opening the mail the authorities might not know who the real owner is."

This is because many clients operate through a series of buffers — often law firms or trust companies — which insulate them from traceable involvement. Liechtenstein may be almost a caricature of this need for ownership privacy, but the same basic need by owners holds true with the controlling shareholders of some of the biggest land companies in Canada — including the biggest of them all, Canadian Pacific Ltd. (see Chap. 5). Tracing the ownership of such companies, even though they may have no known involvement with Liechtenstein, Panama, Andorra or any of the other such laundries, is often as difficult as if they were registered at 236 Kirchstrasse itself.

One reason clients are drawn to Liechtenstein is that it offers an unique form of incorporation called the *anstalt,* or in English the *establishment.* Liechtenstein's government describes it as intermediate between a corporation and a foundation. It is unique in that it has only one block of capital — no shares. The best part, however, is the fact that taxes on anstalts are only one mill (*i.e.,* one one-thousandth per year) of capital and reserves. There are no taxes on earnings or profits.

This saves a lot of money for the clients of Hilti and of such leading Vaduz law firms as that of Gregor Steger, whose clientele includes numerous Canadians as well as people of other nationalities investing in Canada. But for every dollar that their clients save by not being incorporated in Canada, less enterprising Canadians — the shopkeeper on St. Hubert St., the secretary in Place Ville Marie, the widow in Toronto with her pension checks, the tenant at "The Boulevard" — have to pay out of their own pockets: the books at the Department of National Revenue have to be balanced. It is generally those who are not rich, who are not well-connected, who wind up paying the tab. Federal officials and outside observers are unable to even guess just how many hundreds of millions of dollars of potential revenue are legally evaded every year through the use of such shelters in Liechtenstein, the Bahamas, the Grand Cayman Islands, etc.

Gregor Steger was unavailable when I was in Vaduz, but I spoke to an associate, lawyer Kurt Martschitz. The Liechtenstein government, following the national tradition of silence, declines to offer data on the importance of these absentee com-

Henry Aubin

Lawyer Kurt Martschitz: "This is not good for Canada".

panies to its own coffers. But Martschitz estimates that through various taxes and fees they account for between 35 and 40 per cent of the government's annual revenue. That may sound like a lot, but with such a tiny budget this comes to only roughly $12 million. However, there are at least 30,000 such companies — more than one per resident — and that's been more than enough in recent years to relieve Liechtenstein citizens of the need to pay any regular income tax at all.

The Liechtensteiners who benefit most, however, are that privileged caste of about 100 men — mostly lawyers like Steger or bankers like Hilti — who set up these dummy companies (or, as Prince Franz Josef's government prefers they be called, "domiciliary" companies). In addition to establishing the firms, these men collect fees as members of their boards of directors. For as little as three or four hours' work per year, Martschitz calculates, a Liechtenstein citizen can earn some $2,000. Multiplied by scores or hundreds of companies, it is, he acknowledges, "a good business."

For the clients, too, it represents a significant savings over Switzerland. In Switzerland, for example, you need three citizens to serve as directors, each collecting their fees.

There is a fundamental irony involved in the willingness with which Liechtenstein and, as will be seen in greater detail later, Switzerland profit from the business activities of such real estate interests. Both countries have laws which prohibit the sale of property to foreigners. They want their land for their own people, not as a speculative commodity for outsiders. In the case of Switzerland, measures were invoked making it practically impossible for foreigners to buy land after Germans and Italians had bought vast tracts of the Tessin region near Lugano.

Yet the secrecy surrounding the activities of domiciliary companies prevents proper appreciation of this irony. Even Louis Burke, the business specialist at the Canadian Embassy, said he had no idea Liechtenstein was being used as a jumping off place by real estate companies active in Canada.

Indeed, the most dramatic evidence of the success with which Liechtensteiners have insulated themselves from awareness of their role came at the end of my conversation with Martschitz.

In passing an open window, overlooking the red tile roofs of small homes and office buildings and offering a vista on spectacular mountains, I praised Liechtenstein for its beauty.

He returned my platitude.

"Montreal is a nice city," he said, "I was there just last year, you know. No, no, not on business, just as a tourist."

And how did he like it, I asked, approaching the door.

"Oh, I liked it," he said. "But there were too many skyscrapers, high-rises. I could not live there. Too many skyscrapers are not good for Canada."

Surprised at his attitude, I told him my reason for visiting Liechtenstein was precisely to trace involvement of domiciliary companies in the city's development. This included the encouragement of the same kind of construction he disliked.

Taken aback, Martschitz grinned tightly at the irony and said, "That is an abuse."

"It is not good for Canada," he said pensively.

Then, recovering his more detached air, he added, "But of course I do not know. I do not know the problems over there."

Footnotes — Chapter 1

1. According to the evaluation rolls of the City of Montreal in early 1976 and *Rudner's Directory of Apartment Buildings* (Montreal: Alex S. Rudner, Jan. 1976).
2. Hearing of November 18, 1975, before the Quebec Rental Board.
3. Sampson, Anthony, *The New Anatomy of Britain* (London: Hodder and Stoughton Ltd., 1971), pp. 655-6.

Chapter 2:
"La Fuga"

THE ABOVE ADVERTISEMENT in a leading Italian magazine[1] had a poignant Christmas message for 1976. It exhorted the rich to take the money and run — to "la provincia del Quebec and western Canada."

This is but one of the more overt efforts by companies in Canada and Europe to steer the massive flight of Italian fortunes into Montreal and other Canadian cities. Though eco-

nomic uncertainties caused by the election of the Parti Que-
becois on Nov. 15, 1976, have helped cause a marked slow-
down in foreign real estate investments in Canada, particularly
in Quebec, the appearance of such post-election ads shows the
kind of background forces anxious for Montreal to resume its
role as a target of international speculation. For those who
have already speculated there, as has the company which
placed the ad, it is essential that there be a return to the norm
if they are to avoid enormous losses; the speculator always
needs to re-sell, and for that there have to be buyers.

In all, hundreds of millions of dollars — perhaps over $1 bil-
lion, say some land dealers — have flowed into Canadian property in the 1970's while Italy's economic depression deepened.
Most of that money has been concentrated in the Montreal
area. Indeed, if one is to estimate property investments here on
the basis of national origin, Italy has been in the period of
1975 to November, 1976 the largest source of real estate capital
— by far.

The "flight" of Italian capital — or "la Fuga" as the phenomenon is familiarly called in Italy — has had vastly different effects on both sides of the Atlantic.

In Montreal the money has given momentum to a form of
urban growth which the sellers and developers of property see
as healthy: it stimulates the economy. Critics, however, con-
tend that much of this growth — high-rises and urban sprawl —
meets the needs of overseas financial interests and their local
associates more than the needs of the people who actually live
here.

In Italy, on the other hand, the mass evacuation of capital to
Canada and other "nest-eggs" outside the country has aggravated the nation's worst depression since the 1930s by remov-
ing money which might otherwise generate productivity and
jobs. The flow of money here goes back to the 1960s but
reached flood proportions during that anxious year following
the Communists' successes in the June, 1975 local elections.
Many wealthy Italians, particularly industrialists from the
north, feared confiscation of their fortunes if the Communists
eventually formed the national government (a fear which was
somewhat mollified by the June, 1976 national elections).

One high-ranking Italian diplomat says he has been troubled how officials in all levels of government in Canada have

permitted foreign money to swamp the domestic real estate market. Aldo Bettini, commercial counselor at the Italian embassy and its chief business expert, acknowledges that the massive flight of capital "has created problems for us (in Italy) and I would say to an extent it has created problems for Canada."[2]

For one thing, he notes, it has "pushed the price of real estate up, up, up" in cities like Montreal. Such investment "should worry local authorities because it is not a reliable source of capital. It is a speculative source. And it really does not add much. What is the interest in building more skyscrapers?"

A more sensible kind of investment from the point of view of an underdeveloped host country, he goes on, is money which goes into the industrial sector — building factories, adding productivity and employing many times the number of people who obtain permanent jobs through a real estate investment.* A factory might employ scores or hundreds of workers, while an apartment or office building will only employ a handful of janitors and other service personnel. Most Italian investors, however, prefer real estate in Canada because it contains fewer risks and requires less attention — it is not always easy to keep abreast of local strikes and market problems from Milan.

There is a second aspect to the Italian money which has flowed into Montreal real estate: an incalculably large portion of it, say Italian diplomats, has arrived here illegally, in defiance of Italian regulations. Much of it has first been "laundered" in banks in Switzerland or Liechtenstein before going to Canada and other investment havens, many of them in the U.S., Latin America or Australia.

For decades Italy had ineffectual restrictions on the export of capital. Then in May 1976, as the flight of capital was peaking, the Italian government with broad public support enacted a law that for the first time would have imposed jail terms instead of simply fines on those who took capital out of the country without government permission. The following October the

---

* Such investments, while relatively infrequent, do happen. Thus in early 1976 Ottawa's Foreign Investment Review Agency approved a plan to establish a plant in Granby, P.Q., to make plastic parts for toys and musical instruments. The Swiss company which owns the project, Internote Financial Holdings, is in turn controlled by Paolo Bontempi, of Italy.

government passed another law requiring residents who have invested in real estate outside the country to bring back to Italy the net income received on it.

Thus, a resident of Italy who, without government permission, bought an apartment building in Montreal — whether in 1976 or 1966 — would have to repatriate the profit he makes on rent. Those who owned such property had to declare that fact to the Italian government before a deadline of Dec. 4, 1976. Many of the Italian landlords in Montreal are known to have ignored the deadline, confident that their government's investigative abilities on this side of the ocean are all but non-existent. If their assets in Canada are valued at over five million lira (roughly $6,000), which is the case with virtually everyone here, then in theory their defiance of the law could carry penalties of up to six years in jail and fines of up to four times the amount of the original investment.

The flight of Italian capital, in short, has helped make Montreal an international haven for illegal money.

There are many reasons for this: investors' reassurance by the political and economic stability here during the 1971-76 period under the provincial Liberal government; the virtual open door policy toward foreign property investments by the provincial and municipal governments; the perception abroad of Montreal as the most "European" city in North America (hence making many European investors feel more at home here than in, say, Calgary or Los Angeles); the additional fact that many Italians speak French — rather than English — as a second language and, extremely importantly, the fact that Montreal's business community is known throughout Europe for its hospitality and efficiency in selling Montreal real estate to foreign investors.

These allies in the business community include developers, lawyers, notaries, property agents, bankers and trust company officials. For years they have ignored the illegal origins of their Italian clients' investments, saying this was Italy's business, not Canada's. They have argued that these investments are good for Canada — not to mention, of course, themselves through the fees and commissions they collect — because their clients re-invest their profits in Canada. Enactment of this new Italian law, however, weakens that argument, requiring as it does that these profits be taken out of Canada and returned to Italy.

The Gazette (Len Sidaway)

Row housing on Dorchester Boulevard belonging to Placements Camillus.

Albert L. Bissonnette, a Montreal lawyer, typifies both the respectability and the aloofness of this breed. Today he is commissioner of the federal government's Anti-Dumping Tribunal. But as late as 1974, prior to his appointment to that post by Prime Minister Pierre Elliott Trudeau, his name turns up on provincial registration records as the president and director of a Liechtenstein-owned company, Venicana Investments Ltd. The firm owns land in Kirkland evaluated at $191,000; it lists Leonide Berti, of Treviso, Italy, as its parent company's largest shareholder. Bissonnette, then with the politically well-connected law firm of Riel, Vermette, Ryan Dunton & Ciaccia,*

---

* Bissonnette's appointment to the tribunal is but part of a pattern of interplay between this firm and government. For example, partner John Ciaccia, a former federal deputy minister, is a Liberal member of the Quebec National Assembly and helped negotiate the biggest land deal in the history of the province: the agreement between Quebec and the native people in 1976 which gave the province the go-ahead for completing the James Bay hydroelectric project. Also, senior partner Maurice Riel is a senator, having been named to that position by Trudeau. There is nothing unusual about such ties to the political sphere: a number of other Montreal law firms, far more deeply involved in the transfer of local real estate to foreign firms, are considerably closer to government. Indeed, Sen. Riel himself left his own firm in 1975 to join just such a practice, Stikeman Elliott. The role of Montreal's highest legal circles in the foreign land trade will be explored later.

was also a director for several years of a company called Placements Camillus Inc., whose president and principal owner is Elisa Scheibler, of Rome.

Camillus is a classic example of an absentee landlord letting its property slide into disrepair. In the late 1960s it bought the entire downtown block, within hailing distance of the Canadian Broadcasting Corp. tower, which is bounded by Dorchester Blvd. East and Lagauchetière, St. André and St. Timothée Sts. The block contains one of the last remaining rows of inhabited graystone houses along that stretch of Dorchester Blvd. The deterioration of these turreted buildings is manifest to any passerby; the exterior window sills and frames, for example, are largely bare of paint and beginning to rot, and broken glass panes are unreplaced.*

Whether Berti's and Scheibler's investments here received approval from the UIC, the Italian agency responsible for authorizing the export of capital, is not known; in an interview, Bissonnette said he had never heard of the UIC.

But Camillus' record of maintenance at its Dorchester Blvd. property raises questions more pertinent to Montrealers. Asked if such investments were good or bad for the city, Bissonnette replied, "Quite frankly I have not thought about it at that level. I don't think a solicitor thinks of it on that wavelength.

"He carries out his instructions. That is what he is paid for.

"You would not expect a solicitor to discuss social philosophy with a client."[4]

The evident blitheness with which some property companies have regarded Italy's restrictions against the exodus of capital is illustrated by the advertisement which opens this chapter. Even some old-time hands in Montreal companies specializing in "la Fuga" business have been stunned by its audacity. It ran in Panorama, the Milan-based newsweekly, for many months after the government's enactment of its first laws imposing jail terms on unauthorized exporters of capital. The ad, of course,

---

* Though Bissonnette no longer represents Camillus since his Ottawa appointment, his old firm still handles its affairs. Jean-Louis Tetrault, another lawyer at the firm, says one possible scheme is to sell the property to the city for demolition and construction of new structures. "I can say," said Tetrault, "that we do not have an interest in keeping land which is half-vacant and half-filled with old buildings."[3]

is implicitly appealing to people to disregard the law. Its sponsor is safely tucked over the border in Switzerland.

The sponsor is called Gruppo Fidinam, or the Fidinam Group. It shares many characteristics with Valorinvest mentioned in Chap. 1: it, too, has headquarters in Lugano, thrives on a secretive clientele from Italy and other European countries, is closely tied with a Swiss bank (in this case Banca della Svizzera Italiana) and operates on a multinational scale. It pumps its clients' investments into property in such other countries as Spain, Venezuela, Brazil and Australia.

But Fidinam is much bigger than Valorinvest. And so are its controversies.

Fidinam may be only one of a score of Swiss or Liechtenstein related organizations contributing to the transformation of urban Canada over the past decade. But few have equalled its agility in skating quite so close to the thin line separating the lawful from the illegal. And few have left such a money-strewn trail of involvement in Canadian politics.

In Canada the Fidinam Group has more than 20 subsidiaries. Based in Toronto, the Canadian arm controls real estate assets throughout Canada of more than $350 million.[5] This puts it among the top dozen real estate organizations in Canada. In all, Fidinam is landlord to 15,000 or more Canadians, most of them in the Toronto area (where some $200 million of those assets are located), western cities like Winnipeg and the Quebec cities of Hull and Montreal.

The picture of the unidentified Quebec property in the advertisement is of the Royal Dixie Apartments along Route 2 & 20 in the Montreal suburb of Dorval. One of the largest "garden apartment" complexes of its kind in Eastern Canada, the Royal Dixie consists of 30 buildings, each one three floors high, containing a total of 630 lower-middle income apartments. Fidinam acquired ownership of the complex in 1974, and since then it has gone through the same barrage of tenants' complaints (deteriorating conditions, rocketing rent increases of up to 28 per cent) of which Valorinvest and so many other European landlords are targets. The president of the local tenants' association, Jean-Charles Bourguignon, refers to Switzerland's restrictions against foreign landonwership when he says of Fidinam's investors, "They can't screw around at home. So to be perfectly free to' screw around they come here."

Michael Dugas

The *Port de mer* (foreground), belonging to the Fidinam Group, is one of the largest appartment buildings on the South Shore.

The Royal Dixie is but one of the more antiquated fragments of Fidinam's string of Montreal holdings. Others include: the third largest shopping centre in the metropolitan area, Centre Laval; perhaps the largest apartment complex on suburban Ville St. Laurent's skyline, the 600-unit "Joie de Vivre" which consists of three towers, each 20 floors high; and one of the South Shore's biggest apartment complexes, "Port de Mer," whose 400 units and 4,600 square feet of office space are located in towers of 26 and 29 floors next to the Longueuil Metro. To buy "Port de Mer," Fidinam required federal approval from the Foreign Investment Review Agency; in mid-1976 the agency decided (without, characteristically, giving reasons) that the purchase would be of "significant benefit" to Canada and approved it.

Despite the rental rollbacks for which the Quebec Rental Board has become generally popular with tenants and notorious among foreign investors, Fidinam appears to have emerged remarkably well in the profit column. Proponents of foreign ownership of apartment buildings say such owners are more interested in security for their money than in high prof-

its, being satisfied with returns of six or seven per cent.* Indeed, in its ad for investments in the Royal Dixie, Fidinam
guarantees returns of 6.5 per cent to investors. But the president of Fidinam (Canada) Ltd., Fausto C. Rusca, suggests that
the company itself, as middleman between the individual investor and his real estate investment, is clearing a lot more
than that. "You try to squeeze as much as you can," says
Rusca. "For commercial, office and residential properties, we
aim for yields (returns on investment) of about 8 to 10 per
cent. For apartments alone we push for more than that — we
truly insist for about 10 per cent. By pure efficiency of management, cost control and economies of scale, we've been able to
get this in Montreal so far."**6

* As the Quebec Real Estate Association put it in a statement urging the provincial Liberal government in mid-1976 to continue its non-discriminatory
policy toward foreign buyers of buildings: "Unlike their North American
counterparts, European investors are less interested in high yield investments, and this is a safeguard against inflation" through fast-rising
rents.

** A 6-10 per cent return may not sound like much. After all, it is only keeping pace with Canada's inflation rate. It might appear as though an investor could make as much money by simply putting his money in a bank
and letting it accumulate interest.
  But his moderate income is only a small amount of the profits to be
made. The real profits lie in reselling the property — assuming the market
is not depressed and he can sell at a profit. This is the main reason these
speculators seek to sell their properties so rapidly.
  How rapidly? Perhaps the best study has been made by Johan Draper,
head of a Montreal firm called Multiple Real Estate Ltd. Draper told me
he surveyed 204 Montreal apartment buildings sold in 1975; all were
priced at over $100,000, with the average price just shy of $400,000.
Draper calculated that the average building had been held by its owner
only *four years* before being resold. This tells us something about the difficulty for a landlord to feel much loyalty towards his building and tenants.
  It also tells us something about the profits involved. Draper found that
the average annual increase in the price of these 204 buildings was 7½
per cent. That does not sound like much — again, it's comparable to the
inflationary rate of that period. Over the four year period the price increase would come to 30 per cent. But look again.
  It is common to buy these buildings with just a fraction of the selling
price — that is, the buyer pays 25 per cent of the purchase price, say, and
borrows the rest through mortgages. Thus if you bought a $100,000 build-
ing with $25,000 of your own money and sold it four years later for
$130,000 (four years multiplied by 7½ per cent annual price increase),
you are not making a mere 30 per cent profit. Your profit has actually
gone up 120 per cent (minus mortgage expenses) — because your original
investment is only $25,000 and your profit is $30,000.

Who are these investors, these clients of Fidinam? Some, says Rusca, are institutions or individuals in Italy, German or Switzerland. The small-fry, of course, are those most likely to clip out the mail-order form on the ad and send it in. But there are clients of a more substantial sort, as well.

In the winter of 1976-77 the world came very close to knowing, for the first time, just who are the illegal Italian investors in such a firm.

A list of facts and figures on clients made its way out of Fidinam's Lugano headquarters. It ended up in the hands of extortionists who demanded a ransom for the document, threatening otherwise to reveal the names to the authorities. Eventually police recuperated the list, but not before triggering widespread panic among clients in Italy. While the Fidinam Group's head, Tito Tettamanti, sought to reassure investors that the blackmail threat had been blown up out of all proportion, in 1977 the company's frenetic activity had clearly arrived at a turning point. The incident also represents one more element in the growing crisis of confidence over Switzerland's once-fabled discretion.

In late 1976 another controversy erupted, this time in Ottawa. It was a affair reminiscent of numerous recent scandals in the U.S. where multinational corporations like Lockheed Aircraft Corp. and Gulf Oil Corp. were found to have practiced bribery abroad as a means of obtaining contracts. But Canada topped this now-familiar story: this time it was not an ordinary company which had made questionable payments overseas but a government-owned corporation, Atomic Energy of Canada Ltd.

In 1974 the AECL and a partner, Italimpianti of Genoa, had been trying to sell a nuclear reactor to Argentina. In April of that year AECL paid a $2.5 million "agent's fee" to a Liechtenstein company called Intercontinental General Trading Co. The proliferation of the AECL's nuclear reactors, with their potential for being used for making bombs, was controversial enough. Was bribery being used as a means of speeding proliferation? The AECL only thickened the intrigue when it protested it did not known who Intercontinental represented nor the name of the agent involved in the sale.

It was not until 1977 that details began to emerge as to who stood behind the dummy company. The $2.5 million had, it developed, been paid to Intercontinental's account in a Lugano bank. The bank happened to be Banca della Svizzera Italiana, Fidinam's largest shareholder. Indeed, the Liechtenstein company's founder was none other than Tito Tettamanti, chairman of Gruppo Fidinam. Tettamanti had also been president of the company at the time the fee was paid.

However, Tettamanti, like Herr Hilti in the previous chapter, says he is dumbfounded about who might really be behind some of companies he founded. He was, he says, only a nominee director of Intercontinental — a front man. "I am not nor was I ever an owner of Intercontinental," he told the press. "The receipt and disposition of funds paid to Intercontinental were never in any way under my direction or control. I had no knowledge whatsoever of the 1974 payment by Atomic Energy of Canada Ltd. As for the coincidence that he resigned only two weeks after Canada's auditor-general, who touched off the controversy, began investigating the agent's fee, Tettamanti said: "The two events (resignation and investigation) are not related in any way."[7]

Fidinam is no stranger to Canadian political life.

A Conservative member of Parliament who later went on to seek his party's leadership in 1976, James Gillies of Don Valley, Ontario, was a director of Fidinam in 1971.

It was that same year that Fidinam received a highly advantageous deal from the Tories in Ontario, in so doing inadvertently affording us with an insight into the kind of rapport such a firm may achieve with domestic government.

Fidinam has been building many projects in Toronto in recent years,* among them an office-apartment complex at Yonge and Bloor Sts. In 1971 Ontario Premier William Davis' cabinet approved a deal whereby Fidinam (Ontario) Ltd. would receive a $15 million loan from the Ontario Workmen's Compensation Board to build that project; the board would also rent part of the building for 20 years.

Just one month later, in July, Fidinam made a $50,000 contribution to Davis' Ontario Progressive Conservative Party.

---

* In 1972 it completed the $20 million construction of what was then the world's largest Holiday Inn, adjacent to Toronto City Hall. Subsequent projects include a $20 million office-retail complex at Wellington and University and a $12 million office-condominium complex at 920 Yonge St., where Fidinam's Canadian arm has its headquarters.

That November the company did a peculiar thing. Fidinam's Toronto office actually sent a Telex message to Lugano headquarters saying a check had been issued to the Tory treasurer "for $50,000 . . . a political donation related to Upper Canada Place — Workmen's Compensation Board."

Cries of political corruption erupted in the Opposition rows of the Ontario legislature when news of the telex message became known. Fidinam spokesman explained the Telex message had been in error — the loan and the lease contract were in no way tied to the donation. The Conservatives said the same. The storm eventually subsided.

Some Italian investments in Montreal property are, of course, quite on the up and up. As the Toronto representative of one Italian bank notes, "You have to suppose that some of the interests here have either had their money out of Italy long enough not to run afoul of the law, or else they have received from the government one of the rare approvals to export capital."

One such company whose propriety is not questioned is Società Generale Immobiliare, of Rome. The Pope was behind it — it was an open secret in Rome — during its most active years in downtown Montreal and is shares were publicly traded. Also unquestioned is its enormous impact on downtown Montreal. In developing in the early 1960s what is still the city's tallest building, the Stock Exchange Tower, the company transformed an area of the business district around Place Victoria. The Vatican-backed company also developed Montreal's most expensive residential highrise, bar none, and has been active in housing developments on the West Island. One of the world's largest multinational builders, Immobiliare will be examined at greater length in another chapter.

Today the 41-floor Stock Exchange Tower, with its numerous corporate, legal and chartered accountant offices, serves as a roost for some of the largest Italian interests. At the end of a corridor on the twenty-first floor, for example, is a door marked "Acmon Investments Ltd." In unravelling control of the company, one ends up with one of the leading families in Italian business.

Acmon declined to tell me what it owns here, but in leafing through property records I stumbled across the fact that it manages a million dollar apartment building at 5501-5505 Cavendish Blvd. The building's owner is a Liechtenstein company, Gasse Finanz Anstalt. It must be assumed, however, that this building only scratches the surface of a mini-empire.

Two Acmon directors are Alberto and Adolfo Cefis, associated with a number of other real estate holdings.* Alberto lives in a house on Summit Circle atop Mount Royal, one of the most prestigious addresses in Canada. The name Cefis is little known in Canada, but in Italy it is celebrated. Alberto and Adolfo's big brother is Eugenio Cefis who is head of the largest private company in Italy, Montedison. He is also a director of Banca Commerciale Italiana. He was the head of ENI, Italy's state oil company, before going to Montedison in 1971. With over $12.4 billion in assets in 1976, Montedison — a chemical and petroleum company with diversified interests — is twice the size of either of the two biggest Canadian industrial companies, Bell Canada and Canadian Pacific Ltd.

Acmon points up how some of these large Italian investors have planted relatively deep roots here. It was incorporated in 1965 when Italy was still enjoying "Il Boom." The presence of the Cefis family (pronounced CHAY-fees) here only hints at the attraction Montreal's development has had in recent years for some of the biggest names — dwarfing the Cefis — in world business.

It is not a presence which advertises itself. As Miss Joan Fobin, a director of Acmon and many of the related companies said in turning down my request for an interview with Alberto Cefis, "Mr. Cefis is rather hesitant to be quoted or interviewed on anything of this nature. It is a ticklish situation."[8]

To smuggle their money to Montreal, some Italians have actually concealed it in their baggage or clothing and brought it in physically. One gentleman stuffed $2.1 million worth of lira into his moneybelt and arrived in Montreal direct from Milan

---

* Alberto is also a director of Metrinvest Development Ltd., a former owner of the apartment high-rise at 1460 McGregor St. He is also president of Investissements Montfin Ltée., which owns the luxury Chequers Place apartment complex at 3033 Sherbrooke St. W. Another company located in Acmon's office, Briginvest Ltd., is in turn owned by a Swiss company called Hoolie S.A.; it owns an office-building at 485 McGill St. Two companies which are tenants of that building have filed suit against Briginvest for letting the building deteriorate.

on an Alitalia flight in early 1976. But such daring, at a time when passengers are often searched by Italian authorities, is as unnecessary as it is unsophisticated.

One of businessmen's favorite techniques is the 'overcharge.' An Italian industrialist might, for example, order rolls of paper from Canada for $100,000, when the price is actually only $90,000. The remaining $10,000 will be his when he comes to Canada to claim it. Repeated enough times over, fortunes of several million dollars have found their way here in this way.

The registry offices of municipalities throughout the metropolitan area abound with names of residents of Italy. Fausto Catto has snapped up 1.2 hectares of St. Bruno for $42,733, for example. Paolo Bertino paid $73,631 for a lot in Longueuil. And Renato Desalvo acquired 2500 Bates St. in Town of Mount Royal for $130,000.

But these are the midgets. The bigger investors, of course, tend to avoid the use of their names. Some of them had enormous impact here over the years without receiving any recognition.

The Aster Corp. is a notable instance of such determined modesty. Without any doubt Aster is one of the biggest single corporate influences in determining the growth patterns on the South Shore, the fastest growing area in suburban Montreal. It is the father of South Shore sprawl.

Founded as far back as 1959, the far-sighted company began buying up farmland in Brossard — that land which now lies at the foot of the Champlain Bridge, the largest of the bridges between the City of Montreal and the South Shore. At one point Aster owned almost five square kilometres of land there. Much of this land it developed itself (or through a subsidiary called Floreal Corp.) and much it sold off to other developers as the land rose sharply in value. In short, it was the guiding force behind the South Shore's first modern bedroom suburb and set the pace for most other development in that booming sector.

Who deserves the credit — or, as urban planners would have it — the blame? Provincial registration records show that Aster is owned by a Swiss bank in Lugano. According to Aster general manager André Vadeboncœur, the bank has been acting on behalf of clients of several nationalities — with Italians figuring prominently among them. He will say no more.

The Gazette (George Cree)

Identifying myself as a reporter, I answered the above ad, which appeared in Milan's *Corriere della Sera* in March, 1976. I was quickly escorted out of the offices of Lumont Consultants Canadian Construction Ltd. in plush Westmount Square.

Lumont's president has "an innate reluctance toward public exposure", an aide explained after repeated requests for interviews.

To underline the point on my next visit, the aide explained that the president, Rico Ellmenreich —born in Germany but raised in Italy and having a roster of mostly Italian clients— is "very, very shy of publicity — very, very shy". Evidently.

The aide, Umberto Sgherri, also declined to identify the extent of the Lumont group of companies' activities in Canada. But local property records provide at least a partial picture.

Lumont has just finished building two high-rise condominiums on Rembrandt St. (above photo) across from Cavendish Mall (prices for a two-bedroom suite start at $60,000). The group also owns the "Hampstead Terrace", an apartment building at 5475 Rosedale Ave. And it manages roughly 10 other properties around the city.

Of all these interests with a proclivity for anonymity, none have more flair for facelessness than those behind "Les Dauphins." This is the biggest single apartment building in all of East End Montreal, and it comes close to also being the ultimate example of how a single project can radically transform a residential neighborhood.

The 28-floor, 416-unit bloc at 3535 Papineau Ave. has dominated the skyline around Lafontaine Park since 1971. With its population of more than 1,000 persons (not to mention their hundreds of cars), the project has in effect superimposed a separate, new neighborhood on what had until then been a rather sedate one of two and three storey houses.

To try to trace the interests behind this building is to embark on a headspinning international merry-go-round.

The company which originally built "Les Dauphins" is Gotthard Realty Investments Quebec Inc. Not one to take the

This ad, which appeared in *Le Monde* of Paris on July 8th, 1977, invites French investors who are anxious over the political and economic climate in Europe to have confidence in their Canadian cousins.

banal course of going to Liechtenstein, Gotthard opted for a somewhat more adventurous mountain tax paradise: it is owned by a bank of Andorra.

No sooner had it built "Les Dauphins," than it sold that property to two related firms, Gotthard Realty Investments and Gottard Secondo S.A. Tropical climes were more congenial for them: both are incorporated in Panama.

But if a tenant wants to complain about something, he goes not to them but to the building's administrator, Europrogramme Management Consultants of Canada Ltd. This firm is owned by a company incorporated in another mini-country back in Europe — not Liechtenstein or Andorra this time, but Luxembourg.

However, when Europrogramme seeks to communicate with the real owners for financial policy directives it does not contact any of these aforementioned places. According to a Europrogramme administrator who asked not to be identified, the company communicates with its higher-ups through Switzerland.

Switzerland is not the end of the line, though. Europrogramme has three directors and all three list their addresses as being in Chiasso, a Swiss town right on the Italian border. It is, like Lugano, a favorite channel for money from Italy to which Europrogramme also directs an ad campaign.[9]

Who, if anyone, will succeed the Italians as big real estate investors here? The answer, of course, depends not just on Canadian politics but on conditions in investors' native countries.

La Fuga may have dried up since the election of the Parti Québécois — its disappearance was due to a combination of political and economic uncertainty in Quebec and of changing circumstances in Italy itself. But the drop in foreign real estate investments in Quebec promises to be only a temporary hiatus. Property values in Quebec are unlikely to fall very far before they will lure other speculators who will make them rise again. Just where these investors will come from is uncertain. But there are indications the leadership will be from France.

This is not so much because France has a cultural affinity for Quebec nationalism (investors tend to be unsentimental about where they put their money) as because France is experiencing roughly the same kind of internal leftist pressures which Italy has undergone. The country-wide municipal elections in March, 1977, which saw large gains by leftists, has fueled the same kind of fears among the wealthy. There is also a sense that political relations between France and Quebec will strengthen, and this can bolster confidence.

It is interesting to note that in the period immediately following the election of a separatist Quebec government France has been the country showing the most confidence — such as it is — in the province's economy. There are a number of examples of this.

Thus after the November, 1976, election, we had to wait four months — a remarkably long time — before the first major construction project was announced for metropolitan Montreal. When it came, the announcement was for a 14-storey, $6.5 million office building at 2075 Stanley St. The developer was a local anglophone firm, First Quebec Corp., but the critical financing* came from a Paris-owned company, Crédit Foncier Franco-Canadien.

The same month that this project was announced — March, 1977 — La Société Générale, France's No. 2 bank, established a Montreal office. It said it intended to promote commerce between France and Quebec and do other kinds of business as well, including real estate.

In April a vice president of the Canadian subsidiary of France's No. 1 bank, Banque Nationale de Paris, noted that his firm had already been in Canada for 15 years but that it now had far more clients from France than ever before. Most clients were interested in investing in Canadian industry, but there were inquiries for acquiring rural land as well.[11]

A fourth instance came in May when the local promoter of the giant, partly Liechtenstein-financed housing project on 25 square kilometres of land near Mirabel Airport told me that four different francophone groups (from either France or other French-speaking countries) had approached him that month about the possibility of investing a total of $6 million in real estate. These groups, said Claude Lafleur of Les Constructions

---

* "Lenders," as notes one Montreal developer, Matthew Hudson, "are probably more important to the development process than the developers themselves. Lenders control what gets built and what doesn't, determine what it looks like, etc. It's their ballgame."[10]

Promirad, were not committed to investing in Quebec — but sniffing the political wind, pawing the ground and poised to spring.[12]

In August the industrial and commercial real estate manager of a Montreal trust company, just back from a trip to Europe to peddle local property, told me exhuberantly: "The French money is coming in like I've never seen it before. There's a tremendous interest in Montreal over there. People are scared silly about the likelihood of a Communist-Socialist win in the next election, in March '78. A lot of the money is coming in from Liechtenstein."

Plus ça change . . .

Footnotes — Chapter 2

1. Panorama magazine, Dec. 21, 1976, p. 165.
2. Telephone interview, Mar. 11, 1976.
3. Telephone interview, Mar. 8, 1976.
4. Telephone interview, Jun. 7, 1976.
5. Telephone interview Aug. 26., 1976, with Fausto C. Rusca, president of Fidinam (Canada) Ltd.
6. Telephone interview, Dec. 2, 1976.
7. Toronto Globe & Mail, Jan. 14, 1977, "Swiss bankers deny agent role in sale of Candu," by Ross Henderson.
8. Telephone conversation, May 28, 1976.
9. One example of such an ad by Europrogramme appeared in the news magazine L'Espresso, Feb. 22, 1976, p. 90.
10. Interview with Hudson, then president of Groupe Canest, Nov. 24, 1975.
11. Telephone interview with Michel Durand, vice president of BNP Canada Inc., April, 1977.
12. Telephone interview, May, 18, 1977.

Chapter 3

A Cluster of Giants

DURING THE 1970s multinational corporations like IBM, Exxon, ITT, Fiat, Nestlé, and Mitsubishi have become household words everywhere. Fanning out across the continents, they have changed local tastes and objectives so as better to peddle their wares or extract resources.

However, multinational companies operating in the real estate development field remain virtually unknown to the public. Because of their low profile, we have greatly underestimated their influence in changing the form and character of cities across Canada and around the world. Each operates under a variety of different names. They themselves tend to be satellites of greater companies which are in the fields of gravity of still vaster corporate galaxies.

In this chapter we shall look at two such companies and begin to trace their chains of command back through a series of strata. The first is English Property Corp. Ltd., of London. It operates in North America through its Montreal subsidiary, Trizec Corp. Ltd., perhaps Canada's best known developer. In the organization which looms behind English Property are some of the biggest names in the British aristocracy, financial world and political intelligence. The leadership of this organization contains enough peers, lords of the realm and Rothschilds to seem to belong to another, earlier age (which in a sense it does). This leadership is part of an old-fashioned, genteel tradition which appears in sharp contrast to the futuristic, ultra-modern generation of glass-box skyscrapers it has helped spawn in Canada and in at least ten other countries.

The second company is Abbey Glen Property Corp., of Toronto, one of the several major companies to follow Trizec's lead in developing urban Canada. Its influential ownership has roots stretching back to the troubled goldfields of South Africa. Via a circuitous route, profits extracted with the miner's shovel in that country have been plowed into some of the largest buildings built in Montreal and other Canadian cities during the 1970s.

If the organizations behind such companies were selling toasters or other consumer products they, like Westinghouse, might want their names familiar to the public — since brand-name identification builds sales. But in the real estate business fame often works against you.

For one thing, quite apart from increasing your accountability, it can raise the price of property you want to acquire. If persons in a position to sell property to these companies knew who was ultimately behind them, they could charge much more. This is one reason such companies use so many fronts, employing various differently-named associated companies to do their buying or engage a trust company or other intermediary to buy for them. For another thing, this is an age when land developers and speculators are widely resented. They are often outsiders — or locals who represent outside interests — with little feel for the traditions and sensibilities of the communities they are seeking to transform.

In a world which wants increasing democracy, the only acceptable justification for action is "popular" approval, and the need for such interests to function behind a facade of "local" front companies grows ever more acute.

The biggest example of such so-called "indigenous" company is Trizec Corp. Ltd.* In the view of many developers, Trizec has been the most influential company in the postwar transformation of urban Canada.

It was formed in 1960 to complete Montreal's Place Ville Marie, then the largest office complex of its kind in North

* With assets of $896 million in 1976.

America and the pivot around which subsequent downtown development turned. Trizec makes its headquarters there today.

In his book on Vancouver's growth, Donald Gutstein assessed PVM 15 years later from the perspective of the other side of the continent: "Place Ville Marie became the prototype for all that is happening in downtown Canada — huge skyscrapers, vast bleak plazas, underground parking lots and underground shopping malls."[1]

But Trizec is not one to rest on its laurels. In addition to building, buying or managing scores of office high-rises, hotels, and shopping centers in other cities in Canada and the U.S., the company today is preparing skyscraper complexes in four cities — Saint-John, N.B., Quebec City, Winnipeg and Calgary — which a spokesman describes in these terms: "Relative to their surroundings, yes, I guess you could call them comparable to what PVM is to Montreal."*

---

* All these projects were conceived and set in motion prior to the 1976 arrangement whereby certain Trizec functions, to be described shortly, were transferred to Canadian hands.

Michael Dugas

Place Ville-Marie (background, center), the *building that has had the most extensive impact on the development of urban Canada.*

Also, Trizec has become Montreal's No. 1 private land-lord — it owns a dozen office buildings around town. If all their rentable floor space in 1977 were added up it would come to a remarkable 122 acres, or 48 hectares. It also owns several blocks of property downtown with development potential, a couple of shopping centres and vast empty tracts in Brossard.

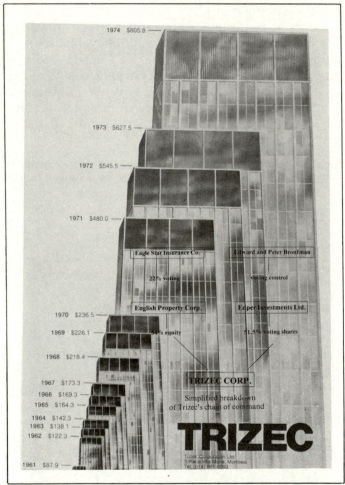

Real Estate Development Annual (1975)

A simplified "family tree" of Trizec's control is superimposed on a company trade advertisement showing how it has grown between 1961 and 1974.

Almost everyone has heard of Trizec. But almost no one — and that includes some of its senior executives — has known who has been ultimately behind it, as it spearheaded changes in urban Canada . . .

Much of Trizec's ownership is a matter of public record and fairly well known. Prior to transfer of stock in mid-1976, of which we will talk a little later, it was 64 per cent owned during the 1970s by English Property Corp. Ltd., of London. English Property is the largest multinational real estate corporation in the U.K., with assets of well over $1 billion* in 8 countries.

English Property's major shareholder, in turn, is Eagle Star Insurance Co. Ltd., also of London, whose 22 per cent of the stock — far more than any other party — is highly influential.

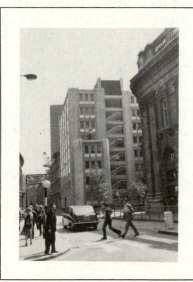

Henry Aubin

Eagle Star's London headquarters overlooks Threadneedle Street, in the City.

* £821,952,000 in fiscal 1975.

Eagle Star is publicly-owned, but who is behind it? What are they doing elsewhere in the world? Is Eagle Star itself but a part of a still larger skein of interests?

These are questions which this triple-tiered organization — that is, Trizec, English Property, Eagle Star — is not anxious for outsiders to explore. My own trip to London as a Montreal newspaper reporter trying to examine the roots of such organizations provided me with a clear picture of how their desire for "discretion" can resemble a brick wall. When I asked for an interview with the chairman of Eagle Star, Denis Mountain, on the subject of Canadian real estate, his secretary referred me, after consulting Mountain, to the chief executive of English Property, David Llewellyn. When I wrote Philip Shelbourne, the deputy chairman of English Property and director of Eagle Star, also requesting an interview, he replied by letter that he was "not suitable" and that I should speak to Llewellyn. When, obediently, I then did ask for an interview with Llewellyn, the public relations officer for English Property, Miss Sally Upson, said after conferring with Llewellyn, "He doesn't feel it would be helpful to grant you an interview."

Canadian operations are "independent" of London, she said, so only executives in Canada could talk about matters relating to Canada — this is surprising news to some London reporters who say that Llewellyn often phones them to boast about the Canadian assets. Miss Upson referred me to James Soden of N.D.G. in Montreal, who was at that time chairman and chief executive of Trizec.*

This kind of runaround is an apt reflection of the chameleon-like idiosynchracies of such companies, and only served to stimulate my curiosity about the organization. They seek to

---

* Soden was not any more receptive than his superiors to an inquiry into the organization. After repeated calls to his office after my return to Montreal, his secretary referred me to the company's vice president for public relations, John Meyer, who also writes a business column for the Toronto Star and Montreal Gazette. Said Meyer of Soden: "He's really not free to talk." Meyer said he was to take the job of answering any questions I might have.

take on the coloration of their host country. They want to be perceived as Canadian by Canadians, and to be frank, they have been quite successful at it. As the property correspondent for the London Financial Times wryly wrote after a visit to Montreal in the early 1970s," Canadians regard Trizec as a purely Canadian real estate company — an unusual distinction . . . There may/be more than a tinge of xenophobia in all this, but this is where the key to Canada lies (for British property firms)."

By 1976 this xenophobia had become quite intolerable for the organization: federal and provincial legislation in Canada were inhibiting acquisitions by foreign property firms. English Property decided to lower its profile still more. It agreed to sell what was defined as "voting control" of Trizec to Canadian interests, headed by one wing of Montreal's Bronfman family. With a depressed property market back in the U.K., English Property could use the money earned from such a sale.

Edward and Peter Bronfman, acting through a family trust called Edper Investments Ltd., obtained directly and indirectly a 51.5 per cent voting interest in the company, enough to satisfy Ottawa that control was no longer in foreign hands. This was widely publicized by Trizec through press releases, messages to shareholders, etc. The Bronfmans lost no time replacing some of the top managers with their own men. "We have absolute voting control of Trizec," an Edper vice president assured me . . . Presto, Canada's most influential real estate company had suddenly become Canadian.

Or so it seemed. But at the same time on the other side of the ocean something quite different was going on. English Property was suggesting to its shareholders that all this was, in effect, part of the old chameleon act.

English Property was to retain enormous veto powers. In a letter to shareholders dated June 3, 1976, Llewellyn stated that under the terms of the sale there cannot be "any change in the nature of (Trizec's) business nor change in Trizec's constitution without English Property's prior consent." It also says that if the Bronfman interests one day want to sell their voting control, then English Property will have the right of first refusal. If English Property decides not to buy it itself, it is insured of having a say in to whom else the Bronfmans might sell. It appears to be much like a corporate counterpart of Canada's constitution, the British North America Act, which makes Canada governmentally subordinate to the British. Let the Canadian Parliament make laws within certain parameters defined by the act, says the constitution; but if it wants to change the rules of the game and reform the constitution it must get approval from the British Parliament.

In the case of Trizec, however, the relationship is enhanced by another matter: ownership. English Property may have sold some of its 64 per cent interest in Trizec to the Canadians, but it still retains about 54 per cent of Trizec's equity, or combined non-voting and voting shares. Thus, regardless of how "voting control" is interpreted, the British still *own* Trizec.

Llewellyn's June 3 letter is very blunt about the relationship: "Trizec will remain a subsidiary of the company."

Trizec's power structure thus remains quite ambiguous. One can get into vigorous semantic debate about what "voting control" means and what "subsidiary" and "equity ownership" mean, as defined by the various partners, and not prove much of anything. It is enough to say that the terms of the arrangement — as described to different audiences on either side of the Atlantic — have left some observers wondering if this is a case of the British selling Canada back to the Canadians or of trying to sidestep such laws as the federal Foreign Investment Review Act while meeting their own cash problems back home. Anyway, the nationality switch worked. In 1977 Ottawa ruled that Trizec could buy all the property here it wanted because it was no longer foreign. Meanwhile English Property remains a major force within Trizec, providing it with most of the share capital to continue the Montreal company's role in North America as well as maintaining veto power over how it plays that role.

Projects started in the days when English Property held clear control are still in the process of changing Canada's skyline. In Quebec City, for example, Trizec is still planning to add a high office tower next to the 23-floor Quebec Hilton which it has already built as part of its "Place Quebec" complex. In Saint John, N.B., work proceeds on "Brunswick Square", to consist of a 33-storey office tower and an adjoining retail-hotel wing.

In Winnipeg, the company is considering several plans for the historic corner of Portage and Main streets; one plan calls for twin 34-storey office towers. And meanwhile in Calgary, its just-completed 40-floor Scotia Centre was filling up with corporate tenants in 1977.

English Property's headquarters are in a rambling Edwardian house on London's Grosvenor St. It is rather quaint, with curving staircases, gleaming old woodwork, and a little elevator that takes forever. It might provide the perfect setting for an Evelyn Waugh farce. Indeed, the company in recent years has presented a cast of characters whose contrasts have all the makings of a drawing room comedy:

— As its influential chairman, we have a superannuated baronet, Sir Brian Mountain who finally died in February 1977. He had about him an air of select private clubs and a passion for racehorses. But he was not to be underestimated.

— As one of the financial advisors who piloted English Property through its period of biggest growth through takeovers, we discern the legendary merchant bank of N.M. Rothschild & Sons, then headed by Edmund de Rothschild. The Rothschild bankers, with their passion for discretion, prefer to stay out of the spotlight, but without their work, the company would be of only minor importance.

— As its major individual shareholder — for a lighter touch — a young man who also owns one of Britain's leading pornographic cinema chains. He is Laurie Marsh, known for his flair: once, in making a point, he is said to have turned the boardroom table upside down at a meeting of the directors of another company. Marsh was once managing director of English Property, but in the era since the Mountains and Rothschilds came in, he has quietly left the board.

— As the largest overall shareholder, the tens of thousands of policy holders in the baronet's family insurance company, whose operations are to an important extent in strife-torn southern Africa.

— As the ramrod of the outfit and second largest non-institutional shareholder after Marsh, David Llewellyn. A pudgy chartered accountant from the Isle of Jersey with a fondness for jewelry, his passion is putting up high-rises. Says a friend:

"He started playing with blocks at age three, and he just never looked back."

In association with some less colorful characters, this cast has turned English Property into the second largest real estate company in Britain and the largest one operating internationally.[2] This is no mean ranking; British companies are far bigger than any North American-owned companies in this field and, indeed, one can almost say that Britain is to international property development what the U.S. is to the world automobile business.

Trizec is by far the brightest star in English Property's constellation of holdings. Its assets accounted for 51 per cent of English Property's total consolidated assets in 1975. Trizec also has subsidiaries in France, Belgium, the Netherlands, Luxembourg, and the Republic of Ireland as well as Britain. Trizec itself has three subsidiaries in the U.S. where about 20 per cent of its assets are located.

Many of the cities where English Property owns property — whether Montreal, Halifax, Paris or Brussels — might once have had their own distinctive architecture. But from photos of these English Property buildings it is virtually impossible to tell in which city, country, or even continent they are located. Architectural differentiations are as blurred as for mobile homes trailer camps — of which, incidentally, Trizec owns 35 in North America, mostly in Florida and the western U.S. A touch of Old World individualism might be fine around English Property's Grosvenor St. headquarters or Sir Brian Mountain's country home at Dunley Manor, but when it comes to making money for its stockholders — English Property's *raison d'être* — what matters is that high-rises provide more tenants from whom to collect rent, and standardized box designs require lower architectural and labor fees.*

This is, of course, the simple and unsentimental perspective from which our cast of characters views English Property: it is a vehicle for investments, an instrument to help attain broader

---

* As we will see in a minute, the one building which does contain considerable originality and remarkability, the cruciform tower of Place Ville Marie, was conceived when the project was under the direction of entrepreneur William Zeckendorf, Sr., not English Property or its antecedent company.

development of capital. Though it may be among the two or three largest multinational landlords in the world, from this perspective English Property is really not very big at all. In fact, the company received Trizec in 1970 as a kind of hand-me-down from a far more important company.

This is the insurance company headed by the family of Sir Brian Mountain.

London's Threadneedle Street has a quaint name, but that's about all that's picturesque about it. A never-ending of stream buses and cars roars by, scattering the rather well dressed pedestrians, in black bowler hats. This is the financial district — the "City", as Londoners call it. No. 1 is but one of a number of post-war buildings on the street: grey concrete with infrequently-washed windows.

In fact, the building would be totally unremarkable except for one thing. It has no neon sign declaring the name of the corporation headquartered here; but the owners, displaying a flair for discreet symbolism, have perched a lifesize statue of a rather grand-looking eagle on a ledge five floors up. The eagle's wings are outstretched, and it is painted gold. Passersby occasionally notice it, and they ask the doorman if this could be the U.S. Embassy. He just smiles patiently and shakes his head. The statue isn't the American emblem, but the corporate symbol for the company which occupies the building: Eagle Star Insurance Co. Ltd.

If the statue is an appropriate symbol for the company, then the direction in which the bird casts its eagle-eye is just as fitting. It looks due west, straight toward Canada. Canada may not be much of a market for the insurance policies that Eagle Star underwrites; — at least 60 other companies sell more there. But, excluding banks, Eagle Star is the single most important company in the world involved in re-shaping Canadian cities since 1960. It was in that year that it co-founded Trizec, which completed the PVM and propelled urban Canada into the ongoing development revolution.

Trizec is only one part of Eagle Star's empire in Canada. In recent years it has also had major investments in three other substantial real estate development companies as well as in a company specializing in real estate mortgage loans.*

The title of "most important company" in shaping Canadian cities may seem a peculiar distinction for a British company, and an insurance company at that. Innumerable recent articles have described the diminishing global influence of Britain, not so long ago the leading colonial power. British business has the image in some quarters of being listless, stuck in its old ways, easily eclipsed by U.S. companies; the British hardly appear to be the investment strategists behind the bold, super-modern skycrapers which are the very antithesis of tradition. Indeed, within Britain itself Eagle Star is not known for any originality or adventurousness except possibly as a pioneer in *pluvius* — the business of insuring cricket matches, horse events and ladies fairs against cancellation by rain.**

---

* These four other vehicles, while smaller individually, comprise a remarkable collective presence:

— Eagle Star has been substantial shareholder in another major British real estate firm, MEPC Ltd. In 1972 it had seven per cent of the equity of MEPC, whose Toronto-based subsidiary, MEPC Canadian Properties Ltd., is one of the dozen largest publicly owned property firms in Canada. And English Property, on its own, held another nine per cent.

— Until 1975 Eagle Star also held controlling interest in Canada's seventh largest publicly owned development company, Bramalea Ltd., according to Bramalea's executive vice-president, Kenneth Field. Field says Eagle Star sold its stake to Canadian interests because of anticipated problems from the Foreign Investment Review Act.

— Eagle Star has the second largest shareholding (13 per cent) in the Rank Organization, the British entertainment consortium which is active in Canadian real estate — besides owning the bulk of Odeon, one of the country's two main movie theatre chains. Through a division called Rank City Wall it owns commercial and residential properties in Toronto, Calgary, and Vancouver, as well as in France, Belgium, and England. According to a Rank spokesman, it also owns many of the 131 Odeon theatres it operates across Canada. Rank and Eagle Star have had close relations since World War II, and today there is a top-level exchange of seats on the board of directors: the chairmen of both companies sit on each other's boards.

— It is the second largest shareholder in United Dominions Trust Ltd., a London bank with four subsidiary companies in Canada. They handle industrial and commercial installment finance as well as real estate mortgage loans. Its Canadian assets in 1975 stood at $165 million, and were rapidly growing.

** In August-September 1974, when five inches of rain fell on London, Eagle Star found itself drenched with compensation requests from charity fairs and sporting events. Few firms sell *pluvius,* and none are larger than Eagle Star. It should be noted, however, that this is just a sideline for the company; the bulk of its business is in property, automobile, aviation, marine, life and other conventional forms of insurance.

But behind Eagle Star's plain-looking exterior are arrayed some of the biggest names of the international economic varsity. In an age of multinational corporate giants, Eagle Star may seem a somewhat modest cog, but it is a cog which turns large wheels.

Just as the presence of Canada's constitution in Westminster, just west of the City, betokens the fundamental political relationship of Canada to Britain,* so the presence of Eagle Star's investment strategy in Canada underscores the economic ties.

Eagle Star is part of an informal cluster of relatively little-known companies which have been transforming much of Quebec and the rest of urban and rural Canada in their own image. Their influence here has as much to do with large energy projects in the north as it does with skyscrapers in the south. By no means do these companies dominate their fields; but they are leaders, showing direction and instilling change.

Nor do they operate here in a political vacuum. A glance at the roster of directors of Eagle Star's Toronto-based subsidiary, Eagle Star Insurance Co. of Canada Ltd., for example, turns up the name of the Progressive Conservative Party's leading financial specialist, MP Sinclair Stevens. In 1976 Stevens was a prominent candidate for his party's leadership post, but his rightwing base was too narrow for success. Stevens is a director of few other firms, and his presence here signals the stake Eagle Star and other companies in its cluster have in Canada.

Stevens' rightist politics mirror those of Sir Brian Mountain, the septuagenarian baronet and patriarch of the Mountain family which has provided the chairmen of Eagle Star for three generations. Under Sir Brian the company amassed large —

---

* The British Parliament retains power of veto over any changes in that constitution requested by Ottawa. Many people say Canada's subordinate status is more apparent than real. That's what the Australians said about their country prior to 1975 when the Queen's representative to Australia — the governor-general, whose function until then was widely assumed to be ceremonial, as is that of his counterpart in Canada — stripped the prime minister of his office during a labor crisis which was weakening the economy and replaced him with the leader of another party. No outsider, the governor-general was not only Australian by birth but nominated to his post by the same prime minister he later ousted.

and, until recently, quite lucrative — real estate investments, directly and indirectly, in countries whose current instability makes Canada, separatist threat and all, seem almost placid. They include South Africa, Rhodesia and the Republic of Ireland. Indeed, the company's biggest overseas insurance operations are in South Africa. There is nothing unusual in Eagle Star's staunchly conservative reputation.* It is consistent with a common correlation between political conservatism and major property owners — those who, among other things, have the most to lose when governmental instability lowers property values.

It is easy to underrate Britain's importance in global business today. Hardly a month goes by without new headlines bewailing the worsening U.K. economy, new tidings of the decline of the pound. But despite the erosion around it, the City remains the world's leading centre for international finance. Eagle Star and other insurance companies — gray, amorphous institutions that they may seem — are one of the key underpinnings of this centre. Despite mounting competition from New York and the Continent, far more international insurance passes through Britain than anywhere else.

Canada itself is a poignant example of a country standing in the shadow of British insurance. Asked to name the three biggest general insurance companies in their country, most Canadians would probably name some of the widely advertised domestic or U.S. firms. Actually, all three are British controlled.** What's more, British-controlled companies hold an even bigger share of property and casualty insurance in Canada than do Canadian-controlled companies: 28.1 per cent of the net

---

* Eagle Star's 1974 annual report, for example, notes the company made a political contribution of £25,000 — substantial by U.K. electoral standards — to the Conservative and Unionist Party. The party is an amalgam of Northern Irish Unionists, who seek to maintain ties with Britain, and the British Opposition party.

** The biggest is Royal Insurance Co., which wrote over a quarter billion dollars in property and casualty premiums in 1975 and accounts for 8.7 per cent of the total market, according to the Canadian Underwriters' Magazine 1976 statistical review. Runnersup are Lloyd's of London (5.3 per cent) and Commercial Union Assurance Co. (4.3 per cent).

premiums written in 1974 versus 22.1 per cent for the Canadian,* according to the latest Ottawa figures. In all, foreign-
controlled firms of all nationalities — U.K., U.S., Swiss,
French, etc. — claimed 78.9 per cent of all premiums written in
Canada.

Just how vital this industry is to Britain is summed up by the
chairman of Eagle Star to the company's shareholders. "The insurance industry," he says flatly, "is the biggest contributor to
this country's invisible balance of payments."[3]

Britain has more than 550 insurance companies. Eagle Star
is ninth largest in the "life" field (with funds of £586,018,000
in 1974) and is the eighth largest in the "non-life" field (that is
property and casualty, where it had a premium income of
£158,882,000.).

Though some companies are bigger, none are closer to the
heart of the City establishment.

For one thing, it has longstanding rapport with probably the
most reknowned insurance company in the world, Lloyd's of
London —Britain's largest underwriter and Canada's second
largest general insurer. It has come a long way since its founding 300 years ago in Edward Lloyd's coffee house, insuring
everything today from supertankers to nuclear power plants. In
a hard-won, overly brief thirty-minute interview in his pan-
elled corner office atop the Threadneedle St. headquarters, Sir
Brian cordially led me through the genealogical maze linking
the two firms — typical of the kind of old family friendships in
the City which determine longlasting corporate friendships. Sir
Brian's father, who founded Eagle Star and became the first
baronet, founded Lloyd's first brokerage firm, called Gardner
Mountain. And Sir Brian's uncle, Rex Mountain, was at one
time chairman of Lloyd's. Also, Sir Brian's son, Denis Mountain, was with Lloyd's some 14 years before eventually succeed-
ing Sir Brian as chairman of Eagle Star in 1974.

---

* This represents a small narrowing of the gap since 1971, when the British
controlled 29.8 per cent versus the Canadians 20.1 per cent. (Source: Report of the Superintendent of Insurance for Canada, Vol. 1, table 5A, both
1973 and 1974 editions).

Henry Aubin

Sir Brian Mountain

Sir Denis Mountain

The Mountains are the family most closely identified with Eagle Star, but they do not control it* — as with most of the big insurance companies there are many hands on the tiller. Indeed, the Mountains are eclipsed socially, financially and in many other ways by other parties associated with the firm.

Consider, first, the social world. The old-fashioned tradition we saw reflected in the *pluvius* policies for horse shows and polo matches is one many directors can empathize with. The 21 directors include a marquess, an earl, a viscount and two baronets; and two of the six knights on the board have married the daughters of peers. Viscount Cobham, for one, has been lord steward of Her Majesty's Household. While he was in that

---

* Nor, as some on Fleet Street have suggested, are they complete figureheads. For years the various members of the Mountain family on the board of directors had more stock in the company than any other directors. Then in 1975 a dynamic property man, John Danny, obtained 1,800,000 ordinary 25 penny shares and became a director, outweighing the Mountains who by the end of 1975 had 606,292 shares. This gives Danny clout but not outright control. (Source: 1975 annual report).

post from 1967 to 1972, Debrett's Peerage ranked him No. 2 in the Buckingham Palace pecking order, behind only the lord chamberlain. Today he is chancellor of the Order of the Garter.* Many large U.K. corporations have peers on their boards, of course, but few have quite so many.

It would be easy to dismiss this as a collection of blue-bloods brought into Eagle Star for decorative purposes. But Eagle Star draws most of its directors from the uppermost levels of diverse spheres, and proximity of some of them to the monarchy only conforms to that pattern. Also, it is interesting to note that directors like the Earl of Cadogan, who owns a vast part of London's fashionable Chelsea area and is a former mayor of Chelsea, are not necessarily useless fuddy-duddies from the viewpoint of a firm like Eagle Star with extensive investments in property. As a class of landowners, peers have an unmatched understanding of real estate: they are to property what industrialists are to industry.** In such families the value of property has been instilled for generations — and some of the Eagle Star directors' titles go back a few. The Earl of Cadogan's earldom goes back seven generations. Viscount Cobham's title spans 10. And the Marquess of Linlithgow may be only the third marquess in his line but he also bears a Scottish baronetcy which goes back 11 generations.

Like Eagle Star's conservatism, there is nothing extraordinary about encountering an old aristocracy in new multinational property ventures. It is part of a pattern which will be unfolding throughout this book. It testifies to the durability of these families. Dispossessed of much of their land over the course of time in some cases, or fearful of expropriation by leftist governments in others, or simply willing to apply the kind

---

* Not a bad move for our upwardly mobile viscount. Of Britain's nine orders of knighthood, the Order of the Garter is the highest and the most coveted. It dates back to the 14th century and membership is limited to 24 persons. These include today King Léopold III of the Belgians, Prince Paul of Yugoslavia, the King of Norway, the Emperor of Japan and the Duke of Edinburgh.

** Their titles are in fact *functions of their property*. A monarch named a man duke of such-and-such a place because he was to control that place — a duke-dom — which might consist of several thousand square miles.

of knowledge acquired over the generations, they associate themselves with real estate investments in Canada and other distant countries.

Next we come to the bankers in Eagle Star's entourage, perhaps the most critical element in such a company's growth. And here we discern the most legendary name in world finance: Rothschild.

Evelyn de Rothschild, a member of the London branch of the family, was first elected to the board in 1975.* But the family and its merchant bank, N.M. Rothschild & Sons Ltd., have enjoyed a rapport with Eagle Star well before this. In 1963, for example, Eagle Star and N.M. Rothschild joined with four other City firms to form a debt collecting firm called Shield Factors Ltd. (Leopold de Rothschild and Sir Brian's son, Nicholas, were both directors). In 1967 the two got together again with others in a small circle to form a London-based multinational bank, Rothschild Intercontinental Bank. And for many years one of the partners at N.M. Rothschild, David R. Colville (the first non-Rothschild to be named to the bank since its founding a century and a half ago) has been one of Eagle Star's three deputy chairmen.

Sir Brian and Evelyn de Rothschild have a lot more to chat about after annual meetings than just investment depreciation: there's also horses. Sir Brian, voluble on the subject, is a former chairman of the prestigious United Racecourses Ltd., while Rothschild was also a director of that and a former champion polo player.

Another important banker is Sir Kenneth Keith, who stepped down from the board about the same time Rothschild came on but who was especially influential in the company in the early 1960's when it was establishing Trizec. Sir Kenneth is chairman of the Hill Samuel merchant bank, advisor to Eagle

---

* The Rothschild bank was advisor to Grovewood Securities Ltd., a property and investment holding company with an excellent profit record, earlier in 1975 when Eagle Star bid to take it over. The bank advised Grovewood shareholders, chief among them chairman John Danny, to sell their shares in exchange for Eagle Star shares. As a result Danny became by far the largest shareholder in the insurance company with family and friends holding about 5 per cent. Both Danny and Evelyn de Rothschild joined the Eagle Star board that fall.

Star for many years. Many self-made men aspire to owning a Rolls Royce; Sir Kenneth, who comes from a Norfolk farming community, did one better. He is chairman of the company that makes them. While Evelyn de Rothschild is chairman of the influential *Economist* newsweekly, Sir Kenneth is a director of *The Times*.

One of the leading figures in British intelligence also served many years on the board. He is Sir Kenneth Strong, a Sandhurst graduate who headed Gen. Dwight D. Eisenhower's intelligence staff in 1943 and continued with the Supreme Commander of Allied Forces until the end o the war. From 1945-47 he was director general of political intelligence in the British Foreign Office (where Sir Kenneth Keith was his assistant). And in the 1960's he was director general of intelligence for the Ministry of Defence.

In a 1961 book, one researcher, S. Aronovitch, described Eagle Star as belonging to a loose group of interlocking inter-

Evelyn de Rothschild receives the Queen's Cup from Queen Elizabeth II after a victorious polo match.

ests which featured the Midland Bank, the Drayton group and what is now the Hill Samuel group; he says, "This grouping may be held overall to be the most powerful in British television, film and theatre."*4

But for Canada what is most important is its ties with the companies most active in transforming Canada.

Eagle Star, like many influential investors in Canadian cities, did not start out with a carefully planned strategy for involvement in Canada. It began, so the record says, quite by default.

The U.S.-controlled company, Webb & Knapp (Canada) Ltd., which was building Place Ville Marie ran into financial problems in the late 1950s. Looking for $25 million, the U.S. entrepreneur William Zeckendorf, Sr. got a promise for it from a London land tycoon, Jack Cotton. But in order to export that capital Cotton needed special permission from the Bank of England, which has restrictions on money draining out of that country. Zeckendorf sent his son, Bill Jr., over to London to close the deal. The day of the signing, however, young Zeckendorf received a call from Cotton saying the Bank of England had shot down the deal.

Zeckendorf had had earlier conversations with Eagle Star's banking advisors, Sir Kenneth Keith and Henry Moore (who were both with the bank which has since evolved into Hill Samuel). He had told them if anything happened to the Cotton deal he would be back to see them. Now he called them and, over lunch in a London restaurant, they struck a deal. Why the Bank of England approved their application and not Cotton's remains one of those little mysteries. Says one London insider: "We were able to phrase our application correctly. Maybe Cotton didn't try hard enough."5

Cotton died four years later. The elder Zeckendorf, whose reputation for flamboyance was equalled only by Cotton's, went bankrupt shortly thereafter and died in New York in 1976. Eagle Star, though its stake in Canada's development has had its ups and downs since then, has stayed the course.

Eagle Star is one of three companies which founded Trizec in 1960 to complete PVM. Originally, it was owned 50-50 by

Zeckendorf's Webb & Knapp and two U.K. partners, Eagle Star and Second Covent Garden Property Co. Ltd.* Since Eagle Star was the largest shareholder in the latter company and Sir Brian was chairman of both, it quickly became an Eagle Star operation. When the price rose for the steel needed to construct PVM, the British companies provided extra capital in exchange for a majority interest in Trizec. Reflecting Eagle Star's control of the company, Sir Brian became its chairman.

In 1970, however, a fast-growing London-based real estate company bought control of Trizec. This was English Property Corp. Ltd. (before a name change it was Star [Great Britain] Holdings Ltd.). Its growth was due largely to a series of take-overs of other British property firms at about this same time. N.M. Rothschild & Sons was highly influential during this period, serving as financial advisor to English Property for the takeovers. In a sense, the transfer of control of Trizec from Eagle Star to English Property was an all-in-the-family transaction: Eagle Star became by far the biggest shareholder in the property company with 22 per cent of the voting shares, Sir Brian became its chairman and two other Eagle Star directors also joined its 17-man board.

In the interview, Sir Brian at first denied Eagle Star had control of English Property. I then asked if its shareholding and interlocking directorate did not give it *effective* control. He was less definite. "We have 22 per cent of it," he said. "Whether you call that control or not I don't know"**

Laurie Marsh, true to the less circumspect tradition of his sex theatre-chain, gave this candid appraisal. "Eagle Star is the controlling shareholder to all intents and purposes," he told me. "They're 10 times bigger than anyone else."

---

* Trizec derives its name from this deal. The "Tri" refers to the three partners; the Z refers to Zeckendorf, the E to Eagle Star and the C to Coent Garden. To this day, however, some of Zeckendorf's friends insist the "zec" refers exclusively to Big Bill.

** Eagle Star's interest in the property company goes well beyond 22 per cent of the voting shares. It also owns 90 per cent of the convertible preference shares, 100 per cent of the first mortgage debenture stock from 1983-87 and from 1987-92 and 28 per cent of the unsecured loan stock from 1998-2003. (Source: Eagle Star's 1975 annual report).

Laurie Marsh, colourful London theater owner; background, a Marsh-owned porno mill.

Yet, stellar force that it may be, Eagle Star is but one twinkle in the little-known galaxy of international finance which has been changing all of Canada.

The insurance company is an associate of one of the true colossi of global resource development, the Anglo American Corp. of South Africa Ltd., of Johannesburg. This is one of the least recognized conglomerate wonders of the world: incredibly, corporate 'hit parades' like Fortune magazine's annual listings of the world's 50 largest industrial companies do not mention it. Indeed, Anglo American does not even place on Fortune's listings of the *500 largest* corporations outside the U.S.; this is because of the complex intertwinings of South African mining companies and their accounting procedures. Yet the Anglo American group of companies has been estimated by Forbes magazine as having combined operating assets in 1973 of over $6 billion, enough to place it among the top couple of dozen corporate groups in the world, at least.[6]

It is the world's largest gold-producing corporation; it is also into everything from uranium to computers to . . . well, yes, insurance. It is co-owner with Eagle Star of South Africa's largest corporate life insurance firm,[7] African Eagle Life Assurance Society Ltd., founded in 1904 (Sir Brian was a director).* It also has a nominee director on the board of a second important arm of Eagle Star in that country, South African Eagle Insurance Co. Ltd., (of which Sir Brian was also a director); this company markets all classes of short term insurance, directly and through subsidiaries, in South Africa, Rhodesia, South West Africa, Lesotho and Botswana.

Indeed, southern Africa is much more than just another market for the Eagle Star group, which peddles policies in over a dozen countries. South Africa itself is the group's *biggest* overseas operation.[8] What makes this interesting is that Anglo American, of all companies, should be a pivotal associate in .that country. This puts matters into a much vaster framework of global finance.

Earlier the ties between the Rothschilds and the Eagle Star/ English Property twosome were touched on. Now the Rothschilds surface again. They maintain an investment presence in South African mining today through two other major mining firms: De Beers Consolidated Mines Ltd. (the world's largest diamond producer) and Charter Consolidated Ltd. Both companies are even closer associates of Anglo American than is Eagle Star.

How is this relevant to Canada 18,000 kilometres away? Because these three mining companies (Anglo American, De Beers and Charter) are all partners in one of the five largest mining companies active in Canada. This is Hudson Bay Mining & Smelting Ltd., a leading producer of copper, zinc and gold.**

* Eagle Star owned 25 per cent as of late 1976, with Anglo America holding the remaining 75 per cent. Anglo American lists it as being "within" its group; Eagle Star lists it as one of its "associate" companies, as distinct from a subsidiary. However, Eagle Star owns 56 per cent of South African Eagle and counts that company as a subsidiary.

** Other companies the trio owns in Canada are Francana Oil & Gas Ltd., Whitehorse Copper Mines Ltd. and Western Decalta Petroleum. It is worth noting that the Anglo American group's nominee director on the board of South African Eagle is Gavin W.H. Relly, who is also a director of Hudson Bay, representing a further tie between the two groups. These companies, and also Hudson Bay, are held through a Canadian holding company called Anglo American Corp. of Canada Ltd. ("Amcan"). Anglo American Corp. of South Africa holds a controlling 30 per cent interest in Amcan; the Charter Consolidated interests own 24.8 per cent and the De Beers group owns 28.8 per cent, as of mid-1976.

Thus while one Rothschild-related group, (Eagle Star/English Property) has been at the forefront of the development of urban centres in Canada, another such group has been among the front-line companies developing natural resources in the North. It is another version of those inter-connected spheres of Canadian development we saw first with Liechtenstein's Hiltis, where the same family is tied in with both real estate and industry, in Montreal.

But it doesn't end there with Eagle Star's friends, Anglo American and the Rothschilds.

Certainly one of the two or three most important companies in the overall growth of the Quebec economy – and hence, of the city of Montreal, whose transformation is a direct expression of this industrial development – has been Brinco Ltd., of Montreal. This is the truly bold, adventurous company which in the 1950s and 1960s planned and then built the Churchill Falls hydro-electric project in Labrador. The province of Quebec is dependent upon it for almost one third of its total electric needs today – over the last decade many industries pumped investments into this province and built factories here because they knew this electricity, which began flowing in 1972, would be available.

We find in Brinco, itself a consortium, two of the same forces we encountered in Hudson Bay Mining. The first is the Rothschilds – the N.M. Rothschild merchant bank headed the consortium. And the other is Anglo American, one of the original partners in the consortium.*

Eagle Star is also laced in with Brinco, which itself is ultimately owned by Rio Tinto-Zinc Corp. Ltd., of London, another global resource company. Though not quite as big as Anglo American, its presence in Canada is larger: it has been active here in many other industrial sectors ranging from mining uranium to manufacturing auto parts, and it will be explored at greater length in a later chapter on the Rothschilds.

* Indeed, one of the first two people the late Anthony de Rothschild, then the head of N.M. Rothschild & Sons, approached in 1952 to set up Brinco was the late Sir Ernest Oppenheimer, then the head of Anglo American. (Source: The Atlantic Advocate, July 1967, "Brinco: The Early Days," by Edmund de Rothschild, p. 32.)

Harry Oppenheimer (centre) maps global corporate strategy around a coffe table with his Anglo American Corp. aides.

David Colville, who, as seen before, is deputy chairman of Eagle Star and a partner at N.M. Rothschild & Sons, is also a director of Rio Tinto-Zinc.*

Trizec thus emerges as much more than just an isolated giant of a city developer. It is an adjunct, ultimately, of a global insurance company which itself is a member of a loose-knit team of companies, British and South African, which have been at the vanguard of Canada's postwar industrial growth.

... massive high-rises in Canada ... old line British aristocrats ... tea-time at Buckingham Palace ... deep-shaft mines in South Africa ...

It may sound like a peculiar combination.

But it finds its echo in another super-developer in Canada, a company with the curiously rustic name of Abbey Glen Property Corp. Ltd., of Toronto.

From 1974 to 1976 this was the sixth largest publicly-owned real estate developer in Canada. It owns about 20 square miles of prime land in and around Canadian cities – property appraised at over half a billion dollars. Its greatest strength is in Western Canada., particularly in cities like Regina, Winnipeg, Edmonton, Calgary and Vancouver. But it is influential in Quebec, too.**

---

* There is also a lower-level interlock. Montreal lawyer E.-J. Courtois is a director of both Trizec and Brinco.

** Abbey Glen's Montreal interests include:
　　— Two-thirds ownership of Place du Centre, a 22-storey office-retail complex above the McGill Metro station.
　　— Thirty-seven per cent ownership of the 17-storey office block at 2075 University, which it originally built.
　　— A stone's throw away, almost the entire block bounded by Sherbrooke, McGill College and Victoria Sts. This prime land, most of it a parking lot, features one of the few remaining rows of Victorian houses along Sherbrooke St., facing the McGill campus's dwindling green space. As of 1976 the company planned to convert the site into a large office development.
　　In the suburbs, Abbey Glen built one of the West Island's largest office buildings, the eight-storey Point Claire Commerce Centre. And at Jolibourg, Laval-sur-le-Lac, it owns 120 hectares of land on which it has already built the first 140 of a potential 2,000 homes.
　　Abbey Glen also developed the 18-storey Holiday Inn in the provincial capital last year, and it still owns the building.

Its profits, incidentally, have been unusually high in the property field since the firm was created in 1974 from a merger of Great Northern Capital Corp. Ltd. and Western Realty Projects Ltd. Abbey Glen reported after tax profits of $6 million in 1974, $9.3 million in '75, and $8.3 million in '76.

Like Trizec, it specializes in high-rises and skyscrapers — though the buildings it has developed across the country are box-like to a degree that makes Trizec's counterparts look almost distinctive by comparison.

There are many uncanny similarities between the two.

Like Trizec, it was formed as a subsidiary of a leading British multinational real estate company, Capital & Counties Property Co. Ltd. Like English Property, Capital & Counties develops real estate on three other continents.

Like English Property, this parent company is headed by an aging baronet. Indeed, Sir Richard Hilton Marler Thompson, chairman of Capital Counties, is — like Sir Brian Mountain — a member of a family (in this case the Marlers) which gives the company a somewhat dynastic tone.

The organization and its members have also served Her Majesty's Household well — Sir Richard was named vice-chamberlain in 1956, with his baronetcy created by the Queen seven years later. And they both have a firm interest in politics — not surprisingly, they too are involved in the Conservative Party. In fact, Sir Richard himself has been a member of parliament on and off since 1955. He was minister of health from 1957 to 1959 and has also been under-secretary of state for Commonwealth relations, a job which took him to Canada. Nor is he the only political link between company and party.*

But these are just sociological parallels. There are also financial ones.

Thus, just as English Property draws much of its capital from an insurance company, so does Capital & Counties.

---

* Another member of Capital & Counties board is Adam Courtauld Butler, also a conservative MP. His father, incidentally, was Baron Butler, leader of the House of Commons (1957-61) and also a former chairman of the Conservative Party. Mother was a Courtauld — as in the multinational rug company, Courtauld's Ltd., which is also active in Canada. "Young" Butler, a director of seven Courtauld subsidiaries, is no stranger to Canada: he was an aide de camp to the governor-general in the 1950s.

Standard Life and Norwich Union are among its leading insurance investors.

Furthermore, Capital & Counties is even more closely tied in with South Africa than is its colleague. Its biggest and most influential shareholder is neither Standard Life nor Norwich but another giant Johannesburg-based company specializing in gold. This is Union Corp., South Africa's third largest gold producer.*

After talking about Anglo American it is hard to make Union sound like a big deal. But Union Corp. calculates that it has been digging up one-twelfth of all the gold produced by the non-Communist world in recent years. And it is one of the mainsprings of the South African economy for more reasons than that: it holds a 46 per cent interest in the world's second largest platinum producer, Impala Platinum Ltd., and is prominent in such other aspects of the South African economy as paper supply (where it is No. 1), shipping, printing, engineering and road construction.

Union holds a 24.4 per cent interest in Capital & Counties — far more than anyone else. Like Eagle Star's 22 per cent stake in English Property, this does not represent outright control — but it is not far from that. As Capital & Counties managing director, Dennis Marler, summed it up for me in London, "We're very close." Union has even been sending one of its directors to Abbey Glen board meetings in Toronto.

That both Trizec and Abbey Glen should arise from interests closely allied with South Africa — the world's most condemned practitioner of institutionalized separation of races — perhaps underlines the hard-eyed attitude with which such investors invest.** A moralist might say that these organizations,

---

* South Africa produces about 75 per cent of the non-Communist world's gold every year, according to the International Monetary Fund.

** In fact, as further evidence of the relationship between Trisez and Eagle Star and South African mining — it can be pointed out that Sir George Harvie-Watt, the president of another major mining company investing in South Africa. Consolidated Goldfields Ltd., is also an Eagle Star director. Sir George is also a director of the Midland Bank. This is the large British bank which owns the Samuel Montagu merchant bank which, along with N.M. Rotschild and Hill Samuel, is a financial advisor to English Property.

tolerant of *apartheid*, can hardly be expected to show much concern for human-scale projects when they go about transforming cities in Canada.

But it would be unfair to lump all these companies together as one big exploitative gang. Anglo American, perhaps more than any other major company in South Africa, has been a proponent of relaxing *apartheid* for many years, well before the new round of riots and civil strife which began in 1976-77. Its chairman, Harry Oppenheimer, is something of a maverick social reformer and is seen as a leftist by many in the business community (though he is considered a conservative by radicals.)* Many individual members of the Rothschild family have also placed themselves in the more innovative, humanitarian side of bid business. The tradition seems to be: always stay a step ahead of the rest of the business community — whether it be in social relations or technology or in developing new parts of the world (like Canada). They are leaders. They set things in motion. This is why they are such an important factor in trying to assess the overall development of Montreal, Quebec and Canada.

The same cannot be said for Union. In contrast to Oppenheimer's pronouncements on the needs of Anglo American's 120,000 black underground workers. Union Chairman Edward Pavitt (who is also a director of Capital & Counties) strikes a bitter note as, addressing shareholders in the 1975 annual report, he assesses his company's pay raises to its miners: "It is disappointing that these substantial increases in wages have not been matched by material improvement in productivity." When in May, 1976, a large Afrikaaner company, General

---

* He is, let it be said, mostly a pragmatic businessman. Back in 1973 Forbes magazine assessed him this way:

"In a society that is pretty well convinced that God is on *apartheid*'s side, Oppenheimer does not waste his time on moral arguments. Instead, he maintains that apartheid is an economically wasteful system, bad for the corporations that he heads and bad for the country that he is so passionately devoted to.

"Oppenheimer, though, is no limousine leftist. The more radical students in South Africa's universities . . . argue that if he only dug in his heels and those of the corporations he heads, Harry Oppenheimer could single-handedly topple *apartheid* and the government that supports it." (Forbes, June 15, 1973)

Mining and Finance Corp. Ltd., won a takeover battle for control of Union, the chairman of this company, W.B. Coetzer showed a similar flair for idealism: "The profit motive," he told shareholders, "lies at the root of the capitalistic system and in my view a sound level of profit is vital to the continued welfare, growth and survival of the company and the fulfillment of its obligations towards its shareholders, its clients, its employees and to the country."

There are more important questions than nationality, however. The key parallel between Trizec's and Abbey Glen's backgrounds are the links going back to the natural resource sector.

It may seem peculiar for a conglomerate dealing in the rugged mining industry to become even indirectly involved in the social crafts of developer and landlord in the urban environment. But it is part of a pattern which goes far beyond Trizec and Abbey Glen. Numerous other large urban developers such as Canadian Pacific, Gulf Oil Canada and Bovis also have strong links to the natural-resources sector out in the boondocks.

The reasons for these companies' investments in real estate differ sharply in each case. But a common element would be the large risks in the resource market: the plummeting price of gold in 1976 illustrates this in the case of Union Corp. By investing in that most secure of all holdings – land – such companies are insuring themselves against financial hard times. This helps explain the popularity of pumping investments into large property firms – especially multinational ones. These firms spread their risks in many countries so that if property values sink in one country there are enough assets abroad to keep afloat.

For those companies with large property holdings in Britain, those values of course sank as part of that country's overall economic depression. Because of this both English Property and Capital & Counties found themselves in 1976 in need of strengthening their cash positions.

This brings up the final parallel. Partly because of the Foreign Investment Review Act, both companies sold off varying portions of their subsidiaries here in mid-1976. But while English Property held on to a majority of Trizec's issued share capital, Capital & Counties sold Abbey Glen outright — all of it. Today Capital & Counties is but a memory here — leaving behind a legacy of large permanent buildings in many cities.

Still, one of the most interesting aspects of the sale of Abbey Glen is the identity of the buyer.

Of all the financial interests in Canada which could have bought Abbey Glen, the purchaser was Genstar Ltd. — another company with particularly strong ties to the natural resources sector, including mining. Indeed, Genstar, as we will see in Chap. 7, is itself an arm of another of the world's super-size resource developers.

The pattern rolls on . . .

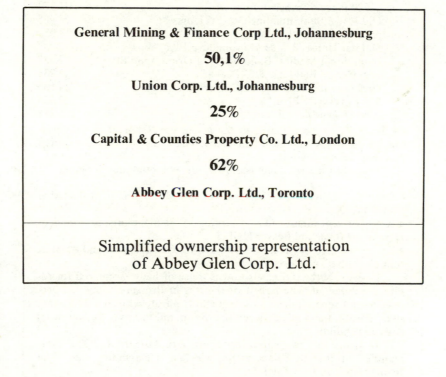

General Mining & Finance Corp Ltd., Johannesburg

50,1%

Union Corp. Ltd., Johannesburg

25%

Capital & Counties Property Co. Ltd., London

62%

Abbey Glen Corp. Ltd., Toronto

Simplified ownership representation
of Abbey Glen Corp. Ltd.

**Trizec's
Portfolio**

Ownership of the following commercial properties makes Trizec the city's No. 1 landlord of office space. The figures refer to the number of rentable square metres of each property.

Place Ville Marie (three buildings)	272,104
2020 University St.	49,330
Banque Canadienne Nationale Building, 500 Place d'Armes	47,379
Old Royal Bank Building, 360 St. James St.	28,985
555 Dorchester Blvd. W.*	18,952
Domtar House, 395 de Maisonneuve Blvd. W.	18,487
Drummond Medical Building, 1414 Drummond St.	17,837
Peel Centre Building, 2055 Peel St.	15,236
Orpheum Building, 515 St. Catherine St.	14,585
505 Dorchester Blvd.*	7,525
5165 Queen Mary Road	5,388

Of these, Trizec participated in the actual development of only two, Place Ville Marie and 2020 University. The company says it acquired all others in existing form.

Prime downtown land acquired for potential development includes:

• Southeast corner of Dorchester Blvd. and Mountain St., evaluated at over $880,000.

• A 50 per cent interest in the parking lot at the southeast corner of Dorchester Blvd. and Beaver Hall Hill.

• Entire east side of Bleury St. between St. Catherine St. and de Maisonneuve Blvd., now occupied by stores.

In the suburbs, Trizec also owns tracts of land earmarked for future development. The largest of these is in Brossard some 360 hectares (or 1.4 square miles). In Longueuil it has developed a 24-hectare site, "Port St. Laurent", between the Metro and the river for industrial and office buildings.

It also owns two shopping centres in Montreal: "The Normandie", at 2628 de Salaberry St., which it is expanding, and "The Jean Talon", on Jean Talon St.

* It was announced in 1977 that the building was sold to Italian interests.

Two views on development

«We have no figures to tell us how the urbanite reacts to the adamant geometry of the glass box, or how the bleakness of our main streets, studded with parking lots, hits small-town and rural folk.

«Who can doubt, though, that our architecture of the slick, boring highrise, the empty plaza, the desolate shopping mall in the suburbs — all those structures that forbid human congress contribute to the poverty of ... public life.»

Jane Holtz, urban planner

«The principal objective of Abbey Glen will be: to continue to assemble and acquire significant land banks in major growth centres in Canada and the U.S.: to develop its land banks to create satellite and suburban communities which produce prime commercial sites for the development of income properties; to emphasize the development and retention of large city-centre complexes in major Canadian and American cities.»

Abbey Glen statement of goals
1975 annual report

The Mountains: *From Churchspires to Skyscrapers*

It is impossible discuss the rise of Protestantism in Quebec without speaking of the Mountain family. Members of that family dominated the Anglican clergy for nearly 70 years after 1793 when George III personally appointed a Cambridge-educated cleric, Jacob Mountain, as the first Anglican bishop of Quebec.

Jacob had a brother who became rector of Trois-Rivières, and he also had three sons who joined the clergy. The second son, George Jehoshaphat Mountain, became bishop of Montreal in 1837 and a year later took over his father's old job as bishop of Quebec.

The younger bishop also founded one of the province's leading English-speaking educational institutions, Bishop's College, of Lennoxville. It is named, in fact, after him.* He also helped lay the groundwork for a second such institution, McGill University, of Montreal.

. . . today another branch of the family which remained in England is near the top of the ladder in a more secular line of work: the property business. In overseeing Eagle Star Insurance, Sir Brian Edward Stanley Mountain, together with his relatives and associates, has helped fill the skyline of Canada not with spires but skyscrapers.

Sir Brian is not actually a descendant of that pious Quebec line. "That was a branch of the family that died out," he told

---

* However, one thing which is commonly supposed to be named after his family, Mountain St. in downtown Montreal, in fact has nothing to do with it. In the 1940s there was an outcry among many Protestant citizens when City Hall Proposed to start calling the street "Rue de la Montagne." When they protested that the street commemorated their first bishop, an ancient French map, dating back to before the first Mountain ever set foot here, was produced. It showed there was then a path at this side called "Chemin de la Montagne" - clear evidence it was named after Mount Royal. Yet the misconception persists.

me in an interview. "But I still have a maple leaf in our coat of arms."

Nonetheless, the family trait of swarming collectively all over an enterprise is alive and well. He himself, chairman of the company for 26 years, was the son of its founder. His own son, Denis, succeeded him as chairman in 1974. A younger son, Nicholas, is a general manager. Another relative, S. Walton Mountain, was a director until recently, and an in-law, Peter Kirwin-Taylor, was until 1976 a director of both English Property and Trizec. Sir Brian himself was also a former chairman of Trizec and until his recent death was chairman of English Property and president of Eagle Star.

Sir Brian seemed to want to dispel any notions of nepotism. Referring to Denis' elevation to the chairmanship, he stressed that the entire "board of Eagle Star asked him to take on the job."

Who is the company's major shareholder? "My family has only ½ or 1 per cent," the portly, second generation baronet replied. "Most of the major pension funds have shares. No one has enough to mean anything – to mean a controlling share."

The accorded interview had to be postponed until the royal week of horse racing at Ascot was over, and he seemed much more at ease discussing horses and genealogy than finance.

The mention of Trizec, for example, prompted Sir Brian – a member of council of the Racehorse Owners Assn. – to launch into a triumphant tale of how the son of one of that company's directors, ex-Sen. Lazarus Phillips' son Neil, had a fine horse, Snow Knight, which won the derby. "I introduced him to horses, you know," he said casually, knocking the ashes off the end of his cigar.

"After it won," he said, alluding to Snow Knight, E.P. Taylor bought the major share of it."

For all his love of racing, he spoke impersonally of the horses themselves. He kept referring to Snow Knight and other horses as neither "he" nor "she" but as "it" – objects to be bought and sold like a company or a building.

In addition to its real estate interests in Canada, Eagle Star has many in South Africa. It owns three property companies there and four development companies.

One of Eagle Star's biggest friends in Canada is the Bank of Nova Scotia. With worldwide operations, the bank has more than $16 billion in assets, and Sir Brian was deputy chairman of its subsidiaries in four countries: Bank of Nova Scotia Trust Co. (United Kingdom) Ltd., Bank of Nova Scotia Trust Co. (Bahamas) Ltd., Bank of Nova Scotia Trust Co. (Caribbean) Ltd. and Bank of Nova Scotia Trust Co. (Cayman) Ltd.

Thus the Eagle Star organization has a key interlocking directorate with a Canadian financial institution. An *interlocking directorate* occurs when a member of one company's board of directors (which presides over management and generally has the capacity to hire and fire top executives) is also a member of another company's board. Sometimes this means little; a company may simply want the business acumen of an experienced professional to help pilot its course. But sometimes (and always in the cases enumerated in this book) there is a larger dimension: the "interlocks" point to a close rapport between organizations, a sense of shared interests, interwoven decision-making and reciprocal benefits.

In the case of Sir Brian, we find that his organization's reciprocal relationship with the Bank of Nova Scotia helped account for far more than just his tropical tan. For example, three of Trizec's four monumental projects of the 1975-78 period (see p. 70) show that, after more than a decade of closeness, the two are still firm friends: one is the 40-floor Scotia Centre in Calgary, where the Bank of Nova Scotia is a 50 per cent joint venture partner with Trizec; another is the Portage & Main complex in Winnipeg where the two are partners; and there's the Brunswick Square in Saint John, where the bank and Trizec are again joint venturers. In each the bank supplies needed construction capital while Trizec is assured a major prestige tenant.

Most of the big companies, though, require the services of more than just one bank: just as English Property had three merchant banks as advisors in London, so Trizec draws on two other Canadian banks besides the Scotia for loans and other banking services: the Royal Bank (one of the initiators, along with William Zeckendorf, of Place Ville Marie and now that project's main tenant) and the Toronto-Dominion Bank. It has interlocking directorates with these banks, too.

Footnotes — Chapter 3

1. Gutstein, Donald, *Vancouver, Ltd.* (Toronto: James Lorimer & Co., 1975), p. 28.
2. Report from the London stockbroking firm of de Zoete & Bevan, May, 1975.
3. Mountain, Denis M., 1974 statement to shareholders of Eagle Star Insurance Co. Ltd., p. 5.
4. Aronovitch, S., *The Ruling Class*, (London: Lawrence & Wiseheart, 1961), p. 104.
5. This account is pieced together from several sources who asked not to be identified.
6. Forbes' magazine, June 15, 1973, "Black, White and Harry Oppenheimer," p. 38.
7. 1975 Annual report, Anglo American Corp. of South Africa Ltd., p. 76.
8. Eagle Star's 1973 interim report.

Chapter 4
A Colonial Heritage

2.

3.

1.

4.

5.

Cities and countries once had distinctive styles of architecture. The growth of multinational real estate companies such as English Property Corp. and its Trizec subsidiary, have contributed to the global uniformity in building design. Can you tell where in the world these English Property/Trizec buildings are located? Answer on page 103.

WHEN THE DEVELOPERS of one of Montreal's largest high-rise projects, La Cité, were looking for money to build that complex, they got help from a powerful source with a quaint name: The Post Office Staff Superannuation Fund of the United Kingdom. With assets of more than $1.5 billion, the postal workers' retirement plan is the biggest pension fund in Britain.

The investment of a morsel of this money (no one will reveal the exact amount) in La Cité in 1974 is an illustration of how the British are contributing to changes in the skyline of Montreal and other cities. Almost all strata of English society — from peers to postmen — are involved in feathering this huge glass-and-steel nest-egg called urban Canada.

Of all world sources of capital, Britain has been the pacesetter in Montreal through its last decade or two of radical urban change. As one veteran backstage dealer in the Montreal property scene says flatly, "The Brits have been the top influence here. Period."

Why? Why not the Canadians? Or the Americans?

Of the 20 or 30 discussions I had with British property men, perhaps the exchange which shed the most light on their pre-eminence in Canada was a not-for-attribution interview I had of all places, in Paris. From there, one could get a fresh perspective on their Canadian activity.

I was talking with a young English executive of the French branch of a London-based multinational real estate company. His secretary, dressed in particularly tight *haute couture,* brought us second cups of coffee and left the room, forcing our attention back to real estate. Through the window, he pointed out the large office buildings on the Parisian skyline which had been developed by the British.

"I had no idea," I said, "the British were such a factor here. There's a certain logic to your being so large in Canada — one country's the offspring of the other and there are still strong bonds between them. But *France?* There's been more antipathy between the two of you over the years than anything else."

"Well," he grinned, snapping his cuff-links, "most French-men don't know the extent to which we're here, not that we're secretive.*

"Here in Paris," he said, "the property boom didn't begin to gather momentum until the mid-'60s and didn't really become an evident boom until about 1970 — I suppose that this time-frame corresponds very roughly to your own in Montreal. A lot of the activity here was due to English developers. We came because the return on investment here was higher. The French themselves were't doing much property-wise — they aren't, uh, very adventurous in property."

Why, I asked, should the British be the ones to show so much initiative?

As he paused a minute to reflect on his answer, it was clear that part of the overall answer — though he himself would be too modest to voice it — would be the legion of British prop-erty men like himself. Unlike so many of the sideburned huck-sters attracted to real estate in North America who are basi-cally without much classroom training, this urbane young man in conservative pinstripes belonged to a very special profes-sional breed called chartered surveyors. There is no equivalent for this in North America, but it is analogous to being a char-tered accountant. It has little to do with surveying the land with a portable tripod and everything to do with earning the

---

* In London I had sat down with this company's high-powered public rela-tions man. "We help the branch in each country *be seen* the way it wants to be seen," he said. "In some countries the branch wants to be seen as part of a much bigger, British-based organization. In others, like with the Dutch office I'm helping set up, they want to be seen as being by them-selves." He was at the time trying to settle on a solid-sounding Dutch name for that new subsidiary.

Answers:

1. Brussels, Belgium.
2. Calgary, Canada.
3. Southampton, Great Britain.
4. Quebec City, Canada.
5. Los Angeles, California.

Peninsular & Oriental
Steam Navigation Co. Ltd.,
Londres
|
Bovis Ltd.,
Londres
|
Bovis Corp. Ltd.
Toronto

Henry Aubin

Henry Aubin

In Paris (left) as in Montreal (above), London-based Bovis Ltd. *is active in real estate.*

complex legal, financial and architectural aspects of the business. In addition to this disciplined background, I was struck by his intellectual level — an uncommon degree of inquisitiveness and, to use the word he chose to describe what the French did not have, professional adventurousness. Clearly, British property has a long enough tradition — his own company was over a century old — and social status, not to mention remuneration, to attract a kind of person who in North America might follow more "prestigious" callings.

"The blitz was very important," he said, looking up. Seeing my incomprehension, he added, "Well, in London we've been rebuilding since the war, you know. So much of the city was destroyed we had no choice. We developed a lot of expertise. Paris, however, was left fairly intact. They didn't need to build much after the war. It wasn't until the mid-'60s or so that the French realized that if they were going to put Paris forward as an international business centre, then they better build new office accommodations. The same was true in Canada. The blitz, you might say, gave us one up on every one else. If you look at another country badly demolished by the war, Germany, you'll find that they're pretty adventurous in real estate also.

"Also, you know, the British have an unusual tradition in property going back to feudal times. We're the only country, I think, that's developed a leasehold concept.

"You don't see it often here in France, where a developer builds a building and then sells it. With British companies, the developer leases out the building and holds it for a long-term investment. The companies benefit from growth in their investments which enables them to revalue their assets periodically, and this allows for security for further loans.

"But the underlying reason goes much deeper than that. The English have been able to benefit from the City — with its sources of financing. After all, the property business couldn't put up a shack without financing. And no other country has the City.

"In the City, the merchant banks are one of the two big components. They've got the financial expertise to let us do all kinds of things we mightn't do otherwise. The second component is the presence of the large insurance companies and pension funds, like the post office fund which you mentioned. They're sitting on these incredible pools of capital and they've got to invest it somewhere."

He put his thumbs in his braces and leaned back in his chair.

"Hell, I guess you could also say we've got a colonial tradition. We're used to looking outward, to investing in land overseas and putting down roots. "Outward expansion's been extremely useful to us. The North American market is what has kept a lot of British property companies buoyant. It's the obvious conclusion."

Britain's starring role in Canadian urban development, then, comes from a combination of many enterprises — banks, insurance companies, pension funds, investment houses and, of course, the development companies themselves.

Two such development companies described in the last chapter, Trizec and Abbey Glen, are two of the six biggest publicly owned real estate developers in the top category — those with assets between about $400 million and $1 billion. But those two companies, which grew up as subsidiaries of London based multinationals, only scratch the surface of British involvement.

In other important categories down the line that same kind of proportion — i.e. a few British companies controlling about 30 to 40 per cent of a market — also holds sway. Take the second tier, that is, the medium size publicly-owned development companies with over $100 million in assets. In this group are at least six such British companies: Bovis Corp. Ltd., MEPC Canadian Properties Ltd., Hammerson Property Corp. Ltd., Hambro Canada Ltd., Slough Estates (Canada) Ltd. and the Rank City Wall division of the Rank Organization's entertainment conglomerate.

Or take Canada's eight largest homebuilders over the past two years as estimated by the Housing and Urban Development Association.[1] These companies, mostly privately owned, seldom release production figures. Each of these, according to the association, is building more than 1,000 housing units annually. And until 1975 four of them were largely British-backed: Consolidated Building Corp. Ltd., Wimpey Homes Ltd., Richard Costain (Canada) Ltd. and Bramalea Ltd. After building Bramalea to its present stature, British interests (Eagle Star Insurance) sold the company to Canadians in 1975.

There are numerous other British interests of a smaller scale to round off the picture. Monarch Investments Ltd., to cite just one local example, built numerous subdivisions and shopping centres in the Montreal region as well as in Ontario during the 1970s.*

---

* One could also cite Canadian-owned firms with substantial amounts of British financial support. Perhaps the biggest of these is the Hudson's Bay Co. In addition to being Canada's second largest department store chain, Hudson's Bay has owned Markborough Properties Ltd., with assets of about $150 million, since 1973. As of April 8, 1977, Hudson's Bay was 65.3 per cent owned by Canadians and 28 per cent by British interests. This is a far cry from earlier years — as recently as 1970 it was 88 per cent owned by British interests — but the British are still quite influential. The secretary of the company, Rolph Huband, reports that no shareholder owns more than two or three per cent of the stock, not enough for clear control, and that the company is largely controlled by its board of directors. Four of the 16 directors are British.

Important as these builders are, however, they constitute only the bricks and mortar side of an industry which depends on finding backers as a prerequisite to building anything.

This is where the power is felt of the "institutions," as they are called in financial circles. Dull and anonymous, they are the insurance companies and the pension funds. Their importance, say property people, is difficult to exaggerate.

An executive of a fast-growing U.K.-controlled firm active in western Canada and the Maritimes made a comment about his company in a telephone interview which reflects on the overall British presence:

"We are trying to keep a very low profile. One of our operating philosophies is to let the big guys make all the noise and to just do our work."[2]

His company, Canadian Freehold Properties Ltd., of Vancouver, is controlled by Canadian Industries Ltd., of Montreal, which is in turn controlled by Imperial Chemical Industries (ICI), of London. Though only fully operational about four years, Canadian Freehold had assets of over $80 million in 1976. ICI's assets of more than $7 billion rank it second among U.K. corporations to British Petroleum (which itself is a major Montreal landowner with an East End refinery which covers over 40 hectares).

But the real power behind Canadian Freehold Properties' expansion is ICI's billion dollar pension fund. It holds no less than 40 per cent of the Canadian company's equity, the executive estimates.

Through vigor, know-how and ample financing, the British firms may have been the leaders of Canadian urban development over the last 15 years — but that is not to say they dominate this complex field. Interests from no single country — including Canada itself — are in a position of domination.

Perhaps the only facet of the development business in which the British are not a major force is the apartment field. They tend to shy away from residential high-rises not only in Canada but in most other countries because of long experience with rent control in Britain. Most British property men consider their country's rent regulations, which date back to before World War II, to favor tenants, and they are wary of the inherent problems in rent control systems wherever they may be.*

Because industry and government collect only fragmentary data on this sector of the economy, it is difficult to specify the extent of the overall British presence in urban Canada. However, the Canadian Institute of Public Real Estate Companies and Canadian Building magazine both publish incomplete directories of firms. By combining their overlapping data it is possible to obtain a rough sampling of U.K. influence.[3]

Of the 35 largest companies — public and private — whose assets are listed in either directory for 1976, the major shareholdings of 11 of them can be traced to Britain. Assets for the top 35 range from $60 million to just under $1 billion.**

Insurance companies and pension funds like the Post Office Staff Superannuation Fund have long been investing in property, but until 1974 or so they had not been a major collective force within the Canadian property scene, according to insiders like John Donald of Marcil Mortgage Corp., a Montreal-based investment property broker.

Says a manager of one major Canadian pension fund, "The future landlords of this country are going to be the institutions."

"If you look at the size of today's projects," he adds, "the institutions are almost the only ones who can afford them."

* Trizec, for example, has had only one apartment building in Montreal in recent years (the Sherbrooke-Crescent Apartments at the the corner of those streets) and it sold that off in 1976. At last count, the company owned 45 office buildings, 37 mobile home communities, 19 retirement lodges and 12 shopping centres in Canada and the U.S. — and only three apartment buildings (all in Halifax). It has a policy of "phasing out of its residential investments." (Source: Trizec 1975 annual report, pp. 9-10) It's much the same with other companies. Thus of MEPC Canadian Properties' $179 million in assets in 1975, only 2.5 per cent were in apartments (all in Winnipeg). (Source: 1975 annual report, p. 10)

** Though assets are the best standard measure of a real estate company's size, they actually understate the real value of a company's property. Assets refer to the value of property when it was acquired, or when last appraised, and since this was often some years ago the assets bear little correspondence to the property's present market value if it were to be sold off today. A firm with $60 million in assets thus might really own $100 million worth of real estate by today's prices, and a firm with listed assets of $500 million might really own $700 to $900 million worth of property.

The British insurance firms and pension funds are "in the forefront" of this trend, Donald notes. [4]

They have not only been among the first institutions in the world to get involved in property — thus showing how it's done. They themselves have also become very active in investing in North American property.

But their power is not newfound. In his 1971 socio-economic study, The New Anatomy of Britain, Anthony Sampson says of London: "The financial giants of the City today are not the bankers or the financiers, but the money-managers of the insurance companies and the pension funds.

"In the field of investment it is they, as trustees for millions of individuals, who have taken the place of magnates, dukes and Rothschilds who dominated the City a century ago."

"Their power has grown up outside the traditional mythology of Britain: there are no good novels about insurance, no fashionable memoirs of '40 years with the Pru (Prudential Life).'

"Decisions are taken by clerkdoms more remote than the civil service, away from parliamentary questions, and the (companies) emerge into the headlines even less than bankers.

"But their decisions are not only important to the stock exchange and to millions of policy-holders: they are also crucial — or could be crucial — for the climate of industrial competition ... They represent the largest chunks of capital in the country, and their use of it affects the whole temper of British capitalism." [5]

The Canadian and Montreal holdings of a company such as Standard Life Assurance Ltd., of Edinburgh, exemplify the kind of far-reaching influence that U.K. insurance companies can have. Though Standard Life is listed in neither of the aforementioned Canadian real estate directories, it is, says one knowledgeable broker, one of the true eminences grises in property development.

In Montreal, for example, in addition to its 20-floor Canadian headquarters at Mountain and Sherbrooke Sts., it owns industrial property in the Côte de Liesse Road area as well as the Four Seasons apartment high-rise opposite Cavendish Mall. Downtown, it is part owner of Les Terrasses, the 10-storey retail-office centre completed in 1976 on de Maisonneuve Blvd. next to Eaton's.

In association with a Montreal company owned by the local Mashaal brothers, Standard is also a 50-50 partner in Hamilton's $100 million Civic Square office project — largest high-rise scheme in that city. (The Iranian-born brothers, frequent associates of the Scottish insurance company, also manage the Four Seasons for Standard.)

It is also a shareholder within many development companies. Figures for 1974, for example, show that it was the second-largest shareholder in Monarch Investments with a 28 per cent interest. And it owned 21 per cent of the issued share capital of Hammerson Property & Investment Trust Ltd., of London, which has $120 million worth of assets and commitments in Canada. Indeed, its Canadian subsidiary is now building what it touts as the biggest office complex in Canada west of Toronto — the four-tower Bow Valley Square project in Calgary, intended workplace for 10,000 Calgarians and with over twice the floor-space of Trizec's Scotia Centre. In Vancouver it owns the twin towers of 700 and 750 West Pender, that city's fifth largest office complex. (In Montreal, Hammerson has purchased 465 Dorchester Blvd. W., a prime site for potential office development.)

In addition, Standard provides what its top property investment manager will only describe as "a lot" of mortgage financing for commercial centres.

As for the pension funds, information on their operations are still harder to come by.

One of the rare studies of pension funds is an MBA thesis written in 1975 by Charles Stough at the London School of Economics. Stough estimates that British pension funds control not less than $24 billion in investment capital.[6]

Despite the size of this money, Stough points out, "there are no statutory or professional disclosure requirements for pension funds, and the funds themselves are largely ignored by the press."

Because of its publicized economic problems, Britain is sometimes written off as an obsolete financial power. It remains, however, the world's most important centre in at least three sectors:

Property companies, banking and, as seen in the previous chapter, insurance.

The three act interdependently, putting U.K. interests in the vanguard of Canadian metropolitan development. The interaction is such that in looking at specific interests, names of individuals keep turning up in what first appears to be wholly separate entities.

For example, Philip Shelbourne, a banker, mentioned in the last chapter for his inaccessibility, is not only deputy chairman of English Property Corp. Ltd., which is the largest shareholder in Trizec, but also is a member of the board of trustees of the Post Office Staff Superannuation Fund.*

London Financial Times (Freddie Mansfield)

Philip Shelbourne, one of the gnomes of London, is a quiet force in international finance.

* The Post Office fund has so far invested more than $30 million — it won't say how much exactly — in Canadian real estate. The secretary to the fund's board of trustees, Frederick "Jock" Clark, identifies these other main (non-controlling) investments as the Norcen Tower in Calgary and an office building across from the legislature in Victoria, B.C.

Shelbourne is also a director of Eagle Star Insurance. He is certainly one of the most pivotal individual bankers behind the entire Canadian urban transformation process. Indeed, when he was still a partner at the N.M. Rothschild merchant bank in the late 1960's, it was he who was in charge of stitching together the takeovers by English Property which led to its rise. And as late as 1976 he surfaced again as chairman of another merchant bank, Samuel Montagu, which was the advisor on that intricately-crafted deal which does/does not transfer control of Trizec to the Bronfmans.

It is commonly maintained that foreign investments in Canadian real estate are good for Canada because they bring in fresh infusions of capital. This is in fact what happens with many of the surreptitious Italian investments here — the money is sometimes even physically hauled in by the suitcase. Then it can be argued that such investments do in fact benefit the economy — even if the argument is somewhat tarnished by Italy's recent law decreeing that profits earned by those investments must go back to Italy. But it is very difficult to make such a case for many of the British investments here.

This is because the Bank of England, in order to shore up the eroding British economy, has banned most outflows of money from Britain — in the same way as the Italian government. Rather than spirit their money away illegally (though some do that, too, of course) many of these major property investors have called on their City merchant bankers to devise legal ways to invest abroad. Bankers like Shelbourne have come up with the so-called "back-to-back" method, among others. The back-to-back is used when, say, the Post Office fund wants to pump millions into Canadian real estate; a group of Canadian interests wanting to get their own money *out* of Canada will reach an agreement with the fund's bankers whereby the two parties pull a swap. That is, neither takes its money out of its own country; each simply leaves $5 million worth of currency, or whatever sum is agreed upon, for the disposal of the other. It's a nifty technique to get around currency controls, but it results in little if any surplus in capital for Canada.

There's another reason these British investments do less for the Canadian economy than than one might think. Rather than bring in new capital they actually borrow money from Canadian financial institutions. With their impeccable credentials, these multinational corporations often find it far easier to get loans here than do relatively small Canadian entrepreneurs. They thus help dry up the domestic sources of capital which might otherwise be available for local interests.

Abbey Glen is a good example of such a company. While it was still under British control it was employing primarily domestic sources of finance to buy domestic land and develop it. Abbey Glen "never did any financing to my knowledge with British institutions," a company director, Clair D. Smith, told me. "All our financing was done through Canadian sources, though some money may have come from U.S. institutions."[7]

This is a normal, not an aberrational way of doing business here. What it boils down to is that Canada is selling its own land to foreigners who *are paying for it with Canada's own money.*

This, of course, is much more than just an irony to ruffle nationalistic feathers. It may be good business for the British multinationals and the Canadian banks which service them, but it raises sharp economic questions for the rest of the country. It contributes to what small businessmen call a credit-short market and inhibits growth of a truly indigenous form of development here.

There's a noteworthy sequel to the Abbey Glen example, pointing up the actual drain of capital from Canada involved in this process. Not only was Canadian money employed by Abbey Glen to buy its properties, but in 1976 after that property had accrued in speculative value and the British/South African interests who owned Abbey Glen sold their controlling interest in the company to another foreign-owned company, Genstar Ltd., it was Canadian money which paid a large part of the $49 million price. Genstar President Angus MacNaughton disclosed in an interview that, while some of the money was internally raised from within his organization, the outside financing came from the Toronto-Dominion Bank.[8] Thus people with savings accounts at the T-D Bank in effect helped bankroll the transfer of more than 13,000 acres of prime real estate across Canada from one foreign-owned organization to another. If they didn't do much for the Canadian economy, T-D depositers can console themselves that they helped pump millions of dollars into the troubled economies of Britain and, indirectly, South Africa.

To what extent are the major British developers enriching the architecture of Canada?

Citizens' groups and sidewalk critics may often denounce the British-promoted generation of high-rises across Canada in such terms as "sterile," "impersonal" — and, in the case of apartment buildings, "machines for living in."

But it is interesting to also go elsewhere for a value judgment: to the development industry and design profession. How do their experts rate their peers?

Let's check the performance of the British companies over the years in what is this country's only award competition in the residential field, the Canadian Housing Design Council awards.

Since 1964 the council, a branch of the federal government's Central Mortgage and Housing Corp., has been issuing awards to "focus industry and public attention on examples of well-designed houses and housing developments built in Canada."

All kinds of housing (ranging from single-family homes to high-rise apartments) are eligible. Criteria include "livability, appearance and the relation of design to the site and climatic environment."

The latest five-member panel consisted of two presidents of development companies, one fellow and one member of the Royal Architectural Institute of Canada and — representing consumers — one member of the National Council of Women with an architectural degree.

The performance of British firms in these competitions is startling. With the British controlling four of the eight largest house-builders in Canada in recent years as well as many smaller builders, one might expect them to garner a significant portion of the awards.

But of the 214 awards and honorable mentions bestowed out of 1,320 entries since the competition started in 1964, only 3 —

or 1.4 per cent — have gone to firms known to be British-controlled.

These winners were: Wimpey Homes Ltd. in 1964 and Bramalea Ltd. in both 1971 and 1974. (Since its last award, Bramalea has been sold to Canadians).

British companies' contributions to local design have been the target of considerable debate in many countries besides Canada (often with Britain itself left out of discussion because the critics did not realize the ultimate ownership of the companies). France is one example, particularly in Paris where, as we have seen, the British have led high-rise office-building construction for a decade.

One foreign architectural expert, New York Times architecture critic Paul Goldberger, viewed the City of Light, listened to the debate and cabled back:

"The new buildings in and around Paris have been designed to an extraordinarily low standard — so low that the modern architecture of the city may, arguably, be called the worst in the world."[9]

Today's "glass box" form of global high-rise architecture owes far more to Britain than the fact that a lot of British development companies and investors happen to have helped popularize it. The glass box is also an architectural form which owes its genesis as much to Britain as the Corinthian column owes its origins to ancient Greece.

Until the late 1950s or so most high-rises or skyscrapers around the world — the Empire State Building or Rockefeller Centre in New York are examples that leap to mind — had exteriors made mostly of concrete or metal and had relatively small, conventionally-sized windows. But in the '60s and '70s buildings sheathed mostly, and sometimes entirely, in glass proliferated throughout the world. Often using glass which is colored or reflecting, these buildings make it difficult for the community outside to look in; it is as hard to establish rapport with one of these buildings as it is with a man with opaque wraparound sunglasses. Despite all the glass not much light can get in, so demands for electric light are high. Also, there are no functional windows — the glass walls do not open — so natural ventilation is impossible and additional air conditioning is necessary. The heat loss due to the poor insulating quality of the glass leads to even steeper energy demands.

Ironically, it is the British, who in the '70s are suffering from energy shortages, who can claim credit for the popularity of this form of architecture.

Back in the mid-'50s a glass company in Merseyside, U.K., called Pilkington Brothers Ltd. invented a special process to make thick, heavy-duty glass with far fewer optical distortions than ordinary glass. It is called "float" glass. Its mass production goes hand in hand with the rise of the generation of glass box architecture. Today in Canada, glass marketing experts say, 99 per cent of the glass which goes into the outside of large buildings is float.

Pilkington is an old family firm — Lord Pilkington is president, Sir Alastair Pilkington is chairman and four other Pilkingtons are board members. Their company did more than just invent float. It has become one of the world's largest glass manufacturers and sells float and other kinds of glass to over 100 countries. Because it cannot possibly produce enough float to meet worldwide demand, the company has also licensed its patented float process to 24 manufacturers in 14 countries.[10]

In Canada, Pilkington completely dominates the market. The company's subsidiaries here manufacture 100 per cent of all the float glass made in Canada. Because about one third of all float glass used in construction in Canada is imported, this gives Pilkington control of about two-thirds of this market, according to a reluctant executive at Pilkington Brothers Canada Ltd., of Toronto. Since Pilkington licenses the remaining one third, one can say that the company has a *de facto* monopoly.

Pilkington additionally plays a major role in the non-float glass field: it and Canadian Pittsburgh Industries, a subsidiary of the U.S. manufacturer, produced about 65 per cent of *all* the glass used in 1976 in construction, whether it be for bungalows, skyscrapers or the pane of glass you buy at the hardware to replace the broken basement window. This is a remarkably high degree of market control by two companies: economists generally consider that whenever *four* companies control *50 per cent* of a market you have a situation ripe for

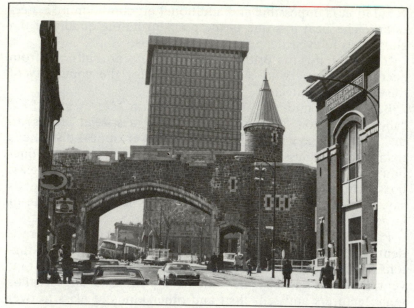

This MEPC-built high-rise dominates the skyline of old Quebec.

Henry Aubin

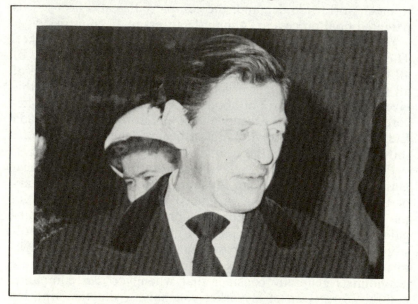

Angus Ogilvy, director of MEPC Canadian Properties Ltd. He is married to Princess Alexandra, cousin of Queen Elizabeth II.

oligopoly, or the absence of genuine price competition.[11] My figure of 65 per cent held by the two glass companies comes from an executive at Canadian Pittsburgh who acknowledged, "There is really damn little competition in this field."

"Don't use my name or I'll be shot at dawn," he added. "The boys at the combines branch (the federal Bureau of Competition Policy) are watching us like hawks."

Be that as it may, the Pilkington company is regarded a bit more reverentially back at home.

The Royal Society, the British club of 700 top scientists, took note of Sir Alastair's accomplishments, notably his developing of a global market for float glass. It awarded him a medal for contributions "leading directly to the national prosperity."

With the state of the British "prosperity" in decline in recent years, it is not surprising that the sheer scale of British involvement in Canadian property should also be ebbing. It is a gradual process.

The turning of the tide of this participation here came dramatically in the summer of 1976 with transactions involving the two largest British-owned companies: this is, of course, when the majority interest in Abbey Glen was sold and the voting control (but not majority interest) in Trizec was unloaded. As said earlier, both sales were partly motivated by the desire to avoid problems with recent federal and provincial laws inhibiting the expansion of foreign real estate ownership.

The sales also reflect the troubled financial state of the parent companies in London, where the property market has suffered recent reversals. To raise capital to reduce their borrowing, such companies have been selling their holdings in places like Australia and Canada.

But it would be premature to assume that there is a generalized withdrawal of the British real estate presence in Canada. The property market tends to run in cycles. And the tide could come back in.

Many companies have extremely lucrative holdings in Canada and are reluctant to sell them. A company like MEPC Ltd., active in four continents, was anxious to remain in Canada, as its 1976 annual report makes clear: "Our principal overseas subsidiary company, MEPC Canada, prospered in 1976. Earnings and cash flow from operations showed an increase of 11.4% and 15.5% respectively. Throughout the year the company remained in a strong financial position and it enters the new year with significant resources available for new investment."

So reluctant has MEPC been to sell its overseas holdings that in January, 1976, one of its directors — none other than Jacob Rothschild — resigned over the issue. Rothschild, whose N.M. Rothschild bank was one of the firm's financial advisors, reportedly wanted MEPC to sell off some of its overseas properties in order to raise cash to reduce its debt in England. The alternate view was to sell holdings at home. [12]

Ironically, 16 months after Rothschild's abrupt departure, MEPC apparently swung around to the spirit if not the letter of his advice. In May, 1977, it announced that it was negotiating the sale of its majority interest in MEPC Canadian Properties.

The buyer? Interestingly, as part of that trend that had been anticipated for several years, it was a group of pension funds which MEPC declined to identify.

One British property man who scoffs at any notion of a generalized pullout of U.K. real estate firms from Canada is James Appleyard, president of the Toronto-based subsidiary of Slough Estates Ltd.

The firm expanded into Montreal in 1974, building a 10-hectare industrial park on Cote de Liesse Rd. And despite the troubled U.K. economy, the Parti Québécois victory in November, 1976, and everything else, it is still considering further long-term growth in Montreal, said Appleyard in a post-election discussion.

"The Montreal market has been a good market," he said flatly.

"I think most British companies must be pretty well pleased with their investment in Canada and Montreal and will be staying.

"*We* are." [13]

The chapter opened with a look at one quaintly named organization, the Post Office Staff Superannuation Fund. Let it close with another: the Peninsular & Oriental Steam Navigation Co. Ltd. This company has an exotic aura rooted in its Victorian past, a time when it provided transport for pith-helmeted gentlemen and long-skirted ladies between England and India. Nevertheless, it is representative of the remote and seemingly old-fashioned forces that are a major factor behind the stark high-rises and sprawling subdivisions of Canadian cities.

When the sun finally set for the British Empire, it kept on shining for "P. & O." Adapting from the age of Conrad to that of the conglomerates, P & O today owns airlines, container fleets, and construction and property companies around the world. It is still Britain's largest shipowner. One of its supertankers, the SS. Ardshiel, which is as long as the Empire State Building is high, was the subject of Noël Mostert's "Supership," the best-selling 1974 book on the ecological dangers of such vessels.*

Today Montreal is but one of its many ports of call in Canada. It is not a transporter but a major land developer.

Advertisements in travel magazines ask "What in the world is P & O up to?" Caribbean cruise liners aside, it is a good question. What are its goals in developing urban Canada, what are its perspectives? In trying to obtain answers, I encountered that same "high-handed style and flair of a feudal barony," which Mostert remarks prevailed formerly aboard P & O ships. Replies to elaborately-phrased letters requesting interviews, written in consultation with my senior editors, were never received. Even repeated written requests for that most public of corporate documents, the annual report to shareholders, were to no avail.

---

* Mostert delights in contrasting the atmosphere of Stanley Kubrick's *2001,* which he found aboard the Ardshiel during his voyage on it, to the company's origins in another age. He writes: "After 1840 P & O was as potently symbolic of the British empire and its mercantile hegemony as the Royal Navy itself, and perhaps even more so, for if the navy suggested power, P & O conveyed the realities of it. Kipling seemed never able to keep the company out of his verses, and small wonder. It was *the* imperial connection: and there was nothing more persuasive of the fact than the sight of a big P & O mailboat on its aloof way through Suez . . . The commodores and masters of these ships themselves stood high in the upper imperial ranks, and often had considerable reknown for their way with these ships, many of which were run with the high-handed style and flair of a feudal barony." ("Supership," New York: Warner Books, pp. 195-196.)

What in the world is

P&O

up to?

World Cruise in January.

P&O's majestic Canberra, by far the largest luxury liner circling the globe this coming winter, will sail west from England January 8. 92 days, 5 oceans, 5 continents, 20 fascinating ports of call. In 1976 she'll take in Hong Kong with opportunities to tour Japan, Thailand and Mainland China.

Your clients can join the cruise in Port Everglades (Jan. 19),

Los Angeles (Jan. 31) or San Francisco (Feb. 2). The voyage ends in Southampton (Apr. 10). P&O offers a wide range of fares and

accommodations. Luxurious suites to economical 4-berth rooms. The ship, of course, is all one class—first.

For details, send for our 1976 World Cruise brochure. Write P&O/Princess Cruises, 2020 Avenue of the Stars, Los Angeles, CA 90067.

FLY FREE Caribbean/Canal Cruises.

There's still time to reserve space on P&O's Oriana for a Transcanal Cruise this year. Next year, too. Your clients can fly free* to Nassau, cruise the Caribbean, transit the Panama Canal, stop in Balboa, spend the day in Acapulco, and sail on to California. Your clients can fly home free* from either Los Angeles or San Francisco. How's that for a package?

Oriana	1975	1976
Depart Nassau	Nov. 4	Nov. 22
Arrive Los Angeles	Nov. 13	Dec. 1
Arrive San Francisco	Nov. 14	Dec. 2

Your clients can also take the cruise in reverse in 1976 with the same fly free* privileges to and from the ship.

Oriana	1976
Depart Vancouver	April 22
Depart San Francisco	April 25
Depart Los Angeles	April 26
Arrive Nassau	May 6

FLY FREE South Pacific Cruises.

You can book your clients on the Oriana or Canberra for spectacular voyages to the South Seas in 1975 and 1976. In each case, your clients can depart from Los Angeles or San Francisco. They'll sail to Honolulu, Suva, Auckland and Sydney. After a 2-day stay in Sydney, courtesy P&O, passengers will fly free* back to Los Angeles.

	Oriana 1975	Canberra 1976	Oriana 1976
Depart L.A.	Nov.13	Jan. 31	Dec. 1
Depart S.F.	Nov. 15	Feb. 2	Dec. 3
Arrive Sydney	Dec. 3	Feb. 19	Dec. 21

In 1976 your clients can also take the cruise in reverse and fly free* from Los Angeles to meet the ship.

Oriana	1976
Depart Sydney	April 5
Arrive Vancouver	April 22
Arrive San Francisco	April 24
Arrive Los Angeles	April 26

Cruise to Europe. Fly home free.

Your clients can sail on the Oriana in the grand manner to Southampton England in April. And P&O will fly your clients home free* to anywhere in the USA or Canada.

Oriana	1976
Depart Honolulu	April 16
Depart Vancouver	April 22
Depart San Francisco	April 25
Depart Los Angeles	April 26
Depart Port Everglades	May 7
Arrive England	May 16

For details on any P&O Liner Voyage, write for our brochures: P&O/Princess Cruises, 2020 Avenue of the Stars, Los Angeles, CA 90067. Or call us collect: Northern California (415) 986-7070; Southern California (213) 553-7000; all others (800) 421-0522. In Canada: Vancouver (604) 682-3811; all others (800) 663-3591.

*Free air fares apply to all accommodations with private facilities. All air arrangements, including complimentary transfers as appropriate, will be made by P&O/Princess Cruises.

Registry: British

Ad of the *Canadian Travel Courrier.*

In urban Canada, it's up to a lot.·

A little anecdote about my experiences in London also tells something about the flavor of the organization and its views on accountability. The P & O headquarters consists of a futuristic black glass blockhouse in the City, and in making inquiries there as to whether my letters had been received, I felt cast in the role of an impudent little colonial sticking his nose into the business of his betters. My request to interview P & O managing director Alexander Marshall got no further than his secretary, Miss Faircraft, who remarked, "If Mr. Marshall submitted to press requests for interviews, he would have no time to run the group." Miss Fletcher, secretary to the chairman, the Earl of Inchcape, maintained a smile as she told me, "Lord Inchcape will be unavailable because of meetings for this week and next, yes, until you go back to Canada."

P & O cruised into urban Canada in 1974 when it took control of Bovis Ltd., of London. This is a real estate developer, whose president was then the Earl of Albermarle, with activities in France, Holland, Rhodesia, Australia, etc. It arrived in Canada in 1970 when it set up a Toronto subsidiary called Bovis Corp. Ltd.

In several ways Bovis is typical of the British firms in urban Canada. In addition to building suburban developments and high-rises,* it is intimately involved in Canada's resource development industries: its own subsidiaries are building roads and bridges in Newfoundland, dredging rivers and harbors (includ-

---

* Bovis as of 1976 had these activities in the Montreal area, according to its executives:
  — Owned some 680 acres (over two and a half square kilometres) in St. Martin de Laval and had plans to build 400 homes, of which many were already finished.
  — Owned about one square kilometre in Pointe Claire near the Trans Canada Highway and Sources Road, where it was building industrial parks.
  — Had built 100 homes at Candiac on the South Shore, 66 at St. Dorothée in Laval, 50 at Ste. Therese and 40 at Blainville. Many of these were built with the Denault Group, a local contractor.
  These projects were intended, as of mid-1976, to be only the beginning of a much wider program of development in the province, including such other cities as Sherbrooke, Trois-Rivières and Québec.

ing the St. Lawrence),* selling construction equipment at James Bay and exploring for oil. Compared to such an axis as Eagle Star/Anglo American/Rio Tinto-Zinc it is quite small. Bovis Corp. had total assets (including urban property) in 1975 of only $117 million, a fraction the size of the Eagle Star crowd but still big enough to rank as the 108th largest industrial company in Canada, as reckoned by the Financial Post.

But Bovis Corp. is bigger than meets the eye. In 1973 it bought 200,000 treasury shares in Canada's oldest real estate company, Consolidated Building Corp. Ltd., making it the largest shareholder.** This makes Bovis a truly major force in the Canadian homebuilding industry. Consolidated has over $100 million in assets (mostly in Ontario) and has been building more than 1,000 houses each year for the last several years; add the 600 per year that Bovis has been building and you have one of the four or five biggest builders in Canada's house construction industry.

Like most of these other London-based multinationals being examined, the P & O is headed by a peer, probably the wealthiest we have yet encountered.*** The election of the

---

* Bovis got itself into some hot water on this account. In 1975 the chairman of Bovis Corp., Harold S. McNamara, and its dredging subsidiary, McNamara Corp., were among these charged with conspiracy involving alleged rigged bids for dredging contracts in Ontario and Quebec. In November, 1976, Harold McNamara resigned as chairman of Bovis and weeks later the Ontario provincial court ordered him and 10 other persons to stand trial in 1977 on those charges.

** An agreement with other substantial minority shareholders allows Bovis the right to increase its holding in Consolidated to 41 per cent by 1978. A Bovis executive strenuously denied that his company exercises "rigid control" of Consolidated. But Bovis has placed three of its directors on the Consolidated board; indeed, the chairman of Bovis is also chairman of Consolidated. Definitions of control may differ, but clearly Bovis has Consolidated within its sphere of influence.

*** To the best of my knowledge, Hilmar Reksten, Norwegian shipowner, is P & O's No. 1 shareholder with about 10 per cent of the equity. The P & O and the Reksten interests, of Bergen, are joint proprietors of Anglo-Nordic Shipping Ltd. (Source: London Financial Times International Business Yearbook, 1975.) Reksten is not a board member and it difficult to assess his influence within P & O.
  The Inchcape family interests are nothing to sneeze at. Inchcape & Co., with after tax profits of £115 million on assets of £1,176 million in 1976, is a healthy worldwide conglomerate rooted in the same exotic imperial tradition as P & O. Among its 131 subsidiaries in 19 countries are tea holdings in India, truck and car dealerships in Ethiopia, Kenya, Thai-

The Earl of Inchcape.

Earl of Inchcape to the chairmanship was not altogether for purposes of adornment. In 1972 his own family company, Inchcape & Co. Ltd., made a conditional offer for the capital of P & O. The merger never took place but Lord Inchcape became chairman the following year. And the acquisition of Bovis came a year after that.

Lord Inchcape, incidentally, shares the same kind of close ties to the insurance industry that we have come to expect among the people behind urban development. He is a director of Guardian Royal Exchange Assurance, which owns Montreal Life Assurance Co. (P & O managing director, Marshall, is a director of Commercial Union, which has financing ties to the P & O group.) Perhaps Lord Inchcape's most significant directorship, however, given the P & O's fleet of supertankers, is his

land and Jamaica, a land development company in Malaysia, oil industry service vessels in Nigeria and the North Sea and a brewery in Tobago. In Canada it makes the same crucial components in buildings as the Hilti family of Liechtenstein — fastenings, as well as the power tools to drive them in. The Inchcapes became major competitors of the Hiltis in Canada when they took over two Edmonton manufacturers of fastenings in 1975 (W.S. Bate Ltd. and Universal Fastening Devices Ltd.) Closer to Montreal, the Inchcapes also own a Granby manufacturer of steel windows, Cresswell Pomeroy Ltd.

presence on the board of British Petroleum. Sir Alastair Pilkington, the glass man, is also a BP director, by the way.

Like the other British real estate interests here, the P & O organization seeks to downplay its Britishness. To win the Foreign Investment Review Agency's favor, it has placed voting control in the hands of three members of its board, Canadians. It would be gratuitous to assume that these three call the ultimate shots without heeding London, but use of Canadian frontmen is a standard device of the 1970s (as we will see in Chap. 7).

Another of the themes running through property development in Canada is the high degree of inter-meshing between the diverse interests. We find this here in the case of one of Bovis Corp.'s three voting principals, Montreal lawyer Paul Beaulieu. Beaulieu is also a director of none other than Eagle Star Insurance of Canada.

At one level or another, many of these major companies are tied in each with the other.

Footnotes — Chapter 4

1. Correspondence from C. Gordon Ryan, dir. of public relations, Housing & Urban Development Association of Canada, dated Aug. 15, 1975, and telephone interview for update a year later.
2. Telephone interview, Gordon C. Jamieson, vice-president, Canadian Freehold Properties Ltd., Oct. 17, 1975.
3. The Real Estate Development Annual (Toronto: Canadian Building magazine, McLean-Hunter Ltd., 1976); Report of the Canadian Institute of Public Real Estate Companies (Toronto, CIPREC, 1976). These publications directories, while the most comprehensive in their field, are quite incomplete: numerous companies, both foreign and domestic, are not included. Their lists are thoroughly impartial, however, and they constitute a representative segment of the industry.
4. Telephone interview, Oct. 9, 1975.
5. Sampson, Anthony, The New Anatomy of Britain (London: Hodder and Stoughton, 1971), p. 512.
7. MBA thesis of Charles Edward Stough for New York University, p. 14.
8. Telephone interview, June 8, 1976.
   Interview, Sept. 8, 1976, and following telephone interview, Sept. 10, 1976.
9. New York Times, July 18, 1975, "Architecture of Paris: New vista is narrow", by Paul Goldberger, p. 2.
10. London Financial Times, Dec. 5, 1976, "First-half fall in profits of £ 5.7 m., at Pilkington Bros.", p. 1.

11. This rule of thumb for finding oligopolistic tendencies derives from numerous interviews in past years with officials at the Bureau of Competition Policy in the federal Department of Consumer and Corporate Affairs and at the U.S. Federal Trade Commission.
12. London Sunday Times, Feb. 1, 1976, p. 54.
13. Telephone interview, Nov. 25, 1976.

Chapter 5
The House of Rothschild

THE ROTHSCHILDS may not own a single square foot of Canadian soil. But in the rarefied air of international high finance, contributions to Canada's growth are not necessarily measured in acres or hectares.

If one were to draw up a list of the top ten people in Montreal's development, one man who would have to be on it is Edmund de Rothschild — not only as an individual but as a representative of the legendary family that has been behind the scenes in building Canada for over a century.

Edmund de Rothschild is a merry-eyed, kindly-faced man of 61 who could be cast by Hollywood as a country doctor.

He has visited Montreal on business about 200 times in the past 25 years but seldom been recognized. Unpretentiously dressed in a baggy suit as he pours coffee for me in a Westmount Square office, at first the only evidence that he is unlike the shoppers below on St. Catherine St. is his initialled gold cuff links — small and functional with the typical understated elegance of the Rothschilds, and an apt reminder of the Rothschild world role. While he fusses with the cream and sugar, my mind wanders . . .

The gold in those flat, oval cufflinks might well have been dug up by any of several of the world's largest mining corpo-

The Gazette (Garth Pritchard)

Edmund de Rothschild: "It's a great country. You still have the potentiality of the frontier... The challenges are still here."

rations active in Canada and South Africa in which Edmund de Rothschild and his various relatives have interests.

Furthermore, there's a good chance that if those grams were mined in Canada — the world's third largest gold producer — they were sold with the help of Edmund's bank, N.M. Rothschild & Sons, Ltd. of London. The bank has a special collaboration with one of this country's two gold dealers, the Canadian Imperial Bank of Commerce.

Indeed, it is virtually certain that on the day those grams were sold the *world* price of gold — the only universally recognized medium of exchange — was fixed at one of the twice daily meetings held inside Edmund's bank and attended by four other London gold dealers. This has been the location for fixing gold prices ever since 1919; even the Soviet Union, a leading gold producer, puts aside anticapitalist ideology to be guided by those prices. Finally, those grams of gold first could have been turned into gold bars at the Rothschild's own private refinery called the Royal Mint Refinery near the Tower of London.

But gold — whether for cufflinks or for bullion — is only a Rothschild sidelight.

Just as gold is the lifeblood of the world monetary system, so other areas of Rothschild involvement here also represent the basic underpinnings of the economy at large.

We have already encountered the family's long-established banking and directorate ties to two important forces in Canadian real estate development and ownership: Eagle Star Insurance Co. Ltd. and MEPC Ltd. But influence in Canada's urban development can extend well beyond involvement in real estate investments *per se* — which are, after all, more a reflection of a city's economic condition than a cause of it.

Through a complex skein of investments, banking functions, interlocking directorates and other advisory positions, the Rothschilds maintain connections with some of the industrial companies at the forefront of Canada's overall development.

These companies include: one of the leading natural resource, transportation and urban development companies in the country, Canadian Pacific Ltd.; the chief pioneer in developing Eastern Canada's hydro-electricity resources as well as a major holder of mining properties, Brinco, Ltd.; the No. 1 uranium producer and specialty steels maker in Canada, Rio Algom Ltd,; two of the leading oil and natural gas producers and distributors, the Royal Dutch/Shell Group and Petrofina S.A.; and one of Canada's leading mining companies, Hudson Bay Mining & Smelting Co., Ltd.

To be sure, the Rothschilds do not own or control any of these companies. Most of them or their parent companies are simply too big and their superstructures too diverse for any identifiable individual or family to have push-button control over them.

But the Rothschilds do provide the supreme example of the unnoticed but fundamental influence of a much vaster cast of Old World groups. For instance, the "City" of London, which, as we saw in Chapter 4, remains the world's leading financial centre, has many merchant banks besides N.M. Rothschild & Sons which are, collectively, playing a major role in Canadian business. The Hambros, Samuel Montagu, Hill Samuel and Warburg banks are among the leaders.

As a young researcher at McMaster University, Ernest Virgint, explains it, "The Rothschilds are part of a complex of power and decision-making that includes other financial groups whose histories are intertwined with the Rothschilds. The Rothschilds represent one strand — albeit an important one — in an international mesh of finance capital which dominates key sectors of the international economy." [1]

There are many qualities that distinguish the Rothschilds from other important groups: unsurpassed prestige, contacts, business integrity and a talent for looking at long-term projects from the perspective of overall economic growth. But there is another key reason: there are simply so many of them — so many Rothschilds, all of them inter-knit.

Edmund is at the fore of the family's London branch, which has the N.M. Rothschild bank as its business focus. The Paris branch is headed by a cousin, Baron Guy de Rothschild, of the Banque Rothschild. Then there are three other associate groups. These are based in: Geneva, where Baron Edmond de Rothschild heads the Banque Privée S.A.; Brussels, where a cousin, Baron Léon Lambert, heads Belgium's second largest holding company, Compagnie Bruxelles Lambert, and, finally, Amsterdam, where there is the Pierson, Heldring & Pierson merchant bank, whose chairman is Allard Jiskoot.

The term Rothschild as used here embraces all five groups. These strategic centres form what the family today calls the "Five Arrows." This alludes to the five arrows in the Rothschild escutcheon, which originally symbolized the five prodigious sons of Mayer Amschel Rothschild, a second hand dealer from Frankfurt-am-Main with a talent for collecting old coins. The sons became the 19th century *eminences grises* behind key economic and political moves in Europe, using banks in London, Paris, Vienna, Frankfurt and Naples as their power centres.

Their heirs prosper today in Canada. Edmund, Guy and Edmond de Rothschild, Léon Lambert and Allard Jiskoot are all

The Express (Cees de Hond)
Baron Guy de Rothschild heads the French arrow in the family quiver.

directors of Five Arrows Securities Co. Ltd., of Toronto, an investment company. Also in Toronto, the Rothschilds own Magnum Fund Ltd., an investment company quoted on the London and Toronto stock exchanges with a diversified investment portfolio. These are hardly the main thrust of family activity here, however.

"It's a great country. You still have the potentiality of the frontier," Edmund de Rothschild said of Canada during the Montreal interview. "The challenges are still here."

Little has been published of Rothschild contributions to this country's growth, and in the two-and-a-half hour conversation he volunteered little that was not already known.

How important are the Rothschilds to Canada's overall development? I doubt if anyone outside the immediate family really knows, and even that is not sure since the various branches of the family, while keeping in touch, do not run in harness. Edmund certainly was not very revealing. Our conversation, dealing mostly with the specifics of the family's corporate involvement in Canada, was characterized by cordial evasiveness.

"Today," says Frederic Morton in his 1961 biography, 'The Rothschilds,' "the family grooms the inaudibility and invisibility of its presence. As a result, some believe that little is left apart from the great legend. And the Rothschilds are quite content to let legend be their public relations." [2]

"They are even more reticient and aloof than other merchant bankers when family matters are concerned," adds Joseph Wechsburg in his more recent book, 'The Merchant Bankers.' "Their family labyrinths are complex, dark and mysterious." [3]

To preserve its privacy, the family has a habit of dividing its affairs among different lawyers or bankers or accountants, so that none of these has the big picture. In Europe, for example, I had lunch with one branch of the family's advisors, to whom I had been introduced by a mutual friend. To obtain his confidence in order to pump him, I told him what I knew. He was flabbergasted.

The interview took place in a parlor inside Brinco's headquarters high in Westmount Square in mid-1975. [4] It was not an uncommon visit for him: fly in from London in the morning, attend a Brinco board of directors meeting*, then perhaps a cab over to the Mount Royal Club for lunch. Finally, a flight back to London in the evening — a timetable which could help explain British businessmen's enthusiasm for the Concorde.

Edmund at first spoke with animation about Canadian development. "It's fascinating," he said. "That's my line."

Why is his family so interested in Canada?

---

* With such fellow directors as Paul Desmarais, head of Power Corp., and E.-Jacques Courtois, a close associate of the Edper wing of the Bronfman family and director of both Trizec and Eagle Star Insurance of Canada Ltd. (and who helped transfer the voting control of Trizec Corp. Ltd. to the former from forces close to the latter).

In a speech he gave to the Halifax Board of Trade in 1974, one seemingly platitudinous passage may help answer that question indirectly:

"You are truly fortunate in Canada for this great country is richly endowed with natural resources ... The real difficulty that faces you in Canada is the priorities of the development of these resources. You have hydro-electricity ... There is also oil and natural gas ... Canada has the uranium to feed the Candu atomic reactors — and these are safe and rank among the finest in the world ... And then you have here in Nova Scotia and New Brunswick the highest tides in the world ..."[5]

Reflecting Edmund's appreciation for Canada's bountiful resources, Rothschild-related interests have played an active role in their development, involving themselves in *every one of the five energy sources,* he mentioned.

Here is a rundown:

1. — *Hydroelectric power.* Without the Churchill Falls hydro project in Labrador, Montreal would be a very different place today.

Many industries made the commitment to come to this city and province in the 1960s with the expectation that the Churchill Falls project, then under construction, would provide a reliable source of energy. After then-premier Joey Smallwood asked for U.K. help, N.M. Rothschild & Sons had begun to plan the financing and organization as far back as 1952. The following year, it helped form a consortium called Brinco to undertake the project. The power started flowing in 1972 and today accounts for a critical 30 per cent of the province's electricity, says Hydro-Quebec.

Edmund calls it "the largest project undertaken until then by private enterprise," covering as it does "a lot of moose pasture" larger than England.

In a surprise move, Newfoundland nationalized the hydro-electricity project in 1974, paying Brinco a handsome $160 million and leaving it with mineral exploration rights for more than 24,000 square miles. Premier Frank Moores of Newfoundland reasoned that the Churchill project's "benefits to this province, apart from the short-term construction employment, have been, and will be, unfortunately minimal." He said that "unless we have control of our resources and their development we cannot control our destiny as a people."

"I would have preferred we could have completed the job — we were 97 per cent complete and we were ahead of schedule and below budget," Edmund commented. But he added, "Power and all forms of energy are very emotive subjects. Generally speaking, power belongs to the people of the country in which the source of energy occurs ... I think we could have come to a very amicable agreement with the Newfoundland government after we completed the job, and then handed it over ..."

Though no longer responsible for Churchill Falls, Brinco, as we shall see, promises to become a major contender elsewhere

The gigantic Churchill Falls hydroelectric project was developed by a Rothschild-associated company, Rio Tinto-Zinc. A main contractor was Janin, also a company with indirect ties to the family.

in Canada in the mining sector. Brinco's owner is the Rio Tinto-Zinc Corp. Ltd. (RTZ), a London-based organization with which the Rothschilds have been associated for generations.*

Because of the different names of its subsidiaries, Rio Tinto-Zinc is not well known. The organization as a whole has little to do with zinc and still less to do with Rio Tinto, the name of a locale in Spain where it began prospecting in the 19th century. The company's 1975 annual report sums up its pervasive influence by saying it has "interests in almost every major metal and fuel," with subsidiaries in about 25 countries.

It is in another form of energy, however, that RTZ dominates the Canadian scene.

2. — *Nuclear Power.* RTZ is a giant in this controversial field — controversial not just for safety considerations but also for questions raised about the free enterprise system.

The U.S. business magazine, Forbes, started a furore when it published an article in 1975 suggesting that world uranium oxide (which is processed into nuclear fuel) production might be evolving along cartel-like lines. One of the parties, the article said, would be the Rothschilds, who "have an interest in nearly every major uranium mine in the world."[6]

When I asked him to comment on the Forbes cartel theory, Edmund de Rothschild put down his coffee cup with a rattle.

"Balls!" he exclaimed.

"No," he quickly added, "you couldn't print that, so 'Baloney!' "

Reconsidering, he said, "I'll use the Japanese word, 'Bakarashii!' It means nonsense."

---

* Asked who was RTZ's major shareholder, Rothschild replied, "I don't know. (The shares are) very widely held. It's certainly not us. The family shareholding is well under 10 per cent . . . There's no controlling shareholder."

The family's connections are nonetheless close. Guy de Rothschild is a director of RTZ and David Colville, the N.M. Rothschild partner who is also an Eagle Star deputy chairman, had been a director for many years prior to retiring in 1975. Also, Sir Val Duncan, longtime chairman and chief executive of RTZ, had been appointed to this job by Edmund's uncle; and Sir Val's successor, Sir Mark Turner, is a director of Magnum Fund, a Rothschild-owned investment firm in Toronto.

Since the interview, the U.S. government has pursued an anti-trust investigation into the possibility of an international cartel in uranium oxide, the price of which has shot up from about $6 per pound in 1972 to over $40 in 1977.

The alleged cartel would have operated in much the same fashion as OPEC vis-à-vis oil, only unlike OPEC this scheme would have been highly secretive, not above-board. It would also have been launched a year earlier, in 1972 (and have lasted at least two years).

The Trudeau government has denounced the U.S. congressional probe and, as late as mid-1977, was still refusing to cooperate — hardly surprising because Canada, as the world's No. 1 exporter of uranium oxide, would have been an active participant in the cartel. The largest participant in any price-fixing would have been a Rio Tinto-Zinc subsidiary called Rio Algom Ltd., of Toronto; as of 1975, Rio Algom accounted for 64 per cent of all uranium produced in Canada.[7] In a related American lawsuit held in the U.S. embassy in London in the spring of 1977, RTZ Chairman Turner and Vice Chairman Lord Shackleton, called as witnesses, have taken the Fifth Amendment.

Rio Algom may have almost two-thirds the Canadian production of yellowcake cornered, but there are four other companies in "competition" here as well. According to federal officials in Ottawa, there should be three more companies in operation by 1980, bringing the total to eight. This may seem like considerable diversity, but look again. Of the three newcomers, the Rothschilds have links to two:

— Brinco. Though better known for its hydro endeavors, this RTZ subsidiary showed an interest in nuclear power as far back as 1968 when it began making plans to set up a facility to make enriched uranium for use abroad. Since then, however, it has dropped these plans in favor of starting uranium production in Labrador.

— Amok Ltd., of Saskatoon. This is a subsidiary of France's Mokta group of mineral companies controlled by Guy de Rothschild (control *is* the case in this instance). It has uranium reserves in Saskatchewan containing an estimated 40 million pounds of uranium oxide.

Aside from the merits or "baka-rashii" of Forbes' and Washington's suspicions, it is hard to ignore the conclusion that in Canada Rothschild-related interests today account for close to two-thirds of the "yellowcake" market, as one of five producers; and by 1980 they should account for three of eight companies with an only-to-be-guessed percentage of the market.

If three out of eight seems a substantial proportion in the area of uranium production, how does three out of seven sound for the most essential energy sector of them all?

3. & 4. − *Oil and natural gas.* The "five arrows" do indeed have connections to three of the largest oil companies in Canada.

To begin with, RTZ has a stake in this field too, with a sizable minority holding in British Petroleum Co. Ltd. (BP), the U.K.'s largest industrial company and one of Canada's major oil and gas producers, refiners, and distributors.

The most important Rothschild involvement with the Canadian oil and gas industry, however, is their connection with the Royal Dutch/Shell Group, of which Shell Canada Ltd.* is a member.

Shell's impact on the Canadian energy scene is hard to overstate. At the end of 1974 the group was the No. 1 holder of exploratory land (with special strength in the Mackenzie Delta), the No. 1 producer of marketable natural gas and the owner of six major refineries.[8] When it expanded its refinery in Montreal's East End in 1953, it became the first oil company in Canada to manufacture chemicals from petroleum.

The Rothschild links with Shell are far more direct than with BP. As Edmund puts it,: "We've always held an interest . . . It's a company we've helped. We are one of their financial advisors." How much stock do they own? "Less than two per cent," he says.** A holding of only one or two per cent is significant in a company with widely dispersed stock like Shell. It is, incidentally, the third largest company in the world.

* Shell Canada reported 1976 sales of $2.1 billion − second only to Imperial Oil Ltd. (Exxon).
** After Exxon and General Motors, according to Fortune magazine.

The Belgian arrow in the Rothschild quiver holds an influential share in Petrofina, S.A. of Brussels. Like BP and Shell, Petrofina Canada Ltd. is active in every aspect of this country's oil and natural gas industry. Baron Lambert's Compagnie Bruxelles Lambert lists a 2.5 per cent direct holding in the global oil company but there may be more indirect holdings; Edmund acknowledges that his cousin has a "fairly extensive interest." The baron is also on the Petrofina board.

Like BP and Shell, Petrofina Canada Ltd. is active in every aspect of Canada's huge oil and natural gas industry. And thus of the seven largest oil companies in Canada, the Rothschilds have significant connections to no less than three of them – a remarkable record.*

5. – *Tidal Power*. This final energy source, a replenishable and non-polluting one, to which Edmund referred in his Halifax speech, is a special favorite for him. In 1970 he and several members of his immediate family spent a holiday at White Point, N.S., he recalls, and "it was then that I first really thought about the power potential of the Bay of Fundy." The chairman of Consolidated Edison, New York City's power company, expressed interest in his idea of harnessing the tides to obtain electricity.

In the Halifax speech he explained the *raison d'être* of his tidal power concept:

"You now in Canada have a chance to help the U.S.A. Their energy problem is something that does need some sort of understanding. This is where I believe you in the Maritimes

---

* And that's not all. The Rothschilds also have indirect ties to several young and growing oil and gas interests. These ties are by way of both Brinco and Hudson Bay Mining and Smelting Co. Ltd., which as seen in Chapter 3 is controlled by three other mining companies associated with the Oppenheimer and Rothschild interests.

Brinco has a large minority stake in Coseka Resources Ltd. (gross 1976 income: $1.5 million) with reserves in Alberta, British Columbia and the North Sea. Hudson Bay controls Francana Oil & Gas Ltd., of Toronto (gross 1976 income: $62 million), which is exploring for petroleum throughout North America; and a Francana subsidiary, Trend Exploration Ltd., is also active in many parts of the world, notably Indonesia. Lastly, Hudson Bay is also the major shareholder in Western Decalta Petroleum Ltd., of Calgary (gross 1975 income: $17 million), exploring in seven provinces or territories as well as in Bolivia, Indonesia and the North Sea.

can not only benefit America but yourselves. It is by the export of power . . .

"It can be either power from the Candu atomic power plants which could utilize the cool water of the Bay of Fundy, or it can be from tidal power itself."

Edmund's idea has not fallen on deaf ears. In March, 1975, a review board set up by Ottawa, New Brunswick, and Nova Scotia announced a $2.1 million study to look into the possibility of building a dam across the bay, thereby forcing the ebb tide through turbines to produce electricity. And in 1977 Nova Scotia said it was going ahead with plans for a prototype power plant on the Annapolis River causeway near the bay.

All this does not mean, of course, that there is a Rothschild presence behind every other dam, nuclear facility, or oil der-

The Express (Julien Quideau)
Elie de Rothschild shows off his new credit card system in front of a PLM hotel under construction in Paris. The PLM chain is owned by the family.

rick in Canada. But it does suggest that the Five Arrows are intertwined in the energy sector as much, perhaps, as any discernible private group, whether Canadian or foreign.

What makes the total picture even more interesting, is that besides simply providing energy for Canada's expansion, some of these same companies or their subsidiaries also supply other building blocks for its growth.

For example, RTZ subsidiaries manufacture many common components of high-rise construction: aluminum, glass, and stainless steel. Each is a leader in its field.

Indal Ltd. in Weston, Ont., calls itself Canada's "largest independent producer of aluminum extrusions." For the layman, that means aluminum window frames and balcony doors, as well as steel girts, purlins, studs, and downpipes eavestroughs.

Tempglass Ltd. of Toronto (actually itself a subsidiary of Indal) boasts "the largest capacity in Canada for the production of tempered glass for the residential and architectural construction markets."

Rio Algom's Atlas Steels division, yet another RTZ subsidiary, is also heavily into this market, as No. 1 manufacturer of

London Financial Times (Nathan)

Sir Mark Turner, a Rothschild associate, is a director of such companies as Rio Tinto-Zinc, Brinco, Rio Algom, Toronto-Dominion Bank and Bank of America International.

stainless steel in Canada, and for that matter, the Common-wealth. A spokesman estimates that over 80 per cent of the stainless and tool steel produced in Canada comes from RTZ.[9] RTZ also finds its way into the home: as one company execu-tive boasts, "Virtually every kitchen in Canada has a sink made of our stainless steel." To imagine the huge demand for this material in high-rise construction, one has only to think of how often one sees it in lobbies, elevators, escalators, as well as exteriors. Think of Montreal's Canadian Imperial Bank of Commerce Building whose vertical steel ribbing runs clear up to its 45th floor.

We cannot complete the tally of Rothschild involvement in Canadian industry and development without another brief glance at the mining industry. Besides uranium and gold, dis-cussed earlier, Rothschild-related companies mine asbestos,* potash,** and base metals like copper, zinc and lead.***

Guy de Rothschild controls a French mining company called Penarroya whose subsidiary here, Penarroya Canada Ltée, is now exploring for minerals across Canada — including copper and zinc in Quebec. The parent Penarroya claims to be the world's largest producer of lead. It joined with Mokta sev-eral years ago in the formation of Imetal, a company which Guy conceived to manage over $1 billion of Rothschild min-eral properties from British Columbia to New Caledonia.

Imetal provides a rare example of an industrial company di-rectly controlled by the Rothschilds.†

In a speech several years ago, Edmund recalled how in 1835 one of his family's correspondents wrote a report saying: "Can-

---

* Brinco has what it calls "one of the largest known asbestos deposits in the Western world" just north of Amos, Quebec.
** Hudson Bay Mining and Smelting's Sylvite potash division was impli-cated (but not indicted) by the U.S. government in 1976 in an alleged price fixing arrangement by Saskatchewan's major producers of potash for the U.S. fertilizer market.
*** Hudson Bay Mining and Smelting ranks as one of Canada's top three or four producers of base metals.
† Its third largest shareholder, incidentally, is Anglo American Corp. of South Africa Ltd. This marks at least the third time that Harry Oppen-heimer's Anglo American Group and the Rothschilds have joined forces in a venture active in Canada. The others are in Brinco and Hudson Bay Mining & Smelting.

ada presents a gratifying spectacle of British institutions free from the moth and rust of ages, of a revenue annually increasing without being oppressive and of property generally and rapidly advancing."

"How true," Edmund said after quoting this passage, "that old letter is today."[10]

In the interview, Edmund did not go into the history of his family's involvement in much depth. N.M. Rothschild, he said, was the Bank of Montreal's first correspondent. Also, "we got a lot of provincial issues in Eurodollars" from Nova Scotia, Manitoba and other provinces. There was "not a lot of investment in Canada until Churchill Falls," he said.

Another of the family's ties to Canada evolved in 1961 when Serena Dunn, granddaughter of Sir James Dunn, the Algoma Steel magnate from the Maritimes who had died five years earlier, married Jacob Rothschild, son of Lord Rothschild. The Dunn estate at one time held a sizable minority portion of Algoma stock. Asked what the current portion might be, Edmund replied: "I think Serena's got some shares — but I don't

London Financial Times (F. Mansfield)

Jacob Rothschild.

know. I don't pry into their shareholdings." The inference was that perhaps I shouldn't either.

Algoma is controlled by Canadian Pacific Ltd. which owns 51.3 per cent of it through a subsidiary. And that brings up another of the Rothschilds' touchstones with Canada: a relationship between the Five Arrows and CP, the largest corporate landowner on the entire Island of Montreal, that goes back to the 19th century.

Allard Jiskoot, who, it is recalled, is head of the Five Arrow's Pierson, Heldring & Pierson bank in The Netherlands, is a CP director. Furthermore, W.A. Arbuckle, a CP director and vice president and director of the Bank of Montreal, is a director of another of the Five Arrows, Baron Lamberts's Compagnie Bruxelles Lambert. This gives CP two interlocking directorates with the Five Arrows.*

Pierson, Heldring & Pierson "has always had a long history with CP," Jiskoot remarked in an informal interview in Montreal, where he was attending an annual CP meeting at the Chateau Champlain. "We listed CP shares in 1882 when its railroad was being built. We have been doing business with them ever since."

"We have quite a bit of banking connections with CP — but we don't talk about it," he added.

The point is not that Rothschild-related interests control CP but rather that they have close banking ties and that these ties go back to the years when the company was largely owned abroad. It gives the Five Arrows a say in Canada's largest overall resource company (its 1976 assets were $6.8 billion). Besides its transport interests, it is a major producer of oil and gas, minerals, coal, forest products, iron and steel (through Algoma)

---

* There are secondary contacts as well. Arbuckle, for example, is also a director of Rio Algom and Petrofina Canada Ltd. Also, Ian D. Sinclair, chairman of CP, is a member of the Canadian advisory board of Sun Alliance & London Insurance Group, often called the "most aristocratic" of all British insurance companies; it was founded by Nathan M. Rothschild in 1824 and Edmund is today a director of it (though he says that today "it's controlled by no single group ... There's no controlling shareholder"). And Donald Curtis, the Ohio-born chairman and president of Canadian Pacific Hotels Ltd., was an advisor to Edmond de Rothschild prior to going to CP. CP Hotels, incidentally, has planned joint-ventures with Rothschild interests to build hotels in Israel and France.

and, of course, real estate development. Indeed, CP owns six square kilometres (2.3 square miles) of the island of Montreal, according to property records.

These calculations, corroborated by Canadian Pacific's computers in May, 1977, comprise scattered railroad yards and conventional landholdings such as industrial parks, office blocks, fields and golf courses which are either developed or available for future development. For the record, it might be noted that railroad yards are by far the largest component, accounting for 4.5 of the company's six square kilometres; the remaining 1.5 sq. km. are held through the company's real estate subsidiary,* Marathon Realty Co. Ltd., according to Marathon's Jean Martineau, general manager for Quebec development. The largest Marathon property, he says, is the West Island's Wentworth golf course, roughly 40 hectares in size.

However, if one were to count CP's active rights of way — that is, the actual rail lines traversing the island for purposes of transportation (as distinct from the rail yards used to store equipment and some of which are potentially adaptable to conventional development) — one would have to raise the company's total landholdings above the aforementioned six sq. kms. How far? "We haven't got a clue," says Martineau.

To conclude: Canadian Pacific is the largest private landowner on the island of Montreal and all of urban Canada, but much of this land is devoted to transport functions and is not available for development. The largest owner of *developable* land in urban Canada will be the subject of Chap. 7.

Who owns Canadian Pacific? That is "one of the most closely guarded secrets in Canadian finance," concludes Robert Chodos in his 1973 book, "The CPR." "Control of the Canadian economy is in large measure anonymous ... Within this secretive web, Canadian Pacific is perhaps the most secretive of all." [11]

---

* The bulk of this is freightyards or other railroad-related land, but there are other developed properties such as Place du Canada, the Chateau Champlain Hotel and the old Laurentian Hotel. CP's plans to demolish the Laurentian, the last remaining moderately-priced major downtown hotel, to make way for an office building encountered widespread protests from citizens groups in 1977.

Chodos could not be more right. This passage from the 1962 by-laws of a key CP holding company (through which most of the subsidiaries are controlled), Canadian Pacific Investments Ltd., gives a feeling for the organization's Liechtenstein-like zeal for privacy: "No shareholder shall be entitled to discovery of any information respecting any details or conduct of the Company's business which in the opinion of the directors it will be inexpedient in the interests of the shareholders of the Company to communicate to the public."

In 1946 only nine per cent of Canadian Pacific's voting stock was held in Canada. Most of the rest was held in Europe. CP's chairman, Ian Sinclair, told the Royal Commission on Corporate Concentration in 1975 the reasoning behind the subsequent campaign to "repatriate" CP's stock: "We're a high profile Canadian company ... And sometimes I wish the profile was a little lower, but it seemed that people felt that to have this company with a large number of shareholders ex-Canada bothered them and it bothered me to a degree also, but maybe for different reasons ... We deliberately attempted to repatriate the stock ..."

So by 1975 the company had returned 66.2 per cent of its stock to Canada (with 16.4 per cent remaining in the U.S., 8.6 per cent in the U.K. and 8.8 per cent elsewhere). CP accordingly says it is a Canadian-owned company. But there is not a scintilla of evidence that it is levelling. What CP means, when you examine its claim, is that most of this 66 per cent of the stock held in Canada is held by unknown persons through nominee accounts (i.e., untraceable, anonymous accounts) in banks or trust companies physically located in Canada. By far the largest shareholding in CP, Sinclair told the Royal Commission, was for 7.37 per cent of the voting shares held by a trust company. He did not say which trust company. Nor did he give the names of other trust companies or banks holding significant nominee accounts. Remarkably, the Commission, which was supposed to be looking into such things, did not ask him.

When I asked CP the names of these banks and trust companies, I got this reply from a public relations man: "It's not the policy of Canadian Pacific to release that information. There's no way of identifying the nationality of the shareholder. You can only identify the place where the shares are registered. The presumption has to be that the majority of the people who register in Canada are citizens."[12]

That's like saying it's logical to presume that the people who register companies in Liechtenstein are Liechtensteiners.

Every day at 10.30 a.m. and again at 3 p.m., representatives of four venerable London gold dealing houses pass through a gate on a narrow, winding street in the City called St. Swithin's Lane. On the gate there is no name or other external indication that this is the entrance to the N.M. Rothschild &

Henry Aubin

St. Swithin's Lane: behind the bland façade of the N.M. Rothschild & Sons bank building, some of the world's most extraordinary financial transactions take place.

Sons merchant bank — there is only a small escutcheon on the gate showing five arrows. There is no need for a bolder proclamation of the bank's presence here; as the name merchant bank implies, it does not serve the public but merchants and, more generally, corporations and enterprises of all kinds.

Toting briefcases and often wearing the bowler-and-pinstripe uniform of the City, the four enter into a courtyard and then walk through the doors of a sleek postwar building made of black marble and aluminum. Inside, the four men meet with a fifth, a representative of the Rothschild bank. Then, under the gaze of portraits of such old Rothschild clients as the Czar of Russia and the Emperor of Austria, the five go through their twice daily ritual of determining the world price of gold on the basis of that day's supply and demand.

One of the men sitting at that table comes from Samuel Montagu & Co., the merchant bank whose chairman, former Rothschild partner Philip Shelbourne, we keep bumping into as we trace back the lines of responsibility in urban Canada. Another of the men there comes from Mocatta & Goldsmid Ltd., the oldest bullion broker of them all, founded in 1684. Today it endures as a subsidiary of the Hambro interests.

This is an interesting coincidence, underscoring the tightness of that small circle of people, with mutual interests in various different fields, who are at the heart of so many different decision-making processes.

The Hambro family, descended from a 18th century Danish silk merchant, is in some ways a parallel family to the Rothschilds so far as Canada is concerned, and a quick glance at its activity here helps put the Rothschilds in perspective.

At about the same time the Rothschilds were emerging from a German ghetto to set up one financial dynasty, the Hambro

---

* Word of their decision is flashed immediately to dealers around the world, including Canada's two principal dealers: the Bank of Nova Scotia and the Canadian Imperial Bank of Commerce. Ties between N.M. Rothschild and the latter bank are especially close. Says a gold trader with the Commerce in Toronto: "We have considerations for them (Rothschild) and we approach them first on a deal and I hope they would approach us first." But the rapport between the Commerce and the family goes much deeper than gold. Though the London family has dealings with other major Canadian chartered banks, its main bank in Canada for general matters is the Commerce, according to a close associate of the London branch.

family was coming out of Scandinavia to set up another. Like Nathan M. Rothschild, the Hambros moved to England from the Continent in the early 1800s. The two families have known each other since the very beginning: Nathan's father, Mayer Amschel Rothschild, the coin-dealer who founded his dynasty, was a Hambro client in the 1830's.

In Canada in recent years, the Hambro family interests, under the tutelage of Jocelyn Olaf Hambro, have been active on the real estate scene — more directly than the Rothschilds. They own Hambro Canada Ltd., which owns Ontario Trust and held more than $100 million in real estate assets, mostly through a subsidiary called Peel-Elder Development Ltd. Most of Peel-Elder's activity has been in building shopping centres and residential developments in the Toronto, Winnipeg and Cambridge, Ont., areas.

The family has also been quite active here on an indirect basis. Remember, for example, South Africa's Union Corp., the gold mining company in Chapter 3 which was the most influential shareholder in Abbey Glen Property Corp.'s parent company? Well, the Hambros have substantial undetermined holdings in Union, and members of the Hambro family have for many years been members of Union's board of directors.[*] And remember that mention in Chapter 2 of Società Generale Immobiliare, the Rome-based development giant which has built Montreal's tallest skyscraper among other things? Well, the Hambros have been deeply involved in that as well through their banking association with the Vatican and with former Immobiliare chief Michele Sindona. And then in Chapter 4 there was also a passing reference to the British-owned Monarch group of companies which have been active developing Montreal-area subdivisions. A British company, Taylor Woodrow Holdings Ltd., owns the controlling interest — and the Hambros are tied in with Taylor Woodrow.

The Hambros also own Berkeley Hambro Property Co. Ltd., which has a Canadian subsidiary headquartered in Mon-

---

[*] Close ties exist between the two organizations in Canada, as evinced by interlocking directorates between the Hambro organization and Union's direct investment arm in Canada, Canadian S.A. Union Corp. Ltd., of Toronto.

treal.* Executives there, however, say it owns no real estate in Montreal; it does own some in Ottawa (e.g., Westgate shopping centre) and in Western Canada. Much of its real estate is in the U.S., where the family has also been involved significantly. For example, the Hambros, along with Jack Cotton, played a critical role in financing the famed Pan American Airlines Building in New York City.

So the point is that the Hambros are meshed into a lot of things just as the Rothschilds are. The Rothschilds would probably have to agree with this generalized view of a City bank's corporate involvement, as summed up by a Hambro banker to Joseph Wechsburg: "We take a minority interest (in companies), but never control. We believe management should be left to the managers. We want to keep a sensible influence — after all, we're involved with our money — but we don't want to run hundreds of companies."[13]

"The role of the merchant banker," Edmund de Rothschild noted in our interview, "is to tie things together." It is not to hustle about trying to control things *per se*. The fact that only two companies in Canada that I could confirm are actually controlled by the Rothschilds, — Mokta and Penarroya (by the French branch in both cases) — says as much. But tying things together, though it may not sound very dramatic, is often what counts at a time when it is not so much individual companies as *networks* of companies which determine the major direction of development. Brinco is the ultimate example. Much of this does not come from waving a magic financial wand but

---

* The precise address of this subsidiary, Berkeley Property Corp. Ltd., happens to be 630 Sherbooke W., a highrise office building called Montreal Life Insurance Building. Most of the executives who work there are ignorant of it, but that location has its own inner logic which demonstrates the kinds of tugs exerted by corporate interconnections. Montreal Life is owned by Guardian Royal Exchange Assurance Ltd., one of Britain's four biggest life and non-life insurors, and whom do we find on its board but Charles E.A. Hambro, chairman of Hambros Bank. The Guardian Royal Exchange connection also illustrates the degree to which interests involved in Canadian land development do rub shoulders: also on the board are the Earl of Inchcape, head of the organization which owns Bovis Corp. Ltd., and Angus Ogilvy, the Queen's cousin-in-law who is a director of MEPC Canadian Properties Ltd. and also a close associate of Philip Shelbourne.

from sheer dint of personality. As Edmund says of the Churchill Falls project, "I helped, encouraged, cajoled, pushed it."

But within individual companies, too, the merchant banker can play a critical role — the best example here is the way N.M. Rothschild & Sons vaulted English Property Corp. into

London Financial Times (Corinne McCarthy)

Jocelyn Olaf Hambro heads the Hambro's banking dynasty. Legend has it that the fortune began in the 18th century when a Hambro sea captain was the first Dane to learn the Queen of Denmark had died in Paris. With no one else aware of this he quickly cornered the black crepe market in Copenhagen and made a killing.[14]

the international big leagues after putting together for it a series of mergers. There is a special kind of power that goes with the role of financial advisor to a company. As one associate of the London Rothschilds explains it: "(N.M.) Rothschild is influential because it puts together deals for clients and is retained afterwards as a financial advisor. It is consulted on most major policy. A company can't make a move without its consultation." This is where the Five Arrows' influence within Canadian Pacific, for example, would play a role. The banker also is the means for a company's capital expansion; thus in 1976 when Canadian Pacific Securities Ltd. floated a $35 million bond issue in Europe, for example, the underwriters' syndicate included Pierson, Heldring & Pierson.

What ultimately separates the Rothschilds from the Hambros and the other merchant bankers, beyond the measure of size or other tangible criteria, is imagination and élan. They have a sense for the strategies rather than the tactics of international development. This is something they have had since the 19th century when they, more than any other group, put their financial shoulder behind the bringing of railroads to Europe and goldfields to South Africa, which revolutionized those two places. Since the last war they have been key influences in the economy of the state of Israel, in the global nuclear energy industry and in providing much of the foundation for industrialization in places like Eastern Canada. They believe in a distinctly *creative* financial role. They have an ability to anticipate historical developments and to get there first. As Jacob Rothschild has said, "We have learned that the merchant banker must not wait for an opening, an opportunity. He must create them ... We must be the catalyst who helps the development of trade. We must never remain static, always attempting to maintain our initiative." [15]

This pioneering role has in the past made them controversial. In the 19th century there was dispute as to whether they were the archangels or archdemons of progress. It is not so much them as the progress they promote which is at issue: if you like technological progress *a priori* you'll probably revere the Rothschilds; if you're wary of it you may have mixed feelings about them. However, since the war few people have known what they are up to — besides a few fragmentary activities here and there — and so few people today have opinions either way. To most people the Rothschilds are just classy gentry who made their money a long time ago and today populate the 'beautiful people' sections of the magazines. It is this lack of accountability that is one of the most striking aspects of their power.

The Rothschilds are, finally, the quintessence of a special order of the Old World. They, and other families or groups also active in Canada and with whom they have much in common, are not necessarily linked by "conspiracies" *per se* or anything sinister of that sort. In the main these groups tend to be competent, independent — if ultimately interdependent — organizations, which share a very specific view of how business and the economy should operate. They tend to think and act alike not because there is any nerve centre on St. Swithin's Lane or elsewhere firing off orders to the Mountains or the Oppenheimers, any more than they do to even more famous families we will come across later; none of these would very likely dream of taking orders. But the very fact that these families have made it to the inner circle means that they can be counted on to think much like each other and to act in harmony with each other's interests. They may share common schools, clubs or company boards, etc. However, when one considers that their decisions affect the economies of entire nations and the lives of millions, perhaps their lack of accountability should be seen in a more critical light — not as a conspiracy but as a form of non-representative power, in the sense that they don't represent the people of their host nation, or if they say they do we'll have to take their word for it. They do not encourage scrutiny by the public of those nations.

Edmund de Rothschild then, this man who looks so much like a rumpled country doctor, journeying regularly to Canada to tend to its economic ills and develop its strengths, is of course much more than that. He is a medicine man of the highest secular order, helping guide Canada toward participation in a grand industrial design.

"To be an optimist today needs courage," Edmund said in a speech on the future of mankind which he made before a business symposium in Tokyo. Then, using an image which could have been drawn from Genesis, the image of the Tree of

Knowledge, he added: "But this is what we all must have — courage, and linked with this must be self-discipline — and I for one have great faith that man will go forward and reach the top of the tree and ultimately find the flower that he is seeking." [16]

Footnotes — Chapter 5
1. Virgint, Ernest, "High Finance and Empire: The Rothschild Nexus," a paper presented to the McMaster In-house Conference on Class and Power, Aug. 31, 1975.
2. Morton, Frederic, *The Rothschilds: A Family Portrait* (Greenwich, Conn.: Fawcett Publications, Inc., 1961), p. 19.
3. Wechsburg, Joseph, *The Merchant Bankers* (Boston: Little, Brown, 1966), p. 337.
4. Interview, Jun. 3, p. 1975.
5. Address by Edmund de Rothschild, Halifax, Apr. 22, 1974.
6. Forbes Magazine, Jan. 1975, "It worked for the Arabs..."
7. Telephone interviews with officials at the federal Dept. of Energy, Mines and Resources, Ottawa, Aug. 30, 1976.
8. Montreal Stock Exchange Monthly Review, Aug. 1975, p. 3.
9. Telephone interview with Terry Brammell, manager of sales promotion, Atlas Steels division of Rio Algom Ltd., Aug. 31, 1975.
10. Keynote address by Edmund de Rothschild at the Manitoba Business Summit Conference, Winnipeg, Jan. 16, 1968.
11. Chodos, Robert, *The CPR: A Century of Corporate Welfare* (Toronto: James Lewis & Samuel, Publishers, 1973), p. 134.
12. Telephone interview with Robert Rice, a spokesman for Canadian Pacific, Nov. 24, 1976.
13. Wechsburg, op. cit., p. 45.
14. Ibid., p. 47.
15. Ibid., p. 357.
16. Address by Edmund de Rothschild at a symposium organized by the Yomiuri International Economic Society, Apr. 26, 1973.

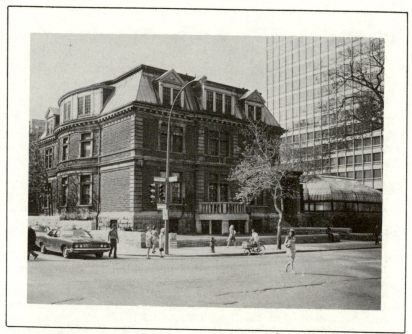

The Van Horne mansion as it once stood...

MONTREAL, July 27 — A group of citizens are fighting the proposed demolition of a stately Victorian mansion here in a battle that reflects the new concern among Canadians about the future of their cities...

— New York Times, July 28, 1973.

Chapter 6
"Das Mekka"

...the transition phase...

BY 1973 THE FEVER OF DEMOLITION and construction in Montreal was beginning to reach unprecedented levels, with entire blocks and neighborhoods razed to make room for high-profit parking lots and high-rises. At first the public reacted with a sense of numbed awe in the face of the seeming absence of social sensitivity among the forces responsible for much of this change — whoever they were.

Then suddenly and dramatically in the summer of that year public sentiment crystallized around efforts to stop the threatened destruction of a highly familiar building, the Van Horne mansion on Sherbrooke Street. Attempts to dissuade the developer who had just bought it, a reclusive Westmounter named David Azrieli, were unsuccessful.

And no wonder. Though protesters at the time had no way of knowing it, Azrieli was just a pawn of much bigger forces. Appeals to his civic conscience by Montrealers meant little to him because Montreal was not his constituency.

The mansion's destruction, which many citizens see as a symbol of architectural sacrilege, may also be regarded as a symbol of an unseen phenomenon which money men call fiscal "recycling." The "story behind the story" of the mansion is the way in which European money — mostly German, in this case — in effect made possible the replacement of that mansion by the 16-floor office tower which Azrieli built on the site. Without downplaying Azrieli's responsibility for decisions on where and what to build, it is certain that his influence and financial status are to a great extent derived from this foreign presence. In this he is typical of the vast majority of local Montreal developers.

A glance back to the days immediately preceding Azrieli's acquisition of the mansion shows how this process can work (and how it still works today).

Until the Van Horne mansion purchase, Azrieli had been a relatively obscure builder, mostly concerned with duplexes and a few high-rise apartment blocks. But only shortly before that transaction, he completed a major deal. His company sold the "Embassy Terrace" apartments it had built at 3440 Durocher St. for $2.9 million to a free-spending German millionaire named Guenther Kaussen.

Michael Dugas

... and the "1155" Sherbrooke St. west, the high-rise that supplanted it.

Deeds at the registry office also show that a week before that Azrieli's company, Scanti Investments Ltd. had sold the "Westside Terrace" apartments at 3464 Hutchinson St. to another German speculator, Achim Luft, for $605,000.

One property agent says he sees this kind of thing all the time: "A developer plows his profits from sales to foreigners into new projects. It's recycling. There's no one-to-one correlation, but it's safe to say that foreign money from Azrieli's sales and others like it effectively built the new office building at 1155 Sherbrooke."

This type of foreplay to the Van Horne affair illustrates a critical undercurrent in Montreal's development: in addition to developing or directly financing new projects, or buying up existing ones, foreign money invested in local real estate continues to have an impact long after it has become "Canadian."

This is why one well-placed Montreal notary, Volker Mehnart, flatly declares: "Most of the development here was generated by capital which was brought in by Europeans and paid to developers for what they had produced or would produce. The profit which the developers made would then be used for new development."

It is a remarkable conclusion: the vast majority of downtown development, starting in the late 1950s, has been generated directly or indirectly, by outside capital, most of it European. Mehnart's conclusion, which confirms my own sampling of real estate documents, is based on the most solid research one could ask for. Besides seeing a lot of sales to foreigners — mostly Germans — cross his desk and serving as a director of some of their companies, Mehnart has been visiting the municipal archives since 1962 to make property-title searches for clients. Combing through those files to see how a piece of land has changed hands in the past, the discerning notary becomes something of an historian in detecting the broad patterns of ownership.

"Montreal fell under the spell of a lot of people coming here and saying, 'My God, look at the potential here,' and then investing here in all kinds of real estate — residential, commercial, industrial," he says.[1]

The extent of these investments has far-reaching implications. It has, for one thing, contributed to the evolution of a development economy of dependence on external, rather than internal, initiative and risk-taking. This may have perpetuated the psychological trappings of colonization here, but on a purely economic level most of the money men involved in real estate believe that this is a healthy state of affairs.

Fausto Rusca, president of Fidinam (Canada) Ltd. which has poured tens of millions of dollars into Montreal for European clients, feels that "it does good for Canada" because "it increases the assets of the country as a whole . . ." The billions of dollars foreigners have pumped into Montreal in recent years "circulate around, generally end up in the pockets of local developers and thus lead to more development."

Gernt Damerau, a colleague with a German firm, Hansa Financial & Corporate Management Inc., would agree. "It gives Canada needed capital," he says. "There is simply not sufficient money available within Canada (to support growing urban development) unless Canadian pension funds and insurance companies divert their funds to real estate."[2]

"There are not enough Canadian buyers for apartment buildings and land here," says Herschel Rosen, president and owner of the local Delrose Development Corp. which has advertised for investors in the German and Italian press. "The volume of European investors has allowed Canadian developers to develop. If you're sitting on a lot of inventory, you can't develop."[3]

Most critics would agree with these views so far as they go. But there is good reason to ask if this superabundance of outside capital can be absorbed here in an orderly fashion. The surge of billions of outside dollars into local real estate investments may well be upsetting the equilibrium in the community's growth.

Furthermore, critics warn that the money has helped transform the local builders and other property professionals into a "semi-parasite" group which, while not foreign itself, is more beholden to foreigners than to the community for its profits and position. They point out that the quality of what it often builds — characterized by *quelconque* high-rises and sprawl — may partly reflect these loyalties. Name almost any local developer — including Max Zentner, Ben Saskin and others whose demolition plans have generated the same kind of controversy as Azrieli — and it is possible to trace foreign sales as playing a key role in their affairs.

While opinions vary as to whether the phenonemon represents an economic blessing or a sell-out, there is little doubt about the principal source of the cash flow — West Germany.

Azrieli's sale of the "Embassy Terrace" to Guenther Kaussen illustrates the vigor of some of these German buyers. On the same day that Kaussen, a bachelor from Cologne, gave Azrieli a down-payment of $350,000 (on the $2.9 million selling price of the Embassy Terrace), he also plunked down another $303,164 on the $1.2 million apartment building at 1225 Sussex St.

And he was only warming up. About this same time he bought an apartment building at 5301 Sherbrooke St. W., evaluated at $1.4 million. Then he quite outdid himself by buying the "Drummond" Court at 1455 Drummond St., evaluated at $3.1 million.

Incredibly, this absentee landlord never even laid eyes on any of the buildings Azrieli sold him. According to an Azrieli aide, Kaussen remained in Germany while a German attorney handled the sale.

Kaussen is but a minor figure in the over-all flow of German capital here. A survey of the 113 apartment properties in the City of Montreal, evaluated at $1 million or more, revealed that at least *40 per cent are owned by Germans* — either directly or through holdings in other countries (usually Switzerland or Liechtenstein). Foreign interests as a whole own about two-thirds of these 113 properties, as seen in Chapter 1; thus this makes the Germans by far the biggest high-rise residential landlord nationality, including Canadians.

In industrial real estate (like warehouses) as well as in office buildings, the Germans have also come on fast. Mehnart reports, for example, that one of his clients is now involved in a warehouse in LaSalle which will be the largest of its kind on the Island of Montreal.

It is locally based companies, incorporated in Canada and generally headed by people with European background, who help steer the investors here, then manage their properties.

One of the leaders is Caresta Services Ltd. of 4467 St. Catherine St. W. which manages, according to an employee's estimate, some 40 buildings, big and small — most of them owned by Germans, reflecting the background of Caresta head, Victor Denning.

Another important management company in both the apartment and industrial park fields is Valver Real Estate Inc. at 2075 Blvd. de Maisonneuve W. owned by Georges Rickli. The company uses the capital of a mostly German and Swiss (reflecting Rickli's background) clientele to develop industrial parks. In 1975, it reported a land bank of about 40 sites for industrial development throughout the island of Montreal.

Groups representing property professionals like these companies, for example the Canadian Real Estate Association, have lobbied against government restrictions on sales to non-residents. Their argument is that foreigners who buy downtown real estate are not in it for the fast buck. The buyers are, says CREA, primarily long-term investors who are contributing to the stability of the market rather than to speculation.

I found numerous exceptions to that generalization, and Azrieli's sale of the "Westside Terrace", mentioned earlier, is a case in point.

The evening of the first anniversary of the Van Horne mansion's demolition. Citizens filed through the streets to demonstrate their opposition to the continued destruction of their heritage.

Azrieli sold that building on May 9, 1973, to Achim and Charlotte Luft, of Sonnenhof am Chiemsee. Only 54 days later, on July 2, the Lufts themselves sold the building. Their profit cannot be determined from the deeds: They bought the building for $605,000 but sold it for $1 and "other considerations," a term often used by speculators seeking to mask their dealings.

Nor is that an isolated example. On Dec. 20, 1971, Azrieli's company sold the "Hampstead Terrace" apartments he had built at 6820 Cote St. Luc Road to a company called QAN Investments Ltd. for $1,125,000. Eight months later it was sold for $1,300,000 to Giovanni Dondena, of Pontestura, Italy — a $175,000 gain.

A sampling of scores of such buildings shows that turnover in ownership is far greater than suggested by the property lobby in its 1975 testimony which sought — successfully — to soften the Foreign Investment Review Agency's restrictions on real estate sales to foreigners. By comparing Rudner's annual lists of local apartment buildings, a privately circulated guide for realtors, one can calculate that 28 per cent of the apartment buildings in the city of Montreal which were owned as of November 1974 by persons giving addresses in Germany had been sold to others (often other Germans) as of November 1975.[4]

With a foreign market so willing to pay higher prices than Canadians for real estate, it is natural that many Montreal developers almost seem to ignore the Canadian market for the new projects they build.

One Swiss-born executive emphasizes that he is seeking more Canadian investors, "because it breaks my heart to see outsiders making the money when the Canadians could be making it."

He says, however, that his search is often frustrating. "Canadians are unwilling to do this — they just like to sit on their land, letting it rise in value. Germans are prepared to delegate responsibility to us to bring development in, make creative use of their capital." Canadians, he says, are "too damn passive."

Though Germans were outspent here in 1975-76 by the Italians, and though they have been following a trail blazed by the British, they still own more property than either group.

It is impossible to calculate precisely how much Canadian real estate they do control. No one keeps statistics on foreign property investments. The investments come in bits and pieces without a central clearing house, and the investors themselves often shun identification, but my calculation is that at least $4 billion worth of real estate in Canada is controlled by Germans. It could go as high as $10 billion.

Complicating the calculations is the fact that the investors often own their property through locally incorporated companies with local-sounding names — like Mountain Place Ltd.

In addition, if we count German money routed through Switzerland and Liechtenstein, we would have to add on several billion more.

These figures may seem high, but they are based on my interviews with property people here and in Europe and on whatever recorded evidence was available. In my research, I stumbled across several individual companies which alone control in the neighborhood of half a billion dollars in assets — each. This would put them easily among the top half a dozen or so real estate companies in Canada, although they are virtually unknown outside their immediate business circles.

"Oh, you haven't seen anything till you've seen Lehndorff," confided an executive at a company with more modest assets.

He and two other executives of companies working with German investors estimate the total Canadian real estate assets of the Lehndorff group of companies at close to $1 billion. This would make it the first or second largest real estate company in Canada.

But Louis Matukas, the vice-president of Lehndorff Management Ltd. of Toronto, laughs when he hears this. "I know, I've heard the rumors too. Bankers and others tell me our assets might be worth $800 million — but that's only if we decided to sell all our real estate today."[5]

He pegs the "book value"* of the group's assets at just under $500 million. Nonetheless, under this standard unit of measure only three or four other companies here are known to be bigger.

---

* The price at which the real estate was bought, not counting depreciation.

The Lehndorff group first became active in Canada in 1966. Though one member of the group, Lehndorff Corp., was established in 1973 and began offering shares to the public, the group as a whole gets much of its money by tapping several German funds (roughly comparable to mutal funds in which relatively small investors pool their resources).

The group, which comprises over a dozen companies, gets its name from Nona von Lehndorff, sister of the Prussian countess Verushka. Verushka, the famed fasion model turned actress, portrayed the bold model in the film "Blow-Up". Nona's husband is Hamburg merchant Jan von Haeften, who co-founded the group with Prof. Hans Abromeit.

Matukas says von Haeften and Abromeit are "Canadians", later amending this under questioning to "Canadian residents". Nevertheless, in three calls over nine months to Lehndorff's Bay Street headquarters, receptionists said von Haeften and Abromeit were both in Germany.

The group is especially active in the Maritimes and Western Canada, where it owns shopping centres, industrial warehouses and apartment and office buildings. Its biggest holding in the province of Quebec is 75 per cent interest in 368 acres in Le Bourg Neuf area of Quebec City. As of mid-1976 there were plans to construct 4,300 housing units there by 1979.

While there is nothing else on the scale of Lehndorff. There are several other German companies with big money to spend. For example, several months before the Nov. 15, 1976 election, "Mountain Place" at 3450 Drummond St. changed hands. With more than 700 apartments in its three towers, it is one of downtown Montreal's biggest apartment blocks, if not *the* biggest.

The buyers were RWI Holdings Ltd. and a sister company controlled by West German limited partnerships. The seller — as happens increasingly in this city where few large projects are Canadian owned — was another European-owned company, Mountain Place Ltd., controlled by German and Swiss interests.

Another example of a company already well-established in Montreal is Polaris Realty (Western) Ltd., a management company with a close association with West German syndicates.*

* The company's registration forms in Ontario list its president as Karsten von Wersebe.

It manages about $200 million in assets across Canada, according to a company source, but their executives were extremely tight-lipped about their holdings. In separate telephone interviews, two executives at the Toronto headquarters reluctantly acknowledged that their firm holds the 28-floor office building at 800 Dorchester Blvd. W. overlooking the Queen Elizabeth Hotel. They refused to identify any of their other Montreal properties.

Property records, however, divulge that the company also has the Northern Building at Dorchester and Guy St., the Confederation Building on St. Catherine St. at McGill Ave., a highrise apartment building at 1400 Pine Ave. W. and two other apartment buildings in LaSalle.

But the bulk of German investments, say brokers here, come from individuals rather than large companies like these.

The flow of German investments to Montreal peaked in 1974-75. That was when a leading German news magazine, Der Spiegel,[6] went so far as to dub Montreal "Das Mekka" for wealthy Germans trying to avoid the twin hobgoblins of surging inflation and creeping socialism.

Old private fortunes, however, which make little noise even in Germany have been investing here for decades. One of the most eminent is Prince Johannes von Thurn und Taxis, a mem-

---

* Prince von Thurn und Taxis, a fifty-ish bachelor living in a huge castle overlooking the Bavarian city of Regensburg, illustrates this species. An interview in the New York Times published Nov. 13, 1976, included the following:

" 'We,' the Prince said, meaning his family, 'invented the mail and got the monopoly on mail service for the Holy Roman Empire in the 15th century. Before that we were robber barons, pirates really, in northern Italy.' The emperors and popes and the Prussian kings rewarded the family with titles of nobility and landed estates — and that is why the Prince is wealthy.

"His family was out of favor during the Nazi regime. After the war its vast estates in Poland and Yugoslavia were seized by the new Communist governments there, and the money it had in West Germany became worthless. But land — more than 80,000 acres of forest and farm in the southern part of the country — kept its value.

The family began anew after the war with that base, plus the Thurn und Taxis brewery in Regensburg and the Fürst Thurn und Taxis Bank, with five branches in Bavaria — and eight castles. Building on the profits from the enterprises, the Prince bought more tens of thousands of acres of cheap rice plantations in Brazil, forests in Canada and a series of precious metal interests . . .

"Cautious, careful management has built the fortune into one of the biggest in the world. How much is it all worth? 'One doesn't have to estimate the value of a thousand-year-old fortune,' Prince Johannes replied."

ber of the Hohenzollern royal line, who has bought land in British Columbia.

Largely because of new economic and political problems of Canada, much German money which heretofore came to Canada had been deflected south to the United States by 1977. Thus in Kossuth County, Iowa, for example, we find another hallowed Teuton name, the Metternichs. Unlike most Canadian provinces, Iowa may have set its defenses against outside landowners: non-resident aliens are not allowed to own more than 640 acres (one square mile). The Metternichs got around that with a facility that would have given their ancestors, the clever 19th century Austrian statesman-prince, a chuckle: Franz Albrecht Metternich-Sandor, Prince of Ratibor and Corvey, owns 611 acres; his wife, Princess Isabelle, owns 470; and Isabelle's sister and her husband own 610 and 440 acres, respectively.[7]

"I have quite a few as clients but I don't like to give their names," says Gernt Damerau, a Toronto-based investment advisor, referring to a string of barons, counts and "fürsts." "Their investments always have been in land — they've owned large parcels of Germany for centuries," he notes.

The presence of a few "vons" in the German investment scene betokening a substantial aristocratic involvement, calls to mind the array of lords, earls and the like involved in the heavy British investment in this country discussed earlier. A certain affinity for land seems to be an attribute of the nobility regardless of nationality.

"There is a definite fear," continues Damerau, "that the government may become too socialistic, whereby free enterprise and capitalism are killed off. And these people with inherited money are concerned it may be taken away."

Marching with this old money is the new.

Among the members of Germany's postwar industrial elite coming here are the Monheim (chocolate), the Burda (publishing), and the Hertz (coffee) interests. Meanwhile in the U.S., the Flick family, the Daimler-Benz people, paid a cool $42 million for the Entex office building in Houston.

Leafing through property records, I happened on a big political name as well. Mrs. Franz Josef Strauss, wife of the chief of the Bavarian wing of the rightist Christian Social Union, holds in trust two apartment buildings at 2705 and 2755 Kent Ave.

Her husband is a possible candidate for the chancellorship in West Germany's 1980 elections.

A few chapters ago, we may recall, we identified Britain as the clearcut overall leader in the urban development process which has been transforming Canadian cities over the past 15 years or so. Britain and Germany both own about the same

Kate McGovern

Franz Josef Strauss, a heavyweight of the German right wing. His wife holds in trust two apartment buildings on Kent avenue.

amount of assets, but the British still can claim the distinction of leadership. The reason is twofold:

— The U.K. has been involved in this process from the start, unlike Germany which only came aboard in earnest within the past decade.

— Britain's investments here are of a fundamentally different nature. U.K. interests have probably acquired no more than two or three apartment buildings, for example. The British like to *build* and be creative. The Germans on the other

Henry Aubin

Most German investors buy already-completed buildings. One of the rare exceptions to this rule is Shercon Plaza, at Sherbrooke and City Councillors' streets. The project was begun by IWF Canada Corp., a company having access to German capital through the Gut Streif Bank in Zurich. The above photo shows a group of German investors at the official ceremony marking the beginning of construction in 1975.

hand largely have preferred to *buy* what others have already built.

Far less familiar with Canada and its traditions than the British, and having the additional barrier of language, the Germans have preferred to help build up a class of local Montreal developers who do the actual work for them and who are beholden to them.

Who's responsible for this state of dependency? The developers themselves, people like Azrieli?

Not really. Developers go where they can get the money to build. They go to foreign sources because they can't get financing from domestic sources.

There are enormous pools of capital in Canada. They could easily be tapped for real estate ventures. There is nothing mysterious about these pools of capital — they are made up of the savings of ordinary Canadians. They are mostly in the form of bank savings, insurance premiums and pension fund premiums — the Canadian Pacific and Canadian National pension funds and the Caisse de Depots are among the biggest such pools. Their potential for investment is enormous.

The common explanation from the Canadian business community as to why foreign investments are needed in real estate is that there just isn't enough money here at home to do the job. Again and again we hear that refrain: Canada is starved for capital.

Matthew Hudson, one of a number of inquisitive young developers on the Quebec scene today, disagrees. Hudson knows something about foreign capital — he worked as president of Groupe Canest, a subsidiary of Toronto's Greater York Group which was in large part dependent on German investments, before breaking out on his own in 1976 to form his own company, Les Associés Sierra, Ltée., which specializes in "human-scale" office and apartment buildings and shopping centres in the Montreal area.*

---

* An example of his work is the harmonious brick office building at the southeast corner of Guy and Ste. Catherine Sts., pleasant-looking, remarkably low — only 3 stories — which he built when with Canest. "My role," he says, "is to produce shelter in hopefully aesthetic ways, in profitable ways, in ways which are of benefit to the community in more than simply the economic sense."

Hudson sees some truth to the excuse that Canada does not have enough capital to develop its own cities, but only *some*.[8] "I don't say Canada could go completely without foreign investment, but what's happened is that it's disproportionately dependent on it."

Urban development, he says, could be financed with much less reliance on outside investment — but "not under the present system."

"These Canadian pools of capital" he says, "would have to become much more attuned to the needs of the real estate market."

The big domestic funds, he says, are managed by very cautious, conservative people, unsure of their own expertise in real estate. They prefer not to take the risk invovled in investing in property development when government bonds present an even smaller risk — and smaller return on investment. This, coupled with the fact that all levels of government in Canada are enormous borrowers (see Chap. 15) and provide a ready market for bonds, means that relatively little of this money trickles into real estate.

This presents a problem for developers. Once they build an office or apartment building they would, under ordinary circumstances, like to hold onto it to enjoy the fruits of their labor and make profits on the rent; this would be socially useful as well, since if you make something to keep for yourself you will tend to make it better than if you're going to make it for "some guy from Frankfurt with money in his jeans," as Hudson puts it. Another word for this is pride.

But the developer cannot build *another* project without getting more money from somewhere. Since he has such a hard time getting a loan from domestic sources he often finds he must sell the project he has just built to raise the capital to build the next project. Since foreign investors are willing to spend more money to buy their Canadian nestegg, the developer naturally sells to foreigners.

"Local people don't own enough of their own real estate," says Hudson. "Having absentee landlords does not make sense for a lot of social reasons.

"Instead of selling property to raise more money, I — or any developer — should be able to go to Canadian lenders and get the money. But there's no enthusiasm on their part. They'd rather invest in stocks and bonds.

"Mind you, I'm not saying that foreign capital is bad *per se*. We should *borrow* money from foreign sources — that way, after we pay back our debt, we still own our real estate. What we shouldn't have to do is *sell* the real estate to foreigners in order to be able to build. That's selling our birthright."

What can ordinary persons do about this? Well, for openers, says Hudson, they can put pressure on their pension funds to invest in Canadian real estate. And they can put pressure on their elected representatives to help promote these objectives.

That may not sound like much. But the problem, he says, is, "There's very little leadership in Canada — either in politics or in business. Either we don't produce leaders or we don't respond to them.

"We've got to begin somewhere."

Michael Dugas

Place du Cercle: a "housing machine" located at 3545 Berri St.

Here are some of the individuals and companies from West Germany who/which own apartment buildings in the City of Montreal, according to data in municipal evaluation rolls and provincial documents as of November, 1976.

Listed are the properties' addresses, the owners' names and addresses and the total 1976 evaluation of the land and building.

3545 Berri St., "Place du Cercle" $5,110,000
          Afra Holdings Ltd., Ontario
          President: H. Schreyer
          Musshacherstr.
          Munich

5035-45 Clanranald Ave. $617,000
          Mrs. Ulrich Layher
          7129 Eibensbach
          Wurttenberg

4935-42 Cote des Neiges Rd. $62,600
          Mrs. Joannes Fromming
          Hamburg

2715 Darlington Place $403,000
          Bernard Guenther Frese
          Gmund am Tegernsee, and
          Wolfgang Greichgauer
          c/o 2015 Drummond St., #652

2840 Darlington Place $125,500
          Jurgen Madsen
          73 Leinbergerstr.
          Dortmund

6190-6210 Decarie Blvd. $111,650
          Josef Pirk
          Marchenwg 6
          Munich

5650 de Salaberry Ave., "Le Cavalier" $233,200
          Johann Moeller-Soenke et al
          2341 Rabenkirchen-Fauluck
          Rabenkirchenholz 13

2605 des Trinitaires Blvd., "Parkview" $277,500
          Mrs. Dieter Beer
          8 Regerstrasse
          Wiesbaden

2775 des Trinitaires Blvd., "Royal Garden" $278,000
          Mrs. Dieter Beer
          8 Regerstrasse
          Wiesbaden

1455 Drummond St., "Drummond Court"
    Guenther Kaussen
    20-26A St. Apernstr.
    Cologne
	$3,120,000

3450 Drummond St., "Mountain Place"
    RWI Holdings Lt., RWI Holdings Two Ltd.
    c/o Westdeutsche Landesbank Girozentrale
    4000 Dusseldorf 11
    RWI-Haus
	$11,666,000

3440 Durocher St., "Embassy Terrace"
    Guenther Kaussen
    20-26A St. Apernstr.
    Cologne
	$2,916,000

3190 Edouard Montpetit Blvd.
    Volkmar Schniewind et al
    AM Kircheck 26
    Dreichenhain
	$443,500

6890 Fielding Ave., "Fielding Towers"
    Alfred Viebig
    Wilhelm Koppe Str. 2
    Wiesbaden
	$323,000

1180 Fort St., "Fort Chateau"
    Harold Gerstner
    78 Freiberg
    Bresigau
	$422,000

2250 Guy St.
    Gottfried Gunther
    Hauffstr. 25
    Karlsruhe
	$3,281,000

2705 Kent Ave.
    Mrs. Franz Josef Strauss — in trust
    Listseeweg 7
    Munich
	$206,050

2755 Kent Ave.
    Mrs. Franz Josef Strauss — in trust
    Listseeweg 7
    Munich
	$195,550

2240 Madison Ave.
    Peter Rixner
    12 Georg Hirth Str.
    Rotach Egern am
    Tegernsee
	$233,200

2260 Madison Ave.
    Gerhard Maute et al
    Haldenweg 81
    Pforzheim
	$214,000

2310 Madison Ave. $209,200
        Peter Rixner
        12 Georg Hirth Str.
        Rotach Egern am
        Tegernsee

2361 Madison Ave. $115,400
        Horst-Dieter Gross
        Leonberg

1945 de Maisonneuve Blvd. W. $143,000
        Gisbert Milanowski
        13 Isestrasse
        2000 Hamburg

2050 de Maisonneuve Blvd. W., "Renaissance" $1,660,000
        Walter Drummen
        94 Erfstrasse
        Neuss

2150 de Maisonneuve Blvd. W., "Weiss Towers" $1,970,000
        Hortense Weiss, Irmgarde Schiele
        Hornberg

9740 Papineau Ave. $219,000
        Dr. Kurt Mueller
        c/o W. Griechgauer Inc.
        2015 Drummond St., #652

9900 Papineau Ave., "Terrace Papineau" $219,000
        Edmund Shoher
        Borngasse 9,
        6442 Rotenburg, Fulda

3404 Prud'homme Ave., "Waldorf" $2,003,200
        Fritz Prager
        Munich

3615 Ridgewood Ave. $498,000
        Hans Herbert Plazig et al
        Neve Weinsteige 46
        7 Stuttgart 1

1 Cote St. Catherine Rd. $925,000
        Mrs. Heinrich Langensiepen
        Brockwede am
        Wittenbrink 28

7 Cote St. Catherine Rd. $1,293,000
        Mrs. Heinrich Langensiepen
        Brockwede am
        Wittenbrink 28

2055 St. Matthew St., "Maisonneuve Tower" $2,885,200
        Guenther Kaussen
        20-26A St. Apernstr.
        Cologne

2300 St. Matthew St.	$2,818,000
Alguvic Properties Ltd.	
major owners:	
Mr. and Mrs. T. Albrecht	
58 Westerwaldstr.	
Essen Bredeny	
4355 St. Zotique St. E.	$140,000
Mrs. Julein Gort	
5/711 Arabellastr.	
Munich 81	
3645 Sherbrooke St. E	$938,000
Gerhard Ludwig Holywart	
7032 Sindelfingen 6	
Im Pfalsterle 37	
205-245 Sherbrooke St. W., "Le Colisee"	$3,302,500
Mrs. Ferdinand Langer et al	
Eibensbach	
5301-15 Sherbrooke St. W., "Marquis"	$1,450,000
Guenther Kaussen	
20-26A St. Apernstr.	
Cologne	
6651 Sherbrooke St. W., "Kerwin"	$494,000
Friedrich Wilhelm Kertz et al	
att: Crown Life Insurance Co.	
4115 Sherbrooke St. W., #230	
1537 Summerhill Ave., "Lew"	$368,000
Rolf Dieter Volberg	
24 Gottfried-Herder Str.	
Kettwig-Ruhr	
1225 Sussex St., "Sussex House"	$1,300,000
Guenther Kaussen	
20-26A ST. Apernstr.	
Cologne	

Footnotes — Chapter 6

1. Telephone interviews, Jun. 3 and 4, 1976; interview, Aug. 17, 1976.
2. Telephone interview, Dec. 10, 1975.
3. Telephone interview, May 31, 1976.
4. *Rudner's Directory of Apartment Buildings* (Montreal: Alex. S. Rudner), editions of Nov. 1974 and Nov. 1975.
5. Telephone interviews of Nov. 28, 1975, and Jun. 3, 1976.
6. Der Spiegel, Oct. 21, 1974, "Neues Mekka Montreal."
7. Newsweek, Aug. 1, 1977, "Europe's money of the run," p. 59.
8. Interviews of Dec. 14, 1976, and Apr. 25, 1977.

Chapter 7
Canada: The Surrogate Congo

(above) Katanga, Belgian Congo; 1955 — Young King Baudouin of Belgium is welcomed at a uranium mine controlled by Société Générale de Belgique. The company, in which the royal family has interests and which is the axle of his country's economy, suffered huge losses after the Congo subsequently declared independence from Belgium.

(below) Quebec City, Canada; September 1977 — King Baudouin, uncertain of the political stability in Canada to which the same company has transferred large investments, visits Quebec to confer with Premier Lévesque (right).

IN THE ELEGANT BRUSSELS RESIDENCE of Canada's ambassador to Belgium, young Joe Clark, just elected head of the Progressive Conservative Party, tugged nervously at the collar of his dress shirt as he was introduced to the assembled guests. Around the table at this black-tie, candlelight dinner in September, 1976, were, among others, two barons, a count and two bank presidents, representatives of a Who's Who of Belgian finance. They were here, at the ambassador's invitation, to take the measure of this baby-faced politician from High River, Alberta, who had suddenly burst into a dramatic lead over Prime Minister Pierre E. Trudeau in the Gallup poll. Indeed, at the time of this small dinner, which took place toward the end of a six-country, 17-day tour of Europe, Clark, now trying to suavely dissect his braised pigeon, was widely regarded as Canada's next prime minister. For him, this whirlwind trip represented an opportunity to begin building an image, which he lacked, of familiarity with foreign affairs. But it was also an introduction to one of the least-known lynchpins of Canada's own domestic economy.

That night's welcoming party included not the biggest names in Belgian business, but their right-hand men. There was Jacques Thierry, Baron Lambert's representative and president of the executive committee of the Banque Bruxelles-Lambert, one of the Rothschilds' five arrows described in Chap. 5. There was J. Glorieux, president of the Banque Belge pour l'Industrie, part of Baron Empain's group of companies whose importance to the suburbs and subway of Montreal will be described in Chap. 13.

And then, over there in the corner, was a man who needed to ask Clark few questions during the after-dinner question period. His name was Baron de Fauconval, representing a bank called La Société Générale de Banque, the financial pinion of a group of companies which have done at least as much to change Canada in the last quarter century as all the arrows in the Rothschild quiver combined.

"It was quite surprising," a Clark aide said later. "I was really struck by how much these men knew about Canada. They have, I understand, a lot of investments in the country. They seemed extremely familiar with it."

His surprise is understandable. To most people around the world Belgium is just a dreary industrialized patch about half the size of Nova Scotia — a mini-country whose main claim to economic fame is its partnership in Benelux. Being an important company in Belgium would not, it might appear, make a company very big in absolute terms. Despite its small size and lack of natural resources, however, Belgium has one of Europe's highest standards of living — and one reason is that it has deliberately fostered very large corporate units whose size and anti-competitive nature would run afoul of anti-combines or anti-trust laws in North America. For example, Société Générale de Banque holds the savings of fully 40 per cent of all Belgian depositors. It in turn is held by a holding company which controls one-fifth of all Belgian industry and which, stacked up against Canada's two biggest holding companies, Argus Corp. and Power Corp., would make them look like *patates frites* operations. Belgian government policies allowing this kind of size have enabled such companies to expand abroad and wield tremendous influence in foreign markets. It is because of this strength in international markets, rather than because of any intrinsic benefits of a poor competitive climate at home, that corporate gigantism has brought wealth to Belgium. In the past this strength often took the form of outright colonization.

The Belgian Congo was the foremost example of this process. Prior to its independence from Belgium in 1960, the Congo — now Zaïre — was in effect a fiefdom for a group of companies which, like Baron de Fauconval's bank, were controlled by a central holding company called *Société Générale de Belgique*. With investments focusing mostly in the mining in mineral-rich Katanga province, "La Générale" controlled two-thirds of the Congolese economy.[1]

It is a shadowy holding company, many of whose investments are secret. But its imprint outside Belgium on the history of the 20th century is clear. In addition to being one of the prime exponents of African development in the early part of the century, it was perhaps the first enterprise in the world to have realized the military potential of nuclear power and push for it: it provided the uranium ore used in the A-bombs at Hiroshima and Nagasaki. Later, when it was faced with the loss of much of its Katanga holdings following the independence of the Congo in the early 1960s, it became a prototype of the now familiar tendency of multinationals to become involved in Third World politics, though La Générale did it with a panache that has yet to be duplicated: it was the behind-the-scenes financier of the bloody Katanga secessionist movement led by Moise Tshombe. Indeed, in 1961 a senior U.S. State Department official, Carl Rowan, characterized La Générale's prime affiliate in the Congo, Union Minière, as being "at the heart of a colonialism that Africa abhors."*

Today "La Générale" has been dispossessed of most of its old Congo holdings, but it has landed on its feet. It has shifted its overseas focus from Africa to Canada, which is even more blessed with natural resources than the Congo and which, rather than resenting foreign takeovers of its economic life, on the whole welcomes them so long as certain formalities are observed. It is a country where nationalism, while quite alive, is containable, and where unlike the Congo, Belgians can blend in.

But it is not a question of marching in and imposing themselves. At this dinner, for example, it was not the companies who invited young Clark to speak to them; on the contrary, it was at the behest of Clark and the ambassador that they came. And it was Clark who assured them — the point was so much taken for granted it barely needed to be stated — that he was no more against Belgians expanding into Canada than the present prime minister.

Yet Clark's entourage had only a vague idea of what La Générale controlled in Canada. It is, for example, by far the biggest shareholder in the company which is the No. 1 owner of developable land in all of urban Canada, and that is only a fragment of its influence. Its role in Canada, and around the world, is scarcely visible.

Founded by the Dutch royal family in 1822**, it is the oldest development company in the world. The Belgian Catholic review, La Revue Nouvelle, makes an apt comparison of it to the systematically sleek counterpart, ITT: "The latter is like a mod-

---

* Its Congo holdings made the company the world's third biggest producer of copper and its biggest producer of cobalt. Time magazine in its Jan. 18, 1963 issue had this vignette: "To charges that the company has been meddling in Congolese politics, Union Minière Director Herman Robiliart snaps: "The policy of Union Minière is to produce copper."
** Belgium at that time was part of Dutch territory.

ern building, functional and produced at one go, whereas the Société Générale reminds one of an old chateau, patched and ill-assorted, where different styles and epochs are super-imposed and co-exist come what may."[2]

Its headquarters is not quite a chateau, but it might as well be. It occupies an elegant but drab, three-storey mock-Georgian building across from King Baudouin's palace in Brussels. High-ceilinged and drafty, the clang of street cars intruding into its inner sanctums, it looks just the opposite of the stream-lined skyscrapers big corporations have today. La Générale's entire payroll is not more imposing: it consists of less than 100 persons, including janitors. But it is the companies it in turn owns or is associated with that make it a bigger factor in economic decision-making than perhaps even the Belgian government itself.

Over the years the secretiveness of the company had contributed to a rather sinister reputation and on the occasion of its 150th anniversary festivities in 1971, recognizing that public relations did have a role in modern multinationals, it opened its

Henry Aubin

The headquarters of Société Générale de Belgique in Brussels.

doors a bit for the financial press. What these normally blasé business reporters glimpsed left them flabbergasted.

"The size and complexity of (its) empire boggles the mind, if not the imagination, and it must be difficult for even old hands to keep track of," gasped Management Today.[3]

"The tortuous interlocking nature of La Générale's interests makes it an opaque subject for financial analysis," said a bewildered Times of London. "Control over members of the group varies widely, and depends on historical and personal factors as well as purely monetary ones."[4]

---

* On paper La Générale's direct interest in a company may appear insignificant. But passivity of other shareholders plus the holdings of its affiliated companies can multiply its voting interest many times.

Thus La Générale has only a 5.9 per cent interest in Union Minière. Through other affiliates it has an additional 30.1 per cent — more than enough to give it the upper hand in the administration of the firm. Indeed, La Générale's governor, Paul-Emile Corbiau, is also chairman of Union Minière. Union Minière, in turn, has vast holdings in other companies: for example, it has a 15 per cent interest in the world's largest zinc producer, Vieille-Montagne (in which La Générale holds another 10 per cent directly), a 24 per cent interest in a leading European chemical company, PRB (in which La Générale holds another 21 per cent directly) and a 44 per cent interest in Metallurgie-Hoboken-Overpelt (in which La Générale owns another 13 per cent directly).[5] And so on. Metallurgie-Hoboken-Overpelt, incidentally, was according to its 1972 calculations the world's leading producer of radium, germanium and cobalt salts, oxides and powders; it was also Europe's largest refiner of copper and silver and a major producer of zinc.

La Générale also: owns 8 per cent of Glaverbel-Mécaniver, a worldwide firm which was third largest distributor of glass in Canada before it sold its Canadian subsidiary to Pilkington Brothers in 1976; controls CMB, Belgium's largest ship company which has had a major impact on Eastern Canada's container industry; has the largest shareholding in Petrofina with a 7.2 per cent (though less influential than Baron Lambert's stake); and has a substantial shareholding in Diamant Boart, world's leading producer of diamond tools, commonly used in Canada's oil and mining industry.

It has substantial interest in three leading European steel companies, Cockerill, Arbed and Sidmar, controlling interests in Cimenteries CBR Cementbedrijven, biggest cement manufacturer in Benelux, substantial interest in Belgonucléaire and MMN, two firms which help make La Générale's group the key contributor to Belgium's ambitious nuclear power program, and interests in so many more other major companies that it would take an equal amount of space to describe them.

It is impossible to say how big La Générale is. It does not consolidate its accounts — partly for privacy, partly because.in many cases it does not actually exert outright control over the companies it helps to administer. For this reason it, like Anglo American Corp. of South Africa, does not even appear on Fortune magazine's list of the top 300 companies outside the U.S.

"It is the world's largest non-ferrous metals group, Europe's largest steel maker, the largest maker in the world of diamond tools," said the Times of London, grazing the surface in another article. "The company's size and power cause concern to many people in Belgium ... The company says it keeps well out of politics, but the fact that it needs to emphasize that is a sign of how much the doubts still persist."[6]

In Canada today La Générale is perhaps the singlemost important corporate force in the development of cities. Yet it says most of its activities here are Canadian-controlled. Because of the Foreign Investment Review Act it masks its presence here behind Canadian frontmen.

What is it up to?

In 1920 six brothers from a Quebec family called Miron started digging into Montreal soil in search of a fortune. They had two horses, a scoopshovel, $7 capital and little else. But through long hours and a knack for buying some of the most centrally-located deposits of limestone, the vital ingredient in cement, they drug quarries and built up a mammoth cement company, Miron Co. Ltd.

Forty years later the Mirons sold their company for a handsome $50 million. There was little comment in the press other than congratulatory chuckles for "les gars Miron" — their limestone mines had turned out to be gold mines. Today, however, it is the purchaser who can chuckle, for the company is worth many times that amount.

It is easy to underestimate the importance of the Canadian holdings of the group which bought Miron Co., La Société Générale de Belgique. The acquisition of Miron Co., for example, included the title to that company's main quarry site. When the Miron family first purchased this land it was located on the distant outskirts of populated areas. Today this land is smack in the middle of a densely crowded tenement area in north central Montreal. Driving along Papineau or Metropolitan Blvd., which bound it on the west and south, it is hard to see just how big it is: it is separated from the roads by chain-link fence and mounds of earth which block entry and view. You have to see it from the air to gain appreciation of it: a barren, treeless expanse marked by craters, some of them hundreds of feet deep.

This land is 450 acres in size, which makes it the largest single piece of private property in the entire city of Montreal. In fact, it is bigger than two municipalities on the island, Montreal West and Ste Geneviève. It is four times as big as Lafontaine Park and almost twice as big as Angrignon Park.

What's it worth?

Driving past it one day along Papineau with a developer I asked him that question. He rolled his eyes and with his cigar still between his teeth said that whoever owned it was in luck. It was, he said, close to being the ultimate piece of empty real estate on the entire island. Hell, he said, some of those pits you could use for foundations of skycrapers — Place Ville Marie had been built into a hole no one had been able to find any use for, and the same applied here. Or, if you wanted to build single-home residential development, you could fill the pits with water and create artificial lakes; along the shore you could build high-priced homes. Or, if the city bought the land, it could use it for parks.*

Société Générale de Belgique

From mines in the Congo...

As he spoke we had to roll up our windows. A great cloud of dust was blowing from the quarry area across the autoroute and towards the tenements. The head of the Montreal Urban Community's air pollution unit, Jean Marier later told me that the Miron Co. quarry was the No. 1 source of dust (particulate) pollution on the island. It has been taken to court about half a dozen times in recent years, he said, describing it as "the quarry against which we have made the most complaints." The fines are only on the order of several hundred dollars, he said.

In May, 1977, for example, after a trial which heard testimony from 53 witnesses, Miron was fined a total of $750 in municipal court despite the evidence of MUC tests which showing dust levels were three times the maximum permissible norm in

* Montreal has an estimated 1.08 hectares of parkland for every 1,000 residents. By comparison, Toronto has 1.44 hectares per 1,000, Ottawa has 2.2 hectares and Edmonton, the country's urban leader in green space, has 7.32 hectares. (Source: Edmonton Journal study transmitted by Canadian Press on Jan. 20, 1977.)

Michael Dugas

...to the heart of Montreal.

the surrounding residential neighborhood. Forty of the witnesses were residents, some of whom testified that the dust on cars was so thick that the only way to clean them properly was by washing them with vinegar: others said that even with doors and windows shut tight, furniture often had to be dusted several times a day.

A 1976 study by Jean Hétu, an environmental law professor at the Université de Montreal, concluded that Montreal pollution levels will remain among the highest in Canada unless court fines for multiple offenders are more than token amounts. One also notes that Hétu's study, compiled from municipal court dossiers on all MUC court convictions, singled out another company in which La Générale is the major shareholder, Petrofina Canada Ltd. Its East End refinery, it said, has been taken to court 23 times since 1970 and has been convicted 10 times, but the total amount of fines it has paid is $5,000.[7]

On the scale of La Générale's total activity across Canada, the Miron quarry is little more than a speck. But, size and pollution aside, there are a number of interesting things about it.

First, it is one of the first major landholdings for La Générale's group in North America. Since purchasing it the group has gone on to become the owner of approximately 35,000 more acres of prime developable land in and about Canadian cities. Most of this was acquired in the 1970s. No other company — not even Canadian Pacific, most of whose urban property consists of land employed for rail-related purposes — owns more metropolitan land in Canada suitable for speculation or development.

Second, the date of this purchase, July 14, 1960, came just 15 days after Congolese independence. Both independence and the purchase were in the works months in advance, of course, but the timing symbolizes the overall pattern: ouster from the Congo, full-scale entry into Canada.*

---

* La Générale actually arrived in Canada several years earlier, setting up a company called Sogemines Ltd. in 1951 to supply ores needed by Belgian smelters. As the riots grew in the Congo in the mid-1950s and La Générale saw the writing on the wall, so did its investments grow in Canada. The Miron acquisition, though, represents one of the first major commitments to an industrial presence in Quebec.

Third, the purchase of Miron betokened an overall *modus operandi* of expansion in Canada: acquisition. Unlike the Rothschilds, La Générale in Canada has not employed its capital for very creative purposes. Instead of building new enterprises, it tends to buy up existing ones. Indeed, few other interests have gone about this with quite as much fury: Miron was one of the first of the dozens of companies in Canada it has acquired, most of which were, like Miron, Canadian-owned. From a viewpoint of traditional free enterprise, as articulated by such members of Joe Clark's own party as Ron Huntington, an MP from Vancouver, this represents a significant diminution of competition and growth of concentration. Says Huntington: "Genstar is sucking up the industrial capacity of Canada in widely diversified fields. Why should ownership all go into the hands of a few? It stifles the economy."[8] From La Générale's point of view, however, it is the simplest way of entering a market, avoiding the high costs of starting up an enterprise and then of competing with other firms. The La Générale group buys up the competition as well: since acquiring Miron, for example, it has also acquired two other major cement companies,* giving it a combined output which now has about 17 per cent of the entire Canadian market, the third largest cement production in the country. Corporate takeover also represents the best way of bypassing Canada's tariff walls. As La Générale, Belgium's biggest cement producer, said in 1960 when buying Miron: "Many overseas countries are closed to the import of Belgian cement, so that the best course is to establish production inside their markets."[9]

Fourth, Miron fits into a pattern of vertical integration for which La Générale has become perhaps the leading exponent in Canada. Vertical integration is the process whereby one corporate unit manufactures a product which is then sold to another unit of the same organization. In the case at hand, for example, Miron sells a huge portion of its cement (as much as 30 per cent, according to the company) to another wing of the same company which specializes in construction and which uses this cement in its work. Critics say such all-in-the-family

---

* They are: Inland Cement Industries Ltd. and Ocean Cement Ltd., both of Western Canada.

buying and selling further diminishes price competition since it eliminates bidding and drives other suppliers out of business. But La Générale says it streamlines the development process and is more efficient.

Fifth, Miron exemplifies the ability of La Générale to get along fruitfully with government here. Year in year out, Miron is, for example, one of the two major construction contractors for the Montreal Department of Public Works. Without insinuating an unduly cozy relationship at City Hall, it is worth noting that Miron is hardly a stranger there. Miron's chairman, a local lawyer named Louis A.-Lapointe was, prior to going to Miron, a civil servant who from 1946 to 1952 was director of municipal services for the city. One encounters the same kind of interplay with government throughout the organization. In 1977, to cite just one recent example, Jacques van der Schueren became a director of La Générale; from 1958 to 1961 he was Belgium's minister of economic affairs. Between leaving government and being appointed to the most powerful board in his country he was president of the executive committee of one of La Générale's key construction subsidiaries, Société de Traction et d'Electricité.

Sixth, Lapointe also points up the proximity of La Générale to other major industrial forces in Canada. He is a director of Rio Algom and Trizec, giving him ties to two other Rothschild-related endeavors. As we shall see, the Rothschilds have had ties with La Générale ever since 1830.

Finally, Miron illustrates the ability of the diverse components of La Générale's farflung machinery to work if not in harness then in harmony. In 1976, for example, the Montreal Urban Community floated a $50 million bond issue in Europe to obtain more money with which to build its subway extensions; one of the underwriters for that bond issue was Société Générale de Banque, the same bank which was represented at Joe Clark's dinner and which is an affiliate of La Générale. It's interesting that another affiliate, Miron, is the second biggest contractor on the extension of the Montreal subway system.*

Thus, one member of La Générale's family helps supply the Montreal Urban Community with money which goes to help

---

* With contracts which by the end of 1976 totalled more than $35 million.

pay another member of the family. It is, in effect, almost vertical integration with the Montreal public in the middle.

It may at first seem bizarre for this sprawling moonscape,
the Miron quarry, to be located close to the heart of Quebec's
metropolis. It is a bit as though part of the Bois de Boulogne in Paris or Central Park in New York City were to be
turned into clay pits. If the mineral at stake here were valuable — something like gold or uranium — it might seem more
logical. But limestone is one of the cheapest, most abundant
minerals in the Montreal region — and could be easily mined
by Miron away from populated areas. On the South Shore in
and around Delson, for instance, the company owns about 750
acres of undeveloped real estate below which are located
prime limestone deposits. Urban planners are perplexed as to
why the quarry remains in centre city. After all, they reason,
Montreal has a housing shortage and it also has the lowest per
capita amount of parkland of any city in Canada. Why isn't it
being used to alleviate either of those conditions, which might
seem much more pressing than limestone?

But the quarry's ultimate owners know what they are doing.
They have a source of cement in the middle of one of the nation's fastest growing areas, reducing the need to haul it far to
job sites, and there is no economic reason why they should
leave. Nor is there a social reason: after a newspaper, Le Devoir, wrote an outraged story on the pollution, Miron's vice
president of public relations, Jacques Langevin, argued his
company's case on a we-got-here-first basis."The public should
take into account that the Miron Co. has been in this location
for more than 35 years, since a time when the area was fields,"
said Le Devoir, summarizing Langevin's point. "The people
who have come to live near the quarry have done so because
they wanted to."

The new owners of the quarry are not naive about the land's
potential. They are waiting for it to accrue in value before using it for something other than limestone.[10] They know full
well — certainly as well as any other group in the country — the
land's potential in terms of residential development: not only
do they own more developable urban land than anyone else in
Canada, but they build more houses in Canada than anyone
else. They build on the order of 2,500 houses every year. In-

deed, in Calgary one of their subsidiaries has made artificial lakes around which it has built high-price housing — the same scheme some people envisage for the Miron land. But right now they have more land in Canada than they know what to do with — in 1976 they almost doubled their landholdings when they bought Abbey Glen Property Corp. The Miron land is much more useful as a production centre which can facilitate the La Générale group's involvement in providing building materials for Montreal's next building boom. There is no incentive to agree to the "greening" of the Miron quarry: years from now it will be much more valuable as open land on the island becomes increasingly scarce.[11] Unlike the Miron family, the new owners have a decidedly long-term view of their investments here.

The holding company which owns Miron and about 50 other companies is Genstar Ltd., a member of La Générale's group. Formed in the 1950s, it now commands more than $1 billion in assets — enough to make it one of the top 20 industrial companies in Canada, as ranked by assets. In influence in Canada's *overall* economy, however, it would perhaps have to rank among the top four companies,* because (as with, say, Canadian Pacific) it is highly diversified. That is, unlike such bigger corporations as Ford Motor Co. of Canada Ltd. and George Weston Ltd. which focus on a specific industrial sector like vehicles or food, Genstar is involved in a whole smorgasborg of sectors. Besides being first in urban developable land, first in house-construction, third in cement production and a leading manufacturer of other kinds of building materials such as gypsum wallboard, it is also first in tugboat and barge operations in Canada, second in shipbuilding on the West Coast, first in making nitric acid and one of the leading fertilizer producers. Nonetheless, by the company's own estimate, 98 per cent of the Canadian public has never heard of Genstar.[12]

---

* The others would be Argus Corp. Ltd., Power Corp. of Canada Ltd. and Canadian Pacific Ltd. Power and Argus, however, are holding companies which preside over relatively loosely-knit subsidiaries. There is no real vertical integration between the various subsidiaries, unlike that within the Genstar organization.

What kind of people are ostensibly in charge of Genstar? Canadians.

You walk into its headquarters on the top floor of Place Ville Marie and you are confronted with a virtual showcase of Canadiana. Inuit art covers the walls of the lobby and halls. In the chief executive's office there are paintings of Canadian rural scenes.

Actually there are *two* chief executives — the only known company in North America to have two. They are a couple of young Canadians, Angus MacNaughton and Ross Turner, "co-chief executives" since their appointment in April, 1976. Both are in their early forties and joined the company as accountants, working their way up through the ranks. Turner once

A cordial meeting in Winnipeg between four Genstar directors and three Manitoba political leaders, June 19, 1974.
From left to right, Angus A. MacNaughton, of Genstar; W. John McKeag, lieutenant-governor of Manitoba; Stephen Juba, then mayor of Winnipeg; Saul Simkin, of Genstar; Edward Schreyer, then premier of Manitoba; August A. Franck, of Genstar, and W. Earle McLaughlin, of Genstar and chairman of the Royal Bank of Canada.

self-effacingly called themselves the Bobsey twins, and they look it. The day of our interview the following September they were both wearing black shoes, blue socks, blue woolen suits and blue shirts. Turner, however, wore a black belt while Mac-Naughton wore a brown one.

Genstar may be one of the Canadian economy's most powerful corporations and its critics may call it a predatory and insensitive organization, but its two top managers come across as somewhat insecure, clean-cut college boys rather than scheming *grands seigneurs*.

My first question would, I thought, be the easiest. What were they planning to *do* with the land they had just bought from Abbey Glen several months before? Genstar had paid $49 million for controlling interest of the company, and I expected them to be brimming over with ideas of what to do with it.

But the question seemed to stump them.

"To make money to start off with," said MacNaughton, laughing.

But did they have any specific plans?

Turner frowned. MacNaughton pursed his lips.

Their silence did not seem evasive, so I tried to be more specific. I asked them their plans for the Abbey Glen real estate which happened to be closest to Genstar's headquarters, a full block of prime land a couple of blocks away on Sherbrooke St. adjacent to office towers. One of the most valuable undeveloped chunks of downtown, it contained only a parking lot and a row of deteriorating Victorian houses. Abbey Glen's previous owners, South Africa-U.K. interests, had planned a major office-building for the site.

"Where is it?" said MacNaughton, peering down from his 41st floor window in PVM. The block was quite literally in PVM's shadow. He said something about driving to work down Sherbrooke every day.

"Down there, see those seven houses at the corner of Sherbrooke and McGill College, and all the land behind them.

He squinted.

"Do we own that? Gee."

"The whole block, except for maybe the building on the corner," I said.

"I didn't know that."

MacNaughton went back to his sofa, hitched up his pants, crossed his arms and frowned. "Abbey Glen," he said, "owns hundreds pieces of land like that across Canada, and I'd say we don't have any plans for any of them." He looked over at Turner. "Well, maybe one or two of them, but that's not one of them."

A latent tension is noticeable between the two men. Being appointed co-chief executives makes each really half a chief executive. The job is generally that of intermediary between the board of directors and the management; it should mean the chief executive carries out the policy decisions of the board and runs the company, but power divided is perhaps power not really exercised.

The two are elaborately polite to each other and go to great lengths during the hour-long interview not to ruffle each others' feelings. "Don't you think so, Ross?" "That's absolutely right, Angus, that's right, but . . ." A whole ritual has been created by which they maintain their equality. They are paid exactly the same salary. If Turner was paid $125,300 that year and Mac-Naughton $124,700, the reason for the discrepancy is that Turner missed a couple of board meetings. My interview had to be delayed several weeks so both could be present: I would have settled to talk to either one, but one of the company's unwritten rules was that they had to give joint interviews. One must not upstage the other.

Both, of course, must have *corner* offices. But here a problem arises: the interview cannot be held in both offices simultaneously; it will have to be held in either Ross's or Angus's. What to do?

I have no idea of how the mechanics of that decision worked, all I know is that MacNaughton's office was the one selected. As Turner is introduced to me he makes a little joke about how much more neatly Angus keeps his office. Angus's desk, he notes is admirably impeccable. "My office is in such a mess we'd never be able to meet there." We laugh heartily about Ross's untidy habits, but there is an edge to his remark which does not go unnoticed: Angus's desk may be neater because he doesn't have as much to do.

One of my later questions had to do with the actual application of Genstar's concept of social responsibility. The opening words of a booklet distributed to the financial press by

Genstar are: "The company's primary purpose is to provide, over both the short and long term, the optimum return on investment for shareholders of the company consistent with a high standard of corporate social responsibility." How does this high standard square with the ongoing operation of Miron quarry with its pollution?

MacNaughton: "There are tradeoffs. No matter what you do you're going to hurt someone. We try to help 1,000 people and hurt one guy, and some well-meaning television reporter with his television camera focuses on that one guy . . . Media pays too much attention to minority groups."

Turner: "There are tradeoffs. We believe we are doing everything practicable in regard to the pollution problem. We can't open another quarry outside the city: the economics wouldn't support the move."

But how about the company's limestone deposits a few miles south near Delson, 15 minutes from the city centre?

MacNaughton: "Sure there are other locations which have limestone. But the cost of the building a new quarry — it just wouldn't pay off . . .

"My owners, the shareholders, they make that decision."

That was what I wanted to know most — the most influential shareholders. Who were they and what power did they have over the company?

The answer was self-evident: La Générale.

The assertion that the shareholders call the ultimate shots at Genstar would seem at variance with the company's official position, that the shareholders have little power and that it is Turner and MacNaughton and the other members of the board of directors who control the company. The reason the company says this is that the Foreign Investment Review Act would inhibit its ability to acquire companies in Canada if it were foreign-controlled.

Earlier we saw to what lengths Trizec went to show the federal government it was Canadian-controlled. But what Genstar has done in inventively persuading the federal officials of its indigenous character almost defies credibility — yet it worked.

For two years a battery of lawyers for Genstar, many of them from the Royal Bank's* law firm, Ogilvy Montgomery Renault, which is located a few floors down also in Place Ville Marie, negotiated with the Foreign Investment Review Agency. They wanted Genstar to be declared exempt under the act — a technical way of saying, in effect if not in fact, a company was Canadian-controlled. On the surface it would seem like mission impossible. No less than 60 per cent of Genstar's voting stock is owned outside Canada: 52 per cent in Europe and eight per cent in the U.S.

Of the 52 per cent owned in Europe, La Société Générale de Belgique owns, directly and indirectly, 21 per cent of the voting shares. This is by far the largest shareholding; the next largest holding is owned by a foreign company, a subsidiary of Associated Portland Cement Manufacturers Ltd., of London, with 10.8 per cent. For many companies of this size a 21 per cent stake is more than adequate to exercise control — Argus Corp., for example, has controlled Domtar Ltd. and Massey-Ferguson Ltd. for years with less than 17 per cent in each.**

---

* Genstar does much of its banking in Canada with the Royal. The Royal's chairman and president, W. Earle McLaughlin, is a Genstar director — he also lives just across the street from MacNaughton's Tudor-style house in Upper Westmount. According to Genstar's proxy statement of March 1, 1977, at the end of 1976 Genstar and its subsidiaries had short-term borrowings of $24,579,030 from the Royal at its prime rate of interest. But the scale of Genstar's operations necessitates the use of more than one bank. The Toronto-Dominion Bank, as noted in Chap. 4, helped provide the financing for Genstar's acquisition of Abbey Glen, for example.

** Only about 50 per cent of Genstar's voting shares are actually ever voted, because of widespread shareholder passivity, Genstar lawyers say. This doubles La Générale's potential voting power.

Another possible indication of La Générale's voting power within Genstar is that it does not actually cast all the votes it is entitled to. It could, if it wanted, cast 21 per cent of all Genstar voting shares but in recent years it has never cast more than 17 per cent, one lawyer acknowledges. This might suggest that La Générale is sufficiently pleased with the overall direction Genstar is taking that it does not have to use all the strength at its command to fight off challenges.

Leading the way at opening ceremonies for the new Brussels headquarters of Société Générale de Banque, financial lynchpin of the Société Générale de Belgique group, are (l. to r.): King Baudouin; Prince Louis-Napoléon and Max Nokin, then governor of La Générale.

The bonds to La Générale are further strengthened by the fact that the top two members of the Genstar board, Chairman August Franck, and Deputy Chairman Charles de Bar, are both Belgians associated with La Générale. Three other Genstar directors — for a total of five out of 20 board members — are also associated with La Générale, including La Générale's own longtime chief executive, Max Nokin. If you count four

other directors who are executives of Genstar or its subsidiaries (MacNaughton, Turner, Lapointe and Saul Simkin)
and who thus are not wholly independent of their owners, you
have eight of 20. Two others are directors of the UK-owned Associated Cement interests, another is a president of the
French-owned Crédit Foncier Franco-Canadien and two others are chairmen of U.S.-controlled firms in Canada. It would
not appear to be very Canadian.

Genstar general counsel A. James Unsworth recalls the company's dilemma vis-à-vis Ottawa. "What we had to do," he
says, "was come up with an argument as to why Genstar was a
Canadian company."

What they came up with, Turner says, was a two-pronged
strategy. First, each Genstar director filed affadavits "saying
that no one controls the company," he says. What, a dynamic
company with over a billion dollars in assets floating around
Canada and no one controls it? A kind of headless horseman?
Turner admits the idea sounds odd, but then came the second
prong: the board of directors argued that it — that is, the board
collectively rather than any shareholder *per se* — controlled the
company. The board was packed with a majority of Canadian
citizens — even though 13 of the 20 are principally employed
by foreign-owned organizations. They also promoted the Canadian Bobsey twins to the chief executive position, which required moving Franck, the Belgian, from that position up to
the "non-executive" role of chairman.

Ottawa bought it. It ruled in May, 1976, that Genstar was
free to acquire any company it wished without having to first
convince the Foreign Investment Review Agency that the acquisition would be of "significant benefit" to Canada. The effect of this ruling was immediate: within weeks Genstar went
ahead and made the biggest acquisition in its history — buying
Abbey Glen.

Thus La Générale was able to have its cake and eat it: it was
able to keep Genstar (named after it, "Générale" + star) in its
sphere of influence while at the same time Genstar was able to
act as though it were independent.

What precisely is Genstar's relationship today with La Générale? As with Trizec's organization, Genstar's says one thing on
one side of the Atlantic and another thing on the other.

Though Genstar minimizes its relationship to La Générale, La Générale trumpets its close rapport with Genstar. Even after Ottawa's ruling that Genstar was Canadian, for example, La Générale's information bulletins to shareholders were still describing Genstar as "one of the companies belonging to the Société Générale de Belgique group."[13]

The term group, as used in Europe, does not necessarily mean an outright hammerlock relationship. La Générale itself has spelled out what its relationship to the "group" involves: "It (La Générale) intends to use all its resources — the men which constitute it and the capital which it can command — as the animating force of a group of companies. Thus, by the continued renewal of the policy of 'association', it has formed an industrial family from which its action can no longer be dissociated."[14] Elsewhere, it notes, "The shareholding, which is the instrument of the financial connection, is extremely stable in character, and amounts only in exceptional cases to a majority shareholding. The administrative organization of the group is widely decentralized. This results in the initiative centre and the decision powers lying primarily with the subsidiaries themselves. Société Générale is always represented on the boards of directors of these companies. It is through this representation that Société Générale takes part in the running of the subsidiaries, at the level of general policy and basic decisions, amounting to a concerted approach with the higher administration of the companies concerned."[15]

Ottawa's decision to overlook La Générale's relationship to Genstar was greeted with hoopla in Brussels. It had been a close call, La Générale told its shareholders that year:

"From 1974 onward, the Canadian government had made known its intentions to exercise stricter control on the economic and social repercussions of the large foreign industrial and commercial interests on the common good. It was as a result of this attitude that Genstar made application to be recognized as a Canadian company. This recognition was granted in the spring of 1976.

"Genstar was then free to implement its expansion program which comprised the following main objectives:

"— increase or extend its investments in all parts of the North American continent . . .

"— strive to achieve a prominent position in each of the fields of activity with which the company is already concerned . . .

"— enlarge and develop its sources of revenue by extending its industrial, real estate and financial operations . . ."[16]

In other words, if La Générale seems big in Canada today, this is just the beginning.

Indeed, Genstar is one of *two* companies – or "investment poles," as a La Générale executive put it to me in Brussels – being established by the organization in Canada.

The other is Union Minière. This is the organization which was dispossessed of much of its mines and plants in the Congo after that country's independence from Belgium. The company managed to hang on, offering jobs and foreign exchange to the Congolese, until Jan. 1, 1967. It was then that Congo President Joseph Mobutu, charging Union Minière with cheating the Congo out of its rightful share of the profits, nationalized the company. Said Mobutu: "If we have to go hungry to be free and independent, then we will go hungry. We prefer to remain poor and free to being rich slaves."[17]*

Union Minière had very skilled engineers and other staff as well as substantial financing. What to do? It has dispersed throughout the world, prospecting from Australia to Brazil as well as on the ocean floor to look for nodules. But increasingly it is looking towards Canada as an area of major strength. It started serious exploration here within a year of its ouster from the Congo and – because of the long time required between exploration and actual production – it is still small. It has begun developing copper and nickel deposits in Thierry, Ont., and is prospecting in Quebec in association with the Quebec government's mining arm, Soquem. Its two main subsidiaries here are Union Minière Canada Ltd. and Union Minière Explorations and Mining Corp. Ltd. (Umex).

---

* But only for so long. In October, 1976, P.-E. Corbiau, governor of La Générale and chairman of Union Minière, visited Zaïre at the invitation of none other than President Mobutu. Corbiau and Mobutu agreed to two important joint ventures by La Générale and Zaïre in the non-ferrous metals sector and in marine transport.[18]

Watch for them. In the 1980s and 1990s they should, according to the expectations of their executives, be among the giants of Canada's mining industry.

Incidentally, La General keeps much of its business in Canada under one roof, 1 Place Ville Marie. Not only does Genstar and its main law firm have headquarters but also its main bank, the Royal, and Union Minière make use of the building for their head offices. Petrofina Canada Ltd., in which La Générale is the biggest shareholder, also has its head office in the building, making the Trizec-owned megalith a real beehive of Belgian activity — even the Belgian consulate is there.*

In addition to these two main poles of La Grande Dame's activity here, Genstar and Union Minière, there are also a number of other interests which have an impact on Montreal. We already mentioned the fact that Société Générale de Banque sometimes underwrites local bond issues and that Petrofina, whose subsidiary here is Canada's seventh largest oil company, is a kind of associate member of La Generale's family. It's also worth noting in passing that Petrofina has an impact on the local landownership scene: in addition to owning 1.3 sq. kms. in East End Montreal for its refinery, it owns about 80 per cent of its 160 "Fina" gas station properties throughout the metropolitan area (the company is fifth largest retailer of automotive fuel the Montreal area and also owns Joseph Elie Ltée, the home heating oil company).[19]

Another company whose actions have had a major but unpublicized bearing on the Montreal economy is CMB, La Generale's shipping company. CMB is the initiator and mainstay of a three-firm consortium which owns Dart Containerline Co. Ltd.; this is today one of the three biggest container companies operating in and out of Canadian ports. In 1969 Dart, an aggressive, go-ahead firm, became the first company to employ large container vessels on the Europe-Eastern Canada run.* So successful was its innovation that by 1974 it accounted for a remarkable 29 per cent of all cargoes going in and out of Eastern Canadian ports.[20]

---

* On the 22nd floor, right next door to Petrofina.
** In fact, one of its ships, Dart Europe, was the world's largest container ship when launched, according to La Générale.

Wamboldt-Waterfield

CMB, La Générale's shipping company, is the n° 1 shipping company serving Eastern Canada. This ship, Dart Europe, was the world's largest container carrier when built in the late 1960s. The large metallic boxes, or containers, are filled with cargo and can be transferred directly to trucks (see insert) or trains for transport to inland destinations.

But the reason Dart was so influential on Montreal was not because it came here — it was paradoxically, because it did *not* come here. That is, by making the decision to go to Halifax rather than downriver to Montreal the company started a trend which is still accelerating. The other two main East coast container companies, Canadian Pacific Ltd. and Atlantic Container Line (Canada) Ltd. followed suit; in 1977 a fourth major firm, Cast Transportation Ltd., likewise made moves to go to Halifax amid howls of protest from local union leaders and businessmen. The reason behind the trend which Dart pioneered was simply that with today's technology it made good business: ships from abroad can save several days by unloading in Nova Scotia, where their cargo can be transported inland by rail, instead of making the journey up the St. Lawrence to Montreal.* Halifax's gain in this area was Montreal's loss; it is one reason why the port of Montreal is now languishing.

The point of all this is not that a group of men sitting around a board table in Belgium consciously set out to debilitate the port of Montreal and create a loss of jobs; from a business point of view it was an excellent decision. Rather, the point is that critical policies like these are being made not within the society which is most affected by them but by remote** people with their own financial self-interest in mind. A decision like this is not made by Montreal or even Haligonian businessmen, much less by a government in Canada as part of a comprehensive transport policy. The *animating force,* to use a La Générale idiom, behind decisions of whether or not to develop a land bank in and around Montreal, or whether to close or keep open a centre-city mine or whether to stimulate or take business away from the port, consists of people whose isolation from the city makes it difficult for them to understand, much less identify with, its social needs. Their loyalties quite natu-

---

* Dart's supremacy in this is indicated by one statistic, courtesy of an executive within Dart who asked not to be identified: 65 per cent of all containers going in an out of Halifax in 1974 were on Dart ships.
** Indeed, the control of three of the four above-mentioned container lines is foreign; control of the fourth, Canadian Pacific, is uncertain.

rally lie with their group's balance sheet and with their own country's welfare. Indeed, La Générale describes itself almost as the economic guardian angel of the Belgian people: "The group, as a whole, is a creator of employment, of profits for the capital and of well-being for everyone . . . (It) seems to have secured a reputation and standing from which the whole country may benefit."[21]

Incidentally, this is not to say that La Générale is not interested in the port of Montreal. Quite the opposite. What few ships do come to the hub of French Canada today are welcomed with toots by a fleet of tugs owned by a firm called McAllister Towing & Salvage Ltd. Years ago there used to be several competing tugboat companies in the port, but now McAllister has an effective 100 per cent monopoly on all berthing there. And Genstar, playing both sides of the street, owns it.

The diverse members of La Grande Dame's family tend to wheel and deal among each other — critics might call it anti-competitive incest, but the mother company calls it a spirit of "mutual helpfulness" which increases efficiency and profits. We can see this on two levels.

First, it can take the form of vertical integration within simply Genstar alone. This company has put together a system of vertical integration which is second to none in the Canadian economy. Just as Miron construction crews use Miron cement, so many vessels in Western Canada's largest tug and barge fleet owned by Seaspan International Ltd. are manufactured by Vancouver Shipyards Co. Ltd., both of which are Genstar subsidiaries.* But the best illustration of this is in home construction. Testifying before the Royal Commission on Corporate Concentration, urban affairs critic Donald Gutstein sketched a "potential scenario" of how the Genstar team works; this scenario applies to Western Canada, where Genstar does most of its home construction, but the company says it may utilize many of the same techniques in Quebec and else-

---

* The Seaspan fleet of 52 tugs and 230 barges represents a prime source of transportation for public and industry alike in and around the islands and waterways of British Columbia; it also comprises, as Genstar puts it, "a substantial segment of Canada's existing merchant marine."[22]

where in Eastern Canada now that, through its purchase of Abbey Glen, it has greatly increased its landholdings there. All companies mentioned here are Genstar subsidiaries:

"BACM Development Corp. buys and assembles the land. Standard-General Construction and other construction subsidiaries may be hired to service and subdivide the land, install sewers, sidewalks, watermains, streets and other utilities. If the subdivision has poor accessibility, BACM Construction Co. may be hired to build roads. Products from other Genstar subsidiaries are used whenever possible. These include ready-mix concrete, concrete block and pipe from Consolidated Concrete (Alberta), Ocean Construction Supplies (British Columbia), and Redi-Mix (Saskatchewan). Precast concrete products come from Con-Force Products. The cement comes from the Inland/Ocean Cement Group in Western Canada or Miron in Eastern Canada. The company has its own pits, quarries and plants to provide the required sand, gravel and aggregates. In British Columbia the agreggates are transported on the barges of Seapsan International.

"The serviced land is then sold to other builders with whom the company has contracts, or to the company's own housebuilders, Engineered Homes and Keith Construction Co. Most of the materials used in the construction come from other subsidiaries. Lumber, cabinets* and windows are provided for the companies' own use, and Truroc Gypsum Supplies provides wallboard for the company as well as other builders.**

"Finally, one more subsidiary (Genstar Chemical Ltd.) sells lawn and garden fertilizer ("Nutrite") to the people who have just bought the homes."

---

* Indeed, Genstar's "Sungold" kitchen cabinets are used "exclusively" by Keith Construction and Engineered Homes,[23] one reason why Genstar can boast of being Western Canada's largest manufacturer of such cabinets.

** In late 1976 Truroc was one of three Canadian manufacturers charged by Ottawa with "conspiring to lessen competition in the production, manufacture, sale or supply of gypsum wallboard" from Quebec to the West Coast between 1968 and 1974. The charge came a year after Genstar testified before the Royal Commission that "Genstar's aggressive investment in low-cost capacity in the Western Canada wallboard market has increased the level of competition and with the pressure of imports contributed to the low level of price increases in that market."[24]

Gutstein cites such practices as exemplifying ways in which Genstar activities "hamper the operation and threaten the viability of smaller Canadian-controlled firms, lessen competition and raise prices and threaten regional and local control over planning and development." Genstar Chairman August Franck, however, says, "The large, successful diversified corporation achieves valid public interest objectives naturally as it pursues an investment pattern based on the efficient allocation of capital in a balanced mix of businesses designed to maximize growth over long horizons."[25]

The credo of "mutual helpfulness" operates in a more diffuse, less structured way among the various components of La Générale. Thus, for example, Genstar acts as purchasing agent for mining equipment for the Zaïre copper mines associated with the revived Générale operations in that country. Genstar and Dart's founder, CMB, are working together in Saudi Arabian marine operations. And Genstar and another Générale affiliate, Union de Remorquage et de Sauvetage, are also working cooperatively in the North Sea oil fields. The list could go on and on.

Genstar's international activity could have far greater relevance to the Canadian economy than meets the eye.

In the late 1970s an intense debate, with very high stakes, is taking place between the government and the business world.* The key question is, should Canada allow very large industrial and financial units to grow unimpeded by tough, U.S.-style anti-trust laws in order that they might become active on an international scale?

La Générale has entered this debate. It wants Canada to permit much the same kind of activity as Belgium permits. As it

---

* Essentially there are two arenas for the debate: the Department of Consumer and Corporate Affairs, in charge of formulating amendments to the anti-combines laws; and the Royal Commission on Corporate Concentration, the only royal commission ever appointed by Prime Minister Trudeau, in charge of studying the pros and cons of allowing large corporations to get larger. It should be noted that Belgian interests are superbly represented on the Royal Commission: one of the three commissioners is none other than the president and chief executive officer of Petrofina Canada Ltd., P.A. Nadeau.

says in its 150th anniversary report, "It may well be asked whether, for companies in a small country with scarce and vanishing resources, and with a capital market of only limited capacity, (La Générale's *modus operandi*) was not the best of all possible ways to face competition in a world which had long been a prey to the scourge of protectionism."[26] Canada, with 300 times its area and more than twice its population might seem to share few traits with Belgium. But from La Générale's perspective the same kind of logic applies. Genstar has been one of the most vigorous voices in the corporate campaign to loosen the competition laws; and, in his brief to the Royal Commission, August Franck (who in addition to being Genstar's chairman is also counselor to La Générale) argued that:

". . . cross-subsidization, concentration and large diversified corporate size are, as long as competition in individual markets is maintained, in the public interest. The successful diversified corporation achieves these characteristics naturally when it pursues an investment pattern which is in the public interest. It is particularly important that public policy in Canada recognize this. Canada, internationally, is in the difficult position of being relatively high wage but relatively low scale among major economies. Its income per capita demands a full range of consumer and industrial products but its production scale in them remains small relative to our (Canada's) major trading partners. This means that Canada must be especially active in concentrating and rationalizing producers in specific markets or endure significantly higher prices and costs than competitor nations."[27]

What does Franck mean? He defines "public interest" as requiring "the lowest prices and costs consistent with a mix of products and services responsive to public demand as well as growth in income per capita and in capital investment." The jargon may be hard to decipher, but basically he is saying that what is good for Genstar is good for Canada. By being allowed to get very big Genstar would be able to produce much more to sell in Canada as well as overseas, hence contributing to Canada's gross national product. But just how much of the profits would remain in Canada is moot. The company is 60 per cent foreign owned. Presumably this means that the bulk of the dividends will be outward bound, and there is a lot of profit involved here.

In 1976 after-tax profits stood at $55.7 million, a healthy 18 per cent increase over the previous year; if Abbey Glen had not been purchased that year, the profits could have been far higher. Indeed, in 1975 profits were $47 million, a 34 per cent increase over 1974. Yet 1974 profits were 40 per cent over 1973, when they were 39 per cent over 1972, when they were 42 per cent over 1971 . . . Canada is indeed, a goldmine.

And the marvel of it is that most of the financing is generated from inside Canada — that is, it is Canadians' money, often that of depositors at the Royal or Toronto-Dominion banks, which is largely financing the company's rapid expansion.* When I asked MacNaughton if Société Générale de Banque had helped finance the acquisition of Abbey Glen, he replied, "They supplied not one cent. Société Générale de Belgique has not supplied money for a (Genstar) project in 15 years."

Who owns La Générale?

That's a good question.

Most of its shares are "bearer shares" — that is, they are anonymously held for tax reasons. The company itself declines to speculate on who its owners might be. It prefers to say simply that most of the shares are very widely spread out with many thousands of Belgians, big and small, owning a piece of the action.

The best evidence is that the largest parcels of shares are held by half a dozen or so different interests. These would include the Belgian royal family and such other eminent families of the realm as the Solvays (of chemical fame), the Lippens, the de Jonghes and the Hamoirs. No single family is considered dominant.[29]

---

* This recalls a point from made by Richard J. Barnet and Ronald E. Müller in *Global Reach*. "The claim that global corporations are major suppliers of foreign capital to poor countries turns out to be more metaphor than reality . . .," they wrote. "Individual investors and banks in poor countries for understandable business reasons normally prefer to lend money to Sears Roebuck or General Motors than to some local entrepreneur without the worldwide credit resources of the planetary giants."[28]

King Baudouin's close interest in the firm is indicated by the fact that one of its auditors is Andre Schöller, former Grand Maréchal of the Royal Court. The Solvays and most of the other families are also represented on the board of auditors.

The fact that King Baudouin and the cream of the Belgian aristocracy are tied in with Genstar would help develop one of the themes of this book: the still vigorous role of the Old World's old families in Canadian development. But, actually, there is a much better example of this theme — the deputy chairman of Genstar, a mild-mannered man with thinning gray hair and the unfamiliar name of Charles de Bar. He does not go around publicizing who he is — and certainly Genstar does not either — but his family would make King Baudouin's family, or for that matter Queen Elizabeth of England and the Windsor family, look rather *arriviste*.

His name in private life is Archduke Charles of Hapsburg.

It's been a few years since we last heard from the illustrious house of Hapsburg. Its empire collapsed at the end of World

---

* Bearer shares are also a common form of shareholding within Genstar, making it difficult to discern some important secondary owners of the company. Incredible as it may sound, MacNaughton and Turner say they themselves do not know who owns 30 per cent of Genstar's voting shares which are in the form of bearer shares. These are held mostly in Europe, often in Belgium, where Genstar stock is publicly traded (it is also traded publicly on stock exchanges in Canada and the U.S., but bearer shares are not traded in these countries). One Genstar lawyer says he "figures" most of the company's bearer shares are fairly well scattered, with no huge parcels among them, but that is only supposition.

Still, these bearer shares could be important factors in any potential fight for control of the company. Those who own them are not wholly apathetic shareholders; in one recent year more than 10 per cent of these shares were actually voted, accounting for 3.2 per cent of all Genstar's voting shares or, because only half of those shares are voted in practice, more than 6 per cent of the actual shares voted.

In theory, it is quite possible that interests allied with La Générale could own substantial amounts of bearer shares, thus swelling the La Générale group's indirect and direct stake in Genstar to above 21 per cent; but, just as easily, another industrial-financial group could own substantial amounts of these shares and no one would be the wiser.

In other words, this is one of the mysterious sidelights to Genstar. But it is all quite legal. In Europe bearer shares are commonly used, often for tax avoidance purposes.

Charles de bar, in private life Charles of Hapsburg, is deputy chairman of Genstar's board of directors.

War I when Charles' father, the late Emperor Charles of Hapsburg, abdicated in Austria. The Hapsburgs had supplied the emperors of the Holy Roman Empire from 1438 to 1806, the kings of Spain from 1516 to 1700 and the rulers of Austria from 1278 to 1918. Today Charles de Bar's brother, Archduke Otto is still pretender to the Austrian throne while Charles himself is playing a pivotal, low-profile role within one of the corporate engines in the Canadian economy.

As deputy chairman, he generally divides his time between Montreal and Brussels, where he makes his home. He is something of a go-between between the two cities. No stranger to Canada, in his student days he took degrees in law and political and social sciences at Quebec's Université de Laval.

There is another intriguing thing about Charles de Bar. His name turns up as a director of a company with the quixotic name of Tanganyika Concessions Ltd. It embellishes another theme being developed in this book: the tie-in between the great industrial interests in colonial Africa and in present-day Canada.

Tanganyika Concessions, headquartered for tax reasons in the Bahamas but basically run out of London, brings together some of the most venerable names in British, Portuguese, Belgian and U.S. high finance. Flipping through its annual reports is like turning back the pages of history, yet it is another one of those companies which has been playing an all but unnoticed influence behind the headlines of the 1970s. In Angola and Mozambique this company has helped form the fibre of Portuguese rule which lasted until these strife-torn countries gained independence in 1975, and the firm is still going strong.

One of Tanganyika Concessions' main holdings is the Benguela Railway Co., which has been to much of central Africa's development what the Canadian Pacific Railway was to Canada's. It links Zaïre and Zambia to the Atlantic at the ports of Lobito and Benguela. In early 1975 when the three main Angolan emancipation movements met with the beleaguered Portuguese government to reach an agreement for Angola's independence, the future of the railroad was a prime topic. Tanganyika Concessions noted in its annual report that the main effect of the decision to grant independence was to move the railroad's head office from Portugal to Angola: "all the movements agree that the maintenance of the railway and its continued efficient running is essential to an independent Angola."[30] More than two years after those agreements the railroad, though its operations had been diminished because of the war, had still not been nationalized; as Mobutu showed in welcoming back La Générale to Zaïre, revolutionaries can need the old corporate infrastructure, too.

There is a very logical explanation to the presence of Genstar's deputy chairman, Archduke Charles, on the board of Tanganyika Concessions. It is the old story of everyone being laced in with everyone else: La Générale is a very large shareholder in Tanganyika Concessions with a 25.5 per cent interest; and, conversely, Tanganyika Concessions is an important shareholder in La Générale's Union Minière with a 17.6 per cent stake. This is why no fewer than four of Tanganyika Concessions' 12 directors, including Lord Clitheroe, who in addition is a Rio Tinto-Zinc director, are also directors of Union Minière.*

Other familiar faces are also interwoven here. Thus Anglo American Corp. of South Africa administers a Rhodesian-based coal company, Wankie Colliery Co., which has mined for bauxite in Mozambique and contains a minority shareholding by Union Minière.

The Rockfellers — whose influence in Quebec development will be touched on in a later chapter — also have a cheek by jowl relationship with these interests. In 1960 they rushed in to help La Générale when the Congo was falling apart, acquiring an undisclosed number of shares in La Générale's Congo holding company; the Financial Times of London interpreted this as signalling "close cooperation" between the Rockefellers and the Belgians.[32] The same four-inch article, typical of the kind of nuggets one finds buried in the financial press, also disclosed that the Rockefellers have a "substantial interest" in Tanganyika Concessions. The ties certainly endure. In 1974, for example, when Angola was torn by guerrilla rebellion the Rockefellers' Chase Manhattan Bank in New York helped Tanganyika Concessions out with the financing of 12 Diesel main line locomotives for its Benguela railroad.[33]

Perhaps the best example of this together-at-the-top syndrome involves the Rothschilds. The Paris branch of the family first gave La Générale its financial support in 1830. During a financial crisis in 1838 Baron James de Rothschild, then the richest man in France[34] and already the banker to the Belgian state, threw a financial life-ring to the weak, 16-year-old company: he granted La Générale a loan which enabled it to float clear of disaster. During liquidity crises in 1846-47 the Paris

---

* It is through this common investment vehicle, Union Minière, that Tanganyika Concessions and La Générale have acquired additional unpopularity in anti-imperialist circles. For example, the London-based Committee for Freedom in Angola, Mozambique and Guiné reports that an affiliate of the "notorious" Union Minière, Compagnia Carbonifera de Moçambique, paid its 897 workers an average daily wage of 14 escudos (about 20p) in 1960.[31]

branch of the Rothschilds again supplied cash to the shaky adolescent organization.[35]

Today, La Générale can stand on its own feet, but is still interwoven with the Rothschilds. Thus Paul-Emile Corbiau — governor of La Générale, chairman of Union Minière, director of Tanganyika Concessions — is also a director of the Paris Rothschilds' giant mining company, Imetal, reflecting La Générale's 4.4 per cent voting interest in the company. The Rothschilds have also had a minority interest in Tanganyika Concessions[36] — indeed, the London branch of the family gave considerable financial assistance to Angola and Mozambique during the last few years of Portuguese rule.*

---

* A paid announcement to exporters by N.M. Rothschild & Sons in the London Financial Times, Dec. 2, 1971, said that the bank was extending its "line of credit covering exports of capital and semi-capital goods to Portugal, Angola and Mozambique." The pamphlet, "British Financial Interest in Angola, Guiné, Mozambique and Portugal," also notes that N.M. Rothschild & Sons headed a consortium of British banks loaning £5 million to the Portuguese government to "buy transport and telecommunications equipment to be used in the wars."

The interplay between these European groups is illustrated by a single transaction in 1974, whereby 1,558,000 ordinary shares of Tanganyika Concessions (at 50p each) were issued to La Générale in exchange for 1,800,000 ordinary shares (of 25p each) of the Rothschild-related Rio Tinto-Zinc Corp.[37]

The alliances between these two spheres are common. Thus in 1970 three Rothschild branches (N.M. Rothschild in London, Pierson, Heldring & Pierson in Amsterdam and New Court Securities in New York) joined forces with Société Générale de Banque and two other major continental banks (Germany's Deutsche Bank and The Netherlands' Amro Bank) to set up European Financial Associates for the purpose of promoting cross-border mergers in Europe and steering European investments to the U.S. And in 1976, a La Générale affiliate acquired 348,000 shares in the Générale Occidentale-Cavenham group, a major Franco-British food conglomerate (it owns Grand Union supermarkets in the U.S.); this is controlled by one of the more off-beat Rothschild cousins, Sir James Goldsmith. Marcel Goblet, a Société Générale director, told shareholders: "Our interests . . . are now at a comparatively high level within the structure of this group with which our relations are developing in an excellent atmosphere."[38]

The Rothschilds, of course, control Belgium's second largest industrial-financial group after La Générale, the Compagnie Bruxelles-Lambert. Though generally considered rivals, they do share some fraternal bonds. In addition to being leading shareholders in Petrofina, the two also have assumed on a joint basis an "active part in the upper administration" of two major industrial corporations, the Cockerill steel firm and S.A. des Verreries de Mariemont.

P.-E. Corbiau, the new governor of La Société Générale de Belgique.

In searching through a morass of evidence a few themes emerge in addition to those already described. One is the way history repeats itself. When La Générale was getting off the ground in the early 19th century, for example, its principal asset was property — 20 million florins' worth of landed estates in Belgium.[39] One hundred and thirty years later when La Générale came to Canada to sire an offspring, one of the first things it did was to acquire enormous tracts of property, an unusual move for a basically industrial enterprise. It bought most of this land not only for immediate development, but to hold in reserve against future contingencies. It was as though we were seeing the reassertion of the nobility's old penchant for land as the ultimate security — as the basic foundation for any future undertaking.

Another lesson of history is the way in which these huge interests tend to land on their feet. La Générale can get kicked out of the Congo, but back it goes in 1976 when the nationalists there realize they can't get to first base without their old antagonists. Its case recalls that of Baron James de Rothschild. He established himself as the monetary arm of the conservative Bourbon monarchy in France, an integral part of the Court of Charles X; thus when the barricades filled the streets of Paris in 1830, and Charles was swept away by the liberal forces of Louis Philippe, many people naturally assumed Beau James' career was over and that he might even have to flee. But so indispenable were his resources and influence, and such was the force of his personality, that Louis Philippe wound up giving him a near-monopoly on state loans. Eighteen years later the barricades returned to the streets, a Rothschild villa was burned, thousands of merchants and bankers were ruined, Louis Philippe fell; but James offered 50,000 francs to all people wounded in the street-fighting, neutralizing criticism against him, and out he came intact.[40]

So it goes with these groups. They have a magical ability to survive political foul weather. On paper Genstar might not have a 100 to 1 chance of being considered Canadian and of outwitting a nationalist law designed to prevent companies like it from expanding, but it did.

Likewise, if Quebec should go independent and socialist, it is a safe bet Genstar would weather that little problem too. To

Advertisement in the Edmonton Journal, Oct. 1, 1977.

Engineered Homes *is a Genstar subsidiary.*

offend La Générale through such acts as expropriation, nation-
alization or by placing a stringent limitation on its growth
might have the cost of alienating an influential member of the
international financial community — on which an independent
Quebec would be even more dependent than it is now for
loans. Any hopes Quebec might have of getting closer to the
Brussels-based European Economic Community might dim
with such hostility.

The odds are good that, rather than playing cool to "La
Grande Dame", Quebec political leaders for some time to
come will find themselves sitting around the dinner table with
her — in the realistic tradition of Joe Clark.

A footnote to history:
La Générale and the A-Bomb

Without Société Générale de Belgique's foresight, the A-
bombs used at Hiroshima and Nagasaki might never have
been produced.

A glance back to the events of more than 30 years ago shows
that the Belgian holding company, which has played an influential role in Canadian development since the war, played a
far from passive role in helping usher in the nuclear age.

One of the company's chief affiliates began preparing for
military uses of uranium at least two years before the U.S. began working on the bombs.

The curious story goes back to 1942. At that time U.S. scientists were making the top-secret A-bombs under the crash program code-named the "Manhattan Project." One of the scientists' basic assumptions was that large amounts of uranium — a
crucial element in making bombs — could be easily obtained.

They were wrong.

U.S. Army Engineers were shocked to discover that uranium, which until then had never been used militarily, was "actually scarce and almost impossible to find in the free world,"
according to Stephane Groueff's book, "The Manhattan Proj-

ect: The Untold Story of the Making of the Atomic Bomb."

Groueff's fascinating book, published in 1967 by Little, Brown and Co., reveals that the Army's frantic global hunt for uranium climaxed when — despite the secrecy surrounding the hunt — a Belgian businessman approached the U.S. government and said he had uranium to sell.

His name was Edgar Sengier. He was president of Union Minière du Haut Katanga, the Société Générale de Belgique's mining arm.

Bachrach

Edgar Sengier.

Army Col. Nichols, wearing civilian clothes so as not to attract attention, quickly called on Sengier at his New York office.

A spokesman for the U.S. Atomic Energy Commission offered Groueff's account of the September 18 meeting as authoritative. Here it is:

> Sengier was an abrupt though very polite man in his sixties, with an unusually pale face and sparse hair. Nichols introduced

himself, but before he was invited to sit down, he was asked, "Do you have any identification? You say you are from the military and yet you are wearing civilian clothes."

Nichols produced his identification card. The Belgian glanced at it and waved his visitor to a chair. "Now what do you wish to see me about, Colonel?"

"I understand you have some uranium, Mr. Sengier."

"Are you a contracting officer?" Sengier asked. "Too many people have been around here about this uranium, and they just want to talk. Do you have any authority to buy?"

"Yes," Nichols replied. "I have more authority, I'm sure, than you have uranium to sell!"

The Belgian thought for a moment, then demanded abruptly, "Will the uranium ore be used for military purposes? I will not sell it for commercial reasons, you see. Military use is the only one I'm interested in."

Nichols hesitated. He was in a quandary: how could he tell an alien anything about the country's most secret war project?

"You don't need to tell me how you'll use it," Sengier went on without waiting for an answer. "I think I know. All I want is your assurance as an Army officer that this uranium ore is definitely going to be used for war purposes."

"You have that assurance," Nichols said solemnly.

"Good, then let's make a deal, Colonel! My company, the Union Minière, has twelve hundred tons of uranium ore stored on Staten Island."

Nichols could hardly believe his ears. While they had been searching desperately for uranium all over the world, the precious ore had been lying unused in New York, right on their doorstep! Nichols was not only delighted but extremely puzzled. "Tell me, Mr. Sengier, how does this ore happen to be in the United States?"

"Very simple, really. In 1939 some European scientists informed me of uranium's potential military value. A year later, when Belgium fell, I had the twelve hundred tons of ore shipped to this country for safekeeping. It has been stored in steel drums in the Staten Island warehouse since 1940."

To Nichols it was now absolutely clear that the Belgian knew how the uranium ore would be used. Was he going to ask any questions about the Manhattan Project?

Sengier smiled as if he knew what was in the officer's mind. "Come now," he said briskly. "I suggest we come to terms on price."

For his services to the Allied cause Sengier was later knighted by the King of England.

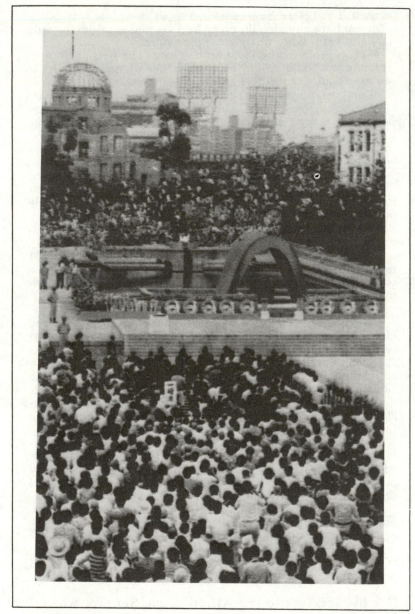

Hiroshima, Aug. 7, 1975. Some 40,000 people gather in the Park of Peace on the 30th anniversary of the city's destruction.

The Société Générale's official history lauds Sir Edgar for keeping the ore out the hands of the Germans and being one of many company people "doing everything within their power to further the common cause." The Germans had been experimenting with the atom, though they failed to develop a nuclear bomb.

The company's official history, published in 1972, spends three pages describing the episode behind the knighthood without disputing Groueff. It also praises him for his "astonishing forethought." But, in a remarkable omission, it never comes out and says what the uranium was actually used for . . .

Footnotes — Chapter 7

1. Fortune magazine, Sept. 15, 1967, p. 187.
2. As quoted in the Times of London, Dec. 15, 1977.
3. Management Today, Aug. 1974, "Belgium's Synergy Société."
4. Times of London, Dec. 15, 1972.
5. Times of London, May 12, 1971, "La Générale — the unique giant."
6. Société Générale de Belgique, Quarterly Information Bulletin No. 26, 1976, p. 10.
7. Montreal Gazette, Aug. 24, 1976, p. 3, "Air of tokenism pervades pollution fines, says study."
8. Interview, Apr. 5, 1977.
9. 1960 annual report of Cimenteries CBR Cementbedrijven, the cement firm which actually purchased Miron and held on to it for several years before passing it over to Genstar in a bit of intra-group shuffling, as quoted in Société Générale de Belgique, 1822-1972, an autobiography of the company, 1972, p. 208.
10. Le Devoir, Mar. 29, 1974, "Miron: poussières et . . . 2,000 emplois."
11. Interview, Angus A. MacNaughton, president of Genstar Ltd., Sept., 1976.
12. Montreal Gazette, May 6, 1976, p. 20, "Genstar's two chief executives look for higher profile."
13. Société Générale de Belgique's quarterly information bulletins for 1976-77.
14. Société Générale de Belgique, 1822-1972, an autobiography of the company issued on its 150th anniversary in 1972, p. 263.
15. Ibid., p. 260.
16. Société Générale de Belgique Quarterly Information Bulletin No. 27, Dec., 1976, p. 6.
17. Time magazine, Jan. 13, 1967.
18. Société Générale de Belgique Quarterly Information Bulletin No. 26, Dec., 1976, p. 4.
19. Interview with Ken S.C. Mulhall, senior vice president and treasurer of Petrofina Canada Ltd. Aug. 14, 1975.

20. Interview with Archie N. Wright, advertising manager of Clarke Transportation Canada Ltd., which then represented Dart in Canada, Jul. 8, 1975.
21. "Société Générale de Belgique, 1822-1972," op. cit., p. 263.
22. Genstar 1975 annual report, p. 30.
23. Stargazer, a Genstar house organ., Sept., 1974, p. 6.
24. Submission to the Royal Commission on Corporate Concentration by Genstar Ltd., Nov. 3, 1975, p. 34.
25. Ibid., p. 41.
26. "Société Générale de Belgique, 1822-1972," p. 263.
27. Genstar's brief to the Royal Commission, op. cit., p. 41.
28. "Global Reach: The Power of the Multinational Corporations," New York: Simon & Schuster, 1974, p. 152.
29. Financial Times of London, Sept. 15, 1972; Management Today, Aug., 1974.
30. Tanganyika Concessions, 1974 annual report, p. 6.
31. British Financial Interests in Angola, Guiné, Mozambique and Portugal, by the Committee for freedom in Mozambique, Angola, and Guiné (Nottingham, U.K.: The Russell Press Ltd., 1973), p. 6.
32. The Financial Times of London, June 28, 1960, "Rockefeller to step up Congo holdings."
33. Tanganyika Concessions, 1974 annual report, p. 25.
34. "The Rothschilds," by Frederic Morton (Greenwich, Conn.: Fawcett Publications, Inc., 1961), p. 68.
35. Société Générale de Belgique 1822-1972, op cit., pp. 24-37.
36. New York Times, Dec. 28, 1961.
37. Tanganyika Concessions, 1974 annual report, p. 10.
38. Société Générale de Belgique Quarterly Information Bulletin No. 27, Dec., 1976, p. 11.
39. Société Générale de Belgique, 1822-1972, p. 18.
40. "The Rothschilds." op. cit., pp. 70-72.

Chapter 8

The Agnellis:
Laying the Groundwork
for Transformation

THE ROUGH AND READY ruling families like the Desourdys and the Donolos who paint their names on every crane and tractor they own are perhaps the most visible names on the Quebec construction scene.

But the family with the biggest name of all remains unnoticed: the fabled Agnellis. Seemingly out of place on Quebec soil, the name Agnelli evokes villas overlooking the Mediterranean, fleets of Ferrari sportscars (which they make), jetset parties, the tinkle of glasses of Cinzano (which they make), marriages to swan-necked princesses — and control of the largest private manufacturing group in Italy, the Fiat automobile-industrial empire.

The Agnellis don't yet sell that many cars here. But they are among those at the helm of several of those pivotal super-projects which are bringing Montreal closer to the "international city of the 21st century" as envisioned by Mayor Drapeau.

Giovanni Agnelli, il numero uno, *answers interviewers' questions on Italian television. His face is reproduced on a giant television screen.*

It will be recalled that many of their anxious countrymen, spurred by Italy's economic and political crises, have also actively changed the city — mostly by getting their lira out of Italy to pump them into local high-rises and land banks ranging from Old Montreal to downtown to the suburbs.

But the main thrust of the Agnellis' presence here is far more dynamic and basic — in keeping with the creative, driving-force personality of the head of the family, Giovanni Agnelli. Long known as *il numero uno* among Italian industrialists, he is the celebrity-businessman who helped lead his country into its economic *miracolo* of the 1960 s.

Now, despite the waning of the flight of their countrymen's capital here since late 1976, the position of the Agnellis here remains firm. Their influence in the transformation of Montreal, like that of the Rothschilds, transcends real estate ownership *per se*. Aside from the normal involvement in trade with Canada (through the selling of Fiat cars, Cinzano, Bantam books and other consumer products) the Agnelli forte is in building things. In this chapter and the next we will look at several of the largest of the more than 15,000 companies in the Quebec construction industry, the industry in which the Agnellis are discreet giants.

In starting my research on land ownership and development I did not expect to get into this area. Construction has a vague reputation for being local and entrepreneurial in nature, and not really a part of international big business. Virtually all the attention the media gives to the construction industry focuses on the employees, not the employers. Strikes, union power structures, union corruption, and labor reform are subjects which comprise the bulk of everyday media coverage; it is easy to come away with a feeling that the owners are really not worth much thought. Indeed, for a reporter, or even for other people in the construction industry itself, the affairs of the major companies are more impenetrable than a construction worker's hard-hat. Most of the companies are privately-owned which means they aren't obliged to divulge very much information about themselves. As one official of the industry's own lobbying arm in Ottawa, the Canadian Construction Association, explained after being unable to tell me which companies had the most contracts or employers, "I know these companies are our members, but don't expect me to know anything about them. They don't tell us anything either, they're secretive as hell and there's no reason why they shouldn't be."

I first got interested in this field because one of the *least* secretive of these companies is — to give you some idea of how secretive the rest are — Genstar. Since its shares are publicly traded Genstar must tell something about itself, and its data on its construction subsidiary, Miron Co., provided an insight into the role these European-backed interests can play in the construction side of the transformation business. In the preceding chapter we touched briefly on how Miron is the second leading contractor on the extensions of the Montreal subway, digging tunnels, and one of the two largest public works contractors for the city of Montreal, paving streets and building sidewalks and the like. But Miron is much more than that. On virtually any major government-financed project in Quebec some of the company's 850-odd orange trucks, power shovels, cranes and vehicles may be seen: it holds major federal, provincial and municipal contracts and helped build such projects as the highway to Mirabel airport ($15 million), the downtown Montreal airstrip used briefly as a STOLport, roads for the James Bay hydro-electric project, the Olympic Village, and even the subsoil under the playing field of the Olympic Stadium. Privately-financed projects such as the building of parking lots for shopping centres are routine as well.

But the closer you look at the construction industry the more likely you are to stumble across other major global interests doing business through inconsequentially-named companies. For example, take the least visible facet of the transformation process, that which takes place completely out of sight but which is a prerequisite for much of the rest of urban transformation: the building of underground sewage systems and of distant energy projects. Here, in these critical underpinnings of metropolitan growth, we find the Agnellis.

For a glamorous family this may appear to be unexciting and grimy work. Sewer-building in the bowels of Montreal may not seem the ideal stomping ground for the Gucci shoe set; and the boondocks of northern Quebec, the habitat of blackflies and riotous labor unions, may not seem like much of an improvement. But such considerations do not mean much for the agressive Agnellis, who are to global engineering what the Rothschilds are to global finance: both families, in their separate ways, are at the tip of the wedge of progress in Quebec and much of the world.

Here is what they are up to locally:

1. Agnelli-related interests are the largest party in a consortium called *Impregilo & Spino Ltée* which is the largest contractor on what could be the world's largest and most expensive construction project, the James Bay hydro-electric scheme.* James Bay, as the project is casually referred to, is the direct heir of the Churchill Falls power project a decade before; just as much of the industrial growth of Montreal which was planned in the 1960s was predicated on the promise that energy would flow from Churchill Falls in the early 1970s, so much of Montreal's growth planned for the 1980s is based on the assumption there will be plenty of kilowatts from James Bay by then.

Impregilo & Spino has the prime contract on one of the project's several dams; this dam, with the uninspiring name of LG-2, will, when completed in 1982, be the most powerful dam in North America.[1] The consortium's contract is for $237,171,241, the largest contract awarded in Quebec's history.

The consortium is 75 per cent owned by Milan-based *Impregilo* (pronounced "im-pre-JEE-lo"). Impregilo, in turn, is

---

* Actually, there are no absolute criteria to determine which construction project is the 'largest'. Does one measure by the amount of earth moved, the size of the worksite, the number of workers employed, the cost, or what?

A James Bay Energy Corp. spokesman says that, taking these criteria overall, no other project in the world is known to be bigger than James Bay — though there is a chance a hydro-electric project in Siberia, on which little information is available, is about the same scale. The spokesman says that the total James Bay project involves 145 million cubic metres of earth and rock being used in dikes and dams, a worksite measuring 150 miles by 500 miles, a workforce expected to reach a high of 14,000 in 1979 and an expected energy output of 67.8 billion kilowatt hours per year. The cost, estimated at $16.2 billion in 1976, could go as high as $30 billion, according to some outside estimates.

owned jointly by three Italian companies, each having a 33.3 per cent stake. In any equal partnership the trick is to discern which partner is more equal than the others: in the case of the Dart Containerline this was La Générale; in the case of Impregilo this is *Impresit,* a subsidiary of the Agnelli-controlled *Fiat S.p.A.* automotive company.[2] Impresit supplies the key financial and administrative resources while the two other partners specialize in the more down-to-earth engineering skills.*

The remaining 25 per cent of Impregilo & Spino which Impregilo does not own is held by *Spino Construction Cie. Ltée.,* of Montreal. Impresit owns 49.98 per cent of that company.

In other words, the Agnellis, having a large piece of each of the two parties in the Impregilo & Spino consortium, are the No. 1 power behind it.

2. Through their stake in Spino Construction, the Agnellis are an important force in another uncelebrated job which is a precondition for further development of the Island of Montreal: digging sewers. Without them the city could not grow any more than a train could go without tracks.

And these are not just *any* sewers. One of them being blasted through the island's limestone bedrock — not far from the Miron quarry — is big enough to hold a single-line of subway. But even this is just child's play for the Agnellis: though Fiat is best known for making cars and trucks, it has also designed and managed construction of such super-projects as the Grand St. Bernard Tunnel under the Alps.

Spino Construction in 1977-78 is carrying out a $27.5 million contract from the Montreal Urban Community to blast a four mile stretch of tunnel at depths of up to 25 metres below ground. It is the biggest contract in the current construction of the huge (up to 5 metres in width) interceptor pipe running along the northern part of the island for over 30 kilometers.

---

* Symbolizing Impresit's pre-eminence is the fact that Impregilo's headquarters are located inside Impregilo's inside Impresit's headquarters on Milan's Via Santa Sofia. Also, Impresit's president, Vittorio Bonadè Bottini, is also president of Impregilo.

The Spino company's construction tower, at a sewer site near Henri Bourassa Blvd. and Meilleur St., is one of the few external signs of the company's mole-like role in Montreal's growth. Note in the foreground a cement truck belonging to Genstar's Miron subsidiary.

The pipe is to deliver waste to the planned sewage treatment plant at Rivière des Prairies.

The company has also landed another jumbo contract: it is carrying out a $33 million contract to build a collector sewer — part of a different system — south of Lafontaine Park. This contract, being paid for by provincial and City of Montreal taxpayers, ranks as the largest sewer or aquaduct contract let in the city.

In brief, Spino Construction has been the No. 1 company digging the island's sewers and aquaducts throughout the 1970s.

3. The Agnelli-interests are important contractors in still a third aspect of metropolitan development: since 1974, Spino Construction, though busy with sewers and dams, rates among the top four or five civil engineering firms in extending the subway system. MUC records show Spino Construction with over $20 million in contracts, mostly for digging tunnels and chambers for stations.

4. The Agnelli interests are also working at James Bay through Spino Construction — that is, independently of the Impregilo & Spino consortium. James Bay Energy Corp. records show the company has been awarded well over $100 million in contracts for work which includes tunnel excavations at LG-2.

5. The Agnellis are also involved at James Bay as machinery merchants. Fiat makes a lot of vehicles besides cars — notably earth-moving equipment. The company owns 65 per cent of the capital in a joint venture it made in 1973 with Allis-Chalmers Corp., of the U.S. Indeed, it estimates that the joint venture, called Fiat-Allis, ranks as one of the four largest companies in the world in this field.

Not surprisingly, a fair measure of Fiat-Allis and Fiat equipment is turning up at James Bay. This includes about half a dozen HD41V bulldozers — the largest in the world. Impregilo-Spino is also using a fleet of 32 Fiat 40-ton trucks.

Whether these contracts call for building dams, excavating sewers or blasting Metro stations, they all have one thing in common: the taxpayer pays for them.

In fact, Spino Construction and Impregilo & Spino between them are getting in excess of $400 million of public money for contracts. This puts them among the very top civil engineering groups in Quebec for public contracts.

Its dependence on public money notwithstanding, Spino Construction maintains a policy of total silence in dealing with the public.

In January, 1976, I asked Spino Construction if it would be possible to visit its premises at 1200 Louvain St. West and interview one of its executives or directors in preparation for a Gazette article relating to the firm's publicly-financed activities.

An executive telephoned back six days later saying that the president of the privately-owned company, Mario Spino, was "not too hot on the story."

"He's a little bit shy. It's part of his nature," he said.

He said no article had ever been written about the firm, even in the trade press, beyond routine announcements on contracts, construction techniques, etc., and he saw no need to break with tradition.

He declined to answer all questions relating to the company, including even the names of its officers, the approximate number of employees and the year the firm was founded.

"Call back in a few months when we're less busy," he said.

In September I did. This time I got through to Mario Spino himself.

"I would prefer to have no article in the papers." he said, declining to be interviewed. "It would cause us more problems than advantages," he added.

"We are not a public company and we don't want to make publicity," he said. "We prefer to remain in obscurity — in the shadows."

Turin's Agnelli family and Montreal's Spino family, though partners in several of Quebec's biggest construction enterprises, are a study in contrast.

Giovanni "Gianni" Agnelli, 55, is one of the world's most famous businessmen — a third generation industrialist who emerged from his partyboy image to become a charismatic folk hero for many Italians after helping push and pull his country to its post-war economic recovery.

During the height of "Il Boom" in the 1960s, Gianni Agnelli (pronounced "Johnny an-YELL-ie") had "a presence not unlike President Kennedy's," writes London journalist Anthony Sampson in "The New Europeans." "Clearly his presence fills some kind of psychological gap."

Mario Spino, 52, is a second generation president of a construction company who seems quite content to have no public image at all. An engineering graduate from McGill University, he prefers to just plug away at his company's mole-like specialty of digging tunnels.

"His work is his life," says one associate who asked not to be identified because of a ban on talking to the press. "He's the first in the office in the morning, and often the last to go at night."

With his wife and five children, he lives a personal life "without extravagance," says the associate. His home is on a small street in Cartierville. His idea of conspicuous consumption is a Cadillac. When he takes a vacation — which is rare — it's to Florida.

His father, Nunzio, founded Spino Construction in 1938, and he is one of four sons now in construction work. His brother, Pascal (or "Pat"), is vice president.

One of the rare times the company surfaced in the news was in December 1975: the company and its president, Mario, were fined a total of $150,000 in Sessions Court for failing to report to tax authorities more than $788,000 in revenue during a 15-year period beginning in 1957.

Gianni Agnelli, meanwhile, makes the cover of Time and the social pages of newspapers around the world. There is always some chitchat in the air about Gianni hobnobbing with Jacqueline Kennedy Onassis, Rainier and Grace or the Rothschilds, or of his younger brother, Umberto, spending weekends in Sardinia away from his wife, whose family makes Vespa motor scooters, and in the company of a girl friend (whom he eventually married), a cousin of Gianni's wife. Time magazine, in a 1969 article which estimated their wealth in those pre-inflation days at $500 million, called them "not a family but an economy."[3] Certainly, without the Agnellis the *paparazzi* would lose one of their staple gossip items.

Gianni's grandfather quit a military career in 1899 to help found Fiat, the cornerstone of the family's holdings. Like many of the backstage figures in urban development in Canada — the Rothschilds, the Hambros, Archduke Charles of Habsburg, etc. — Gianni comes from no mean stock. His mother was Princess Virginia Bourbon.

Gianni was known largely as a wealthy playboy until, driving home from a Monte Carlo party at 5 a.m. one day in 1952, he drove his car into a truck. He spent the next three months in a clinic, emerging with a permanent limp and a toned-down lifestyle. He married (Princess Marella Caracciolo di Castagneto) and set about transforming Fiat from a big industrial firm specializing in cars and iron and steel into a multinational empire with plants in 22 countries.

He works just as hard as Mario Spino — maybe harder. The intensity of his 16-hour days is legendary. But he also goes about his workday with a flair which reflects his personality. In the time it takes many businessmen to eat lunch, he sometimes breaks the day by speeding from his Turin headquarters to his helicopter pad in a $50,000 Ferrari, flies to the nearby Alps for a few runs down the ski slopes, and then goes back to the office.

Fiat moved into electronics in 1957, nuclear energy and earthmoving machines in 1958, gas turbines in 1960 and space research in 1963. In 1970 it was supplying four out of every five cars sold in Italy.

Like the Rothschilds, the Agnellis present themselves as quite humanitarian, a step or two ahead of the corporate pack in terms of social responsibility. In fact, the Agnellis are probably the most politically liberal of any of the major interests encountered in this book. A prototype of industrial paternalism, Fiat operates trade schools, day-care centres and seaside holiday camps for workers and their families. It even sponsors a multi-sport competition event at which employees in Turin compete to win the "Agnelli Trophy". Such social concern helped delay labor discord until 1969 when it began to be overtaken by the overall Italian labor malaise of absenteeism and strikes.

Today, despite several years of bad times caused largely by labour unrest, energy shortages and runaway inflation, Fiat is still the world's fifth biggest auto manufacturer and Italy's largest private employer with 185,000 workers. In late 1976 it strengthened its financial position by selling new stock to the

Libyan government. Oil-rich Libya came to the aid of its former masters (it was ruled by Italy from 1912 to World War 2) by pumping an estimated $415 million into Fiat through this and other financial arrangments. It received a 10 per cent voting interest in Fiat, but the Agnellis retained control through their holding company, IFI.

IFI holds much more than "just" Fiat. It also has vast interests in insurance, finance, cement, real estate, hotels and publishing. But Fiat is still its kingpin — indeed, with sales approaching $5 billion, it is larger than any company in Canada.

The LG-2 project at James Bay may seem impressive. But after a visit to Impregilo's Canadian headquarters in the heart of Montreal's financial district on St. James St. the mammoth project in northern Quebec shrinks somewhat in perspective. In the waiting room are hung poster-size photos of other Impregilo projects around the world. There is the dam on the Bandama River on the Ivory Coast . . . the Chocon dam in Argentina . . . the Kariba Dam on the Zambesi River in Rhodesia . . . a dam on the Euphrates River in Turkey. Each seems bigger than the next, dwarfing the kind of dams which used to illustrate elementary school textbooks a generation ago . . . The receptionist looks up. "Oh," she says, "those aren't anything, you should see the Tarbela Dam they just finished in Pakistan." That one, which Impregilo built in association with German and Swiss groups, is more than three kilometres long and in places about 100 metres high — taller than the 33-floor CIL Building on Dorchester Blvd. Finished in 1975, it is the biggest dam in the world.*

Later, in chatting with Impregilo & Spino's general manager, Paolo Cassano, I ask if he has ever met his boss, Gianni Agnelli. Cassano's eyes light up. "Ah, yes, once I saw him. I was working on a dam on the Volta River in Ghana." He pauses to think back on that momentous occasion. "He came for the inauguration."

But doesn't Mr. Agnelli ever fly into Quebec to check up on things at James Bay? Cassano looks at me as though I have no comprehension of the order of things.

---

* The James Bay scheme is still a much larger project because it involves a total of six dams, of which LG-2 is only one.

"For the Agnellis I woudn't say this is a minor activity," he says, gesturing towards a map of James Bay on the wall, "but . . ." He shrugs.

Still, after looking at what the Agnellis are doing here and around the world, one comes away with a feeling for much more than simply the *scale* of their activities. As with the Rothschilds, it is also the *quality* of what they are doing.

They are involved in creative, leadership-type projects which generate enormous economic — not to mention ecological — side-effects. They make plenty of money in the process, but what they do really transcends the more pedestrian, money-grubbing ways of many of those who follow their lead.

One can argue that there's no reason the Agnellis should be building dams and tunnels in Quebec when local interests could do them; but that's not a rap against the Agnellis so much as it is a reflection of the dearth of indigenous leadership. The Agnellis have *élan* and they're underbidding local firms for the big contracts. They are no more imposing themselves here than are the Rothschilds — just as Newfoundland Premier Smallwood decided to build the Churchill Falls project for which the Rothschilds then prepared the financing, so Quebec Premier Bourassa's government decided to go ahead with James Bay.

It happens, though, that very few interests around the world are geared to do this kind of work. So once a government embarks on a project of this magnitude it becomes in a sense captive of the few groups around the world which can carry it out. This is as true at the money end as at the construction end — thus in the case of James Bay, the Rockefeller interests, who have much to do with the loans for the project, wield a disproportionate influence through the dollars Quebecers already owe them and Quebec's continuing need for more.

This leadership by the Agnellis extends to other areas besides construction. In the town of Orbassano in Italy, for example, Fiat has set up — in response to the 1973 energy crisis — one of the world's newest and most advanced energy research centres. With a staff of 1,700 and a budget of over $40 million a year, it "befits a manufacturer which sees its future more as an energy systems company than just a car-maker," the Financial Times of London observes.[3] Devices to exploit renewable energy sources such as the sun's rays and the wind are in the works. As far as cars go, the Financial Times reports that "the quest has taken Fiat much more deeply into electro-chemistry than car-makers would normally venture," exploring new kinds of battery electrodes. The company is also working on micro-computers for car engines so as to reduce fuel consumption. Some scientists at the centre say the electric car owner of the 1980s will get a battery charge by plugging into his own private windmill. This is not to suggest the Agnellis are by any stretch of the imagination eco-freaks. They are simply trying to devise ways to sell more cars in the petroleum-scarce years ahead.

Other Fiat subsidiary or affiliate companies are involved in designing nuclear reactors, building nuclear islands and experi-

Michael Dugas

A lot of Fiat-Allis heavy equipment tends to turn up at worksites in Montreal and at James Bay where construction is being performed by Spino, a leading recipient of public contracts. It's nothing more than another form of vertical integration. The Agnellis stand behind both companies.

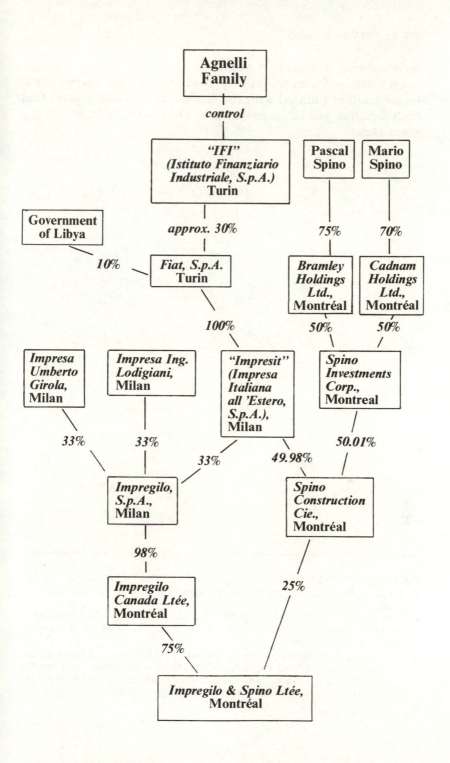

menting with nuclear fuel elements.

This kind of overall priority given to various energy areas forms another parallel with the Rothschilds — and insures that both families will be in positions of increasing influence in the years ahead.

Footnotes — Chapter 8
1. Girouard, Robert, information officer, James Bay Energy Corp.
   Energy Corp.
2. Time magazine, Jan. 17, 1969, p. 59, "A society transformed by industry."
3. Financial Times of London, Feb. 13, 1976, p. 17, "Fiat on the energy road," by David Fishlock.
Note: Most of the information on the extent of Agnelli-related involvement in local development came from records of government agencies (in particular the Service des Compagnies in Quebec) and confidential interviews with government engineers and other officials.

Chapter 9

French Building Blocks

The Gazette (Michael D

Local workers employed by Francon, the Quebec construction arm of France's worldwide Laf *cement interests, build Montreal's Decarie Expressway in the 1960s.*

Question: Name one *single* company without whose products much of Canadian industry would come to a grinding halt.

Answer: Opinions may vary, but you can make a strong case for a company called Canadian Liquid Air Ltd.

The 65-year-old firm, headquartered at 1210 Sherbrooke St. W., may be small — at least 150 other industrial companies in Canada have greater sales. And its main products, industrial gases, are about as drab and unexciting as any products can be in terms of public identity. But as the No. 1 maker of these products with a full 40 per cent of the market,[1] the chances are that if it were to cease production tomorrow many of Canada's steel mills, petrochemical refineries, auto-makers, electronics companies and even lightbulb manufacturers would either have to curtail or stop production.*

* It could be argued, certainly, that petroleum is as essential as industrial gas in keeping heavy industry chugging. But no single company — not even Imperial Oil Ltd., the biggest — has a chunk of the petroleum market comparable to Liquid Air's 40 per cent of the industrial gas market. Indeed, if Liquid Air's supplies were no longer available, Imperial Oil itself — a major customer — might have refinery troubles.

A second reason for making a case for Liquid Air's importance to Canadian industry is that, in addition to gases, it estimates that it makes some 36 million pounds of electrodes for welding each year. That, says one executive, is close to 50 per cent of the Canadian market for the electrodes used in certain kinds of welding.

Without these electrodes, many companies would be unable to perform one of the most basic steps in industry: sticking one piece of metal to another.

Canadian Liquid Air happens to be 100 per cent owned by a French company, Air Liquide, of Paris.* And its role here symbolizes the all-round role of France in Canada's development: inconspicuous and far from dominant in terms of an industrial presence, but nonetheless concentrated in pivotal places.

If one were to wave a magic wand and remove every solid object in Canada built with products or workmanship in which the French have large holdings, we would suddenly have a denuded landscape: between one-third and one-half of all major buidings, highways, bridges and dams would disappear.

Sound bizarre?

Such leverage is due to the leadership role French-related interests hold in two fields: construction materials and construction itself. Let's take construction materials first.

Industrial gases like oxygen and nitrogen may be the ultimate building blocks in heavy manufacturing. But in urban development, it is cement. Today more concrete is used in Canada than any other construction material: in fact, more of it is used than all other construction materials *combined,* whether measured by volume or weight.[3] And by far the most important manufacturer of this material is — no, not the Belgian-backed Genstar organization — but French-owned Canada Cement Lafarge Ltd. Lafarge, as it's called for short, sells fully *twice* as much cement as Genstar or anybody else.[4]

This gives the company a significant role in the shaping of urban growth. As Lafarge itself puts it in its own promotional literature:

" . . . concrete is changing the face of Canada in a multitude of forms: soaring high-rise buildings, sweeping modern structures, pyramid-shaped housing condominiums, multi-level traffic complexes, long ribbons of concrete expressways, expanses of runways to accommodate giant jet aircraft, towering dams to

---

* Air Liquide is the world's largest producer of industrial gases measured by income, just ahead of Union Carbide and British Oxygen. It has operations in 54 countries. No shareholder holds more than about 5 per cent of the capital, and the most important of these are institutional investors.[2] One familiar name, however, appears on the Paris company's board of directors: W. Earle McLaughlin, chairman of the Royal Bank.

hold back the waters of our mighty rivers and to provide much-needed electric power."[5]

But hold on to your hats. We haven't seen anything yet. The rhapsodic Canada Cement Lafarge prose goes on:

"The next few decades will see an even more accelerated pace in the use of concrete. By the year 2000, hundreds of new cities will have been born, some in the form of self-contained communities of concrete and glass built on piles many miles offshore in order to solve the problem of the shortage of building space on land; expressways will have built-in shopping malls; commuters and travellers will be riding to and from work and jetports by means of high-speed air cushion vehicles gliding on wide concrete tracks; massive concrete dams, diversion and irrigation channels will control the flow of our northern waters, diverting water to the dry south."

One of the interesting things about Lafarge is the way it puts Genstar in perspective. It shows that Genstar, far from being an aberration from the corporate norm in Canada's development, is actually part of a broader pattern in several areas of its activities.

In land ownership *per se,* we saw in Chap. 7 that Genstar's 180-hectare Miron quarry, used to get limestone to make cement, was the largest piece of privately-owned property inside the boundaries of the City of Montreal. But right next door to that quarry is a Lafarge-owned quarry, held through its Francon division, which at 140 hectares is almost as big.

And eight kilometres eastward, just outside city limits, in the neighboring municipality of Montreal East, Lafarge owns another quarry — which at 192 hectares is even bigger than the Genstar quarry.[6] If we combined the areas of these two Lafarge tracts we get just under 3.5 square kilometres, or 1.3 square miles.

That's more land than in five municipalities on the island (Hampstead, Montreal West, Roxboro, Ste. Genevieve or St. Pierre). No other company owns more land on the entire island of Montreal, except for Canadian Pacific Ltd. when its rail yards and rail lines are included. Genstar, by contrast, is not quite so strong locally but is the biggest metropolitan landowner nationally, making exception again for the CP railway property.*

Like Genstar, Lafarge says it has no immediate plans to move its limestone-mining operations to less populous parts of the region. Genstar says there is enough limestone in its Miron quarry to last another twenty years and Lafarge's administrative manager and legal counsel, Pierre Maltais, says there is enough limestone at the Montreal East site to produce cement for another *fifty* years.**

What is even more remarkable than these two European-backed companies' landholdings, however, is their grip on the cement market. Nationally, Lafarge, Genstar and one other company control approximately 85 per cent of the cement production, according to estimates at the federal Department of Consumer and Corporate Affairs. In Quebec itself, the trio control 90 per cent of all production, according to an official of the Canadian Portland Cement Association, a trade group.[7] This hammerlock on the market represents one of the most intense oligopolies in North America. As we recall from Chap. 5, in discussing the domination of the construction glass market by the British-owned Pilkington glass interests, the basic rule of thumb for oligopoly is when four companies control 50 per cent of a market. Federal anti-combines officials have long fought these two industries with few notable successes. Roy Davidson, Ottawa's second-ranking anti-combines official, says flatly that "there would be lower prices in cement and glass" without these high concentrations of producers.[8]

And what is this third company? Its name is St. Lawrence Cement Co., which may sound indigenous but is, like the others, basically European. It is controlled by a Swiss company, Holderbank Financière Glaris A.G., which owns 54.4 per cent

---

* That is, the bulk of CP's metropolitan land is used for rail related purposes — tracks, freight-yards, repair yards, etc. Most of this land, with some important exceptions, is devoted to these transport purposes and could not foreseeably be converted into more conventional forms of development. On the other hand, Genstar's land tends to be vacant or almost vacant and is earmarked for eventual development (including the Miron quarry).

** In addition to its quarries on the island of Montreal, Lafarge also owns four quarries on the island of Laval. Company officials estimate them to be 25 hectares or less in size.

of it. In Quebec itself this group has actually grown bigger than the others since its controversial acquisition in 1976 of Ciment Indépendant Inc., a Quebec producer which, interestingly, was owned by the same Miron family which 15 years earlier had sold their original company to the Belgians.

Nationally, anti-combines officials calculate that Lafarge is far and away the leader with over 45 per cent of the market,* while St. Lawrence has a little over 20 per cent and Genstar a little under 20 per cent.

Davidson says these three companies have "lessened competition in Canada and it would be difficult to demonstrate (greater) efficiency" through their increased size. That is, in cement there are relatively few economies of scale.

Lafarge and, to a lesser extent, Holderbank, have done what Genstar has done: they have expanded rapidly in Canada since the war not through underpricing the competition but through takeover and merger of existing companies, which by definition reduces competition. There used to be dozens of these companies. We recall how, for example, a young Maritimer named Max Aitken made a name for himself in 1909 by merging ten cement companies into one, called Canada Cement Co. Ltd.** Aitken went on to become Lord Beaverbrook, but even he never dreamed of the merger process he set in motion in the cement industry. Only 14 years after it came to Canada in 1956, Lafarge became the country's largest cement producer; it did this by snapping up smaller companies right and left, finally climaxing the process in 1970 by merging with Canada Cement itself. Today the French parent company, called

---

* This figure was corroborated by John Tittley, advertising manager of Canada Cement Lafarge. Tittley notes that in some parts of Canada the percentage soars much higher – thus in the Maritime provinces Lafarge controls 75 per cent of the market, he said.[9]

** Its graceful colonnaded headquarters still overlooks Montreal's Phillips Square. Though it looks as though it were made of graystone, the 10-storey building is made of concrete, giving the lie to those who say concrete must necessarily make for austere, impersonal structures. Another building which makes the same point is Place Bonaventure, built 55 years later in 1967 in a modern, geometric style; the mixure of millions of brown pebbles into the concrete gives the squat structure a rough, almost tweedily warm look.

Lafarge S.A., controls 54.5 per cent of that creation, Canada Cement Lafarge.

The federal anti-combines agency, or Bureau for Competition Policy as it has been renamed, strongly opposed this merger. It sought to block it on grounds that competition "is or is likely to be lessened to the detriment of or against the interest of the public." In 1972 it turned its files over to the Justice Department for action against the companies. It was a sensitive case: the prime minister of Canada, Pierre Elliott Trudeau, had just married Margaret Sinclair, daughter of James Sinclair, the deputy chairman of the newly merged company. The Justice Department dropped the case. Why? A department spokesman told me, "There was simply not sufficient evidence on which to get a conviction." Because of the courts' narrow interpretation of anti-combines law, this is a thoroughly plausible explanation and consistent with Canada's law, lax relative to the U.S. anti-trust stance. Rather than insinuate that it would have been somewhat unseemly for Trudeau to go after his father-in-law's company, I would suggest that the government's inaction falls into a pattern of passivity before corporate mergers generally.[10]

In any case, Ottawa was not to show itself as spineless. While it allowed the critical merger to take place, it did later successfully prosecute Lafarge for the relatively minor, if ignominious, offense of price fixing. In 1974 several Lafarge subsidiaries on the West Coast were convicted — they pleaded guilty — on three counts of conspiracy to fix prices. It and its co-conspirator* were fined a total of $432,000.

This is the *highest* penalty inflicted on any companies in any case tried up to that time under the Combines Investigation Act, the basic anti-trust legislation which goes back to 1910.

Construction is the second area in which the French are so important in the urban transformation process.

---

* The other guilty party was Ocean Construction Supplies Ltd. At the time of the price-fixing, this company was owned by a British firm, Associated Portland Cement Manufacturers Ltd. Since then, however, it has been absorbed by Genstar; in an exchange of shares, Associated Portland became the second biggest shareholder in Genstar after La Société Générale de Belgique and its affiliates.

There are two major French-backed companies with great influence in this area. One of these is, again, Lafarge: it has a division, called Francon,* which is even more important than Genstar in the construction industry in Montreal and the province generally. Indeed, Francon is the second largest (we'll get to the first in a minute) construction company throughout the province as a whole, say numerous industry and labor officials.[11]

Its specialty is road building. None of its contracts are as big as those obtained by the various Agnelli interests (Chap. 8), but Lafarge tends to get more middle-sized contracts year in, year out than any other firm.** The second largest road builder in Quebec after Lafarge is none other than Les Mir Construction, controlled by St. Lawrence Cement's parent company, Holderbank. Small world. It may be recalled from Chap. 7 that Genstar's Miron subsidiary was one of the two main companies to get contracts from the City of Montreal for fixing streets and sidewalks and digging open-cut excavations — well, that other member of this dynamic duo is Lafarge's Francon division.

I call these three dominant, remarkably similarly structured organizations — the French Lafarge, the Swiss Holderbank and the Belgian Genstar — the 'three sisters' of the local construction and construction materials scene.

We have already seen how the three sisters have grown so quickly in Canada by swallowing up other companies and thus undermining competition here. Another way they have become successful here is through vertical integration, which also has the effect of reducing competition in Canada by elimi-

---

* Acquired by Lafarge in 1961. It was known formerly as Mount Royal Paving & Supplies Ltd.

** Francon has received, for example, a $19.8 million contract from the James Bay Development Corp. (the highest ever awarded by that corporation, thereby lending symmetry to the sister James Bay Energy Corp., which also awarded *its* highest contract to Europeans, in this case the LG-2 contract to the Agnelli-related interests). This contract was to build a road between the LG-2 dam and Fort George. Francon has also received more than $24 million in assorted other contracts for roads and bridges in the James Bay area. Elsewhere around the province it has helped build Mirabel International Airport, the Metro extensions and the Olympic facilities.

The 'Three Sisters' of Quebec's construction and construction materials industries: Les Mir (St. Lawrence Cement, Holderbank, Switzerland*); Francon* (Canada Cement Lafarge, Lafarge S.A., Francon)*; Miron* (Genstar).

nating competitive bidding.* Critics say that so many of the leading ready-mix concrete and construction companies are controlled by the cement producers that the smaller, independent cement producers have trouble finding customers.

Speaking at an industry convention in September, 1976, William Bateman, president of a relatively small Toronto company called Lake Ontario Cement Ltd. urged the industry to slow down the pace of vertical integration. Otherwise, he predicted, the "government will do it for us" and small companies will "get more protection than they wanted." Indeed, Ottawa's top anti-combines official, R.J. Bertrand, warned the same convention that his agency was taking a close look at the concrete industry.

Nonetheless, a month later Holderbank went ahead and, through St. Lawrence Cement, acquired Ciment Indépendant Inc.; in January, 1977, it obtained approval from the Foreign Investment Review Agency to buy certain assets of the ready-mix concrete division of the Ontario subsidiary of the U.S.-owned Flintkote Co.; and in February, 1977, it announced it had completed the purchase of a cement plant at Hudson, Quebec, which had belonged to a division of the United States Steel Corp. The trend toward increasing concentration in this field seems to be opposed in Ottawa by challenges of a largely rhetorical nature.

It should be noted that these three sisters are only the Canadian offspring of much larger multinational sisters. We already known about Genstar's background, but Lafarge is a major power, too. It employed 23,700 persons around the world in 1973 and, in addition to controlling 40 per cent of the French cement market, also has operations in Senegal, Ivory Coast, Morocco, Brazil and the U.S. (where it is 50 per cent owner of Citadel Cement Corp., of New Jersey.)[12] It began as a small

---

* Lafarge candidly describes its devotion to vertical integration in its aforementioned company brochure: "In the fifties and early sixties, a program of vertical integration was begun; that is, the investing by the company in ready-mix, concrete products, paving and construction companies. Such a program of acquisitions is designed to develop the market for cement by acquiring control of end users of the product and to maintain some influence on the end product, concrete." The acquisition of Francon was part of this strategy.

Olivier Lecerf, head of Lafarge S.A., in his Paris office.

limestone mining operation near the Rhone River, founded in 1830 by the Lafarge family (which still has a member on its board); today it is one of the three largest cement groups in the world.[13] No shareholder has over five per cent of the capital, but we note that its chief executive, Olivier Lecerf of Paris, is a director of the Canadian Imperial Bank of Commerce. He is one of three French directors on the board of Canada Cement Lafarge.*

Holderbank, too, is another of the world's three biggest cement groups.[14] In addition to Europe, it is strong in Lebanon, South Africa, the Philippines, New Zealand, Latin America and the U.S. (where it has a stake in Dundee Cement Corp., of Michigan.) Despite its name, Holderbank is not a bank but a manufacturing company. It is closely tied in with a Swiss family called the Schmidheinys. Located near the centre of the Swiss business establishment, Holderbank has no fewer than six directors who also sit on the boards of Switzerland's Big Three banks — Union Bank, Swiss Bank Corp. and Swiss Credit Bank. They often help underwrite municipal and provincial loans in Quebec. Thus the banks found themselves at one point indirectly helping to finance the Olympic facilities while at the same time one of their client manufacturing companies was an important supplier of cement with which to build the stadium.

The other major French-related construction firm is A. Janin Cie. Ltée. It does more construction work around Quebec — and in fact, across all of Canada — than any other organization,** according to officials of the Canadian Construction Asso-

---

* Two of its longtime directors, incidentally, have also been members of Canada's Senate. They are Jacques Flynn and the late L.P. Gelinas, who died in 1976.
** The Janin group of companies includes more than a dozen differently named entities, including: The Foundation Co. of Canada Ltd., Namur Equipement Ltée., A.D. Ross & Cie., Les Usinages Industriels Ltée., Regional Asphalte Ltée., Carrière St-Maurice Inc., Janin Building & Civil Works Ltd., Pax Construction Inc., Foundation Comex Construction Equipement Cie., Atlantic Tug and Equipment Co., Janin Western Contractors Ltd., Turnkey Development Engineering & Contract Management Ltd. and Janin Construction Ltée.

ciation and the Association de Construction de Québec et de Montréal.

Most of the super-projects of the last decade throughout Quebec have had a substantial Janin input. It has been one of the largest, if not the largest, contractor on the Churchill Falls project, for example. [15] It has done some $40 million worth of work at James Bay, mostly in the form of building bridges and camps for workers. It also helped build the Manicouagan hydro-project. It built the Pierre Laporte Bridge over the St. Lawrence near Quebec City, the longest bridge in Canada. It has helped supply the pre-cast concrete parts for the Olympic Stadium. It is the biggest contractor on the City of Montreal's biggest current capital works project, the Charles Des Baillets filtration plant for drinking water in LaSalle (Janin has a remarkable $125 million contract for that project alone).

Around the world it has had major contracts as far away as Australia and Indonesia. In 1977-78 it is building a large irrigation project in Peru and a metallurgical factory in Algeria.

It is headquartered on the top floor (No. 32) of the east tower of Complexe Desjardins, the four-tower office and hotel complex it completed in 1976 for its owners, the Quebec credit union (Mouvement des Caisses Populaires Desjardins) and the Quebec government. The view from its windows is breathtaking, not so much for the panorama itself but for the *way* that panorama has been moulded by Janin's hand. There is the Stock Exchange Tower, Place du Canada, the Château Champlain Hotel, Central Station, the Quebec Provincial Police headquarters on Parthenais St. and Maison Radio-Canada. Are any other big skyscrapers left out? Well, there's Place Ville Marie which was built by Foundation Co. of Canada — but, shortly after the completion of PVM, Janin acquired control of that company. But these are just *buildings* — isn't there anything else? A stone's throw from Complexe Desjardins is the Ville-Marie Expressway which has sliced through the downtown core despite citizen protests that it was destroying neighborhoods — that's a Janin project. Then there are the bridges: Janin has helped build each of the big ones — the Jacques Cartier Bridge, the Champlain Bridge and the Mercier Bridge. It also built the sole tunnel under the river, the Hippolyte Lafontaine Tunnel. There on the other side of the river one can dimly perceive the St. Lawrence Seaway — that, too, was partly a Janin job.

It is difficult to say who controls Janin today. But a huge French multinational construction firm with the parochial name of Société des Grands Travaux de Marseille (GTM) holds an influential 23 per cent[16] stake in it. Located outside Paris in Nanterre, the company no longer has much to do with Marseilles. It belongs to that same class of construction companies as the Agnellis' Impresit — in fact, it has collaborated with Impresit on numerous projects around the world including the Tarbela Dam in Pakistan. It is also one of France's principal builders of highways, skyscrapers, canals, parking lots and nuclear facilities.

Just as Impresit is controlled by Italy's giant Fiat group, so GTM is associated with — though not controlled by — a very large French transport and industrial firm, Chargeurs Réunis S.A. It controls France's second largest non-petroleum shipping company and its second largest airline (called Union des

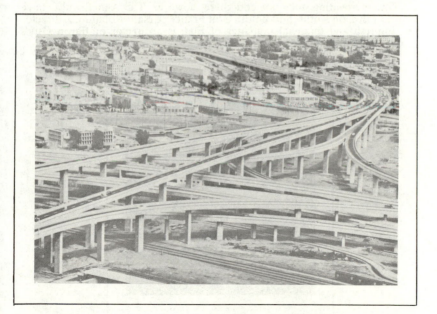

The Trans-Canada Highway's Turcot interchange in Montreal, built by Janin.

Transports Aériens). Chargeurs Réunis is GTM's principal shareholder with 16 per cent of the voting stock.* [17]

In construction and construction materials, as in so many other aspects of urban development, the big interests often are inter-related. Thus Janin — Canada's largest user of cement — is also tied in with Lafarge — Canada's largest producer of it. One of GTM's directors, Robert Gachet, is also a director of Lafarge S.A. in Paris. Rapport between the two groups also ex-

---

* Other major interests are also linked in with GTM. Two of the most discernible are the Lazard Frères banking interests of Paris, who are also tied in with Chargeurs Réunis, and the French branch of the Rothschilds. The Rothschild interests customarily occupy a seat on GTM's board of directors — their current representative is Michel de Bossieu, director of the Banque Rothschild and Baron Guy's Le Nickel.

Chargeurs Réunis is controlled by Francis Fabre and his family. Now in his sixties, Fabre represents the third generation of an armaments family. Not only is he tied in with GTM, he is also associated with Impresit; that is, he is a director of the Agnellis' Fiat group, which controls Impresit. In other words, Fabre has close ties of *three* of the biggest construction interests in Quebec — Janin, Spino and Impregilo & Spino.

The intertwining does not end there, however. The Agnellis also have ties to the main Rothschild holdings in France: Cesare Rolando, a director of Impresit and financial manager of Fiat, is a director of Baron Guy's Compagnie du Nord.

Francis Fabre.

ists here in Canada: for example, when Lafarge in 1966 wanted a large cement factory at St. Constant on the South Shore, it was Janin that built it. Indeed, in the spirit of *fraternité* for which the French are celebrated, the president and managing director of Canadian Liquid Air Ltd., Pierre A. Salbaing, is also a Janin director.

As an anecdotal sidelight, it's worth noting that both Lafarge S.A. and L'Air Liquide, the Paris parent companies of these two pivots on the Canadian industrial scene have the *same* major shareholder. There is nothing grand or aristocratic about this shareholder: it is one of France's leading financial institutions, Groupe de la Caisse des Dépôts, a cooperative. It owns 3.32 per cent of L'Air Liquide and 5.12 per cent of Lafarge, not much — but more than anyone else.

For about eight months I had sought an interview with the president of privately-owned Janin, Henri-François Gautrin. But my messages were never returned. From his photograph in Who's Who he looked like a rather tall man, austere and almost imperious. From corporate ownership records in Quebec City and Ottawa he appeared to hold a key number of shares in Janin and two obscure holding companies (Nootka Investments Ltd., of Vancouver, and Index Holdings & Management Ltd., of Montreal) which, along with the French inter-

Henri-François Gautrin, president of Janin.

ests, own large blocs of voting stock. His son, also named Henri-François Gautrin, was head of the New Democratic Party in Quebec. He himself had been born and educated in France, had worked for GTM as an engineer in France and had lived in Canada since 1949, when he was 30. He was not pleased when my article for The Gazette described him as inaccessible. Prior to publication of this book he accepted to be interviewed.

I found a man who looked little like his picture. He was of just below average height, maybe 5'8" and rather than haughty he seemed rambling and overworked. His eyes were bloodshot. He answered all of my questions graciously and — with the exception of the one seeking the names of the most important shareholders — completely.

The penthouse headquarters itself was also a surprise. Rather than posh and with the kind of thick carpeting one might normally associate with a company doing an average $250 million worth of work every year, it was as sparely furnished as a civil service office. The president's corner office was outfitted in inexpensive imitation-antique Québécois desk and chairs — the kind of rough, unpainted and unstained things one can pick up in a furniture warehouse. It gave the quarters a rustic look which stood in sharp contrast to the rigid modernity of so much of what the firm has built. On the walls were Gautrin's framed engineering diplomas and a *de rigueur* painting of a Quebec village scene in winter. (Pictures of snowbound bucolic villages are surely as common to high-rises as pin-ups are to garages.) On the shelf was a meagre half-dozen books — Who's Who and similar works. Most dentists have grander offices. So unprepossessing were the man and his surroundings that during the interview I kept looking out the window at this vista of skyscrapers, bridges and highways to remind myself that this organization was out of the ordinary.

Gautrin handed me his official biography, consisting of two pages stapled together. Its opening sentence went to lengths to stress the Canadian side of his background: "(He was) born in Breteuil-sur-Iton in Normandy of a family of Flemish origin, but one of his Norman grandfathers claimed that his great-grandmother had come from Acadia."

I had imagined Gautrin to be something of a VIP. After all, as a large shareholder as well as top executive of Canada's largest construction group, he is a general of an army of thousands of helmeted workers. But when I asked him if perchance during his days as the biggest contractor at Churchill Falls, he had ever met Edmund de Rothschild, who had put the project together and made 200 trips to Montreal in the process, Gautrin smiled wanly and shook his head.

"I have no relationship with that world," he said. "I am just a very small contractor when you compare me with the international giants."

Canada's No. 1 construction company is but a midget on an international scale? "Compared to Impregilo and Grands Travaux de Marseille and Brown & Root (of the U.S.) which may be the largest in the world, we're nothing," he said.

Gautrin seemed to have only the foggiest notion of who was associated with Grands Travaux de Marseille. Told that Chargeurs Réunis was the biggest shareholder, he expressed surprise. Thumbing through a GTM annual report together, the veteran engineer also expressed considerable interest that the Rothschild and Lazard financial houses were involved.

His company has passed through several hands. It was founded by a French engineer, Alban Janin, about 1931. After he died in 1948, GTM took control, sharing ownership with the Pallaz family of Lausanne, Switzerland, and Canadian interests, says Gautrin, who has become a Canadian citizen. Shortly after Expo '67 (for which Janin built the Japanese and Czechoslovakian pavillions), GTM ceded control, said Gautrin. "But," he added, "they didn't cede control to somebody else. Management now more or less has control." However, though Gautrin has been the chief manager of the Janin group since 1963, he does not have control, he stressed.* Ideas he pro-

* Who would be a major force in Janin's ownership besides GTM and Gautrin? One of the answers would be whoever has control of Nootka Investments, whose 26 per cent stake represents the largest single holding in Janin. Gautrin controls 20 per cent of Nootka's votes but the records and say nothing about the remaining 80 per cent. "I am very reluctant to talk of such things," he said. Its worth noting, however, that C.W. Brazier of Vancouver, is president and a director of Nootka; he is also chairman of the H.R. MacMillan Family Fund and a director of the British Columbia Hydro and Power Authority, Canada Trust and the Eaton Group of Mutual Funds. Gautrin said that all Nootka's shareholders were Canadian and that they were not fronting for anyone.

poses at board meetings sometimes run into heated debate and he has to quickly "back-peddle," he said.

The ownership appears to be delicately balanced, somewhat like a mobile, with no one group having preponderant weight. My own feeling is that Gautrin is probably quite right when he says no person or organization has outright control of the Janin group. But the group is nonetheless clearly within the sphere of influence of Grands Travaux de Marseille. Not only does it have two directors on Janin's board but its own 1975 annual report puts Janin in the category of "sociétés apparentées." It's an unusual term which suggests a close family relationship — Gautrin used the word "cousins" to describe it.

The significant degree of foreign influence within Janin is rather ironic in light of the great number of construction contracts Janin has won from the federal and Quebec governments, both of which have policies intended to encourage indigenous enterprise. The ultimate example of this is the modernistic Department of External Affairs Building in Ottawa, built by Janin. It is perhaps fitting that the building in which Canada's foreign policy is shaped is itself built by a company with a substantial foreign background.

But *why* are there so many foreign-related construction companies at the fore of development here?

Certainly, some of this engineering work is of a highly technical nature, but surely building a dam or a highway or skyscraper is not like putting a man on the moon. Why are foreign-backed companies like Janin, Miron, Francon, Les Mir, Spino and Impregilo & Spino — plus others which have not even been mentioned, like the U.S.-owned Bechtel group — more often than not the leaders of construction here? If Canadian workers can get callouses on their hands holding the shovels why can't Canadian businessmen hold control of the companies? Why can't labor leaders in this unusually disputatious and strike-affected industry be able to sit down and negotiate contracts with representatives of owners whom they know and who in turn know them and their workers' needs. And why do so much of the profits from these enormous contracts — which are often paid for by taxpayers — have to be drained from the country?

Why, in short, can't Canadian construction companies make more low bids for the big jobs than the foreign-backed ones?*

Gautrin rubbed his chin and thought about that question for several moments.

"It's solely a question of capital," he said. "Europeans succeed in obtaining capital easily, while Canadian companies find it very difficult."

Most of the European companies here, he said, are able to obtain capital through the Canadian operations of their parent companies' associates or through their ability to get credit directly from Canadian financial institutions. In the case of Janin, the latter was generally the case, he said. Most of Janin's banking has been with the Royal Bank.**

Having large financial resources is a critical precondition for bidding on major contracts for two reasons, he continued. For one thing, construction companies — rather than proprietors of projects — must pay a sizable advance on the early costs of projects (in Europe, however, it is often the proprietor who pays the costs). For another, the proprietors in Canada can hold back payments to contractors after projects are completed if they, the proprietors, say they are not satisfied. Under these circumstances, contractors can find themselves financially strapped very easily. The overall system militates against companies getting very big — big enough to compete for major contracts with the solidly-financed, foreign-backed ones.

* Of the 15,000[18] construction companies in Quebec — ranging in size from one-man operations to those with thousands of workers — probably more than 98 per cent are Canadian-owned. But it is the big companies — that is, the ones which do the work which determines the tone and sets the pace for the development of Montreal and Quebec — which tend to be foreign-backed. This is not to say, however, that there are not some major Canadian-owned companies here (that is, they are presumed to be Canadian-owned though little is known about their internal affairs). These would include the Desourdy and Donolo brothers as well as Les Constructions du St. Laurent (owned by G. Lloyd Welch, of Beauport, Quebec) and the Beaver group (owned by John S. Newman, of Montreal), all hard at the heels of the foreign-backed firms in bidding for the big contracts.
** Two other banks with which the Janin group does business to a lesser extent are the Canadian Imperial Bank of Commerce and the Banque Canadienne Nationale.

Another reason why Canadian companies seldom grow big enough to compete with the others is that their ownership "is confined to a small group of shareholders," Gautrin said. If they were publicly owned like GTM or Fiat they could raise money by issuing shares to the public.

But all these reasons do not sound like huge problems. They sound more like excuses than justifications. They are conditions and customs which could be overcome if people put their minds to them.

Isn't there one extremely good, necessary reason why Canadians can't direct the construction of their biggest projects?

Gautrin reflected and came up with just one — that old demon, the weather.

"Canada has a harsh climate and it's hard to predict the weather," he said. "This means it's easy to lose money on a project."

But it couldn't, he suggested, really be called a necessarily deciding factor.

In fact, these isn't any.

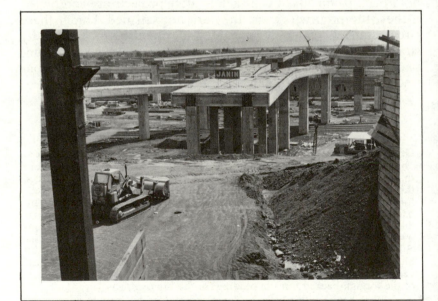

Footnotes — Chapter 9

1. Telephone interview with Guy Murray, manager of gas products sales, Canadian Liquid Air Ltd., Sept., 1976.
2. DAFSA report, Paris, 1975.
3. "The Canada Cement Lafarge Story," a booklet published by the company, Montreal, 1974, p. 28.
4. Estimate by the Bureau of Competition Policy, Department of Consumer and Corporate Affairs, Ottawa.
5. "The Canada Cement Lafarge Story," op. cit., p. 28.
6. The sizes of these properties are derived from Montreal Urban Community evaluation rolls.
7. Telephone interview with Maurice Marcil, regional manager of the association, Dec. 14, 1976.
8. Telephone interview with Roy Davidson, Mar. 18, 1977.
9. Telephone interview with John Tittley, Dec. 14, 1976.
10. The Trudeau government's stance vis à vis mergers and competition generally was the subject of a lengthly analysis in the Gazette, Jan. 5, 1975, pp. 8-9, "Monopoly Power: The years drag on, and still legislation languishes," by Henry Aubin. (Still dragging.)
11. Among them Roger Trepanier, business agent for the Confederation of National Trade Unions, who keeps track of the number of workers employed by the various companies around the province.
12. DAFSA report on the company, Paris, 1973.
13. Financial Times of London Yearbook, 1974.
14. Société de Banque Suisse, étude de placement, Nov. 1974.
15. Interview with Henri-François Gautrin, president of Janin, April 29, 1977. "Of the $600,000,000 worth of general enginneering work at Churchill Falls, I'd say we probably executed more work than anyone else, but it's hard to be certain," he said.
16. The 23 per cent figure is derived from Janin data dated July 1975; it was given to me by H.-F. Gautrin on April 29, 1977, with the understanding it was still basically accurate.
17. Chargeurs Réunis, Exercice 1973-1974, p. 8.
18. Estimate by Robert Nuth, chief spokesman for the Association de Construction de Québec et de Montréal.

Chapter 10

Whiskey à Gogo:
Bronfman Development

JAMES WALKER HARDWARE (1955) LTD. is *not* the place to shop for hammers, nails, mops, or buckets.

Located in carpeted offices on the eighth floor of a downtown office building, the "hardware" company is in fact a land speculation company owned by Montreal's wealthiest family.

In the West Island towns of Dorval and Dollard-des-Ormeaux it owns bits and pieces of land totalling more than 1.3 square kilometres. Evaluated at over $8 million, most of this land is undeveloped.*

Interests closely associated with the Bronfman family control the company. But big as this holding is, it is but a bubble in that family's multi-billion-dollar brew of property interests across Canada.

The original wellspring of the Bronfman fortune** was the world's largest liquor manufacturer, *Seagram Co. Ltd.* But much of the profits from that livelihood have been pumped into a large number of operating companies, holding companies, trusts and old shell companies, like *James Walker Hardware,* active in that mellowest of long-term investments, property.

Add up all the real estate owned by these various firms and one can only reach the conclusion that the Bronfmans are the largest landowning family in all of urban Canada.

The Bronfmans:

— Through a family trust called *CEMP Investments Ltd.,* are main shareholders — with about 35 per cent of the stock — of Canada's largest publicly-owned real estate company, *Cadillac Fairview Corp. Ltd.* With 1976 assets of $1,045,157,000 across Canada,*** Cadillac Fairview owns some of Montreal's largest

---

* These figures are derived from evaluation rolls at city halls of both towns in March, 1976. Twenty-six hectares of this land is in Dorval, most of it near the north service road of the Trans Canada Highway. More than 150 hectares are in Dollard-des-Ormeaux, most of it along Spring Garden Rd.

** *Newsweek* magazine estimated the fortune of the clan, counting both its Montreal and New York members, at over $1 billion in 1975. The closest runner-up in Montreal would probably be the Websters, whose holdings were pegged at over $400 million that same year by author Peter C. Newman.[1]

*** Genstar, which does many things besides just develop real estate, has greater assets ($1,232,843,000) than Cadillac-Fairview; however, a greater portion of Genstar's assets are in manufacturing facilities, transport equipment, etc., rather than in real estate *per se.* Cadillac Fairview was unable to calculate for me how much land in hectares they own across Canada, but it would be less than Genstar.

So this raises the question, How can Cadillac Fairview have more real estate assets than another company yet own less land? The answer is that much of Genstar's land is still vacant whereas Cadillac Fairview's land tends to be worth more, and hence counts as greater assets, because it is filled to a greater degree with shopping centres, housing developments, etc.

shopping centres, office buildings, apartment blocks and suburban housing developments. CEMP also owns James Walker Hardware.

— Are big enough shareholders in Canada's *second* largest real estate company, Trizec Corp. Ltd., to at least technically control it. Trizec's 1976 assets are just under $900,000,000. The Bronfmans own — through another family trust, Edper Investments Ltd. — 51.5 per cent of Trizec's voting shares.

— Have important holdings, through other vehicles, in additional pieces of real estate around Montreal ranging from highrise apartment buildings in Côte St. Luc to historic houses in Old Montreal. They also own the city's principal area for all indoor-sports and entertainment, the block-square Montreal Forum (evaluated at $11 million).

— Are associated with other significant real estate interests here. Take, for example, the case of Baron Alain de Gunzberg, of Paris, who is a Bronfman in-law and a representative of Bronfman interests overseas. Gunzberg's main job is being managing director of the Banque Louis Dreyfus, of France, and that bank has moved several million dollars of investments into Montreal in the mid-1970s. It is one of the partners in the *Les Terrasses* office-retail complex next to Eaton's downtown, which opened in 1976, and it owns prime land for development just across the street on de Maisonneuve Blvd.

— Are, to cite another example, substantial (20 per cent) shareholders through Edper in another of Canada's ten largest public real estate companies, S.B. McLaughlin Associates Ltd. The firm owns four acres of super-prime land, most of it undeveloped, in downtown Montreal on both sides of Dorchester Blvd. West. It also owns more than two square kilometres of land near Mirabel International Airport.

— Are involved in various other kinds of firms which are neither landowners nor developers themselves but are nonetheless closely associated with this field. Thus the Bronfmans, through Edper, ultimately control a residential mortgage company, Niagara Realty of Canada Ltd. which has some 20 branches in Montreal and ten times that number sprinkled around the rest of Canada.

On paper, such highlights might appear to give the Bronfmans an awesome degree of power over the local — and national — property scene. But it's not quite so simple. The Bronf-

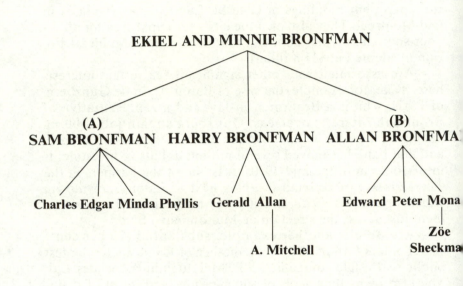

EKIEL AND MINNIE BRONFMAN

(A)
SAM BRONFMAN **HARRY BRONFMAN** **(B)**
ALLAN BRONFMAN

Charles Edgar Minda Phyllis Gerald Allan Edward Peter Mona

Zöe
A. Mitchell Sheckman

Note: This family tree only includes members of the Bronfman family pertinent to this chapter. There are scores of other members as well.

(A.) Charles Bronfman, of CEMP...

David Bier Studios

(B.)... and Peter Bronfman, of Edper.

mans cannot accurately be treated as one monolithic family. The elements we tend to lump together under the common surname are really a factionalized cluster of individuals. They all share a bloodline which goes back to the quite recent past. That is, they are all descendants of Ekiel and Minnie Bronfman, who immigrated to Canada from Eastern Europe in 1889. But there is much bad blood between these descendants.

There are two main wings to the Bronfman family, and they might seem to have so much in common that they would get along well. But perhaps it is a case of similarly charged ions repelling each other.

Leaders of both wings make their offices on Peel St. within a couple blocks of each other. Each of the wings owns a major league Montreal sports team, each has interests in the same liquor company, each has large investments in oil as well as real estate. But where they differ most is in their opinions of each other.

Because of the multitude of personal and company names, it may help us keep our heads straight to use two letters, A and B, to identify the two main groups. The first group (A) is composed of the four children of Samuel ("Mr. Sam") Bronfman, Ekiel and Minnie's third son and the driving force behind the growth of Seagram's. These four children, now middle-aged, are Charles, Edgar, Minda de Gunzberg and Phyllis Lambert. With the help of old family confidant and lawyer Lazarus Phillips, Mr. Sam set up a family trust for his children, to settle inheritance matters, before his death in 1971. This is CEMP Investments Ltd., deriving its name from the first initial of each child; it controls Seagrams today, with about 33 per cent of the voting stock and is the vehicle for most of this branch's real estate holdings.

Charles, the youngest of the children, has owned the Expo baseball club since its inception in 1969. Though he is among the wealthiest, if not the wealthiest, of any baseball team owner, the team in its first eight seasons has had among the lowest payrolls and worst overall record of any team in either the National or American league, never once winning more games than it lost. Nonetheless, he said in 1976, "The best thing that ever happened to me was the Montreal Expos ... It

Charles Bronfman is the only owner of a baseball team in the major leagues who has managed to incorporate his personal initials in the team logo. The Expo's stylized «M» —for Montreal— insignia contains a «C» for Charles and a «B» for Bronfman.

was the first thing I ever did on my own without the family to fall back on if I'd failed."[2]

The second branch (B) is composed of the children of Ekiel and Minnie's fourth son, Allan. The two sons, Edward and Peter, have given their names to their trust, Edper Investments which owns a small percentage of Seagrams. It is Edper which, through a variety of intermediary companies, includes among its investments Trizec, S.B. McLaughlin Associates, the Canadiens hockey club, the Forum, Niagara Realty, a seven per cent holding in Ranger Oil Co., etc.

The Financial Post has estimated that, between them, CEMP and Edper have a "big say in assets now totalling well more than $7 billion."[3] But there is little chance that these two branches could ever fall afoul of the anti-combines law, no matter how tough it might be made; a competitive relationship exists between the CEMP and Edper branches that, though they would never advertise it, might almost make them unintended heroes of those who champion the breaking up of monopolies.

The best example of this relationship took place in the small city of Kingston, Ont., midway between Montreal and Toronto. It was in Kingston in June, 1972, that the federal government's Canadian Radio-Television Commission held hearings to review the application of a CEMP subsidiary, a computer firm called Multiple Access Ltd. (A), to buy one of Montreal's principal English language TV-radio outlets, CFCF-TV (tied in with the CTV network and one of the city's two English channels) and CFCF radio, the rock and sports station. The Canadian Arena Co. (B), an Edper offshoot and owner of the Canadien hockey team whose own bid to purchase the stations had been unsuccessful, demanded that the CRTC reject the application. The actual details of the application are not very interesting. But the transcript of these hearings, available from Ottawa for $.25 per page, contains at least 100 pages which are worth their price in cobra venom.

The two sides were represented by the cream of the Montreal legal establishment: working for the challenging Edper group (B) was E.-Jacques Courtois, a longtime intimate of that group, whom we have encountered earlier in this book as an ally of the Eagle Star and Brinco interests. Representing the CEMP group (A) was Philip Vineberg, one of Canada's foremost tax advisers and a partner with Lazarus Phillips in the Phillips & Vineberg law firm.

In the genteel world of the billionaire, one might think that disagreements between members of a family would not be publicly aired. A raised eyebrow, perhaps, or a slight damning with faint praise, might be the only external clues that all was not peace and harmony. But here in remote Kingston, on this obscure matter which would receive scanty media attention, one Bronfman branch went on record accusing another of hiring people who are neither "competent" nor "forthright," of lacking "pride" in Montreal, of abetting the deterioration of the Montreal economy to the advantage of Toronto's, of being "selfish" and of being so shifty with its taxes that it was "causing indirectly Canadian taxpayers to foot the bill" for its own activities.

It is an interesting commentary, raising as it does the question of what Montreal's richest citizens are doing for Montreal's development.

The transcript reads like — to borrow an analogy from the TV medium they were contesting — a comedy-hour takeoff on a VIP catfight. One can almost imagine Harvey Korman and Tim Conway, of the Carol Burnett Show, outfitted in pinstripes, begin with arch-politeness and end by hurling verbal custard pies at each other. Though this catfight took place back in June, 1972, it's well worth reviving.[4]

It would be hard to find two more courtly members of the Montreal bar than Messrs. Vineberg and Courtois. Vineberg (A) in particular expressed discomfiture at being involved in this skirmish between the cousins. As he told the commissioners at the outset, "It falls to my lot to deal somewhat with a certain opposition that has been registered and I hasten to say that this opposition is made by persons with whom I have close personal and professional association and for whom I have the greatest of personal esteem." He pointed out that he was a director of some of this other branch of the family's companies, including even Edper (B) itself.

Vineberg started his defense of the CEMP group's (A) application on a lofty note and tried to keep it there. His pitch was that the application should be approved by the commission because this branch of the family had a record of pouring part of its profits from alcohol into philanthropy (not a word here of tax advantages). "I don't want to sound sanctimonious," he said, "but when you have got money it is much easier to be generous — it takes much less out of you and is much less of a sacrifice, and I am fully aware of that, but on the other hand the family has had a certain background and training of devotion to citizenship duties ... arising beyond the immediate sphere (of wealth) ... Mr. Sam Bronfman in his capacity as

(A.) Philip Vineberg, lawyer, representing the CEMP *wing...*

Arnott Rogers Batten Ltd.

(B.)... and E.-Jacques Courtois, lawyer and hockey club president, representing the Edper *wing.*

head of the House of Seagrams said, and this continues to be our motto, 'The horizon of industry surely does not terminate at the boundary line of its plants. It has a broader horizon, a farther view, and that view embraces the entire Dominion.' And it is in that perspective and in that spirit that we ask for your support and approval of our application."

Courtois (B) was not impressed.

"Mr. Chairman," he began sarcastically," . . . when I listened to the eulogies of the late Mr. Samuel Bronfman I thought for a moment he was the applicant. Mr. Samuel Bronfman was highly respected in Montreal for his philanthropy and his business acumen, but we are not dealing with him here today.

"The financial power and control behind the applicant are his four children. Each of them is most highly regarded but the fact is that of the four only one is a Canadian, resident in Montreal and that is Charles Bronfman," said Courtois, seeking to make indigenousness, or lack of it, an issue in control over leading local media outlets. "One of the sisters, Baroness de Gunzberg, has lived in Paris over 20 years. Another sister, Mrs. Phyllis Lambert, lived in the U.S. and has only recently come back to Canada I am told, but in doing so did not choose to come back to Montreal, she went to Toronto.* So when I talk of Montreal content, when I talk of people who live in Montreal and work in Montreal, I would ask you [the commission] to bear that in mind."

Then Courtois got down to business.

"It is our submission, Mr. Chairman and ladies and gentlemen, that it is not in the interests of the public at large and more particularly not in the interests of residents of the Province of Quebec and of Montreal that the application of Multiple Access [A] to acquire the broadcasting division of Canadian Marconi Co., [then-owner of the CFCF stations] be approved.

"I make this submission based on my belief that the owner of a broadcasting undertaking:

"— first, should be from and intimately involved in the area which is served by that undertaking;

---

* Mrs. Lambert has since this time, however, moved to Montreal.

"— two, should have competent and forthright management which will have the ability to manage a broadcasting undertaking with knowing and understanding;

"— third, should consider the broadcasting undertaking as a principal concern and area of its activity.

"We believe that Multiple Access [A] . . . fails on all three counts."

Tough words. But Courtois, president of the champion hockey club, then knocked the other Bronfmans up against the boards on questions of ethics.

"The main attraction of the acquisition of the broadcasting division of Canadian Marconi is the heavy losses of Multiple Access [A] . . . [The] heavy losses . . . will be set off against the operating profit of the broadcasting division so as to eliminate the payment of Canadian income taxes for many years to come, thereby causing indirectly Canadian taxpayers to foot the bill for the acquisition."

Courtois skated off for a moment and then came back, slamming his opponent even harder.

"I say that nothing that has been done is legally dishonest," he said to make sure he wouldn't be called for high-sticking in the libel court. "I say the way that every turn, at every financing, some insiders [at Multiple Access] seem to make profits shows much more interest in a financial operation than in wanting to operate something for the benefit of the public, because I say when you see people . . . getting 200,000 shares at $.15 and two months later offering the stock to the public at $10.00 per share, I say well that is rather selfish."

"I say," said Courtois coming back later for more, ". . . that the radio and TV station should be sold to a group who is interested in the Province of Quebec and in Montreal and who has some pride in wanting to make this a success, not somebody who says, 'Well we have got a tax loss and that is a wonderful tax shelter for the profits of our other division.'"

Now Vineberg (A) threw off his gloves.

"I don't want to go into each and every one of the items." he said. But "there is a great deal of irrelevance to the submissions that are made and they represent a kind of resentment on Mr. Courtois' part and that of his clients, a resentment which is unfounded . . ."

Courtois, said Vineberg, "seems to have studiously over-looked" the fact that the branch of the Bronfmans he represents is not so very indigenous either. He recalled that Courtois had said Edward and Peter Bronfman (B) controlled Ecco Securities, which controlled Place La Rondel Ltée., which controlled Canadian Arena. But, said Vineberg, pulling out some of the knowledge he has acquired as a confidant of this other branch of the family, "what he didn't mention to you was Zoë Sheckman," who was a "principal stock holder in Ecco Securities."

"Zoë Sheckman," he announced, "is a niece of Edward and Peter Bronfman, the sole child of the deceased sister, who was born in New York, lives in New York, she is a very fine girl, and she represents on . . . their branch of the family what Edward does on our side of the family — a New Yorker. I would not have thought either that he would have forgotten our mutual friend and she is a friend of his and mine, a mutual friend . . ."

It all goes to show, said Vineberg, that the "kind of problems he is charging us with he has in greater measure himself."

Now Courtois' own rectitude was being questioned. Rising to his feet and speaking from the audience, he said, "It has been suggested to the Commission that I misled them. I state categorically that Zoë Sheckman is not a trustee of the trust. I state categorically that she is not a shareholder of Place La Rondel,* I don't want to pursue the debate but I am not going to be accused of misleading the Commission and I would ask Mr. Johnson [special counsel to the Commission] to investigate the matter, we will open our books to show she never was and is not a trustee of the trust."

Unless there is a retraction by Mr. Vineberg," he added indignantly, "I would ask you to do that, Mr. Chairman."

Vineberg was not intimidated.

"I would reiterate the statement that I made, that Zoë Sheckman's trust is a shareholder in Edper, which in turn is a shareholder in Ecco to which my learned friend had referred."

---

* Which, according to the transcript, Vineberg had never said was the case. He had said she was a principal shareholder in Ecco Securities.

The abundance of shell companies was confusing everyone, even their own directors.

"That is a different statement," said Courtois. "I said that Zoë Sheckman is not a trustee and she has no control over the trust. I believe it would be worthwhile to have Mr. Johnson investigate and report to the Commission on that."

Unabashed by Courtois' continued indignation, Vineberg delivered the squelch.

"I would also remind Mr. Courtois," he said, "that he participated in the decision to name Zoë Sheckman a trustee."

"Thank you, gentlemen," said the chairman.

At this point, one almost expects to see Carol Burnett, playing Zoë Scheckman, wander out on stage with wide-eyed bewilderment.

But the theatrics in Kingston were over and the commission went on to approve the Vineberg/CEMP (A) application.

Because of their fortune and influence, it is fair to judge the Bronfmans by high standards. What sense of social responsibility does Montreal's largest real estate family exercise in the community?

At the same Kingston hearing described earlier, the president of Multiple Access (A), John McCutcheon, delivered this praise:

The family of the late Mr. Sam, he said, is "well known for its involvement with the community, both as donors and investors. Examples of direct participation in the Montreal community are the Saidye Bronfman Centre for the Performing Arts and the Samuel Bronfman Faculty of Management Building ... on Sherbrooke St. on the McGill campus ... The family of Mr. Bronfman makes substantial contributions to several Canadian universities, to museums and public institutions and through the Fairview Corp. of Canada Ltd.,* is helping to change the face of Canada. In fact only 10 days ago announcement was made of another large Fairview investment — a major commercial development in the City of Laval which will not only provide shopping amenities, but create a substantial

* The company is now part of Cadillac Fairview Corp.

amount of employment. 'Canada, the Foundation of its Future,' a Canadian history written by Stephen Leacock, was commissioned by Mr. Bronfman, as was a series of paintings by Canadian artists on the cities of Canada. Because of the great financial strength of the family, they are able to hold to a policy of establishing and maintaining high standards and quality in their many activities."

Courtois, of course, raised some different points, questioning the willingness to shoulder the responsibility of paying taxes and the extent to which there was pride in the community.

The family's contributions to excellence in urban real estate investments is a matter of record. The 38-storey Seagram Building in New York City, completed in 1958, is deemed by many design critics as that city's finest postwar skyscraper. As New Times architecture critic Paul Goldberger has written:

"The Seagram Building is one of New York's most copied buildings. Its dark bronze exterior and two-storey high travertine lobby have provided the inspiration for countless office towers around the world, most of which have been far less refined than the New York original.

"Indeed, much of the Seagram Building's importance comes from aspects of its design that are now common, but were dramatically new in the 1950s, such as the wide plaza in front of the building, the tinted-glass curtain wall and the elegantly crafted interior hardware."[5]

The project was largely due to Phyllis Bronfman Lambert (A), one of the CEMP children, who urged Mr. Sam to go all out in building a New York headquarters for Seagram's. Lambert herself chose Mies van der Rohe as architect.*

But that's in New York.

In researching Bronfman holdings in Montreal real estate I was unable to find anything remotely comparable. I asked Phyllis Bronfman Lambert, herself an architect, what she con-

---

* Its worth noting that though the building was very costly it has had its dividends. Goldberger notes the "prestige of the tower has translated itself at least somewhat into monetary terms." Even during the 1976 oversupply of Manhattan office space, which saw many office buildings with few tenants, the Seagram tower was 98 per cent full with many occupants paying considerably higher rents than at nearby buildings.

sidered to be the best quality building in Montreal for which hers or any branch of the family was responsible. She said the Saidye Bronfman Centre, named after her mother and located on Cote St. Catherine Rd. was the best (she also was the architect of it). Esthetics are a subjective thing, and perhaps the best way to describe it is to simply print a picture of it. She noted, however — that the building should be judged not just on its appearance but on its purpose as a social centre — for recreation, theatre, etc. As she put it, "It's fulfilling a marvelous social function in its area."

Lambert is also influential in Save Montreal, one of the city's main preservation groups. Several years ago when the Shaughnessy mansion on Dorchester Blvd. was threatened with the same demolition fate that had befallen the Van Horne mansion, Lambert personally intervened and bought it. She says she hopes to make the building available to people in the surrounding neighborhood for some as yet undefined purposes. Construction of houses on the spacious grounds are also a possibility, she notes. Her branch of the family also became involved in 1977 in the restoration of some deteriorating houses in Old Montreal and then reselling them, which makes sense not only in business terms but in helping to revitalize a picturesque but dilapidated part of the city's historic centre.

Outside these bright spots, however, the real estate legacy of Montreal's largest landowning family remains quite unspectacular.

McCutcheon's mention of the Faculty of Management Building, built by Mr. Sam on Sherbrooke St. for McGill University, as part of a campaign to buy respectability,* is a case in point. It required the destruction of numerous old houses of high architectural standards, replacing them with a building whose design Lambert herself terms "unfortunate." "It's not a good building," she says.

---

* The Bronfmans have been dogged by a less than pristine image, partly because of making and selling hard liquoir, especially during Prohibition, which is considered by some to be a less than gentlemanly vocation. As Newsweek has written. "Sam Bronfman never denied that [U.S.] Prohibition made him rich — "I never went on the other [U.S.] side of the border to count the empty Seagrams bottles," he averred — but he was self-con-

The family has also been an integral part of the so-called "Manhattanization" of Montreal, but it has done so without the flair of the Seagram Building. The office building at 2055 Peel St., where Edper has offices, is a case in point. Banal though it seems today, it was something of a pioneer. As Peter Bronfman (B) once told The Financial Post, "We decided to put up this building at 2055 Peel St., but I was pretty inexperienced. In those days, most of the new buildings in New York were installing air conditioners, self-service elevators and recessed lighting. These were the three new things, but the trend to them hadn't started in Montreal. It was a big added expense, and some of the builders were advising against it, but in the end I decided I'd be more worried if I didn't put them in than if I did."[7]

The Rockefellers in the U.S. may have pumped many millions into such socially useful projects as Rockefeller Centre in New York or the restoration of colonial Williamsburg. But when one scans the accompanying list of Montreal real estate owned by the Bronfmans, the Rockefellers' counterparts in this city, it is difficult to point to much that rises above the ordinary, the average. In shaping the urban environment here, the

---

scious about it. He became an active philanthropist, particularly for the state of Israel, and in time accumulated a vast store of art treasures . . ."[6]

In 1977 one member of a third branch of the Montreal Bronfman clan appeared as a witness before the Quebec Police Commission inquiry into organized crime. Mitchell Bronfman, grandson of Ekiel and Minnie Bronfman's second son, Harry, was questioned. Mitchell, a local business executive, obtained more than $1.4 million in loans from alleged underworld financier Willie (Obie) Obront. The commission said Mitchell paid more than $1 million in interest on the loan between 1967 and 1974. Other borrowings had been made as early as 1962. Mitchell testified he borrowed the money because he had "just nowhere else to go."

Another of Ekiel and Minnie Bronfman's great-grandsons has been making the news. Samuel Bronfman II, son of Edgar (A), disappeared from his parents' New York state residence for nine days in August, 1975, in what appeared to be a kidnapping. However, the two men he accused of kidnapping him for a $2.3 million ranson were found not guilty by a White Plains, N.Y. court in December, 1976. Several jurors openly accused young Sam, then 23, of having faked his own kidnapping in order to obtain ransom money from his family. Sam hotly disputes this, saying, "The people who know me know this isn't true. If they believe it, they are not worth knowing."

Architecture Bronfman-style:

Henry Aubin

(A.) The Saidye Bronfman Centre...

Michael Dugas

(B.)... and 2055 Peel St.

city's largest landowning family has shown remarkably little of the leadership here which, by default, the Europeans have been exercising.

Emerged from poverty for only 60 years or so, the Bronfmans today are an intrinsic part of the Montreal establishment. This was implicitly recognized in 1976 when three of the city's most important businessmen joined the board of Seagrams: Paul Desmarais, chairman of Power Corp.; Ian Sinclair, chairman of Canadian Pacific; and Fred McNeil, deputy chairman and chief executive officer of the Bank of Montreal.

But the Bronfmans are much more than just Montreal (or New York) poobahs. They are among the very few Canadians who have been accepted by the kind of elite global families described in earlier chapters.

There are two points to be made here: first, they may be new rich, but they are *extremely* rich and this wealth serves as a kind of passe-partout into the top financial circles; second, their interplay with some of the familiar names in this book goes to show once again just how knit together the forces determining Montreal's growth really are regardless of how separate they may appear.

Thus in April, 1976, Italy's Agnellis — the Fiat, James Bay and Montreal sewer kings (chap. 8) — combined with the CEMP wing (A) to buy a substantial 15 per cent stake in one of London's most prestigious merchant bank organizations, Arbuthnot Latham Holdings. The City press referred to CEMP with some disdain as the "American Bronfman whiskey dynasty";[8] but it was clearly further cracking the inner circle.

It had already been there for some time. Minda's (A) marriage to Baron de Gunzberg helped establish a beachhead in Europe. We note that CEMP is now the third largest shareholder, for example, in a major French gas maritime shipping company, Gazocéan, with 6.6 per cent of the shares and with Baron de Gunzberg on the board; also on the board, representing the 8.1 per cent second largest holding, is Francis Fabre, representing Chargeurs Réunis S.A., which is tied in with Canada's biggest construction company, Janin (Chap. 9).

But my favorite example is a most unlikely one. It involves a business venture which has absolutely nothing to do with big urban development companies or with any other aspect of cities. In fact, it has everything to do with getting *away* from them.

It's Club Mediterranée. Ironically, it promises one million white collar workers in Europe and North America "total escape" every year "from the daily, mechanized routine of everyday living"[9] which the owners of Club Med have, perhaps as much as anyone, helped foster. "Come play with us," says the promotional literature. "Club Mediterranée is for you, a place in the sun, where you can give your vacation dreams free rein to live out your fantasies in a special world"[10] in holiday villages scattered throughout the world.

In its original post-war form, Club Med was largely held by Edmond de Rothschild's Compagnie Financière. Since the late

Club Méditerranée

Club Med: Consumer society takes a breather.

1960s, however, he has brought in new partners. Today there are seven partners with carefully equalized holdings, which at last count were at exactly 10.4 per cent.

They include a Who's Who of the interests mentioned in this book. In addition to the Rothschilds, there is: CEMP (A), IFI, the Agnelli's holding company, Compagnie Financière de Paris et des Pays Bas, to be seen in Chapter 15 as the largest shareholder in a major Montreal landlord, Crédit Foncier. While the secretaries, salesmen and executives mingle in "a special world where rules do not exist . . ., where fantasy turns into actuality and desire becomes reality,"11 around the board table back in Paris some of the top personalities involved in European and Quebec development do a little shoulder rubbing themselves. We find Edmond de Rothschild, Alain de Gunzberg, Giovanni Agnelli and Francis Fabre as directors.

For them, too, like the "gentils membres" of the Club, it is a "special world, where rules do not exist."

Here is a partial list of Bronfman real estate in the Montreal area.

Holdings through CEMP Investments Ltd.:

CADILLAC FAIRVIEW

Shopping centres:	Site's hectares:	Stores:
Maisonneuve	3.6	30
Domaine	5.2	60
Greenfield Park	10.4	45
Fairview Pointe Claire	29.6	79
Le Carrefour Laval	29.6	128
Les Galeries d'Anjou	26.8	145

Office buildings:

Dominion Square Building, 1010 St. Catherine St. W.*
550 Sherbrooke St. W.
1400 St. Catherine St. W.*
2100 Papineau, "Bell Telephone Bldg."
5250 Decarie Blvd., "Zeller Bldg."
(*acquired, rather than developed)

Residential, single family houses:	**approx. number:**
Brossard	150
Kirkland	145
Pierrefonds ("Woodview Park")	175

Residential, high-rise:

Les Habitations Malicorne, 6400 Place de la Malicorne

Twin towers at Cavendish Blvd. and Kildare Rd., Cote St. Luc

ISLAND PARK HOMES

Housing development on Ile Perrot

JAMES WALKER HARDWARE

Land:
Dorval, 26 hectares
Dollard-des-Ormeaux, 112 hectares

SEAGRAM'S

Headquarters, 1430 Peel St.
Historic house, 160-162 St. Amable St., Old Montreal
Plant site, 225 Lafleur Ave., LaSalle, 9.5 hectares

SHORE HOLDINGS

High-rise residential buildings:	1976 building evaluation:
7431 Kingsley Road , Cote St. Luc	$1,829,250
7448 Kingsley Road, Cote St. Luc	$ 614,200
414 Trent Ave.	$1,322,000

Holdings through Edper Investments Ltd.:

TRIZEC

(See list, Chap. 3)

S.B. McLAUGHLIN ASSOCIATES (NON-CONTROLLING)

Undeveloped land bounded by Dorchester Blvd. W., Drummond St., Lagauchetiere St. and Mountain St.

Land across street along Dorchester Blvd. for a two-block strip between Stanley St. and Mountain St., including the land on which the world's largest Holiday Inn is built.

CANADIAN ARENA

Montreal Forum

(**Note:** Other members of the Bronfman family own additional property. For example, Gerald Bronfman, a member of a third branch of the clan, until recently owned the Haddon Hall apartment buildings on Sherbrooke St. near Atwater St.)

(**Sources:** Cadillac Fairview annual reports, municipal evaluation rolls, interviews with CEMP, Cadillac Fairview and McLaughlin executives.)

Footnotes — Chapter 10

1. Newsweek, Aug. 25, 1975, p. 16, and Newman, Peter C., "The Canadian Establishment," Vol. I (Toronto: McClelland and Stewart Ltd., 1975), p. 272.
2. The Financial Post, Toronto, Nov. 13, 1976, "The Bronfmans: driving, hugely monied — and mostly very quiet," by Amy Booth.
3. Ibid.
4. CRTC transcripts (Hull, Quebec: Canadian Government Printing Bureau), June 19, 1972, pp. 48-141.
5. New York Times, Nov. 8, 1976, "Seagram Building owners plan to seek landmark designation," by Paul Goldberger.
6. Newsweek, op. cit.
7. The Financial Post, Toronto, Nov. 20, 1976, "The Bronfmans: a liquid legacy for the lineage," by Amy Booth.
8. London Financial Times, April 24, 1976, "Bronfman and Agnelli will acquire Latham stake," by Margaret Reid.
9. "Club Méditerranée" (Paris: Club Méditerranée S.A., 1974), p. 1.
10. Ibid., p. 7.
11. Ibid., p. 1.

Chapter 11

The Vatican Realm

ON DECEMBER 14, 1976, The Gazette ran an article I wrote on local landholdings belonging to various religious units which are under juristiction of the Vatican.

During my research, the various ecclesiastics whom I had approached for help had been, in the main, unhelpful. With smiles and repeated apologies, they had explained that the information sought was simply not available.

The reaction of the archdiocese to the article after it appeared is a story in itself.

Here is the original article as it appeared without a word changed.

The Gray Nuns' Motherhouse in downtown Montreal. In 1975 the Swiss company Valorinvest agreed with the sisters to buy the land in order to demolish the church and surrounding residences and build, in their place, an office-tower complex. The provincial government, however, killed the deal, declaring the property to be part of the province's cultural heritage.

No. 1 private landowner: Church

One of downtown Montreal's most valuable pieces of undeveloped property is the city block located between Place Bonaventure and the Château Champlain Hotel.

At more than two acres, it is one of downtown's biggest parking lots.

The only sign of proprietorship is that of Servoparc Inc. It rents the land from the private group of Canadian real estate interests now helping put up the La Cité project 10 blocks to the north.

But the ultimate landlord — to whom the real estate group pays $225,000 annually as part of a 99-year lease — is one of the various branches of the Roman Catholic Church, in this case the Archdiocese of Montreal.

Michael Dugas

The Servoparc parking lot which belongs to the Archdiocese.

This piece of real estate is part of the largely unperceived, never-tabulated skein of Church landholdings in Montreal. It illustrates the secular uses to which religious land is frequently being put.

No other large city on this continent, north of Mexico, contains proportionately as much real estate owned by a religious institution as does Montreal — with the exception of Salt Lake City, where the Mormon church holds centre stage.

The true extent of the Church's holdings here has long been a baffling mystery. Even the Church's local financial experts, accountants and its lay lawyers — the people who would know if anyone does this side of the Vatican — told The Gazette they could not name more than half a dozen or so holdings of 10 acres or more and that neither they, nor the Church, has any need to know more.

They point out that what is termed "the Church" is in reality an agglomeration of hundreds of separate groups, each with its own parcels of tax-free land and that there is no clearing-house for their financial data.

As the archdiocese's comptroller, Canon Jules Delorme puts it, in order to obtain even a rough estimate of how much land is involved "you'd need a Royal Commission."

Stymied urban affairs experts say that because of the sheer size of these holdings and the frequency with which they are being disposed of, an inventory of these properties is essential for informed land-use policy and planning.

The Gazette today presents the most comprehensive account ever published of Church real estate here. It includes an inventory of 25 of the largest holdings here [ranging from] 10 acres to over 400 acres in size. It is based on a piecing-together of data culled [from] computerized evaluation rolls of municipalities across the Island of Montreal.

This data, while incomplete, shows at the very least that the Church is by far the biggest private landowner in the City of Montreal. It is also the biggest on the Island of Montreal.

By conservative estimate, organizations which are directly or indirectly answerable to the Vatican own at least 2,500 acres on the island. That's about four square miles, or bigger than 14 of the 29 municipalities on the island.

This is well in excess of the land controlled by the largest private business corporation, Canadian Pacific Ltd. with its prime downtown properties and vast railyards.

These acreage statistics do not reflect — in both potential monetary and recreational terms — the extraordinary value of much of the undeveloped Church land.

Within the City of Montreal alone, for example, there are over 900 acres of non-parish, non-cemetery land; they are mostly in the form of open, little-used tracts belonging to religious congregations.

These tracts — ranging from Villa Maria's 38 acres in N.D.G. to St. Jean-de-Dieu's 340 acres on the East End — represent even more undeveloped land than that occupied by the European-owned quarries.

The immensity of the Church's real estate here is, of course, the legacy of the island's original settlement in the 17th century by a French religious order for the purpose of converting Indians to Christianity.

This order — called the Society of Notre Dame of Montreal for the Conversion of the Savages of New France — held on to the island only 21 years before asking the Sulpician order to take over its missionary task — and with it the ownership of every square foot of this 180-square-mile (or 114,000 acre) island.

The Sulpicians disposed of much of their property through gift (often to other religious communities), sale or other arrangements. Today their biggest individual holding consists of a mere 36 acres — albeit it one of the most valuable properties downtown — in the area near Atwater and Sherbrooke Sts.

They sought to sell to developers several years ago before being blocked by preservationists. Their only other major property is the 20-acre College Grasset at 1001 Cremazie Blvd. E.

With verifiable holdings of at least 2,500 acres (and perhaps in reality closer to 3,500 if all were known), the Church overall now owns two or three per cent of the island's territory.

That may not seem like much but land ownership in Montreal is extremely fragmented. Studies of other parts of the country indicate that no other metropolitan area in Canada is divided into nearly so many hands.

The Church's holdings are also highly fragmented.

Most of the major landholdings here belong to the 130 or so religious congregations [also called religious communities] on the island. These groups communicate often with each other on spiritual matters but seldom if ever on such "temporal affairs" as property, notes a tax advisor to numerous local congregations, Brother Pierre-Paul Gougeon.

Loose control over the destiny of the more important pieces of property (including virtually all of The Gazette's list of 25 of the largest) lies with the Vatican. "If religious congregations want to sell an expensive property, they need the permission of Rome." says Brother Pierre-Paul.

Almost any proposed sale of property for more than $300,000 requires the Vatican's stamp of approval, says Father Louis Telmosse, director of the archdiocese's Office for Religious.

Religious congregations, of course, are but one of the Church's two principal wings here. The other is the archdiocese — more formally known as the Archepiscopal Roman Catholic Corporation of Montreal. It includes 256 parishes, of which roughly 200 are on the Island of Montreal.

The archdiocese itself owns only a modest amount of property. Besides the aforementioned Servoparc parking lot, which is located directly behind the cathedral, it owns the cathedral and its headquarters building at 2000 Sherbrooke St. W.

The bulk of property is owned by the parishes. This land tends also to consist of small tracts — Canon Delorme estimates they average 35,000 square feet — less than an acre.

For the record, it may be noted that the archdiocese calculates the 1975 assets for its 256 parish properties — which includes both land and buildings — at $139,416,926. This does not include congregations' property.

As a gauge of true market value, however, these figures are meaningless. The assets are determined by the price of the properties when they were bought — often generations ago.

Sisters own 482 acres

The largest single piece of religious property on the Island of Montreal belongs to the Sisters of the Holy Name of Jesus and Mary.

It stretches out over 482 acres of fields and woods on Cap St. Jacques in the western reaches of Pierrefonds.

The population density is probably the lowest on the entire island; one person for more than every one and a half square miles.

Fewer than 30 people live there, estimates one sister. These include 16 sisters, several farmers and two families who rent houses on the land.

"It is," she notes, "one of the few beautiful corners left on the island."

The MUC for years has talked about transforming the cape into a 970-acre regional park.

But so far it has taken no action.

The sisters say they will sell their land to the MUC if it asks for it. But some neighboring private land-owners on the cape have expressed a willingness to bring in housing developers.

Church's major holdings untangled for first time

Here is the first list ever published of major real estate holdings of the Roman Catholic Church on the Island of Montreal.

The list of the 25 biggest properties is based on a search of thousands of computerized pages of municipal evaluation records across the island.

To give readers a rough idea of the properties' values, the list includes their a) number of acres, b) 1975 evaluation of land, an assessment by municipal officials of what the land is worth for taxation purposes and c) the combined evaluation of both the land and the buildings on it.

The tax value of the buildings can be deduced by subtracting the land evaluation from the combined evaluation.

As a rule of thumb, a property's market value is 10-25 per cent more than its evaluation.

In practical terms, the evaluation of these properties by municipal officials is a meaningless exercise since the property owners, charitable institutions, generally pay no property taxes.

	acres	land	land & bldg	owner
▪80-90 Rosemont ▪vd., Montreal	11.8	$639,000	$2,020,000	Soeurs Franciscaines Missionnaires de l'Immaculée Conception
▪6 Senneville Rd., ▪nneville	12.3	$105,590	$193,990	Religieuses Hospitalières de St. Joseph de Montréal
▪75-5605 Beaubien St. E. ▪ontréal	13.1	$713,500	$3,470,000	Petites Soeurs des Pauvres
▪t, Rousselière St. ▪inte-aux-Trembles	14.5	$111,800	$111,800	Pères Capucins du Québec
▪00 Côte Vertu, ▪lle St. Laurent	14.6	$509,375	$4,122,700	Corp. des Soeurs de Ste. Croix et des Sept Douleurs
▪80 Côte des ▪eiges Rd., Montreal	16.2	$2,759,000	$3,366,600	Prêtres du Séminaire du St. Sulpice
▪5-768 18 Ave. E. ▪chine	18.0	$606,360	$606,360	Soeurs de Ste. Anne
▪0 Bouchard Blvd., ▪rval	19.2	$629,420	$1,166,220	Soeurs de Ste. Anne
▪01 Cremazie Blvd E. ▪ontreal	20.6	$1,900,800	$3,258,800	Ecclésiastiques du Séminaire de St. Sulpice ("Collège André Grasset")
▪t, Bois Franc ▪lle St. Laurent	20.6	$575,525	$575,525	Soeurs Grises
▪t, Vincent ▪ndy Ave, Outremont	21.4	$932,400	$932,400	Fabrique Notre Dame, 4601 Côte des Neiges Rd.
▪00-3820 Queen Mary ▪., Montreal	22.3	$1,867,700	$13,741,500	Oratoire St. Joseph
▪269 Gouin Blvd. W, ▪rrefonds	25.0	—	—	Soeurs de Ste. Croix
▪etropolitan Blvd., ▪inte-aux-Trembles ▪dastre 22 P207)	25.4	$259,600	$259,600	Pères Capucins du Québec
▪0 Rousselière ▪, Pointe-aux-Trembles	26.2	$201,700	$907,500	Pères Capucins du Québec
▪0 Côte Ste. ▪therine, Montreal	27.6	$2,681,000	$6,747,000	Corp. du Collège Jean de Brébeuf
▪5 Gouin Blvd. W., ▪ntreal	28.3	$830,400	$1,532,000	Hôpital du Sacré Coeur
▪1-2065 Sherbrooke W. and ▪0-3880 Côte des ▪ges, Montreal	29.8	$8,660,800	$10,900,000	Prêtres de St. Sulpices
▪5 De Salaberry Montreal	30.5	$1,829,250	$6,729,200	Communauté des Soeurs de la Charité de la Providence
▪0-5600 Gouin ▪d., Montreal	38.6	$1,906,600	$12,081,500	Hôpital du Sacré Coeur

4245 Décarie Blvd., and 700 Claremont Ave., Montreal	38.7	$3,958,900	$5,068,000	Soeurs de Congrégation c Notre Dan ("Villa Maria"
Lot, Gouin Blvd. W., Montreal (Cadastre 11 P94, etc.)	42.1	$355,100	$355,100	Hôpital Du Sac Coe
7025-7225 Maurice-Duplessis Blvd., Mtl	73.0	$800,000	$8,422,000	Collège Mar Victor
3745-91 Queen Mary Rd., Montreal	195.6	$2,718,700	$6,564,500	Collège Not Dame du Sacré Coe
Route 25 and Hochelaga St., East End	340.0 (est.)	–	–	Soeurs de la Providen ("St. Jean-de-Dieu
Cap St. Jacques, Pierrefonds	482.0 (est.)	–	–	Soeurs des Saints Non de Jésus et de Ma

In the days after this article appeared my phone started ringing with people making complaints — the only complaints made at all vis à vis the entire 15-part series in The Gazette. The callers wanted to know why I had "picked on" — as one put it — the Roman Catholics. Why didn't I write about what the Anglican Church owned or the Jewish congregations? The answer, which seemed to satisfy most callers, was that these other institutions simply did not own nearly as much land. Writing about the Roman Catholic holdings was not a matter of bias; the series, by definition, focused only on the major holdings.

Then in January the following article appeared in the Catholic Times, a monthly newspaper associated with the Archdiocese of Montreal.

Gazette Article Off Base
Church Not No. 1 Landowner
By Barry A. Jones

The Montreal Gazette in a series of articles about Who Owns Montreal recently attempted a review of the "Church's" property holdings in Montreal. Written by Henry Aubin, the article has about it an air of look what I found.

Unerringly when the major premise of an article is wrong the conclusions are likely to be wrong. An accompanying article in The Gazette opened with the paragraph: "Here is the first list ever published of major real estate holdings of the Roman Catholic Church on the Island of Montreal". What follows is a list of properties owned by various religious communities in Montreal. Mr. Aubin has made the mistake of concluding that these properties are owned by the "Church". They are, in fact, owned and controlled by the religious communities which are private, non-profit corporations. They are administered solely by the communities themselves and are, under civil law, be-holden to no one but themselves.*

Being members of the Roman Catholic Church, a community of believers, religious orders and communities have a moral requirement under Canon Law (but not under civil law) to consult with the appropriate Vatican congregation before selling major property holdings.

As Mr. Aubin reported: "Most of the major landholdings belong to 130 or so religious congregations on the Island. These groups communicate often with each other on spiritual affairs but seldom if ever on 'temporal affairs', notes a tax advisor to

* Dr. Jones' article challenging mine bears a certain resemblance to the Vatican's response in its newspaper, L'Osservatore Romano, at about the same time to statements in L'Europeo in early January 1977 charging that the Holy See owned one fourth of Rome and was indulging in real estate speculation; Corriere della Sera followed up with a critical editorial on the "Sack of Rome", to which L'Osservatore also replied. Essentially, L'Osservatore stressed the distinctions between the Holy See, the diocese of Rome, and the substantially autonomous religious congregations and ecclesiastical associations and sought to discredit the reporter's findings on grounds he had lumped everything together.

numerous local congregations, Brother Pierre-Paul Gougeon".

The legal name of the archdiocese which united in a moral structure all the parishes of the archdiocese is La Corporation Archiépiscopale Catholique Romaine de Montréal. It owns very little property. An office building at 2000 Sherbrooke Street, West, which serves as the administrative headquarters of the archdiocese, and the Basilique Marie Reine du Monde together with the attached residence. With but one exception that is all.

The exception is a block of land situated between the Château Champlain and the Bonaventure Trade Centre which has been leased to private developers. In effect, under the terms of the 99 year lease, control of the property is in the hands of the lessee. The annual rental revenues of $225,000. are used to help pay the administrative costs of the archdiocese. Further revenues are accrued through a 7% tax levied on the gross revenues of each parish. (For 1975-76 the operating deficit of the archdiocesan corporation is $573,029.)

Parish Properties

All parish churches are owned by individual corporations called "la Fabrique". The parish corporation is administered by a pastor who is appointed by the Archbishop and wardens elected from among the parishoners. The wardens serve without remuneration for a period not exceeding three years. The pastor and wardens are required to administer the fabrique solely for the benefit of the parishioners. The archepiscopal corporation cannot appropriate or direct the property or other holdings of a parish.

"The true extent of the Church's holdings here has long been a baffling mystery" would be a true statement if the properties held by Roman Catholic affiliated organizations were so done in the manner implied by Mr. Aubin.

Urban affairs planners need not be stymied, as Mr. Aubin states they are, by the proliferation of properties owned by religious communities. They simply have to treat them separately and for what they are: properties owned by private, non-profit and legally established corporations. They enjoy certain tax benefits because they earn no profits from which taxes are generally paid. Hundreds of organizations, religious and non-religious, enjoy such benefits.

In the matter of actual cash worth, Mr. Aubin also *errs*. Property evaluations are just that, generally made for the purposes of taxation. The real cash value of a property can only be determined when an offer for sale is made and a potential buyer declares what he is prepared to pay for the property. What is the real value of a parish church property upon which stands a single-purpose and highly unadaptable structure such as a church? Or the real value of a 75-year-old convent? The same evaluation versus real value can be made, by way of example, of the Olympic Stadium of which it is said by one government minister to be a white elephant.

The exploration of the fabled wealth of the Roman Catholic Church will continue no doubt, but it is hoped that future explorers will attempt to be objective. Clearly, a title to a property which earns no revenues and whose real value is largely diminished by the structure which stands upon the property does not make the titleholder a rich landowner.

The "Church" is not a vast holding company. It is not a legal entity and it owns nothing. It is an assembly of believers. The legal non-profit organizations such as religious communities who are members of that assembly are, for the most part and in themselves, the legal holders and controllers of their own temporal affairs.

Contrary to the "Church's major holdings (being) untangled for the first time" as headlined in The Gazette, Mr. Aubin's article has only added to the confusion. The "Church" is not Montreal's number one landowner.

The article had depicted me as incompetent. One of the librarians at The Gazette, who subscribed to The Catholic Times, told me coldly, "Boy, did you ever goof. The Gazette should print a retraction."

I called Barry A. Jones, the author, and asked if it might be possible to write a reply which could be published in The Catholic Times. He said he would be happy to publish such a letter and he suggested I mail it to him personally since, it turned out, he was chairman of the Times' editorial board (as well as a spokesman for the Archdiocese).

20 January, 1977

for requested publication
attn: Mr. B.A. Jones

The Catholic Times
2000 Ouest, rue Sherbrooke
Montreal, Quebec H3H 1G4

Sir:

Please allow me to respond to charges against me which appeared in January's *Catholic Times* under the byline of Barry A. Jones, chairman of the *Times'* editorial board and a public relations representative of the Archdiocese. His front page article (headlined "Church Not the No. 1 Landowner — Gazette Article Off Base") deals with an article in the Montreal *Gazette* of Dec. 14, 1976. It was part of a 15-part series of articles titled "Who Owns Montreal?"

Mr. Jones disputes my conclusion that various branches of the Roman Catholic Church are, collectively, "by far the biggest private landowner" in both the City of Montreal and the Island of Montreal.

He seeks to discredit that conclusion as "wrong" by introducing two arguments, both of them red herrings:

1. Mr. Jones suggests that my article treats "the Church" as a monolithic institution. In fact, early in the article I quote ecclesiastics as noting that "what is termed 'the Church' is in reality an agglomeration of hundreds of separate groups." Later it is further pointed out that the Island of Montreal's 130 or more religious congregations "seldom if ever" communicate with each other on such temporal affairs as property. Some monolith. Where are we in conflict?

2. He says, "In the matter of actual cash worth (of properties), Mr. Aubin also errs. He says the property evaluations which I list for 23 properties ranging in size from 11 to 195 acres are "generally made for the purposes of taxation" rather than actually reflecting the "real cash value" of properties. How true. And how very much in line with what I had written; my story explicitly states that the evaluations are "for tax purposes" and that there is usually a sharp discrepancy between evaluation and market value.

For all the verbal dust the *Times* article kicks up, we are in conflict on no other specific points, either.

Unfortunately, someone reading the *Times* article without looking back to the *Gazette* of Dec. 14 might easily come away with the impression that I am indeed "off base."

It is also puzzling that I was not contacted prior to your article's publication and given the opportunity to reply at once to such personal criticism. This is basic fairplay for articles appearing on news pages; it is incorporated into many newspapers' codes of ethics.

St. Peter's in Rome. The Vatican must approve all sales of land exceeding $300,000 by religious congregations, or communities, in Montreal.

Incidentally, I received no substantive help from anyone I contacted among the major religious communities. People said they were not secretively witholding information — rather, they said they simply did not know much about the entire question of property. So be it. It was much the same story from the big land development companies I approached as well. Fine. I then looked through thousands of computerized pages of property records belonging to municipalities throughout the island, looking for land belonging to secular and religious institutions alike. After double-checking my data with the main religious communities, this conclusion (as quoted from the article) was unescapable:

"By conservative estimate, organizations which are directly or indirectly answerable to the Vatican own at least 2,500 acres on the island. That's more than four square miles, or bigger than 14 of the 29 municipalities on the island."

This makes "the Church," as so defined, the No. 1 private landowner.

If this conclusion can be challenged on the basis of the facts and not shaky semantics I would be delighted.

In my series there is no question of a vendetta against the various branches of this or any other religion. Of the 15 articles in the series, the other 14 dealt with private, secular organizations ranging from those registered in Liechtenstein to Toronto. The story on the various branches of the Church appeared quite far back, I believe eleventh in the series.

On a more personal note, may I add that if all these various landowners were to be presented in order of the social good they have done, and on the basis of the utility and happiness they have brought the Montreal public, the story of the holdings of the various branches of the Church would have to be presented first — far and away. Indeed, rather than just an article it would take many, many volumes!

Sincerely,
Henry Aubin

The next edition of The Catholic Times came out but the letter did not appear in it.

Then this arrived in the mail:

February 23, 1977.

Mr. Henry Aubin
The Montreal Gazette Limited
1000 St. Antoine Street
Montreal H3C 3R7

Dear Mr. Aubin,

Thank you for your letter of January 20, 1977 enclosing your views of the article on property owned by religious institutions which appeared in The Catholic Times' January issue.

Your letter was presented to the editorial board at its last meeting. It is the opinion of the board that sufficient material has been presented on the subject and that further publication of views would serve no purpose, especially since The Gazette had devoted a full page to your articles.

With our best wishes.

Yours sincerely,
Barry A. Jones
Chairman — Editorial Board

So much for promoting secular truth.

Father Jones (yes, it turns out that Mr. Jones is a parish vicar) is quite correct when he says the larger land-holdings are in the hands of *non-profit* organizations. But until recently Vatican-related interests have been among the leaders in the profit-oriented, speculative real estate syndrome which is at the root of Montreal's transformation.

In fact, in the 1960s these Vatican-related interests built Montreal's modern-day temple of capital and profit, the Stock Exchange Tower. They also built the most luxurious and most expensive residential high-rise in the city, the Port Royal Apartments.

The Pope's involvement in the development of these buildings has been the subject of local gossip for years, but few concrete facts have been in circulation. Here is a rundown.

The Vatican's involvement was through a Rome-based firm, Società Generale Immobiliare. This is one of the world's larg-

Michael Dugas
Place Victoria's Stock Exchange Tower, the tallest building in Montreal, and the Hotel Régence Hyatt, the city's newest luxury hotel, are both owned by Immobiliare.

est real estate development companies — bigger, even, than London's English Property Corp., ultimate owner of Place Ville Marie.

Until the Vatican sold most of its indirect interest in the company in 1969, Immobiliare was "the main stronghold of the Vatican financial empire," says an investigative book by Corrado Pallenberg, "Vatican Finances.[1] Pallenberg, noting that four of the firm's nine directors were Church financiers, says "the Vatican strictly controlled (Immobiliare) for many decades by owning only 15 per cent of the shares."

It was during this period that the company built the Stock Exchange Tower at Place Victoria, which opened in 1965. Forty-seven floors high, it is still Montreal's tallest building.

Since the building was developed around the needs of one of its main tenants, the Montreal Stock Exchange, the Vatican held the peculiar position of being patron and landlord of the symbolic citadel of secular business.

This kind of mixture of religion and business underscores a broader pattern. Indeed, some observers have found it hard to reconcile the concept of the Pope as the representative of Christ on earth with that of the head of a global financial empire.

Pallenberg, the Rome correspondent for the London Sunday Telegraph, is one of them. In penetrating the secrecy with which the Church invests money it receives from collections, Pallenberg discovered what he calls a possible "contradiction between the official doctrine of the Church of Rome, as embodied in the encyclical *Populorum progressio,* and her current financial practices.

"The encyclical strongly condemns liberal capitalism, but the Vatican, as a financial entity, has close ties with such arch-capitalistic institutions as the Rothschilds of France, Britain and America, Hambros Bank in Britain, the Credit Suisse in Zurich and London and, across the Atlantic, the Chase Manhattan Bank, the Bankers Trust Co., the First National Bank of New York and the Morgan Bank.

"It also," Pallenberg continues, "owns shares in several of the world's giant international corporations including General Motors, Shell, Gulf Oil, General Electric, Bethlehem Steel, IBM, TWA..."[2]

To his amusement, he also notes, "The situation becomes ironical when one considers that the Istituto Farmacologico Serono (pharmaceuticals), in which the Vatican is interested, is currently making the pill which the Pope has condemned."

Pope Paul has on occasion referred to the Roman Catholic Church as the "Church of the Poor". But, in building the Port Royale, which opened in 1965 at 1455 Sherbrooke St. W., Immobiliare was evidently not catering to the ideal of poverty of St. Francis of Assisi. The going price for ownership of a modest 3½-room suite on the 21st floor is $67,200. The only other such complex which can compare to it today in price is Westmount Square.

Says Pallenberg: "Naturally, those who run the finances of the Holy See are not out to make a personal profit, but to gain money in order to use it to spread the Gospel and for humanitarian purposes. But it is hard to accept that so much Vatican capital should be invested to build luxury hotels, residential quarters with golf courses and swimming pools, and that it should make a profit out of the shares of Radio Corporation of America, Italy's biggest maker of dance music records."[3]

The Vatican's sale of most of its interest in Immobiliare in 1969 was part of a revamped investment strategy. To see how the Vatican sees its financial role, it is worth looking at an explanation of that period given by Cardinal Egidio Vagnozzi, head of the Prefecture of Economic Affairs, to U.S. journalist Paul Horne:

"When the Pope explained that we need more money and are a poor Church, he meant exactly that. We, the managers, want to improve investment performance, balanced of course against what must be a fundamentally conservative investment philosophy.

"It wouldn't do for the Church to lose its principal in speculation. This is even more important as major currencies depreciate and costs rise.

"We have decided to avoid attempting to maintain control of companies in which we invest, as was done in the past... This means we are getting away from the practice of lay Vatican fiduciaries sitting on the boards of companies in which we invested. The Vatican simply cannot afford primary responsibility for business failures requiring transfusions of capital...

"We are reducing our real estate holdings and increasing securities investments.

"The Vatican's investment policy remains basically conservative, although the Church's increasing needs mean that the balance between conservation and the need to increase income has been moving towards the need to increase income."

Just how much stock does the Vatican own in Immobiliare today?

The basic connection "was effectively liquidated by 1971," says Hugo Facci, vice president of Immobiliare's key local subsidiary, Place Victoria-St. Jacques Co. Ltd.

It is possible the Vatican still has a residual interest, he says, but it is not significant.

Immobiliare itself, however, remains a giant.

It owns housing projects in California, is building an airport at Nairobi, sells high-rises in Paris and remains, of course, Italy's largest builder. In 1977 it controlled 120 companies, of which about 70 are outside Italy.[5] Perhaps its most famous property is Washington's Watergate apartment complex.

In Montreal it still owns, in addition to the Stock Exchange Tower and the Port Royal, land for development in Pierrefonds, Dollard-des-Ormeaux and Ile-Bizard. On the West Island it developed, during its papal period, a housing project called "Greendale." But today it is instead selling land to other firms for development. It has sold some land on Ile-Bizard, for example, to the U.S. homebuilder Kaufman & Broad, Inc., says Facci.

Also, it completed development in October, 1977, of the Hyatt-Regency Hotel, a 37-floor tower located next to the Stock Exchange Tower. Its 768 rooms place it among the three or four largest hotels in Montreal.

While Chicago's Hyatt International manages the hotel, the hotel and its land is actually owned by the Immobiliare group. The group, in turn, is renting it on a 50-year emphyteutic lease to a partnership called Regence Associates.

Place Victoria-St. Jacques is a 50 per cent partner but "sort of controls the partnership", says Facci. The other partner is called Refco-Montreal Inc. and is owned by several U.S. groups, he says.

Who owns Immobiliare since the Vatican got out?

That's a dramatic saga in itself. The firm has been squired by some of the world's leading private organizations. And in the process it has become further intertwined with some familiar forces in this book on the many interests that are helping transform Montreal.

Indeed, Immobiliare provides yet another illustration of the 'small world' syndrome whereby a few massive global interests reappear again and again in various corporate incarnations as forces in Canada's urban development.

First, says Pallenberg, most of the Vatican's shares were sold to the Paribas group, one of France's two principal financial-industrial axes. This is the same organization which today is the largest shareholder in another substantial Montreal land-owner, Crédit Foncier Franco-Canadien. By coincidence, this gave Paribas a major indirect holding in the two biggest buildings overlooking the park at Victoria Square — Crédit Foncier's headquarters is catty-corner to the Stock Exchange Tower.

But Paribas was really buying on behalf of a banking client, Charles Bluhdorn, president of the U.S.-owned Gulf & Western conglomerate to be described in the next chapter.[6] Bluhdorn and another G & W executive, Don Goston, were both named to Immobiliare's board of directors in 1970.

However, G & W's stay in Immobiliare was brief.

Taking control of Immobiliare after Gulf & Western was famed Milan financier Michele Sindona, now under indictment for alleged offenses unrelated to Immobiliare. Born in Sicily as the son of farm-cooperative employees, Sindona accumulated a fortune as a lawyer and financier which was estimated at $450 million in his Immobiliare heyday.

Thus the Montreal Stock Exchange now had Michele Sindona as its ultimate landlord. In fact, Sindona controlled it through a Liechtenstein holding company; as said in the opening chapter, Liechtenstein companies own some pretty big properties, and in Montreal this is the biggest one of all.

The small world syndrome does not end here. Sindona had a close financial relationship with the Vatican and also with London's Hambros Bank, a key Vatican banker for generations. As noted in Chap. 5, the Hambro family is another par-

ticipant in Canadian real estate, being active through such vehicles as Union Corp., of Johannesburg, and Hambro Canada
Ltd., of Toronto.

Financial analysts say one of the causes of Sindona's un-
doing was his attempt to take over Italy's largest holding company, Bastogi,* in conjunction with the Hambros. After the
attempt failed, Sindona's relationship with the Hambros
deteriorated. One factor was the retirement of Jocelyn Hambro, Sindona's longtime friend, and his succession by a more
skeptical cousin, Charles Hambro.[7]

In October, 1974, two orders for Sindona's arrest on fraud
charges were issued in Milan. Sindona fled to New York City,
where he lived in high style at the Hotel Pierre for almost two
years. In September, 1976, he surrendered to U.S. officials in
New York on a warrant for his extradition to Italy. He is
charged with fraudulently taking the equivalent of about $225
million from the Banca Privata and two predecessor banks.

Almost ignored in the dustup was Sindona's resignation in
1974 from the board of Immobiliare. His more than 30 per
cent interest in Immobiliare — collateral for earlier loans — was
taken over by the state-controlled Banca di Roma.

The bank, not wanting to operate the real estate company itself, sold the controlling interest to a group of eleven Italian
real estate developers.

The group, which includes such men as Arcangelo Belli and
Roberto Tana, are frequently termed "palazzinari" by the Italian press. It is a slightly derogatory term for large developers,
suggesting a *nouveau riche* flair for the ostentatious.

In 1976, the newsweekly Espresso interviewed Belli in his
Roman villa,[8] styled "midway between gothic and late-fascist"
with a Rolls Royce and telephone-equipped Mercedes lined up
outside.

Why, asked the magazine's reporter, did he and his colleagues buy Immobiliare?

---

* To further thicken the coincidences, Bastogi owned a pivotal block of
shares in Montedison, the massive industrial firm headed by Eugenio
Cefis, whose extensive real estate interests in Montreal were touched on in
Chap. 2. In fact, the Cefis companies are holed up on the twenty-first floor
of — you guessed it — the Stock Exchange Tower.

Michele Sindona, who surrendered here.

The New York Times

Sindona to Face Charges in Italy After Surrender

Financier Is Released on $3 Million Bond

By TERRY ROBARDS

Michele Sindona, the Italian financier who held a major interest in the Franklin National Bank when it failed in 1974, surrendered here yesterday on a warrant for his extradition to Italy to face fraud charges there.

Mr. Sindona, who had vowed repeatedly that he would never return to his native country unless the charges were dropped, was taken into custody at the Federal ... Foley Square ... was

Michele Sindona took over control of Immobiliare shortly after the Vatican sold its controlling interest.

New York Times, Sept. 9, 1976

Belli: "... we all knew Immobiliare was the only concern which in years to come could become a reference and turning point in the changes which will occur in the construction industry. So far we have lived the era of cars; now we will live the era of new use of the land, cities, hospitals and schools."

Espresso: "Very good. You must feel guilty for what you did to our cities then. And how do you want to 'arrange' them now?"

Belli: "... alone I am a nobody; as Immobiliare I can express myself."

Montreal awaits his self-expression.

Footnotes — Chapter 11

1. Pallenberg, Corrado, Vatican Finances (Harmondsworth, England: Penguin Books Ltd., 1973), p. 110.
2. Ibid., pp. 181-2.
3. Ibid., p. 180.
4. As quoted by Pallenberg, p. 195.
5. Financial Times of London, Mar. 25, 1977, "SGI to make public offering."
6. Pallenberg, op. cit., p. 194.
7. Fortune magazine, Aug., 1973, p. 111, "What's behind the Sindona Invasion?" by Don Cordtz.
8. L'Espresso, Feb. 8, 1976, p. 95, "Vorrei baciare i tuoi palazzi d'oro."

Chapter 12
Yankee Peril

IN THE HEART OF MONTREAL giant cranes recently completed yet another tower of the La Cité complex — or, as it was known during more controversial times, Cité Concordia.

The Gazette (George Cree)

La Cité *(foreground and background).*
Canadians started the five-tower project, Americans finished it.

Along with the change in name, there is a change in the people who determine the nature of the five-block project — and thereby help decide the character of much of the downtown area. The privately-owned project's partners refuse to discuss the matter. But an inside source says ultimate control has passed from Canadian hands to a group of Chicago-based businessmen.

If anything, the arrival of such U.S. interests is remarkable because it is so uncommon. With only a few exceptions, one has to go well outside the downtown area before encountering U.S. ownership of other major land-holdings.

Despite U.S. corporations' record of dominating many sectors of Canadian business, they lag far behind European interests in buying and transforming Montreal.

Though there are no published statistics, there are growing signs that there are actually fewer U.S. interests buying and developing urban land in Canada than there are Canadian-based companies — controlled by either Canadians or Europeans — buying and developing U.S. urban property in U.S. cities.

One centrally placed Montreal-born broker, who has been wooing foreign capital of every description for over a decade, spits on the floor when asked about the U.S.

Its influence here is "minimal," he says. "Top influence here is the U.K. After that it's Italy and Germany — they're very close together."

The Americans, then, are just one of a horde of foreign groups who have rushed to this investment Klondike called Montreal.

These foreigners have been buying land, either for speculation or long-term land-banks. They have been putting up the major high-rise complexes and residential developments — and often have a vested interest in them since they also control the companies which sell the raw materials for this kind of development.

They have been building the highways, blasting the subway tunnels, even digging the sewers which in their way allow further metropolitan expansion. They have been even building the distant power projects which are helping spur the overall development climate.

To be sure, they are not doing it all. Not by a long shot. In every category Canadians contribute substantially. But in general these Canadian participants are small- or middle-range outfits. They don't give the direction to what's happening. They conform to the patterns and overall tone set by the dominant interests which are foreign.

In this imported dynamism, Americans play a secondary role. This is not to say Uncle Sam is not big — he is. It is a question of scale. Measured next to the Europeans he makes them look like giants.

Here are some highlights of U.S. stature here:

— The Gulf Oil group, quite aside from owning hundreds of acres in the East End for its pollution-rich refinery, owns more than three square miles of prime land on the South Shore at Laprairie. That makes it one of the two largest privately-owned pieces of land in the entire region, says a Gulf spokesman. (The only thing bigger is the Campeau Corp.'s chunk of Ile Bizard.) Gulf, which bought most of its farmland from the Church, started construction in 1976 on a residential community planned for 30,000 people by 1990.

— The International Telephone & Telegraph Corp. is building suburban housing projects through its Levitt Canada Ltd. subsidiary. Its two biggest projects are at Pierrefonds (1,000 homes planned) and Brossard (1,500 planned), it says. It also owns land in Dollard-des-Ormeaux.

— ITT, through its subsidiary, Canadawide Parking Services Ltd., also is far and away the largest operator of parking lots in Montreal (and the country as a whole). It has 50 parking lots and garages here which the company says allow it to accommodate 28,000 cars at one time — or, by its own estimate, 30 per cent of all parking space in downtown Montreal, including that run by the city government.

— Kaufman & Broad Inc., which calls itself "America's largest multinational housing producer," owns land for developments in Kirkland, Ile Bizard and near the 9000-block of Gouin Blvd. W. in Montreal. It has already built bungalow development on much of this land, including the "Timberlea" project in western Kirkland.

— Metropolitan Structures Inc., a private Chicago company, has leased Nun's Island and is developing it as a community for thousands of persons.

— A company called VK Estates Ltd., in which Miami residents Herman Isis and Alex Engelstein are directors, is one of the half dozen leading developers in Dollard-des-Ormeaux. Samuel P. Sherdell, of New York, is one of the three major landowners in Dorval. And two of Brossard's top 10 landowners are also from the States: the Seltzer Organization, of Philadelphia, and Laprairie Shopping Centre Ltd., owned by Aaron Green and family, of New York.

— In Montreal's dowtown area, one of the most prestigious U.S. development firms, The Rouse Co., worked on the "Les Terrasses" project at de Maisonneuve Blvd. and McGill College Ave.

— YUL Associates, an Illinois partnership, is the group calling the shots at the La Cité project, according to Frederick Clark, secretary to the trustees of Britain's Post Office Staff Superannuation Fund, an ex-officio member of La Cité's management board. With its five towers, La Cité is the fourth largest high-rise complex in town in terms of floor space. If and when more of the remaining 18 of the project's 25 acres are developed, it should be the largest by far.

— Gulf & Western Industries Inc., of New York, through its 51 per cent ownership of Famous Players Ltd., owns the 24-floor Capitol Centre. Built in 1976, it covers a complete city block bounded by St. Catherine, Mansfield, Cathcart and McGill College Streets, in the shadow of Place Ville Marie.

— And, of course, there is the genius behind Place Ville Marie itself, the late William Zeckendorf, Sr. Often called one of the most influential individuals in the shaping of this city over the past two decades, the New Yorker and his company masterminded PVM, in the early 1960's. It is still the city's largest office complex.

At first glance, such a list of highlights might seem to vault the U.S. into its celebrated role as the Mr. Big.

However, closely comparing many of these projects, with those of other national groups, the relative importance of U.S. interests here appears to be qualified.

The answer to the question, "Is the U.S. influential in transforming Montreal?" would seem to be "Yes, but . . ."

Thus ITT and Kaufman & Board may both have launched substantial housing developments, but their combined total of homes here is still overshadowed by those built here by European-backed companies.

ITT may be downtown Montreal's parking impresario, but it owns only one of its 50 lots, leasing the rest, mostly from Canadian or European owners. It is these owners who, in general, have power to decide what is done with the land. (Incidentally, though ITT is the major owner of Canadawide's parent company, Avis Inc., as well as of Levitt, it is under a U.S. court order to divest itself of both. In the meantime it has ownership without control.)

Rouse may have developed "Les Terrasses," but British (Standard Life Assurance) and French (Banque Dreyfus) interests still own more of the project.

YUL may have controlled La Cité for the last several years, but the most controversial decisions for that project were made by the previous owners, a Canadian company. It was associates of that company, Concordia Estates Ltd., which in 1958 began buying up more than 250 houses in the six-block area. They bought them through "about half a dozen" differently-named companies in order to "retain the confidentiality of our intentions," as one of them, Concordia director Norman Nerenberg, puts it. And it was these Canadians who then ousted the residents and bulldozed many of the four-storey homes to make way for the towers.

As for William Zeckendorf, he may have been the high-rolling entrepreneur who developed PVM, but he and his company lost ownership of it well before the complex was ever completed, victims of their own "house of cards" financing. It was the British who carried the project through and who ultimately own it today — along with more commercial property than any other group in town.

Certain other prominent local properties which are commonly supposed to be U.S. generated are in fact not. There are some eight large high-rise Holiday Inn franchises in the metropolitan area, for example. Five of them are operated by Atlific Inns Inc., 50.02 per cent owned by Quebecer Jacques Lalonde, brother of former Quebec liberal cabinet minister Fernand Lalonde. The other three are owned by Commonwealth Holiday Inns of Canada Ltd., of London, Ont. Holiday Inns, Inc., of Tennessee, the wellspring of the worldwide chain, says the 27

William Zeckendorf, Sr. the entrepreneurial dynamo behind Place Ville Marie, in his New York City penthouse shortly before his death in 1976.

per cent it owns of Commonwealth is enough to make it a subsidiary; a Commonwealth spokesman, however, says the majority of the shares are Canadian-owned. In addition, their hotel properties — including the skyscraper which was planned as the "world's largest Holiday Inn" now awaiting completion near Dominion Square — are often leased from Canadian property owners.

All this is not to minimize the U.S. role in developing Montreal, only to put that role in perspective.

It should also be noted that U.S. banks, insurance companies and real estate interests frequently pump financial support into projects here. This is often without equity participation or board membership.

Returning to the example of La Cité, here we have a consortium of banks headed by the First National Bank of Chicago which provides the construction loans. The others are the Bank of Montreal and four U.S. banks (Wells Fargo, Citibank, Morgan Guaranty Trust, and Crocker National Bank). Equity participants are YUL, Cité Concordia Properties Ltd. (the Canadian partners) and the British post office pension fund.

In the area of mortgage loans on real estate, where insurance companies play a large role, two U.S. companies are among the leaders. Prudential Life Insurance Co. of America ranks as No. 7 in Canada ($588 million) and the Rockefeller-related Metropolitan Life Insurance Co. as No. 5 ($622 million), according to from the 1973 Report of the Superintendent of Insurance for Canada.

What U.S. involvement there is in the transformation of urban Canada is amply reciprocated.

One prominent New York real estate executive, with firm contact throughout Canada and the U.S. estimates, "There's far more Canadian real estate money coming into the U.S. now than there is U.S. money going to Canadian real estate."

When that assessment was made during a background interview I was skeptical. But a review of the operations of hundreds of real estate companies on this continent since then appears to bear out that estimate.

Canadian-owned real estate interests which have been expanding substantially south of the border include such big names as Cadillac-Fairview Corp. Ltd., Oxford Development Group Ltd., Concordia Estates Ltd., Bramalea Ltd., Daon Development Corp., Greater York Group and the Webster family of Montreal.

In March, 1977, for example, Olympia & York Developments Ltd. of Toronto paid a cool $350 million for nine New York City skyscrapers including buildings which house such giant U.S. corporations as International Telephone and Telegraph, American Brands and Harper & Row.

Some industry executives estimate that many Canadian developers have as much as 20% of their assets in the U.S. Companies find profit margins there comparatively higher than those in Canada. Also construction costs are more than 15% cheaper in the U.S. and interest rates are lower. In Canada government restrictions like the Foreign Investment Review Act regulations, anti-inflation controls, height limitations and rent controls, as well as high taxes tend to discourage developers while the depressed U.S. real estate market with its bargain prices attract them. (It is a trend which predates by several years the threat to Canadian unity posed by the 1976 election of separatists in Quebec.)

Furthermore most U.S. developers have assets of under $200 million, while at least ten Canadian developers have more than that, and it is on the basis of this backing that they can enter into deals like that of Olympia & York.

European-backed interests based here have also been spreading much of their investment to the U.S. These include Trizec Corp. Ltd., the Hambro family interests, MEPC Canadian Properties Ltd., Genstar Ltd. and the Lehndorff Group, to name just a few.

To be sure, in a very broad sense — looking outside the real estate field *per se* — the U.S. wields great influence in shaping the city's character.

Many of the manufacturing and industrial facilities here are owned below the frontier. And, of course, U.S. interests also own the companies producing most of the automobiles which are having an enormous impact on the patterns of urban growth*, a phenomenon we'll discuss further in chapter 14.

Also, the U.S. has played a critical role in the bond market, for example, the subject of chapter 15, allowing Montreal and numerous other local municipalities and governments to find the financial wherewithal for growth.

---

* The case of General Motors' decision-making power over the fate of more than 40 units of housing on St. Denis St. near Boucher St. illustrates the oblique effects of the auto industry.

Clermont Motors Ltd., a GM concession, is located nearby and owns these rowhouses. GM has indicated it will remove its franchise from Clermont unless the latter boosts its sales, says Clermont.

Clermont says that to attract customers it needs to enlarge its parking lot; to get space for the parking lot it plans to demolish these houses, despite protests from tenants.

"These houses which are worth a great deal, both financially to their owner and socially to the 40 families who live there, are threatened with demolition to make space for car sales," says Lucia Kowaluk of Save Montreal. "We deplore the exalted position of the private automobile in our cities and the collision course we are on between private use and public good."

Why is there so much less U.S. involvement in metropolitan Montreal real estate than in most other sectors of the economy?

Observers point to several reasons.

First, Americans have enough urban property themselves to invest in. Cheap Canadian rural land may attract individuals and families in search of a vacation homes, but the foreign market for urban Canadian land is very different: it is for investors and speculators, not for people wanting to use their property themselves.

Real estate interests are generally more eager to sell land to Europeans than to Americans. As one salesman of commercial and industrial properties for Montreal Trust puts it, "Europeans are satisfied with a lower return on equity — it means you're selling at higher prices. There's more money to be made selling to Europeans."

Europeans are pumping money here often not just for profit but for security. If their countries' economies go down the drain, Canada's may not necessarily follow suit and they will have nest eggs here. But Americans looking for security do not look to Canada: Canada's economy is too closely tied to the U.S. Many reason that if the U.S. economy goes belly up, so will Canada's.

Also, many Europeans feel more at home in this bilingual city than in most other North American centres, say realtors. Government attitudes as well as the business community's already significant orientation toward Europe fortify this sense of hospitality.

Finally there is for Europeans often a kind of mystique about investing in Canadian land that does not exist for Americans. According to many local realtors, this emotional factor is not to be underrated.

European investors — particularly from Germany — frequently spoke in interviews in almost romantic terms of investments here.

As one German investor who had flown here for groundbreaking ceremonies for Shercon Plaza in 1975, remarked looking at the clouds and taking a deep breath, "Investing in a city in Canada is like an adventure — it's part of the great frontier."

Before...
When the Champlain Bridge (built in part by Janin) was completed in 1962, the South Shore was still largely pastoral farmland. The land seen here, part of Brossard, became the property of Aster Corp. and related interests.

After...
The same land 15 years later.

Michael Dugas

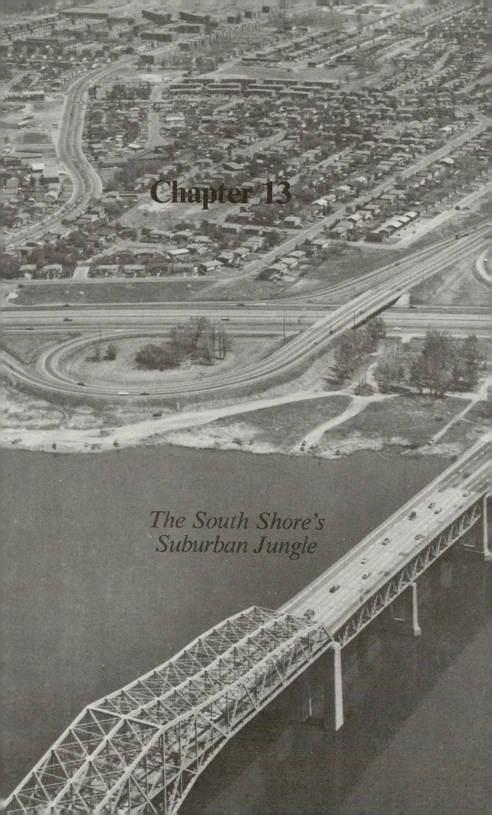

Chapter 13

*The South Shore's
Suburban Jungle*

A NUMBER OF THEMES *have emerged so far in this book: the domination of foreign interests in determining the course and character of Montreal's growth, through ownership of both land and development companies; their resistance to public exposure and accountability; the presence, within this ownership bouillabaisse of sleek corporate multinationals, smalltime individuals out for a fast speculative buck or simply security, and the European nobility; the frequency with which many of these larger interests are extensions of global industrial and natural resource interests; the acquiescence and red carpet treatment given to this leadership by the Montreal establishment and the large municipal debt involved in this kind of growth.*

Now, however, we leave the Island Montreal behind and explore the South Shore on the other side of the St. Lawrence. We will see to what degree these themes are relevant in this, the newest, most rapidly changing part of the metropolitan area.

Less than 20 years ago the South Shore was largely an isolated farming hinterland of quiet towns and some of the most fertile land in Canada. Today, spurred by the opening of the Champlain Bridge in 1962, the real estate boom has arrived and transformed much of it into a controversial crazy-quilt of suburbs criss-crossed by California-style freeways.

Large real estate promoters like Aster Corp. say they are just building and promoting projects which the public wants in as economical a manner as possible.

But urban planners deplore the proliferation of "soul-less" towns often built without centres and without respect for efficient public services, which destroy valuable farmland and which owe their origin to groups of absentee investors.

Who's utimately behind the companies which are setting the tone for South Shore development? Few are eager to claim credit.

Aster Corp., one of the most influential firms over the last 15 years, keeps its ownership concealed behind an anonymous bank account.

And when Jean-Paul Allard, a director of the main organization behind another important company, Candiac Development Corp., was asked who owns his organization, he replied: "The question is the ultimate in indiscretion."[1]

But ownership of such key companies is important, be-cause — given the absence of any effective public planning mechanism — it is up to them, more than anyone else, to deter-mine whether vast parts of this fastest-growing area of the Montreal region are transformed into model communities or into chaotic sprawl. Future generations will have to live with their investment decisions. And so Allard's reticence only served to whet my curiosity.

Michael Dugas

Brossard: A patch of the crazy-quilt.

Urban planners like Prof. Jeanne Wolfe of McGill University raise an even more fundamental issue. They say the South Shore should not be developed – period – until the Island of Montreal itself is thoroughly developed.

This, they say, would not only preserve farmland and the environment, but it would save huge amounts of taxpayers' money. Thin, generalized sprawl makes it nearly impossible for public services – such as mass transit or water and sewer systems – to function efficiently, either on the island or off of it.

My investigation focused on three shoreline municipalities which motorists may encounter after they cross the Champlain Bridge: Brossard, Laprairie and Candiac. The three are adjacent and stretch out over a total of 65 square kilometres of flat territory which ranks among the most valuable in the suburbs.

Two of these towns – Brossard and Candiac – have been the trailblazers of the South Shore's post-war development. The owners of companies like Aster and Candiac Development, which started projects there, helped set in motion the entire process of go-go growth on the South Shore.

To be sure, none of these three towns is "typical" of the South Shore's newly developing suburbs – none of the more than 20 municipalities on the South Shore *is* typical. The trio, however, contain enough variety to provide a cross-section of what's happening. Spot-checks of other areas on the South Shore show the same overall direction – though somewhat less evolved – elsewhere. (Such established pre-war communities as St. Lambert and St. Bruno are of course, quite apart from trends of newly-developing municipalities.)

I found that, despite their many differences, the three towns have basic common denominators:

– In each town one company stands out as the dominant influence in real estate affairs. Other small firms tend to tag along and conform to the character of development established by the leader.

– This dominant company is, in each of the three cases, foreign-owned. Pivotal decisions are being made either by absentee owners or by local managers who owe their appointment to them and who are carrying out the owners' investment objectives.

— The dominant foreign company is, in each case, actively supported by some of Canada's foremost financial and legal firms. There is no evidence, then, of foreigners imposing their will on a resisting Canadian public.

— Two of the three dominant companies are European-owned. The third is U.S.-owned. That ratio is representative of the breakdown of nationalities of foreign development interests on the Island of Montreal.

But what's happening in Brossard, Laprairie and Candiac is more than just an echo of what is happening on the Island of Montreal. It is a far more intensified version of it.

If foreign interests and their local allies are a pervasive force in shaping the course of development on the Island of Montreal, these three towns across the river make the island seem almost Canadian-owned by comparison.

Consider:

Driving down off the Champlain Bridge, motorists see on either side of them block after block of indistinguishable houses stretching into the distance. This is part of Brossard, one of the Southshore's first post-war bedroom suburbs.

Prime mover behind the modern town is Aster Corp. which began buying land in 1959, three years before completion of the bridge. At one time it owned almost two square miles of land, according to Aster's general manager, André Vadeboncoeur. A speculator, Aster has since sold about half of that off.

When Aster arrived the municipality had a population — mostly agricultural — of 2,300 people thinly spread out over its 17 square miles. Today the population stands at about 40,000 and, with three-quarters of the territory still undeveloped, it could eventually reach 200,000, predicts Vadeboncoeur.

In addition to selling off land, Aster has also built some of Brossard's first single-family homes and three-storey apartment buildings, establishing the "tone" of development for the area. Vadeboncoeur says that in selling empty land to contractors it would insist that their own buildings conform to Aster's standards so as not to debase overall land values.

Aster uses two main banks here: the Royal Bank of Canada and the Canadian Imperial Bank of Commerce. But Aster's ownership is a deliberately maintained mystery.

At first the corporation was technically "owned" by a Liechtenstein bank. By refusing to divulge the names of its clients who owned Aster, the Bank in Liechtenstein A.G. could preserve the real owners' anonymity.

Then about 1974 the façades changed.

A Swiss bank became "owner" and serves the same purpose. The bank is the Sintlon Bank (known in Italian as Banca del Sempione), of Lugano. That border town's proximity to Italy often — but not necessarily — betokens the nationality of its banking clients.

But Aster's owners are so mum about their identity that even Vadeboncoeur, a top executive for 15 years as well as a director, says he does not know who his own employers are.

He acknowledges, however, that there might be Italians or Swiss among the owners. One Italian who was active in Aster over the years — living in Montreal while he administered the company's affairs — is Mario Santarelli, a member of a major Italian wine-producing family. One can buy its "Frescati" red table wine at any liquor store. And though he is now back in Italy his memory lives on through Mario St. and Marisa St., named after him and his wife.

Another figure who emerges is Leonard Francheschini, the Italian-born head of the French-owned Lafarge group's Francon construction division, one of Quebec's biggest highway builders. Francheschini is both president of Aster and a director of the Sintlon Bank, and has been for more than a decade.

Residential development by Aster Corp. in Brossard.

The Gazette (Michael Dugas)

Pressed on the ownership question, Vadeboncoeur says: "One has to be careful. One can't indicate anyone. There are political problems of a national nature ... You know in Italy there are laws forbidding the export of capital, so one cannot insist too much.

"The government (of Italy), you know, is on the hunt. So I wouldn't push it."[2]

Ownership aside, Vadeboncoeur acknowledges that Aster has played a role on the South Shore roughly comparable to that which Place Ville Marie played in downtown Montreal. Both pioneer developments, which took place at about the same time, helped stimulate development by others and establish the character of their respective areas.

By concidence, PVM's owner, Trizec Corp. Ltd., a subsidiary of a U.K. company, happens to be Brossard's other major landowner. Trizec and Aster today each own tracts totalling about one square mile, estimates Brossard's director of urban planning, Michel-André Boyer. Unlike Aster, however, Trizec did not enter the picture until relatively recently — 1974 — and so far has not built anything on its land.

A third noteworthy company in Brossard is Cadillac Fairview Corp. Ltd., which has bought land from Aster (about 150 lots' worth, estimates Vadeboncoeur) and is building houses on it. Cadillac Fairview is largely Canadian-owned.

It might appear that these three companies — Aster, Trizec and Cadillac Fairview — are unconnected, coming as they do from different countries. Perhaps by coincidence, they are all interlocked.

Trizec and Cadillac Fairview — the country's two biggest real estate companies — each have a different branch of the Bronfman family as major shareholders. And each maintains close ties with one of Montreal's top law firms, Phillips & Vineberg. One senior partner, Ex-Sen. Lazarus Phillips, is a director of both Trizec and CEMP Investments, the Bronfman trust behind Cadillac Fairview, while another partner, Philip Vineberg, is a director of Cadillac Fairview.

To round out the symmetry, the company which is spearheading Brossard's development, Aster, is also a client of the firm.

The relationship is not an incidental one: Aster's headquarters are physically inside the law firm's own offices in PVM. Indeed, Philip Vineberg is a director of Aster as well as its vice president.*

Behind this cast of foreign and local characters in Brossard comes a parade of secondary ones.

These include, according to Boyer and property records, three U.S. parties** and a number of Canadian ones, notably Monsadel, Inc., owned by John Szaz, of Toronto.

And then there is the usual assortment of untraceable alpine trolls such as Pindar A.G., of Liechtenstein, and Société Internationale de Finance, which calls a Zurich post office box home.

Urban planners may use words like "chaos" and "fragmentation of planning" to describe the South Shore's development. But from a boardroom perspective there is less disorganization than may meet the eye: the private interests doing much of the development may share directors and investment goals.

Some of the interests at work in Brossard also interlock with those at work in Candiac, as will be seen.

In other words, things may look chaotic. But at least in part, it is "organized chaos".

---

* Coincidences do not end there. A fourth company which owns, through a subsidiary, Brossard's largest shopping centre, Champlain Mall, is also a client of the law firm and has interlocking directorates through Ex-Sen. Phillips with Trizec and CEMP. The company is Steinberg's Ltd., the region's largest supermarket chain (with a strong grip on the Brossard market: besides having a supermarket at the No. 1 shopping centre, it also has one at the No. 2, Place Portobello). The company has also evolved into a major South Shore landowner. In a National Film Board documentary several years ago, a Steinberg's executive mentioned on camera that the firm owns some 15 million square feet of choice land (equal to 344 acres or just over half a square mile) on the South Shore, much of it since sold off for housing.

** These are: — Aaron Green, a New Yorker, and his family, who owned about 200 acres of Brossard at one time but have since sold off much of this except for the Portobello Shopping centre.
— Levitt Canada Ltd., ultimately controlled by ITT, which has begun developing some of its 250-odd acres.
— The Seltzer Organization, of Philadelphia, owners of some 300 acres.

Candiac's 7,800 citizens, like a growing number of suburban taxpayers, do not own their own city hall.

It belongs to a company owned by Germans.

The same company — in which one of the principals is someone called Ingeborg Zilch — owns the entire shopping centre in which City Hall is located.

This is only fitting because European interests own actually as much as 90 per cent of Candiac's 12 square kilometres, according to municipal officials.

Candiac stands in visual contrast to most parts of Brossard: It has winding streets, larger yards and a wider variety of housing styles on the same block.

So far as origins go, Candiac and new Brossard have much in common: both were started by European-owned corporations in the 1950s, and these firms are still around today as the major landowners.

Candiac likes to call itself Canada's first independent municipality created by a private development company. The company is the Candiac Development Corp. which began acquiring land in the area in 1953 and four years later helped the town become incorporated by private bill in the Quebec legislature. Indeed, during the town's early years CDC executives regularly served as mayors. CDC owns 70 per cent of Candiac's land.*

As Jean-Paul Allard, director and treasurer of CDC's main shareholder, Sparmont Corp., describes it, the town itself is almost an accident.

---

* The second largest landowner is Diamida A.G., a company registered in Liechtenstein. Lawrence Galletti, a former mayor of Greenfield Park who is an associate of Diamida, says only that its owners are originally from Italy and that they bought their land about a dozen years ago. Its land is undeveloped so far but plans for residential and commercial development are afoot. Diamida owns roughly 20 per cent of Candiac and Morgan Trust five or 10 per cent, say municipal officials.

A group of French-Canadians and English-Canadians sought to "make a fortune" by first buying up agricultural land where the proposed St. Lawrence Seaway would go. But the seaway did not bring them the riches they anticipated, so they decided to create a town on the land. They formed the CDC in which several of Europe's major corporate groups took part and which bought more land.

The most detailed assessment of the town so far is by Bernard Vachon, former Candiac recreation director and now head of the geography department at the Université du Québec at Montreal. His 256-page master's thesis on Candiac in 1971 concludes on this note:

"Candiac, a happy or unhappy experiment? One cannot answer the question with absolutes. Twice voted suburb of the year (by the Montreal Home Builders' Association), Candiac struck us as artificial, under-serviced and de-personalized."[3]

The Gazette (Michael Dugas)
Candiac, a «noble» fief on the South Shore. Baron Empain's company provides the land, the Earl of Inchcape's builds the houses.

The town was examined again in 1976 as part of a master's thesis by Joanabbey Sack of McGill University's urban planning program. She said in an interview that the town appeared to be taking steps to provide more recreational and community services, but that these basic planning flaws remain:

— A lack of community cohesiveness. The town is sliced up by highways 15 and 9-C and there are few public meeting places where community spirit may be fostered.

— The absence of any hub or centre. Zilch's shopping centre is the only place to shop in town. It contains few stores and is so situated as to be accessible to residents only by car. This contributes to the town's car-intensive character and to the fact that over 90 per cent of the residents leave town to shop.

Vachon's analysis shows that as a money-making enterprise, CDC has been only a marginal success. Growth of the town towards its goal of 60,000 people is far behind schedule.

Says Vachon: "Regionally, Candiac today appears to be an enclave poorly incorporated into the metropolitan area; locally, its too rigid masterplan, structured on debateable (financial) choices, helps explain its social problems and the quasi-stagnation of its development."[4]

Despite academia's interest in what Candiac Development has done, virtually no attention has been given to its ownership.

And that, says Allard, is the way it should remain. "We have no accounting to give anyone. We don't need publicity. We are not interested in being known," he said in a telephone interview, explaining that the organization did not sell shares in Canada.

"Here (in Canada) we don't give information to anyone. We don't want anyone looking at our affairs."[5]

He should have known that is the last thing to tell a nosy reporter. Several letters to the Quebec government's company records service showed that Sparmont Corp., CDC's main shareholder, is a wholly-owned subsidiary of United North American Holdings Ltd., also of Montreal. It, in turn, is 64 per cent owned by Schneider S.A., of Paris. This is part of the Empain-Schneider group of companies, France's largest heavy industrial conglomerate.

Schneider was founded in the mid-19th century by two brothers, Adolph and Eugene Schneider, who built France's first steam locomotives and steamboats. But history remembers their company best for cannons and munitions.

As William Manchester writes in his best-seller "The Arms of Krupp": starting in the 1860's Krupp of Germany, Schneider of France and Armstrong of the U.K. became "Europe's deadly triumvirate . . . Over the next eighty years they were to be celebrated first as shields of national honor and later, after their slaughtering machines were out of control, as merchants of death."

In the 1970s the company has been seeking a growing role in Quebec. One subsidiary, Jeumont-Schneider, is part of the consortium which won the $29 million contract to build the control system on the Metro extensions. Another subsidiary, Spie-Batignolles, was a member of a consortium which barely lost out to Agnelli-related interests in landing the prime, quarter-billion dollar construction contract on the James Bay project.

Its history in the arms industry is hard to bury. In 1976 Spie-Batignolles and Framatome, France's nuclear monopoly in which Schneider interests are the major shareholder, agreed to build two nuclear reactors for South Africa for nearly $1 billion. The conservative newspaper Le Figaro said the two nuclear reactors could produce enough plutonium annually to make several hundred atomic bombs of the size exploded over Hiroshima.

South Africa, a leading producer of uranium, has pledged not to use the reactors for military purposes. Protests that South Africa was effectively obtaining the means to produce its own atomic bomb are groundless, said the French government, even through South Africa has not signed the nuclear non-proliferation treaty. The contract has helped fortify France's position as the third largest constructor of nuclear power plants after the United States and Germany.[6]

The French government itself, however, *has* been upset over one aspect of Schneider's affairs. In the early 1960s a Belgian family, the Empains, acquired controlling interest in the company from the Schneider family's heirs. That foreigners should own such a pivotal industrial-nuclear conglomerate prompted Gen. de Gaulle to devise stratagems to keep the Empains from exercising control. Until de Gaulle retired in 1969 the company existed in leaderless limbo.

When Schneider first became involved in Candiac, the company was under control of Charles Schneider, third-generation owner who died in 1960 following a boating accident. Baron Edouard-Jean Empain has been firmly in control of Schneider throughout the 1970s (through a family holding company called Electrorail).

Allard acknowledges that the Empain-Schneider group, as it is now called, is the strongest force behind Candiac Development Corp. Sparmont owns 24 per cent of it and another Empain-Schneider subisidiary, Paramer S.A., of Geneva, owns another 9.2 per cent.

(Another of France's major groups, the Suez complex, owns an additional nine per cent of CDC. A firm called Moncus & Co., which can be traced only so far as a post office box at Place d'Armes, owns another 19 per cent).

All this may make the group seem remote. But some of its key local allies here are the same ones encountered at Brossard. This gives us a fuller idea of the relationships between some of the pioneers behind South Shore development. The skein is complex,* but it comes down to this: Candiac in large

---

* Thus: — Yet another partner at Phillips & Vineberg, Ivan E. Phillips, is a CDC director.

— And one of the main tenants at Zilch's shopping centre, Steinberg's, has maintained bonds with Candiac Development's owners which transcend Candiac itself. The Steinberg organization, which owns the town's only supermarket, as of 1972 owned 11 per cent (through a Steinberg family trust called Rockview Corp.) and Sparmont 19 per cent of a real estate firm called Combined Mortgage Corp. which holds a high-rise property in Montreal's Bois de Boulogne evaluated at $2.3 million. (Largest shareholder in Combined Mortgage is Morgan Trust Co., which by coincidence is Candiac's third largest landowner.)

— One of the shopping centre's other main tenants, Candiac's only bank, the Royal, also fits in as part of this circle: it is one of Aster's two banks and it is CDC's only bank. Moreover another of the Empain-Schneider group's principal arms in this country is Elican Development Co., of which Royal Bank Chairman W. Earle McLaughlin is a director. Another Phillips & Vineberg partner, Neil Phillips, is also a director of Elican, United North American Holdings and the Royal. Until it sold it in 1976, Elican owned Canadian Hydrocarbons Ltd., a major natural gas producer.

— To further carry out the parallels between Brossard and Candiac, E.-Jacques Courtois, the close associate of the "Trizec" branch of the Bronfman family also fits in. He is ε president of both Elican and Compagnie Foncière de Manitoba (1967) Ltée., an Empain-Schneider subsidiary, and a director of Trizec. He is also vice-chairman and president of Eagle Star Insurance Co. of Canada which is an arm of the British insurance company which a main power behind Trizec and another major South Shore developer, Bramalea Ltd., until selling its controlling interest in 1975.

part reflects the same circle of interests which are active in various aspects of Brossard's development, not to mention other parts of the South Shore.

The pattern is remarkably similar. ͟ ͟reign interests put up the risk capital, set the terms by which the investment is to be carried, and a handful of local interests both jump on the band-wagon and help to steer it.

Originally, Laprairie parish included all of Brossard, Laprairie and Candiac. It was divided into the three parts in the early 1950s, and as in Brossard and Candiac, foreign-owned companies took the lead in Laprairie.

This time, however, the major landowner is not European but American: Gulf Oil Corp., of Pittsburgh, acting through Canadian subsidiaries.

(The municipality's second largest landowner after Gulf, according to officials, is a firm with the name of 295514 Ontario Ltd. It owns about 100 undeveloped acres near Gulf's land.)

Gulf moved into Laprairie in 1973, buying up six square kms. of fields and woods from religious orders, farmers and others. Its goal: creation of a "new town" which, as its promotional literature puts it, is "patterned after the highly successful new town of Reston, Va."

Reston has drawn praise from urban planners around the world for its creation of a self-contained community some 30 minutes' drive from Washington, D.C. It is owned by Gulf.

Since work only began in 1976, it is still too early to evaluate the project. But even before construction started, it was drawing raves from officials like then-Quebec Minister of Municipal Affairs Victor Goldbloom who called it "the ideal way to pursue urban development"[7]

The oil company's image as Reston's owner is a factor in much of the advance enthusiasm over the company's plans for Laprairie. However, a check of Gulf's record at Reston shows that the company's contributions there were late — and controversial.

The man who conceived Reston in the early 1960 s was Robert Simon, not Gulf. It was Simon who gave the town its famed lakeside "village" design, its sense of community cohesiveness and its clustering of townhouses to leave large areas of public green space intact.

After this visonary's debts piled up in 1967, he was ousted by Gulf — which had to protect its unsecured investment in Simon's project. That's when Gulf started managing the project itself, and that's when the Reston citizen's groups began protesting that the new managment was trying to create "an asphalt environment typical of suburbia."

In his recent book "Mortgage on America," a Washington Post editor, Leonard Downie Jr., notes that when Gulf came in automobiles began taking priority over pathways, typical suburban detached houses with large lots gained favor over townhouses with large public spaces, etc. Reston, he writes, was "becoming just another middle-class Washington suburb."[8]

In short, though many observers have high expectations about Gulf's Laprairie project in large part because of its ownership of Reston, Gulf's actual performance at Reston suggests it has few laurels on which to rest.

Jeanne Wolfe, the urban planning professor at McGill, makes another point. While she calls Gulf's plans "as good as anything in the area," she notes that the project's location is questionable.[9]

She says it would be far more rational for Gulf to locate its project on the Island of Montreal — either the West Island or Rivière des Prairies where there is still enough empty land to accommodate decades of metropolitan growth.

"The way it is now, the populations of the West Island and the South Shore are simply not dense enough to make public transport, for example, an economic matter," she says.

"To get rid of traffic congestion in the centre city you need more concentration of population on the island so that you can establish well-used transport routes. If you spread development out it becomes a vicious circle.

"People tend to think the island is 'full,' but it's not at all."

Furthermore, the new town, she says, may greatly increase the traffic load in the area. And, since it is located in a limbo area between the Champlain and Mercier bridges, it will perhaps help create demand for another bridge.

The three towns illustrate a basic problem of all the Southshore, urban planners say: towns are being built by private developers where land happens to be cheapest, not where the land is best suited for towns.

A 1964 study by the City of Montreal of Laprairie, Candiac, Brossard and six other nearby municipalities totalling 163 square kms. found that 10 square kms. of this land was abandoned farmland or woodland. In other words, this was land available for development.[10]

In doing a follow-up study in 1976, Joanabbey Sack found that 61 per cent of this old abandoned land was still abandoned, still ripe for development (the remainder having been developed or subdivided). But during the same 12 year interval an *additional* 7.2 square miles had been abandoned, most of it farmland.[11]

"This is devastating wastefulness," says Sack. "New land is being abandoned and developed instead of old abandoned land being used for development.

"Thousands of acres of valuable agricultural land are being taken out of circulation and being bought by speculators."[12]

The fact that Gulf's land is *not* valuable farmland does little to help the generally "anarchistic" situation which planners like Vachon and Wolfe say is unavoidable so long as development races along without any comprehensive plan for the entire area.

For taxpayers of these new communities there is also a burdensome problem: municipal debt. The town fathers of Laprairie, anticipating a burgeoning Gulf community of thousands of additional people — all paying taxes to the municipality — launched a $4.5 million public works program. They borrowed money to construct water mains, sewers and streets. But then came delays in actually carrying out that work: owners of houses in Laprairie's historic old quarter protested Gulf's development on grounds it would ruin the character of the area;

construction strikes have put work even further behind schedule.

Consequently the Gulf project has been unable to provide an adequate flow of taxpayers to help pay for these debts, which must be paid off no matter how much work has actually been done. This has aggravated a situation which would have meant higher taxes anyway: oldtime residents are now stuck with 40 per cent of their taxes simply paying off debt. This is well above the 29 per cent average for municipalities of this size, according to the Quebec municipal affairs department. The department is now requiring developers like Gulf to share with municipalities the cost of sewers, roads, etc.

The circumstances in Laprairie are exceptional but the conditions they have helped engender are not. The high cost of municipal services — particularly an enlarged water filtration plant — in this low-density area is one big reason why Candiac also has a debt service ratio of well over 40 per cent. Brossard is the second-largest debtor in Quebec among towns with population between 25,000 and 50,000, spending 42.3 per cent of its budget paying back its creditors.[12]

In short, this kind of growth is not only often ugly but it is wasteful of energy and agricultural land — and it is inordinately expensive.

The Belgian Baron

Baron Edouard-Jean Empain may have youth, an undistinguished scholastic record and matinee idol looks.

But he is no figurehead sitting passively at the top of the Empain-Schneider group of more than 60 operating companies.

The son of a second-generation Belgian noble and an American burlesque artist named Rosezell Russell ("The Golden Girl"),[13] Empain not only controls France's largest heavy industrial group by virtue of his inheritance.

He runs it.

"Il sait," as one Parisian puts it with ironic understatement, "compter."

Baron Empain.

Now 39, Empain is president-director general of a group of such size that its control of the largest bloc of shares in Candiac Development Corp. does not even receive a mention in its public accounts.

Empain's personal life is almost as international as his industrial empire. He was born in Hungary, retains his Belgian citizenship, lives in Paris and is married to an Italian.

His stepfather bought a major interest in France's Schneider S.A. in 1963. And ever since the French government relented in its opposition to letting foreigners own the country's giant nuclear-steel-construction conglomerate, the young baron has been trying to restore his family's standing as one of the Europe's industrial leaders.

His grandfather, an engineer, built the Paris Metro as well as subways and tram lines as far away as Cairo and Shanghai. Working in conjunction with Société Générale de Belgique, his the grandfather's company built railroads and canals in the Congo. King Leopold II made him a baron.

Two world wars and an anti-colonial war in the Congo have been unable to separate the two Belgian groups.

Both Baron Empain and Max Nokin, longtime head of La Société Générale, are today vice-chairmen of the Arbed Group, of Luxembourg, one of Europe's four or five largest steelmakers. The Empain and Société Générale groups share control of Arbed.

And on the South Shore today it is still possible to find the two groups maintaining the same neighborly spirit. Just next door to the Empain's land at Candiac is the town of Delson. And who is a major landowner there?

Société Générale's principal investment arm in Canada, Genstar.

Footnotes — Chapter 13

1. Telephone interview with Allard, treasurer of the Empain-Schneider group's Canadian operations, Sept. 30, 1976.
2. Interviews with Vadeboncoeur by telephone Feb. 25, 1976, and in person, Mar. 12, 1976.
3. Vachon, Bernard, "Candiac: Un cas particulier de développement peri-urbain au sud de Grand Montréal," département de géographie, Université de Sherbrooke, master's thesis, 1971.
4. Vachon, Bernard, "La création de Candiac en banlieue de Montréal," *Rév. Géogr. Montr.,* 1973, vol. XXVII, n° 1, p. 39.
5. Allard, op. cit.
6. News from France, No. 6, Feb. 1, 1977, (Paris: Association pour la Diffusion de la Pensée Française), p. 16.
7. La Citière press release, June 16, 1975, p. 5.
8. Downie, Leonard, Jr., "Mortgage on America" (New York: Praeger Publishers, Inc., 1974), p. 172.
9. Interview with Wolfe, Oct. 8, 1976.
10. Urbanization study, 1964, by the Département d'urbanisme, City of Montreal.
11. Sack, Joanabbey, "A Study of Exurban Growth," Department of Urban Planning, McGill University, master's thesis, 1976.
12. Montreal Star, Mar. 5, 1977, "Growth dreams turn sour: Gambling suburbs deep in debt," by Terence Moore.
13. Fortune magazine, Aug. 1975, "A Belgian baron fights for his corporate domain in France," p. 171.

Chapter 14

*The Vested Interests
in Energy Waste*

It may seem somewhat bizarre that an energy company like
Gulf Oil should be the promoter of a new town planned for
30,000 people in suburban Montreal.

But there is, in fact, nothing in the least unusual about
Gulf's activity. It is typical of a striking trend discernible in the
companies most involved in land development: of the my-
riad major development interests examined in this book, over
90 per cent of those whose ownership can be traced have ties
to petroleum, automobile, auto parts or automobile raw material suppliers. Curious?

It means that these interests in general have, in effect, a vested interest in perpetuating the public's reliance on the private
vehicle — as well as high energy consumption and the vast
highway network which go along with it. If they push for a
sound, efficient mass transit system, for example, they might be
acting against their own long-term investments in other fields.

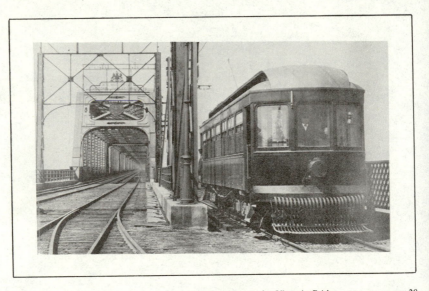

*Electric tramways, here seen crossing the St. Lawrence on the Victoria Bridge, once ran every 20
minutes between Montreal and Chambly. One line went all the way to Granby, 75 kilometres away.
The line was owned by Montreal Southern Counties Railway Co., a subsidiary of Canadian National.
The history of this popular, low-energy, pollution-free communter service is described in* Catenary
through the Counties, *a book by Anthony Clegg and Omer Lavallée.*

This interlocking investment pattern has evolved only within the past generation or so, and it is accelerating. It is during this same period that transportation practices in this area have changed most dramatically.

If development were still taking place here the way it was a generation or two ago, this syndrome of interlocking investments would be irrelevant. Communities were then reached by a network of cheap, frequently-running transit lines.

Older citizens can recall how, for example, electric trolley lines allowed workers to commute into the city from such diverse spots as Lachine, the Back River and even — on the South Shore — St. Lambert and Chambly. New residents on the South Shore are often surprised to learn that these frequently running, pollution-free trolleys crossed the St. Lawrence river over the Victoria Bridge as recently as 1955, when

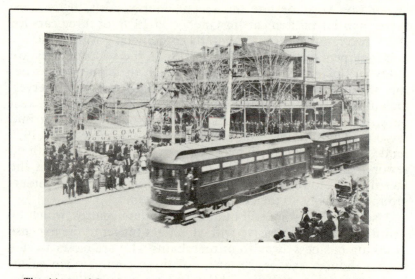

The citizens of Granby turn out to cheer the arrival of the first tram to make the 75 km. run from Montreal on April 29, 1916.

High officials of Canadian National Railways, the government-owned rail network, now acknowledge that their predecessors' decision to close down the commuter service in the 1950s, so as to allow priority of the automobile, was a mistake.

the tram tracks were torn off to make room for automobile traffic.

Also, in sharp contrast to today's amorphous development patterns, communities used to grow up clustered about these transit stations. Thus Lower Westmount, Montreal West, Dorval, Dixie, Valois, Beaconsfield and Ste. Anne de Bellevue were all built around the stops of Canadian Pacific's Lakeshore rail line. Today these same original communities are generally highly valued for their remarkable centralization and sense of identity.

But what was once a transportation system relying on inexpensive rail, tram or bus service based on low energy consumption per passenger mile has turned into a system in which cars are no longer a luxury, but a necessity.

There are at least two main reasons for this:

1. — The housing sprawl has been built without consideration for existing or possible future mass transit systems. It is virtually impossible to get around without a car — which is a key reason why, despite the recent energy crisis, there were more than 2.1 million cars in Quebec in 1976, or three cars for every two families, according to the provincial government.

Developers contribute much to this. In the suburbs, they are today still planning subdivisions in much the same way as before there were projections of diminishing fossil fuel reserves. Downtown, they are still building office high-rises with vast parking facilities, thus encouraging more people to drive into the city. The ultimate example of this was completed in 1976 on de Maisonneuve Blvd. near Aylmer: an office tower with no fewer than *eleven* floors of parking — and this in spite of the fact that the tower is *directly connected,* by convenient underground walkway, to the city's subway system.

Also developers are still building shopping centres, which by definition are car-intensive and which get bigger at the expense of taking business away from merchants who are closer to customers' homes: that is, designers of these centres often calculate that they must draw a clientele from a radius of 20 miles or more in order to make a profit. In October, 1977, for instance, Canadian Pacific was proposing to build a giant, 125-

store regional shopping centre with parking for 4,000 cars on one of its old railyards in the East End. Energy crisis? What energy crisis?

2. — At the same time, the quality of mass transit has declined sharply. This is true anywhere in the suburbs.

Thus on the South Shore — which is booming in residential housing and in highways — there is just one commuter train a day (Canadian National's line to St. Hyacinthe). Bus service on the South Shore has been so infrequent that it became a central issue there in recent provincial elections.

Meanwhile in Laval, all attempts at extending the Metro to that fast-growing island have been beaten back. And on the West Island the Canadian Pacific has more than tripled its commuter fares over the past decade — to the point where many workers find it cheaper to drive into the city even without carpools.*

To be sure, all this cannot be laid at the door of private enterprise. Various levels of government are responsible for much of the decision-making which goes into this deteriorating mass transit. Subways, the CN commuter railroad and highway construction all depend on government. The municipal government owns many of Montreal's parking lots, offering lower rates than ITT and thus luring more cars downtown. And the municipal government also has a bylaw requiring new office buildings to have substantial underground parking facilities — one parking space for every 1,000 square feet of floor space, which works out to about one parking floor for every five floors of offices.

But private interests play a large, often unseen role in guiding these government decisions. Right now, for example, developers like Gulf are asking for new highways on the South Shore so as to better attract homebuyers. Some are also lobbying for a fifth bridge across the St. Lawrence. There is no such corporate clamor for a rail line or for restoration of a

---

* For example, in 1966 the price of a one-way ticket from Pointe Claire to downtown Montreal was $.65. By 1977 it had soared to $2.45, an increase of 276 per cent.

tram (though CN President Robert Bandeen told me it would be feasible, crossing the St. Lawrence on the Champlain Bridge and proceeding inland along the wide centre-strips of highways).

What is true for cars is also true for heating.

A spokesman for Ottawa's Office of Energy Conservation notes that the great majority of developers are building projects — from houses to high-rises — which are almost as wasteful of heating fuels as before the 1973-74 energy crisis.

According the spokesman, Brian Kelly, a government study shows that builders of typical single-family homes could slash these homes' heating costs by one-half if they invested as little as $700 to $1,000 more per house in extra insulation, storm windows, caulking, etc. Kelly estimates that homeowners would get their money back in three or four years through lower fuel bills.*

Canada's approach to urban development is one reason why the country is the worst waster of energy in the world. Statistics released by the federal government in 1977 show that the average Canadian uses the energy equivalent of 49 barrels of oil per year, thus overtaking the traditional leader, the U.S.[2] It is not enough to say that this is because Canada's cold climate re-

---

* Office building construction, too, could be much more efficient. In the pre-war days buildings along most Montreal streets — St. Catherine St., for example — were built lower on the south side and higher on the north side of the thoroughfares so that each could receive more sunlight and hence, heat. So as not to block light for other buildings or create chilling wind canyons, the city's first "skyscrapers" — the old Royal Bank Building on St. James St. and the Sun Life Assurance Building on Dominion Square, for example — were built in a wedding cake manner.

Today these old virtues are being rediscovered — most notably, so far, by the government of Ontario. Its 20-storey Ontario Hydro building in Toronto, completed in the mid 1970s, is among the most energy-conscious in North America. Arc-shaped and with silver-coated glass walls, it acts like a gleaming giant reflector which turns away solar heat in summer and reflects interior heat into the building in winter. It also uses the body heat of its 7,000 employees and the heat of equipment. "About 25 per cent of all energy in North America is used in buildings," says the developer, Gerhard Moog, president of Canada Square Corp. "With application of our ideas and philosophy, you can save a large part of that consumption." He says the building requires less than half the energy used by other buildings of its size.[1]

quires high heating bills. In 1960 Canadians managed fine with half the per capita use of energy they have today.2 Indeed, Finland, a country which has a comparable climate and a high standard of living, still uses half the energy of Canada on a per capita basis.3 The director of Ottawa's Office of Energy Conservation, Ian Efford, says the main reasons for this waste are over-reliance on automobile transportation, insufficient insulation in buildings, poor maintenance of furnaces and an "easy come, easy go" mentality.4

To be sure, industrialism as a whole has a natural stake in generating more public consumption. And in this conglomerate age, many sectors of the economy overlap to some extent with common ownership. But the linkage between urban development interests and the energy-auto interests stands out sharply. (For example, there is no consistent interlocking pattern between urban development interests and either the food or the pulp and paper industries, two other important sectors of Canada's economy.)

Nonethless, it would be simplistic to compare the link between the energy-auto interests and developers to, say, a dentists' association as a major shareholder in the local candy company.

It is not a matter of one company developing a housing project so that a related company can peddle more fuel or tires to it. Many of these organizations are multinational with assets of over $1 billion, and such a "captive market" sales strategy in Quebec would barely tickle their balance sheets. Indeed, some of these companies do not even offer their products in Quebec. They may be involved in real estate here for no reason more sinister than that it happens to be a secure, profitable investment.

But many of these developers are so big and operate in so many places that they help instill the tone and direction of development here and in other provinces and countries.

Here are some of the most influential development interests with explanations of their relationships to auto-energy interests. Examined individually, none of these cases would mean much. Taken collectively they suggest a strong pattern of shared interests. To refresh the memory, some details of ownership mentioned in earlier chapters are repeated here.

— Canadian Pacific Ltd. Through its subsidiary, Marathon Realty Co. Ltd., CP is among the largest landowning and developing companies in Montreal and all of urban Canada. Local projects include Place du Canada downtown, Summerlea Industrial Park on the West Island and land on Ile Perrot for residential development.

Ironically, though the company is best known for its railroad operations, many analysts say it stands to make more money from increased use by Canadians of cars rather than trains.

CP owns PanCanadian Petroleum Ltd., which calculates it is the largest independent "Canadian-owned" producer of crude oil and natural gas. It also has a 12.6 per cent interest in Panarctic Oils Ltd., the industry-government venture which is exploring the Canadian North.

CP also controls Algoma Steel Corp. Ltd., whose products are used by auto-makers, among others. Algoma, in turn, is the major shareholder in Dominion Bridge Co. Ltd. The latter builds local highway bridges, supplies steel frames for some of Canada's tallest buildings and manufactures cranes for the construction of buildings as well as of offshore oil rigs.

Another susbidiary, CP (Bermuda) Ltd. owns a 25-vessel fleet. But the fluctuation of the world's oil consumption has shown just how dependent that company, which owns tankers, is on the public's unslaked energy thirst. As CP glumly reported in its 1975 annual report, "CP (Bermuda) . . . faced severe problems in 1975 as worldwide movements of oil and bulk materials were curtailed due to the economic recession."

GROUPE EMPAIN-SCHNEIDER

— Empain-Schneider group. Gulf may be the owner of the region's newest 'new town,' but this Belgian-French group is the biggest shareholder in the company (Candiac Development Corp.) which founded the first "new town." It began assembling the land for Candiac as far back as 1953. It is still the largest landowner in this South Shore town, regarded as one of the influential "seed" projects in establishing the character of Montreal's suburban development.

The Empain-Schneider Group, headed by Baron E.-J. Empain, has been the No. 1 shareholder in Canadian Hydrocarbons Ltd., of Calgary, the country's leading liquid energy distributor. Subsidiaries have included Quebec Propane Inc., a distributor of petroleum gas and lubricating oils in this province, and Canadian Homestead Oils Ltd., which is exploring and producing oil and gas across Canada.

The Emplain-Schneider group sold its control in Hydrocarbons in 1976, but its overall orientation remains unchanged. In Europe it is involved in shaping growth as a builder of highrises and of super-highways.

In conjunction with La Société Générale de Belgique, it also administers a major metal producer, Arbed, which helps supply the European automotive industry.

— The Bronfmans. Through a family trust, CEMP Investments Ltd., one wing of the Bronfman family has for many years been building housing projects and shopping centres. Today they are major owners of Cadillac Fairview Corp. Ltd., the largest publicly-owned real estate firm in Canada. Locally, it is building homes and shopping centres from Kirkland to Brossard.

CEMP also controls Seagram Co. Ltd., and alcohol is not the only liquid which pours out of that organization: there is also *oil.* Seagram's estimates that a subsidiary, Texas Pacific Oil Co., is one of the five largest independent oil producers in the U.S. The company is developing wells in Western Canada, the North Sea, and the waters off Saudi-Arabia and the Philippines, as well as in the U.S.

In its 1975 report to shareholders, Seagram's provides a glimpse into the rationale behind these energy investments. It says that Samuel Bronfman, the firm's late head, "as early as 1950 saw that within the next quarter century the western world's needs for oil and gas would increase dramatically."

Bronfman, says the report, had this principle in mind when he invested in Texas Pacific: "Identify an important future demand, then start building to meet it."

The report makes no reference to Bronfman's simultaneous real estate developments, but it says he envisaged building an oil firm which would eventually become a "significant factor in coping with the energy-short future he foresaw."

Cadillac Fairview's current construction of metropolitan Montreal's second largest shopping centre (at St. Bruno) is not designed to hold that future at bay. Nor was its expansion in 1976 of Galeries d'Anjou, making that *the* largest metropolitan shopping centre.

But this is not to overlook the other branch of the family.

A company associated with Edward Bronfman, a director of Ranger Oil (Canada) Ltd. which is exploring for energy across Canada and in Europe, took voting control that same year of Trizec Corp. Ltd., Canada's largest publicly-owned real estate firm after Cadillac Fairview.

GULF+WESTERN INDUSTRIES, INC.

— Famous Players Ltd. This company, best known for movies, is owner of the newest and largest office tower on St. Catherine St., the 24-storey Capitol Centre.

Famous Players is part of a conglomerate in which movies play a small role and cars and energy play a large one.

Gulf & Western (no relation to Gulf Oil), based in New York with $3.3 billion in assets, makes car batteries, bumpers, pistons and numerous other automotive parts. In fact, it has one subsidiary, APS Inc., which supplies 100,000 auto parts, says its annual report.

Other subsidiaries make components for oil and gas pipelines, rigmounts for offshore drilling, drill bits, etc.

In partnership with Société Générale de Belgique (more on that later), Gulf & Western also owns New Jersey Zinc Co. which produces zinc for special steels used in automotive manufacturing.

In addition, Gulf & Western has a 37 per cent interest in Flying Diamond Oil Corp., of Utah, which has permits for oil exploration and development in over 200,000 acres of Canada.

The conglomerate has a stake in real estate, incidentally, which goes well beyond Capitol Centre and hundreds of theatre and drive-in properties. Since 1970 it has formed a subsidiary called G & W Realty Corp. and has a broadened real estate stake in the U.S. through a separate company, the Richards Group.

Welcome to your store

— Hudson's Bay Co. This is the prime mover behind Parkade Tower, compared to which Capitol Centre's parking facilities are negligible. It, too, was completed in 1976 and it has 17 floors above and below ground: this is the building which devotes 11 floors to parking. Located just across de Maisonneuve Blvd. from the Bay's downtown store, it connects to the McGill Metro station by underground passage.

Hudson's Bay has major investments in energy. It is one of the principal shareholders in Siebens Oil & Gas Ltd. (with 34.9 per cent of the outstanding stock), of Calgary, which is exploring for petroleum around the world.

Hudson's Bay also has a 21 per cent stake in Hudson's Bay Oil & Gas Co., of Calgary, making it that firm's second largest shareholder.

Besides Parkade Tower, the company has significant real estate holdings. In 1976 it bought 57 hectares from Lebanese interests for a regional shopping centre, on the West Island, for example. And in 1973 it bought control of one of the top 15 publicly-owned real estate companies in Canada, Mark-borough Properties Ltd., which specializes in building large residential, commercial and industrial projects in Ontario.

— The Heitman Group. Looking elsewhere in the downtown area for major new developments, one cannot avoid La Cité, the fourth largest high-rise project in Montreal.

YUL Associates, an Illinois partnership which controls La Cité, is a spin-off of the Heitman Group Inc., of Chicago, which also operates a mortgage banking and property broker-age business in Canada. Heitman is a wholly-owned subsidiary of Cordura Corp., a diversified services company registered in Delaware, with assets of $62 million.

While it itself is not directly involved in the oil business, "72 per cent of the net sales in its marketing services operations were derived from direct mail programs conducted for Gulf Oil Corp.," according to a Cordura report to the U.S. Secu-rities & Exchange Commission.

The health of Heitman's parent company, in other words, is very much tied to the oil industry.

It's also worth noting that the group's most active arm here, Heitman Canadian Realty Investors, consists of 10 trustees of whom five are also directors of firms involved in petroleum. This is an unusually high ratio.

One of these interlocks involves Edward A. Galvin, chair-man and president of Canadian Industrial Gas & Oil Ltd. and also chairman of Norcen Energy Resources Ltd. which ulti-mately controls Gaz Metropolitain.

— Abbey Glen Property Corp. Ltd. Another variation on this kind of involvement existed here, too, when this company helped put up two large office buildings at 2001 and 2075 University St. (Though one of these is built directly over the McGill Metro and the other connects to it by passageway, here too we find, extensive parking facilities.)

It has also begun a large suburban housing development at Laval-sur-le-Lac.

The major shareholder in Abbey Glen's parent company (Capital & Counties Property Co. Ltd., of the U.K.) was South Africa's Union Corp. Union has a stake in North Sea oil exploration and, more importantly, it is a prime supplier of platinum sold to the North American auto industry for anti-pollution devices.

Indeed, in its 1972 annual report Union exultantly said that a long-term contract just signed with General Motors meant extra sales over the next 10 years of some half a billion dollars. Consequently, it was "embarking on a major program of expansion."

As the chairman of Impala Platinum Ltd., the world's second largest platinum producer and a key Union holding, told shareholders in 1976, the auto industry is a customer "on whose prosperity our prosperity depends."[6]

Credit Foncier

— Crédit Foncier Franco-Canadien. This French-controlled company has been lending mortgages since 1880 and its clients today include some of the city's newest high-rises. It also owns scores of small and medium size residential properties around the city and numerous undeveloped tracts of up to a million square feet in the suburbs. Its real estate investments across Canada shot up by 45 per cent in 1976 to $101 million.

The firm has been active in petroleum as far back as 1952 when it incorporated Francana Oil & Gas. Though it sold most of its interest in Francana in 1975 to its long-time partner, the Anglo American Corp. of South Africa, Crédit Foncier still retains over 300,000 shares. In addition to drilling for oil in Western Canada, Francana controls Trend Exploration Ltd. which is searching for oil as far away as Indonesia and Pakistan.

Crédit Foncier's major shareholder is the Paribas Group, one of France's principal financial-industrial complexes. It has large investments in four real estate companies in France, including one associated with Paris' well-known skyscraper cluster, "La Défense". The group's 1974 accounts show that biggest bloc investments (11.5 per cent) are in petroleum; indeed, it has a substantial 4.3 per cent stake in what Fortune magazine ranks as the world's 18th largest industrial company, Compagnie Française de Pétrole. This is the parent company of Total Petroleum (North America) Ltd., the Calgary oil firm which rates as Canada's 92nd largest company in sales in 1976, according to Canadian Business.

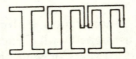

— International Telephone & Telegraph. Through its Levitt Canada Ltd. subsidiary, ITT has projects in the bedroom suburbs of Brossard, Pierrefonds and Dollard-des-Ormeaux which call for a total of several thousand homes.

Through another subsidiary, Canadawide Parking Services Ltd. ITT is also the No. 1 parking lot operator in Montreal. Some 28,000 vehicles can park on facilities at one time, estimates Canadawide's general manager, Eric Pace.

Michael Dugas

ITT has an active hand in both ends of modern-day commuting, as a developer of bedroom suburbs and as the largest operator of in-town parking lots.

— Genstar Ltd. This is the largest home-builder in Canada — until now this has all been in Western Canada but, with the acquisition of Abbey Glen in the summer of 1976 Genstar plans to become a major builder in the East as well.

As described in Chap. 7 through Miron Co. Ltd., a subsidiary, Genstar owns 450 prime acres of land in the centre of Montreal Island and another 750 acres on the South Shore. It plans to build houses, offices or light industry on them eventually.

For years Miron has also been a leading construction contractor on highways as well as a major producer of the cement used in highways, high-rises and other construction. Through other subsidiaries, Genstar is a major supplier of home-building materials.

Genstar also looms large in the oil industry. Subsidiaries are building tankers and oil rigs in British Columbia, shipping the most supplies to oil workers in the Western Arctic, building homes for oil workers at the Athabasca tar sands and making special cement for oil wells.

Genstar's principal shareholder (with 21 per cent held directly or indirectly) is Société Générale de Belgique, of Brussels. It is the biggest shareholder in Petrofina, the multinational oil company which calculates it has some 160 gas stations in the Montreal area). It also has a fleet of tankers and has major investments in mining and manufacturing companies whose products are used by automotive firms.

Bovis Corporation Limited

— Bovis Corp. Ltd. Through a joint venture called Cartier-Denault, Bovis is developing housing subdivisions in Candiac, Laval, Ste. Thérèse and Blainville. Bovis, which itself had $117 million in assets nationwide in 1975, is the biggest shareholder in Consolidated Building Corp. which builds houses and high-rises mostly in Ontario and has $100 million in assets.

Bovis is a conglomerate and one of its companies, McNamara Corp., is exploring for oil and built the super-tanker terminal at Come-by-Chance, Newfoundland.

That is but a tiny sample of the petroleum activities of Bovis' ultimate owners, the Peninsular & Oriental Steam Navigation Co., of London. In addition to carrying out extensive oil exploration projects, the P & 0 runs a fleet of oil super-tankers which are as long as the Empire State Building is high.

The group's orientation to oil is further buttressed through the activities of its chairman, the Earl of Inchcape. In addition to being a director of British Petroleum, he is head of his family's conglomerate, Inchcape & Co. Ltd., which is involved in offshore drilling in the North Sea, Saudi Arabia and Nigeria and sells cars and car parts from the United Kingdom to Guam.

— Lehndorff Group. This German-backed group ranks among Canada's largest real estate organizations with reported assets approaching the half billion dollar mark.

One of the group's Canadian members, Lehndorff Corp., has three Canadian directors — and all three of them are also directors of TransCanada Pipelines Ltd.

Indeed, one of them, Chairman John H. Coleman, is also a director of Siebens Oil & Gas and of the Chrysler Corp. (in Detroit).

Trizec Corporation Ltd.

— And then there is Trizec Corp., the largest developer in Canada after Cadillac Fairview. Through its British owners it has associations with two global mining companies, Anglo

American Corp. of South Africa and Rio Tinto-Zinc Corp., whose Canadian subsidiaries are important suppliers of raw materials for automobile companies. In fact, one of RTZ's subsidiaries, Indal Ltd., is a prime manufacturer of auto parts in its own right. Anglo American also has substantial oil exploration investments in Canada and around the world.

Such a list could go on and on. Even Sir Alastair Pilkington, chairman of the glass company which has popularized the insulation-shorn glass-walled high-rise, turns up as a director or British Petroleum.

I am perfectly ready to concede that a good portion of these interlocks are pure coincidence and no more than that, but when this phenomenon takes place across the board it speaks for itself.

The ownership of some of the key companies is, of course, secret, and so this blocks exploration of their ties to the auto-petro interests. Aster Corp., owned through an anonymous Swiss bank account is one such company; through its development of Brossard, it helped pioneer suburban sprawl on the South Shore. While Aster's ownership cannot be traced, it is worth noting that the president (Leonard Francheschini) of one of Quebec's two largest roadbuilders, the Francon division of the Lafarge cement company, is a director of Aster as well as of the Swiss bank. Clearly these highway-cement interests have as much to gain from sprawl as any automobile or petroleum company.

It is *hard* to find big developers which are not part of this phenomenon. Kaufman & Broad, Inc., the U.S. firm which is developing housing subdivisions on the West Island appears to be one such company, though its own ownership picture is not all that clear. Campeau Corp., another suburban homebuilder which is focusing on a giant scheme on Ile Bizard, could be another such company — though the identity of some of its main backers remains a mystery. In 1972, Campeau, a Canadian company whose chairman and chief executive officer is Franco-Ontarian Robert Campeau, borrowed 105 million Swiss francs to finance the purchase of 48 per cent of its shares from Power Corp. of Canada Ltd. Just who gave Campeau that loan is a well-kept secret. For what it's worth, the company does have a couple of directors tied in with the auto-petro complex.*

It goes without saying that the majority of the secondary companies owned by local builders — like the Zunenshine family's Belcourt group or Max Zentner's companies — may well be independent of the auto-petro sector. For one thing, such interests simply are not big enough to diversify in that direction. You need to be a millionaire many times over before you get seriously involved in these other fields.**

But a couple of points can be made about such local builders.

First, they are not important enough to reverse the mode of development established by their giant international colleagues. They tend largely to mimic the subdivision and highrise formats established by the Cadillac Fairviews and the ITTs.

Secondly, they themselves are often not really quite so independent of the energy-auto sector as might appear at first. This is because, like most developers, they are only as strong as their financial support. And that support often comes from banks with huge investments in that sector.

Thus, for example, the Zunenshines and Zentner are clients of the country's largest bank, Royal Bank of Canada. So are the two biggest single companies in the entire energy-auto sector: General Motors and Imperial Oil. (Indeed, the ties are so strong that the bank's chairman is a member of GM's Detroit board and Imperial's chairman is on the bank's board.)

For that matter, other clients of the Royal include Genstar, the Empain-Schneider group and Aster — with Bank Chairman W. Earle McLaughlin himself as a director of the first two.

For one of the most vivid examples of banks' shared interests in urban development and energy one can turn to the case of the City of London's elite Hambro family.

---

* Frank Stronach is chairman and chief executive officer of Magna International Inc., a manufacturer of automotive products. Robert L. Pierce is president of Alberta Gas Ethylene Co.
** Local families besides the Bronfmans which have done so include the Cummings and the Websters.

The family has vast real estate holdings in Britain as well as this country; its development firm called Hambro Canada Ltd. has more than $100 million in property assets — mostly in high-rise apartments and shopping centres. Meanwhile another arm, Hambros Bank, is one of the largest of London's merchant banks. It, perhaps more than any other London bank, specializes in loans to shipping companies — notably those in the oil tanker business.

Just how tied the family is to the public's energy habits was seen in 1975 with the same downturn in world oil consumption that hurt Canadian Pacific's tanker fleet. With tankers standing idle and unable to get customers, the companies owning or leasing them were unable to pay back Hambros Bank's loans. The bank went through a hammering that was the talk of the City.

In Canada itself they also have a direct tie to the oil industry. R. Nicholas Hambro, one of the younger members of the family, is a director of White Pass & Yukon Corp., which owns and operates oil tankers and an oil pipeline in Western Canada and sells petroleum products there as well.

We are entering the age of the 'new towns,' developers say. And that, they say, means less automobile usage.

Will it really?

Following on the success of its new town in Reston, Va., during the 1960s, Gulf is now at work on an encore at Laprairie.

By planning stores, places of employment and abundant pedestrian and bicycle pathways within its community, Gulf says it hopes to avoid the problems of auto-intensive sprawl which characterizes much of the suburbs. This is what it had said would happen at Reston.

However, in his book, *Mortgage on America,* a Washington Post editor, Leonard Downie, Jr., revisited Reston after its first decade of operations and found that things have not worked out that way. He buttresses personal observation with quotations from the highway industry itself.

He cites how "Highway User," a trade magazine, reassured its readers in September, 1972, that a survey showed that people used the pedestrian walkways in addition to, not instead of, trips made by car. The average Reston family owned 1.8 cars and still made between 11 and 15 daily car trips.

"A Reston wife cannot be left without a car because she needs it for her necessary trips, like most other suburban wives," said Highway User.

It adds that new towns were begun "with the idea that their superior design and emphasis on pedestrianism would substantially reduce the need for cars, [but] the suburban lifestyle replaces expectation with reality . . .

"Auto ownership and parking needs within new communities differ little from those of other suburban developments. It remains high," concluded the trade magazine.

It is still premature to judge how Gulf's project at Laprairie will compare since construction on it has only just begun. But it is worth noting Downie's conclusion on how the new town movement has worked so far south of the border:

"More soil is paved over, more erosion-causing drainage problems are created and more auto exhaust pollutants are added to the air.

"In this, as in many other ways, . . . new towns add up simply to larger-scale suburbia."[7]

If nothing else, Gulf's experience shows just how deeply the energy-intensive development is rooted — in not just the corporate process but in the acquired habits of the public.

When existing petroleum reserves run low, will those metropolitan development interests which have investments in petroleum be left high and dry?

No.

Many of these same interests are busily preparing for the nuclear age which, they think, will succeed the present era's dependency on fossil fuels.

Here is a look at what some of the biggest of these interests are doing:

— Gulf Oil Corp. has followed the trend of many petroleum companies of diversifying into the nuclear field. It has a stake in uranium reserves at Rabbit Lake, Sask., and in uranium prospects in Quebec's Mont Laurier and Fort Chimo areas as well as near Sudbury, Ont. In April, 1976, a partnership between a Gulf subsidiary and the Province of Quebec was announced whereby the two would explore for uranium ore in a 1,200-square mile area of Quebec. The province is seeking uranium for fuel in 35 planned nuclear power stations and for processing at a proposed $6 billion nuclear enrichment plant near James Bay.

Gulf is also 50-50 partners with the Royal Dutch/Shell Group in forming General Atomic Co., a manufacturer of gas-cooled reactor systems for central station electric power plants.

— Genstar's affiliate, Société Générale de Belgique, is a prime mover behind Belgium's well-advanced nuclear power industry.

Numerous companies in La Générale's family take part in this industry, both inside Belgium and abroad: MMN makes fuel elements for nuclear reactors; Traction et Electricité designs nuclear power stations; Cockerill make steel equipment for them, and Belgonucléaire has engineering contracts for power stations as far away as Libya and Pakistan. Belgonucléaire is also making plutonium fuel for the Italian National Committee for Nuclear Energy.

La Générale's 1976 annual report also notes that Belgonu-cléaire has received "an important new order from Japan" for the "treatment and conditioning of radioactive waste". There is a certain irony in this since it was the Générale group which first helped bring radioactivity to Japan by providing the uranium for the bombs exploded over Nagasaki and Hiroshima.

— Empain-Schneider group, the principal organization behind Candiac, is the largest shareholder in Framatome — which has a literal monopoly in France's nuclear power industry. Empain-Schneider holds most of its interest in Framatome through a subsidiary, Creusot-Loire.

In April, 1976, Creusot-Loire announced it would hold an initial 60 per cent interest in Novatome, a new company which is to develop fast breeder reactors in conjunction with France's atomic energy commission.

— Gulf & Western has a big stake in a nuclear future.

In its registration papers to the U.S. Securities & Exchange Commission, it describes its involvement this way:

"G&W manufactures forged fittings, flanges, connectors, valves and a variety of other piping components.

"These products are used in virtually every type of pipeline carrying liquid, solid or gas material, oil and petrochemical refineries, chemical production plants, fossil and nuclear

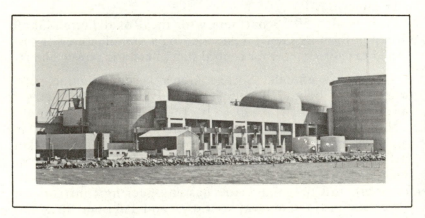

Gulf & Western products are used in many nuclear generating plants, such as this one in Pickering, Ont.

power generating plants, oil well drilling and production machinery, nuclear submarines, liquid and synthetic natural gas tankers . . ."

— Canadian Pacific has been strongly tempted by the idea of getting into the uranium enrichment field in the James Bay area. Though it appears to have dropped any plans for involvement there, it is still involved in the industry through an associated company, Dominion Bridge.

Indeed, Canadian Nuclear Association literature hails Dominion Bridge for playing "a vital role in the fabrication of reactors and major components." Customers from as far away as Taiwan come to the firm's Lachine plant for special parts.

— Union Corp. has also been exploring for uranium in Southern Africa.

In addition to these companies, Trizec Corp. Ltd., owner of Place Ville Marie and other downtown office buildings and land for development in Brossard, has indirect ties to one of the giants on the world uranium scene.

Its parent interests in England have ties with the Rothschilds who also have extensive holdings in uranium mining companies in Canada. These include Rio Algom Ltd., Canada's No. 1 producer, and associates of France's Mokta group of companies, which plan to start production in this country within several years.

All this data provides abundant evidence, I think, that we have to reorient our thinking if we are to come to grips with the forces behind the urban metamorphosis. It is very nice to make resolutions calling for an enhanced role for mass transit and conservation and a reduced role for the car and other aspects of development; but this can be just spinning wheels unless it is understood that those who provide the financial push for metropolitan growth also have an overwhelming vested interest in perpetuating the present waste. The strategy and pressure tactics of such goals should be shaped accordingly.

While many of the local managers of these development interests may quite honestly speak in favor of energy reform and work toward it, the ultimate decisions rest with others well beyond them. Some attempts at amelioration — such as Gulf's

new town and other companies' energy-conscious high-rises —
are being made; but these are only nibbles at the problem. A
new town like Gulf's on the South Shore is located near no
commuter rail line and is not big enough to warrant a regular,
convenient commuter bus service to the city; it brings no help
to the cause of energy-conscious urban planning.

What companies might be looked to — and addressed — to
help turn things around? Logically, the foremost single company would be Canadian Pacific. After all, what other private
organization is in a position to provide rail service *and* the development to go along with it? But its vast interest in energy
consumption makes it doubtful that it would have much incentive to help usher in a return to the more efficient, harmonious type of development it was promoting several generations ago. And if a citizens' group or government sought to
communicate its views to those who control the company in an
attempt to persuade it, to whom should it go? Nobody knows.
The anonymity of the company's power helps separate this
power from responsibility.

Footnotes — Chapter 14

1. Montreal Gazette, April 19, 1977, "Canada near world lead in over-use of
   energy," by the Canadian Press.
2. Toronto Globe & Mail, April 20, 1977, "Who's an energy hog? The Canadian, and his use of cars makes him one," by Mary Kate Rowan.
3. Ibid.
4. Toronto Globe & Mail, Mar. 25, 1977, "Canadians seen worst of energy
   wasters."
5. Montreal Gazette, April 17, 1975, "Building harnesses body heat," by
   United Press International.
6. Statement by I.T. Grieg, chairman of Impala Platinum Ltd., to shareholders, as it appeared in advertisement form in the Financial Times of
   London, Oct. 1, 1976.
7. Downie, Leonard, Jr., "Mortgage on America" (New York: Praeger Publishers, Inc., 1974), pp. 159-162.

Chapter 15
Bonds:
Europe expands its hegemony

"The borrower is servant to the lender."
Old Testament, *Proverbs*, xxii, 7

ON A SPRING DAY IN QUEBEC CITY in 1977, the finance minister of the five-month old Parti Québécois government delivered his government's first budget. The party's leftist supporters had been eagerly awaiting this day, for during the election campaign the party, promising "an economic system eliminating every form of exploitation of workers," had said it would bring in a guaranteed minimum income, indexation of personal income taxes to the cost of living, a massive cleanup of the environment, etc.

They were to be bitterly disappointed, for this year anyway. Perhaps the new locale chosen by the minister inadvertently illustrated his predicament: he announced his program to more than 100 reporters and editorial writers and asked for their understanding, not inside the parliamentary building, as might have behooved a government with a "maîtres chez nous" credo, but across the street in the luxurious new Quebec Hilton Hotel. It is a building (see illustration in Chap. 3) owned by a European-owned company, Trizec, and managed by an American firm, Hilton. In a very real sense the new government was, through no fault of its own, now the financial captive of the play now, pay later form of rapid modernization which had transformed the province since the Quiet Revolution of the early 1960s.

Far from being a *host* to European and U.S. interests coming into the province, the government was now symbolically their *guest* — and, as this 1977-8 budget and many future budgets will show, a distinctly *paying* guest.

The budget announced that day by the minister, Jacques Parizeau, reflected that brutal reality. Declaring that "the road to independence passes through healthy finances." Parizeau offered what his opponents derided as a "status quo" budget tailored for the international financial community rather than for the workers. Quebec's borrowing would go down from $1.35 billion the previous fiscal year to $900 million. Deeply in debt from the prodigal spending of the previous Liberal government, the Parti Québécois government was now forced to cut back on more borrowing (which could have financed the promised programs) to pay back the existing debts and to groom an image of financial conservatism with which to impress lenders in future years.

Unable to be true to its ideals because of this debt, the government was forced — only "temporarily," of course — to let the international financial community determine policy.

It was not the first time Quebec had found itself over its head in debt. In his book describing the Union Nationale Party under Premier Maurice Duplessis in the 1930s, Conrad Black wrote colorfully: "Like gluttonously hungry children . . . the Union Nationale deputation swarmed through the vast kitchen of the provincial government. At first, they advanced timidly. Soon glee replaced respectfulness, intoxication banished continence . . ."[1]

Dominique Clift, of the Montreal Star, recalls what happened next: "The political turmoil and budget problems which ensued caused financial institutions in 1939 to tell Mr. Duplessis that he should seek another mandate before contracting any more loans. Duplessis lost the election and the Liberals were returned to power. The effect on the province was traumatic. There arose an almost superstitious fear of financial institutions and of their ability to thwart collective aspirations. For both the Liberals and the Union Nationale, which came back to power in 1944, it seemed imperative to keep provincial deficits and borrowing at the lowest level possible. The idea was to avoid any situation where 'outsiders' such as banks could dictate policy."[2]

Gradually during the 1960s the province forgot these old restraints as a new generation assumed power and became increasingly determined to make the province a land of superdams, go-go industrialization, autoroutes and cosmopolitan tastes and consumption demands.

Finally, Black's image for how "intoxication banished continence" in Quebec in the '30s became applicable for Canada as a whole in the '70s. In 1975 Canada borrowed more money in the international and foreign bond markets than any other country in the world: $4.5 billion. That represents an amazing 20 per cent of all the borrowing made in those markets by all countries in the world.[3]

Borrowings in 1976, however, put that in the shade. Canada borrowed $9.2 billion in foreign debt markets. The next closest country was Brazil — far, far back with $3.4 billion in borrowings.[4]

In 1975, $.38 cents of every dollar borrowed by municipal and provincial governments* and by companies came from foreign sources. In the first 10 months of 1976 — that is, up to two weeks before the election of the Parti Québécois on Nov. 15 — it was up to $.60.[5]

This mania for borrowing is not some aberration peculiar to governments and companies — the population at large behaves in the same way. It is part of a national enthusiasm for debt which embraces everyone from the milkman to the housewife to the businessman.

Canadians are more in debt than any other nationality *in the world*. The average Canadian consumer was in debt to the tune

---

* The figure excludes federal borrowing which is traditionally in Canadian dollars.

of 21.3 per cent of his personal disposable income at the start of 1973, according to calculations made by federal statisticians and economists at the Royal Bank. That is, if the man on the street earns $10,000 a year after taxes he will owe $2,130 to lending institutions like the Royal, credit card companies, department stores, etc. The figure does not even count mortgages. It is more than 50 per cent above the figure for the average consumer in the United States (where the average is only 14 per cent of personal disposable income).[6]

Of all 10 provinces in Canada, none is so easy-spending as Quebec. The per capita debt in Quebec in 1975 was $924.48 — and that includes every man, woman and child. This figure, which comes from the office of Quebec Minister of Social Development Pierre Marois, covers all the trademarks of the society of consumption — credit for cars, records, televisions, travel, clothes, stereos, etc. (but, again, it excludes mortgages; otherwise it would be much higher). It represents a lusty 86 per cent increase over 1970.[7]

As in government and corporate bonds, in short, so in personal credit cards.

But back to bonds . . .

There are very important strings attached to this kind of indebtedness. It means, for one thing, that enormous amounts of money will be flowing out of Quebec and Canada as this money is paid back in coming decades. Because of the interest rates, much more money goes out than ever comes in.* It

---

* The government officials who arrange the borrowing often say that taxpayers save money by borrowing from overseas because interest rates are lower there than in North America. That's fine in theory, but in practice this has boomeranged. This is partly because the savings on lower interests rares are party wi ed out by the higher commissions and fees entailed in floating a bond issue abroad. But it is mostly because of the fluctuating exchange rates.

Let's look, for example, at what happened to the exchange rate after the Drapeau administration borrowed 100 million Deutschmarks in April, 1969, in order to pay back earlier loans for Expo 67 and to get the Expo's ball park, Jarry Park, ready for major league play. In Canada at that time the interest rate on this bond issue would have been 9 per cent, but in Germany Drapeau was able to get a 7 per cent rate payable over 20 years. It looked like a sweet deal for the taxpayers.

But since then a lot has happened to the worth of the Deutschmark. In April, 1969, it was worth $.26 (Canadian). Eight years later it was worth $.48. Because Montreal taxpayers are paying back this debt in Deutschmarks, rather than in dollars, this means they are heavy losers.

helps weaken the value of the Canadian dollar, which by October, 1977, had fallen to less than $.90 (U.S.).

Secondly, it also raises artificially the standard of living and raises expectations beyond the realms of realism. It makes people think that all these bridges, highways, stadiums, subways and sewage projects, and the development which is dependent on them, are within its natural reach, when in fact it can no more really afford them than a clerk can afford a Cadillac — making the down payment is easy, but paying off the installments is another story. This is why the chairman of the Toronto-Dominion Bank, Allen Lambert, commented at the height of the borrowing orgy in mid-1976, "We have been living well — too well perhaps. We still think we are rich but we are heavily in debt . . . (We) can't afford to borrow abroad to maintain our standard of living."[8]

Such levels of debt have a third effect. They put, as the biblical quotation at the start of the chapter warns, a subtle degree of power over the borrower by the lender.* Duplessis learned this when the lenders caused him to call an election; and New York's Mayor Abraham Beame learned this in the 1970s as banks, doubting New York's ability to pay back loans, repeatedly brought the city to the brink of bankruptcy and thousands of municipal workers, ranging from policemen to schoolteachers, lost their jobs in economy measures. In New York's case, however, most of those lenders were local institutions; their civic conscience, such as it was, could be appealed to, and this helped.

---

* It should be noted that there is, however, one big advantage to obtaining capital from the sale of bonds instead of selling equity. Bonds contain a promise to pay a specified sum of money at a specified date and to pay interest periodically. After the bond is paid back — after five years or 15 years or whatever the specified date — the entire undertaking which was being financed by the bonds is owned by the party which sold them. If you sell equity — that is, stock — the person who owns that stock continues to own it (and thus retains an influence within the undertaking) indefinitely. Thus it is sometimes argued that the sale of bonds is less of a "soul-selling" exercise from the point of view of the seller.

But in order to be able to sell the bonds in the first place, and to be able to continue to sell new bonds in order to get the money to pay back those people who have bought the previous bonds (for this kind of debt is regenerating) the seller must jump through various hoops held by the underwriters.

But even in relatively undramatic times the role of this financial community, particularly the underwriters,* is substantial. The underwriters often exercise an influence on government far swifter than even the most vociferous voter group. If they, and the investment community generally, decide a city or province is badly managed or a poor risk, they can raise the rate that government must pay to borrow money or even deny borrowing completely. This is the nature of the relationship Parizeau was implicitly acknowledging when he handed down his conservative budget. The cornucopia of social democratic programs to which his government was pledged would have cost far too much money to raise through taxes; he would have had to go to a reluctant investment community for vast amounts of money.

In a don't-kick-the-U.S. speech in Toronto, the entire relationship was summed up in a sentence by the chairman of the executive committee of the New York-based First Boston Corp., one of the most active bond underwriters in Canada. Canada is no exception to the rule, said Alexander C. Tomlinson, that "unless you are financially self-sufficient, you better be nice to your banker."[9]

Just who are these influential underwriters and their backers?

The first thing that might leap to mind is "Wall Street." After all, New York is where the money bags have sprung from traditionally. That's where the premier of the Parti Québécois

---

* Underwriters serve as middlemen between lenders and the actual borrowers, though they take on many of the characteristics of the borrowers in that they act as their agents. An underwriter is generally a private firm (in Europe it's often a major bank) which arranges with a government to raise money for it; it determines how worthy the government's management and plans are, what the risks are, what the rate of interest should be: then it advertises for individuals or institutions to buy the government's bonds at that rate. Often, to spread the work load and reduce the risks for each firm, several firms will get together and handle the bond issue as a group or syndicate, with one firm acting as syndicate manager.

A variation of this is the so-called privately-placed bond issue; in this, there is no need to solicit sales from many parties. Rather, one party undertakes to buy the whole bond issue. Hydro-Quebec frequently goes this route.

government, René Lévesque, journeyed early in his term to try to sweetalk the financial leaders into keeping those bags coming. That's where much of the money comes from to finance Hydro-Quebec's James Bay project (the Rockefeller-related Metropolitan Life Insurance Co. is a prime buyer of Hydro bonds, as well as the Prudential Insurance Co. of America).

The Gazette (Len Sidaway)

Montreal, 1976 — New York banker David Rockefeller (right) journeys to the Montreal home of Robert Bourassa, then premier of Quebec. The province then enjoyed the financial blessing of U.S. bond investors.

But in the 1970s a remarkable and little-noted shift has taken place. While the U.S. remains an important debt market, it has been displaced as No. 1 by Europe on the provincial and municipal level.

In isolation, this may not seem important. But taken in conjunction with European pre-eminence in the fields of land-ownership, construction companies, and building materials, it gives Europe enormous influence in shaping growth. It is, after all, these loans which determine so many of the building blocks of urban growth: they are essential to the realization of highways, subways, sewers, water treatment plants and power projects without which Montreal would not have expanded the way it has.

This role of money-lending has a special political character, quite unlike that of the other roles of the European interests ac-

Associated Press

New York, 1977 — Quebec's new premier, René Lévesque, himself travels to New York to see Rockefeller (left), New York Governor Hugh Carey (centre) and others in an attempt to convince U.S. investors that Quebec was still worthy of their confidence. Lévesque fai'.d to allay U.S. wariness, and Quebec's dependency on European capital increased even further.

tive in urban growth. The money lenders have a direct rapport with government. They are cultivated associates of government — unlike landowners, of whose identity government is more often than not ignorant. They have an entrée in the corridors of government. Government, in other words, *needs* them.

The provincial government's financial orientation towards Europe had already begun prior to the election of the Parti Québécois. In January, 1976, the Liberal government floated a Eurodollar issue; in all, it went to Europe three times for a total of $175 million in 1976. By contrast, it went to the U.S. for considerably less, $100 million. It succeeded in raising the remaining $225 million from within Canada.

Early signs indicate that the Parti Québécois government might outdo its predecessors. In May 1977, it announced it had arranged a $300 million (U.S. dollars) loan from a London-based syndicate of European banks, for example.

This came on the heels of $60 million and $65 million bond issues in January and May, 1977 respectively, both in Deutchmarks. By contrast, during this same period, $200 million worth of bonds had been sold in Canada (much of them to Caisse de Dépôt et Placement du Québec, an almost captive buyer) and none in the U.S.

But so far we have talked only of the provincial government. This has been to help put into context what has also been happening on the levels of municipal and regional government.

The City of Montreal is the ultimate example of this phenomenon. Until 1969, when it borrowed once in Deutchmarks, it had never borrowed in overseas currencies in modern times. Then, first tentatively and finally dogmatically, the city has gone to Europe for money. In the two-year period since May, 1975, the city floated 10 bond offerings to raise over half a billion dollars; *not one* of those times did Mayor Drapeau's administration seek that money in Canada.* Indeed, only one time did it seek the money in the U.S. — a far cry from those relatively low budget days of the 1960s when Montreal borrowed virtually all its money inside North America. Nine of

* Of this, only about 40 per cent, or the $214 million raised in 1977, is directly associated with financing the Olympic Games. The rest has gone toward paying for roads, sewers and other more mundane everyday expenses.

the 10 issues were placed overseas — seven in Zurich, one in Dusseldorf and one in London.

Some of the surrounding municipalities have also joined the trend, though less spectacularly — Laval, Montreal East and Pointe-aux-Trembles are among them. The province's two main regional governments, the Montreal Urban Community and the Quebec Urban Community have likewise followed suit.

If one adds up all the bond issues for the years 1975 and 1976 from the cities of Montreal and Laval and the Montreal Urban Community — a fairly broad-based sampling of the province's urban picture — one gets the total of $631 million. Of that total amount of money, 89 per cent was from foreign sources. And of that 89 per cent, 63 per cent were in Europe.[10]*

But *which* European interests are involved in this trend?

Often, but not invariably, it is the same interests who have been active in other sectors — land ownership, construction, etc. Thus, as mentioned in Chap. 7, on one side of the ocean the banking arm of the Société Générale de Belgique family may help underwrite an MUC bond issue to build subway extensions, while on this side a construction arm, Miron Co., may reap the fruit of such investments by obtaining, through competitive bidding, a super-portion of the contracts to build the extensions.

One does not have to read a sinister *quid-pro-quo* into such interconnections to make them interesting. There may be no connection whatever in the fact that Miron gets so many MUC contracts or that Miron's local quarry remains operating in the centre of Montreal island, the subject of trifling $500 fines, despite the MUC air pollution service's statement that it is the island's largest dust polluter. Interconnections like these simply show that these global groups have their fingers in a surprising number of local pots.

---

* This excludes the $214 million package of bond issues to pay for the Olympic Games which were arranged by the City of Montreal in the closing days of 1976 but not actually offered to the public until January 1977. If this were included, the percentages of foreign financing would be even more intense. The lead underwriter was the London-based branch of a New York bank, Citibank.

Similarly, the Swiss Credit Bank and the Union Bank of Switzerland, both of them close to Switzerland's Holderbank cement interests which control St. Lawrence Cement Co., have between them acted as the lead underwriters on no less than six of Montreal's 10 bond issues during the aforementioned two-year period; and St. Lawrence Cement happens to have been a major supplier of concrete to numerous municipal projects, including the Olympic facilities. Whether by offering credit or products, or both, these global interests can cash in directly on what Parizeau, whose government's social policies are now crippled by such expenditures, ruefully describes as "les aventures montréalaises."

France, too, is represented. The Banque de Paris et des Pays Bas, financial arm of the Parisbas Group, has also been underwriting its share of local bond issues. The bank is the largest shareholder in Crédit Foncier Franco-Canadien which has helped finance several new high-rises in downtown Montreal and is also a landlord of numerous low-income dwellings on the immigrant corridor which parallels St. Lawrence Blvd.

But such interconnections go on and on, involving not just construction and building material companies but property-owners as well. Thus when, a month after announcing his first budget, Parizeau floated a $65 million bond issue in order to commence the $900 million in borrowings which his budget required, he floated it through a syndicate headed by Westdeutsche Landesbank Girozentrale. This bank also happens to manage a company called RWI which in mid-1976 had pur-

Henry Aubin

The provincial and municipal governments of Quebec are being attracted toward the money markets of Paris, Zurich, London, Düsseldorf and Brussels.

chased the largest apartment building in Montreal, Mountain Place, among other properties. Another member of that same syndicate, helping Parizeau raise the money, was Banca di Roma, the principal bank behind Società Generale Immobiliare — owner of the Stock Exchange Tower, the Hyatt-Regency Hotel and the Port Royal apartments.

If ever any enthusiasts in the Quebec government attempt a repeat of the shortlived May, 1976, budget proposal to impose a 33 per cent tax on sales of real estate to non-residents, they might recall such interlocking investment by these foreign banks — and understand why the government cannot afford to alienate these institutions. Certainly a heavy tax on sales to non-residents would achieve such an alienation since it would make it virtually impossible for, say, Westdeutsche Landesbank to ever resell its real estate to another foreign buyer — and foreign buyers historically would be the only ones able to pay for the real estate at prices high enough to give the seller a profit.

This docility before the banks is likely to increase in the future. Quebec's (and Canada's) borrowing binge climaxed with the election of the Parti Québécois,* and since then the political uncertainties and emotional hostility on the part of many Canadian investors from outside Quebec helped reduce the amount of money available for bonds from within Canada. This means that Quebec will have to continue to go outside Canada for the indefinite future. What the party calls "independence" from Canada, would also mean increasing dependence on other countries for capital needs.

---

* In the first three months of 1977 Canada fell from first place — as the largest international borrower — to fifth place behind France, Britain, Sweden and Venezuela[11]. Public and private bond financings by federal, provincial and municipal governments as well as by companies fell to $4.6 billion for the first three months of 1977 from $5.6 billion in the corresponding 1976 period.[12]

Footnotes — Chapter 15

1. Black, Conrad, "Duplessis" (Toronto: McClelland and Stewart Ltd., 1977), p. 148.
2. Montreal Star, Mar. 5, 1977, "The politics of Quebec's credit," by Dominique Clift.
3. Calculations derived from "Borrowing in International Capital Markets, Aug. 1976 (Washington: Economic Analysis and Projections Dept., World Bank).
4. Montreal Gazette, Jan. 5, 1977, "Canadian borrowing leads world in 1976, by Peter Cook, Toronto Financial Times. The article uses projections by Morgan Guaranty Trust Co., of New York.
5. Calculations derived from Wood Gundy debt financing report (Toronto: Wood Gundy Ltd.), Oct. 1976, p. 2.
6. Telephone interview with experts at the Royal Bank of Canada's Service des recherches économiques, Montreal headquarters, June 1, 1977.
7. This comes from an aide to Marois, Jean-Pierre Belanger, who specializes in consumer credit. He is author of a study on the subject aptly named, "Le Québec de l'illusion de l'abondance à la réalité de l'indebtment."
8. Montreal Star, Aug. 41, 1976, "We're not so rich as you might think." by Canadian Press.
9. Montreal Gazette, Nov. 10, "Don't tread on U.S., banker warns" by Robert Lake, Financial Times.
10. Montreal Gazette, Dec. 17, 1976, "Foreign influence in urban Canada helped by jump in Canadian debt," by Henry Aubin.
11. Montreal Gazette, Mar. 30, 1977, "Canada bond issues drop sharply," by Peter Cook, Toronto Financial Times. The article uses data from Morgan Guaranty Trust Co., New York.
12. Toronto Globe & Mail, May 3, 1977, "Public, private bond financings decline." The article uses data from Wood Gundy Ltd.

Chapter 16

Conclusion

CONCLUDING CHAPTERS ARE, CONVENTIONALLY, supposed to propose solutions to problems. I cannot offer a neat package of cures, only a description of the situation. In identifying the extent to which Montreal is under the sway of forces beyond the control of the community, this book may sound disheartening. I would argue the opposite, however: before anything effective can be done about a problem, the problem must be understood. In the past, public unawareness of the situation has constituted a virtual *carte blanche* for these forces.

Montrealers have been disenfranchized from their own city. It no longer belongs to them or even to people whom they know or can identify. It is a community shaped most by the anonymous, the absent and the unaccountable.

The Gazette (Len Sidaway)
Three thousand cyclists protest pollution and the privileged status given cars in centre-city.

Wave after wave of foreign investments have rolled into the city since the late 1950s. Through their sheer scale, these investments have tended to:

— Inflate the market price of much local real estate beyond the means of the local buyer.

— Concentrate decision-making over urban growth in the hands of people with few roots or commitments here, giving impetus to an impersonal kind of growth.

— Obtain additional financing from within Canadian financial institutions, thus siphoning off credit which might otherwise go to indigenous enterprises.

— Export a large part of the profits, thereby taking money out of circulation and using up Canadian foreign exchange credits.

— Widen the gap, through absentee ownership, in landlord-tenant relations.

— Encourage the construction of very large buildings — easier to supervise from afar and offering a better return on investment — rather than small projects.

— Dominate the building materials industry — particularly in glass, specialty steels and cement — with the effect of accelerating oligopoly and vertical integration, thus reducing the competitive fibre of Canadian industry.

— Spur energy-intensive development, not surprising considering that many of these investors are also investing in the energy or automobile industries.

A search for those who are responsible leads one through a complex skein of interrelationships between various spheres of influence. When one emerges on the other side it is a little like the voyage in *2001: A Space Odyssey* — at the end one finds oneself confronted with a very simple, elementary truth, stunning in its ordinariness. The power lies with those who dominate Montrealers only so long as Montrealers continue to let themselves be dominated.

It may be fashionable for French-Canadians to blame English-Canadians for their economic problems, and for English-Canadians to blame Europeans or Americans, and for Europeans and Americans to blame multinational corporations, and so on. But pointing the finger at outside scapegoats is not very useful. The problem is a matter of attitude, of self-image, of belief in oneself. One always hears *reasons* why local people

And the winners are...

236 Kirchstrasse, Schaan, Liechtenstein: **The most common place of registry for major apartment buildings in the Montreal area.**

Trizec Corp.: **The owner of the most large office buildings in the Montreal area.**

Genstar Ltd.: **The owner of the largest single piece of private property on the Island of Montreal (the Miron quarry, 180 hectares).**

Lafarge S.A.: **The owner of the largest single piece of property on the Island of Montreal owned by private enterprise (the Canada Cement Lafarge quarry on the East End, 192.4 hectares).**

Congregation of the Sisters of the Holy Name of Jesus and Mary: **The owner of the largest piece of property on the Island of Montreal owned by a religious institution (Cap. St. Jacques, 192.8 hectares).**

Her Majesty Queen Elizabeth II **(as municipal evaluation rolls often officially refer to the federal government of Canada): The owner of the largest single piece of property on the Island of Montreal owned by any level of government (Dorval Airport, 765 hectares) and the largest overall owner of land on the island.**

The Bronfmans: **The largest landowning family in the Montreal area and Canada as a whole (through its interests in various companies).**

Canadian Pacific Ltd.: **Owner of more land on the Island of Montreal and the rest of urban Canada than any other private enterprise (it estimates it controls 600 hectares of land on the island, of which 145 are considered 'developable' and the rest are being used for railroad functions).**

The Vatican: **The owner (indirectly, through the organizations which have allegiance to it and need its permission to dispose of the land) of the most private land on the Island of Montreal (upwards of 1,000 hectares).**

The Royal Bank of Canada: **The most influential bank in Montreal development.**

A. Janin Cie.: **The company doing the most construction in the Montreal area and Canada as a whole.**

The Agnellis: **The family behind companies receiving the most money in public contracts in Quebec.**

and, for a second bow, *Lafarge S.A.:* **The largest producer (by far) of Canada's Nº 1 construction material (by far), cement.**

cannot do local things — the climate is too harsh, there is not enough capital, this society is too "new." But foreigners somehow manage to brave the cold and use Canadian capital to do what Canadians themselves cannot do. "The powerful here," says Peter Newman of Canada as a whole, "have always lived with a colonial mentality which deems that *real* power (and real excellence, for that matter) lies somewhere else — over the water, below the border, among the imperial interest groups who must be viewed with awe, emulated with care, but on no account challenged lest they withdraw their dollars and their moxie."[1]

Who can blame outsiders for coming in? They have filled a vacuum of leadership, of investments, which someone had to fill. International capital goes where there is money to be made and where it is wanted. Foreign buyers of Canadian real estate have been welcomed here by the Montreal establishment — political, financial and legal — with all the enthusiasm of brothel owners when the fleet comes in.

It is against this background of absence of pride or abnegation of responsibility that the Parti Québécois has come to power in Quebec. If it does succeed in getting the economy into gear again — whether as part of Canada or not — Montreal would doubtless attract many of the same kind of investors it has attracted in the past. Because of the short-term benefits from this kind of investment — an initial injection of capital which stimulates business for construction companies, banks, trust companies, law firms, real estate companies, notaries and others with influence — it is to be expected that there would be much support for just such a return. There would also be substantial pressure from existing owners of real estate (whether they be foreign or domestic) for a return to the good old days — since in order to recoup their investments they must be able to find new buyers for their properties.

What to do?

Most laws will not work. Legislation cannot really undo the ways of international capital. Such capital will, when its managers put their minds to it, generally find ways to override or circumvent laws. The best example of this is the facility with which Trizec Corp. and Genstar Ltd. have succeeded in end-running the Foreign Investment Review Act.

Even if one could effectively ban foreign investments what good would it do? Foreign investments in this or any other field are not bad *a priori*. Canada needs outside investments, as does any country — even if it be a prosperous giant like the U.S. or the U.S.S.R. Such investments do, as their supporters in the Montreal building industry maintain, help keep the economic wheels spinning. These outside investments become of questionable value, however, when — as is the case in Montreal — a community grows as dependent on them as an alcoholic does on alcohol. In moderate amounts such investments are helpful, but here they have become a substitute for local initiative.

The initiative must come from the hearts of the people. It cannot be legislated. But though laws cannot create élan and self-assertion they can impede these. Such is the case with what passes for Canada's constitution, the British North America Act. Its existence nurtures this colonial mentality which is the root of the problem. That another government has effective veto power over changes in a culture's fundamental legal foundation, its constitution, perpetuates this sense of emasculation.

Other things can be done, too. To engender corporate accountability, existing disclosure laws for companies could be enforced and beefed up. Major companies like Janin for years have avoided disclosing their ownership to the provincial government — though failure to do so is punishable by loss of their charters. Even Canadian Pacific, one of the most influential forces in not just urban development but many other aspects of the economy, masks its ownership — legally — behind an impenetrable facade of nominee bank and trust company acounts. There are ways to encourage such companies to reveal more than they have up to now — for example, by the withholding of government contracts.

Pollution laws against chronic polluters — Miron, for one — could be strengthened. At present, the $500 fines simply represent a license for doing business. Environmental impact statements could also be required of major projects.

More urban planning by government can also help reduce energy-intensive sprawl, destruction of agricultural land, etc. But this is no panacea for the problems of metropolitan expansion, either. Local and provincial governments are indebted to the same international banks and money markets that nourish the developers and energy interests behind so much of this sprawl; and those who control such sources of capital can be expected to exercise their influence on government to protect their interests.

The executive vice president of Cadillac Fairview Corp., Joseph Berman, has recommended (as an individual, not on behalf of his company) that an "ombudsman director be appointed to serve on the board of all public corporations and their affiliates." With the help of a research staff, the ombudsman director would represent the public interest and "be directly responsible to assorted interest groups otherwise unrepresented at the board level." Berman also suggests that the ombudsman act as chairman at the annual general meeting.[2] Everything would depend on the spine and integrity of the person selected for the job, but on paper it sounds excellent. After all, the local community has an even greater right to be heard in decision-making than small shareholders.

The place for such an ombudsman is particularly needed on the boards of banks. By deciding where to put their loans, the banks determine what companies will rise and which will fall, which neighborhoods or areas will be developed and which will deteriorate. Despite this power, and partly because of it, bankers are exceedingly cautious about discussing with outsiders the ways in which they exercise control over money — which is, in fact, other people's money.

Insurance companies and pension funds, too, sit on enormous pools of capital — which really belong to the public. These could be invested with greater social responsibility within Canada. Informed representatives of the public interest could play a far bigger role in decision-making than they have heretofore. As things stand today, few workers have any idea of how their weekly contributions to their pensions are being invested — it could be invested in sprawl or outside the country and they would not be the wiser. Vast sums of investments have been leaving Canada for years, often to be placed south of the border. The capital exists here to do great things. What is lacking is the volition.

Power in shaping Montreal is held by people, whether foreign or domestic, who are faceless. B⌐ing unknown, they can exercise power without accountability. They are powerful largely by default, by the abnegation of power by the community itself. Their power is waiting there to be shared.

Footnotes — Chapter 16

1. Newman, Peter C., "The Canadian Establishment, Vol. 1" (Toronto: McClelland & Stewart Ltd., 1975), p. 386.
2. Toronto Globe & Mail, Apr. 27, 1976, "Greater disclosure by companies urged," by Graham Fraser.

Index

A

Abbey Glen Property Corp. Ltd.: 64, 88-93, 114, 119, 150, 192, 194, 197, 199, 206, 209, 356-357
Acmon Investments Ltd: 54-55
Afra Holdings Ltd: 74
African Eagle Life Assurance Society: 85
Agnellis (family): Chap. 8 (223-238), 281, 385
Agnelli, Giovanni (Gianni): 225, 231-233, 283
Agnelli, Umberto: 232
Air Liquide: 242, 255
Aitken, Max: 245
Albermarle, Earl of: 123
Alberta Gas Ethylene Co.: 362
Albrecht, T. (Mr & Mrs): 177
Algoma Steel Corp. Ltd.: 144-145, 352
Alguvic Properties Ltd: 177
Allard, Jean-Paul: 324, 332, 334
Allis-Chalmers Corp.: 230
Amok Ltd: 138
Amro Bank: 214
Anglo-American Corp of Canada Ltd (AMCAN): 85
Anglo-American Corp. of South Africa Ltd: 84-87, 90-91, 124, 143, 184, 273, 357, 361
Anglo-Nordic Shipping Ltd: 139
Anstalt: 38
Appleyard, James: 120
Aps Inc.: 354
Arbafin Anstalt: 34
Arbed: 184, 342, 353
Arbuckle, W.A.: 145
Arbuthnot Latham Holdings: 281
Archepiscopal Roman Catholic Corporation of Montreal: (See also: Vatican): 292-293, 295, 300
Argus Corp. Ltd: 181, 197
Aronovitch, S.: 81
Associated Portland Cement Manufacturers Ltd: 199, 246
Aster Corp.: 56, 324, 327-331, 361-362
Atlantic Container Line: 204
Atlantic Tug and Equipment Co.: 251
Atlas Steels: 142
Atlific Inns Inc.: 317

Atomic Energy of Canada Ltd (AECL): 52-53
Auclair, Audré: 26-27, 32
Avis Inc.: 317
Azrieli, David: 158, 160, 162-164, 171

B

BACM: 205
Banca Commerciale Italiana: 55
Banca Privata: 310
Banca di Roma: 310, 380
Banca della Svizzera Italiana: 49, 53
Bandeen, Robert: 350
Bank of America International: 142
Bank of England: 82, 113
Bank of Montreal: 144-145, 281, 319
Bank of Nova Scotia: 97-98, 149
Bankers Trust Co.: 306
Banque Belge pour l'Industrie: 180
Banque Bruxelles-Lambert: 180
Banque Canadienne Nationale: 259
Banque Louis-Dreyfus: 265
Banque Nationale de Paris: 60
Banque de Paris et des Pays-Bas: (See also: Paribas): 379
Banque Privée S.A.: 132
Banque Rothschild: 132
Bantam (editions): 225
de Bar, Charles: 198, 210-211
Barnet, Richard J.: 209
Bastogi: 310
Bateman, William: 249
Baudouin, King of Belgium: 198, 209-210
Beame, Abraham: 373
Beaverbrook, Lord: 245
Beaulieu, Paul: 126
Beck, Ernesto Fabio: 30-31
Beer, Mrs Dieter: 174
Bélanger, Jean-Pierre: 381
Belgonucléaire: 184, 365
Belli, Arcangelo: 310
Benguela Railway Co.: 212
Berger, E. Michael: 26-27, 33, 36
Berkeley Hambro Property Co. Ltd: 150-151
Berman, Joseph: 388

Berti, Leonide: 47-48
Bertino, Paolo: 55
Bertrand, R.J.: 249
Bethleen Steel Co.: 306
Bettini, Aldo: 45
Bissonnette, Albert: 47-48
Black, Conrad: 370-371
Blogg, Keith: 14
Bluhdorn, Charles: 309
Bontempi, Paolo: 45
de Bossieu, Michel: 254
Bottino, Vittorio Bonadè: 228
Bourassa, Robert: 375
Bourguignon, Jean-Charles: 49
Bovis Corp.: 92, 105, 107, 123-126, 151, 359-360
Bramalea Ltd: 74, 107, 116, 319, 336
Bramley Holdings Ltd: 237
Brazier, C.W.: 257
Briginvest Ltd: 55
Brimco Ltd: 86, 88, 131, 134-138, 140, 142-143, 151
British North America Act: 70, 387
British Petroleum Co. Ltd: 108, 126, 139-140, 360-361
Bronfmans (family): Chap. 10, also: 69, 113, 134, 330, 353, 385
Bronfman, Allan: 269
Bronfman, Charles: 268
Bronfman, Edgar: 268
Bronfman, Edward: 69
Bronfman, Ekiel and Minnie: 266, 268
Bronfman, Mitchell: 279
Bronfman, Peter: 69
Bronfman, Samuel: 268, 276, 278-279, 354
Bronfman, Samuel II: 279
Brown & Root: 293
Bureau of Competition Policy: 119, 246
Burke, Louis: 37, 40
Butler, Adam Courtauld: 89

C

Cachet, Robert: 254
Cadillac Fairview Corp. Ltd: 264, 276, 319, 330, 353-354, 388
Cadnam Holdings Ltd: 237
Cadogan, Earl of: 79
Caisse de Dépôts et de Placements du Québec: 171, 377

Campeau Corp.: 315, 361
Campeau, Robert: 361
Canada Cement Lafarge Ltd: 242-246
Canada Square Corp.: 350
Canadawide Parking Services Ltd: 315, 317, 358
Canadian Arena Co.: 270
Canadian Building (magazine): 109
Canadian Construction Association: 225, 251
Canadian Freehold Properties Ltd: 108
Canadian Homestead Oil Ltd: 353
Canadian Housing Design Council: 115
Canadian Hydrocarbons Ltd: 336-353
Canadian Imperial Bank of Commerce: 130, 143, 149, 259, 328
Canadian Industrial Gas & Oil Ltd: 356
Canadian Industries Ltd (CIL): 108
Canadian Institute of Public Real Estate Companies: 109
Canadian Liquid Air Ltd (see also: Air Liquide): 241-242, 255
Canadian Marconi Co.: 270
Canadian National (CN): 171, 348-350
Canadian Pacific Ltd: 23, 38, 55, 92, 131, 145-148, 153, 171, 188, 192, 204, 281, 348-349, 352, 367, 385, 387
Canadian Pacific (Bermuda) Ltd: 352
Canadian Pacific Hotels Ltd: 145
Canadian Pittsburgh Industries: 117, 119
Canadian Portland Cement Association: 244
Canadian Radio-Television Commission: 270-276
Canadian Real Estate Association: 163
The Canadiens (hockey team): 264
Candiac Development Corp.: 324, 332, 336, 342, 353
Candu (nuclear reactors) (see also: Nuclear power and: Uranium): 135, 142
Canest Group: 171
Capital and Counties Property Co. Ltd: 89-93, 357
Capitol Center: 316, 354
Caresta Services Ltd: 162-163
Carey, Hugh: 376
Carrière St-Maurice Inc.: 251
Cartier-Denault: 359
Casellini, Claudio: 31, 33
Cassano, Paolo: 234
Cast Transportation Ltd: 204
Catholic Times: 298-304
Catto, Fausto: 56

Cefis (family): 55
Cefis, Adolfo: 55
Cefis, Alberto: 55
Cefis, Eugenio: 55, 310
CEMP Investments Ltd: (see also: Bronf-
mans): 264-265, 268, 270, 281, 283, 330,
353
Central Mortgage and Housing Corp.:
115
CFCF-TV and CFCF-Radio: 270
Chargeurs Réunis S.A.: 253-254
Charters Consolidated Ltd: 85
Chase Manhattan Bank of New York:
213, 305
Chodos, Robert: 146-147
Chrysler Corp.: 360
Churchill Falls: 86, 135-136, 144, 151-152,
227
Ciaccia, John: 47
Ciment Lafarge S.A.: 242-255, 385
Ciment Indépendant Inc.: 245, 249
Cimenteries CBR Cement bedrijven: 184
Cinzano: 225
Citadel Cement Corp.: 249
La Cité (apartments complex): 313, 316,
319, 356
Citibank: 319, 378
City Concordia Properties Ltd: 319
City of London: 73, 76-77, 80, 106, 109-
110, 113, 123, 131, 148-149, 151
Clark, Frederick «Jock»: 112
Clark, Joe: 180, 182, 189-190
Clermont Motors (see also: General
Motors): 320
Clift, Dominique: 370
Clitheroe, Lord: 212
Club Méditerranée: 282-283
CMB (see Compagnie Maritime Belge)
Cobham, Viscount: 78-79
Cockerill: 184, 214, 365
Coetzer, W.B.: 92
Coleman, John H.: 360
Colville, David R.: 80, 88, 137
Combined Mortgage Corp.: 336
Commercial Union Assurance Co.: 76,
125
Commonwealth Holiday Inns of Canada:
317-318
Compagnie Bruxelles-Lambert: 132, 140,
145, 214
Compagnie Financière de Paris & des
Pays-Bas (see Paribas)
Compagnie Foncière de Manitoba (1967)

Ltée: 336
Compagnie Française de Pétrole: 358
Compagnie Maritime Belge (CMB): 184,
202-203, 207
Compagnie du Nord: 254
Concordia Estates Ltd: 317, 319
Concrete: 185, 206, 242-245. See also:
Ciment Lafarge S.A.; Ciment Indépen-
dant Inc.; Cimenteries CBR Cement;
Citadel Cement Corp.; Miron Ltée; Cana-
dian Portland Cement Association; Con-
solidated Concrete; St-Lawrence Cement;
Dundee Ciment Corp.; Ocean Cement Ltd.
Con-Force Products: 206
Conin Establishment: 34
Conservative Party (British): 76, 89
Consolidated Building Corp. Ltd: 107,
124, 360
Consolidated Concrete: 206
Consolidated Edison: 140
Consolidated Goldfields Ltd: 90
Corbiau, Paul-Emile: 184, 201, 214-215
Cordura Corp.: 356
Corporation des Soeurs de Ste-Croix: 297
Coseka Resources Ltd: 140
Cotton, Jack: 82, 151
Courtauld's Ltd: 89
Courtois, E.-Jacques: 88, 134, 270-275,
336
Crédit Foncier Franco-Canadien: 60,
199, 283, 309, 357-358, 379
Crédit Suisse: 36, 306
Creswell Pomeroy Ltd: 139
Creusot-Loire: 365
Crocker National Bank: 319
Curtis, Donald: 145

D

Damerau, Gernt: 161, 168
Danny, John: 78, 80
Daon Development Corp.: 319
Dart Containerline Co. Ltd: 202-204
Davidson, Roy: 244-245
Davis, William: 53
De Beers Consolidated Mines Ltd: 85
Deckelbaums (family): 25
Delorme, Jules (Canon): 293, 295
Delrose Development Corp.: 161
Denault (groupe): 123 See also: Cartier-
Denault

Denning, Victor: 163
Desalvo, Renato: 55
Desmarais, Paul: 134, 281
Desourdy (Enterprises): 223, 259
Deutsche Bank: 214
Diamant Boart: 184
Diamida A.G.: 332
Dominion Bridge Co. Ltd: 352, 367
Domtar Ltd: 197
Donald, John: 109
Dondena, Giovanni: 164
Dongof Anstalt: 36
Donolo Construction Ltd: 223, 259
Downie, Leonard Jr.: 338, 363
Drapeau, Mayor Jean: 223, 372, 377
Draper, John: 51
Drayton Group: 82
Drummen, Walter: 176
Duncan, Sir Val: 137
Dundee Cement Corp.: 251
Dunn, Sir James: 144
Dunn, Serena: 144
Duplessis, Maurice: 370-371
Dussault, Madeleine· 23, 27

E

Eagle Star Insurance Co. Ltd: Chap. 3,
(67-98), 107, 113, 124, 131, 134, 137
Eagle Star Insurance Co. of Canada Ltd:
75, 126, 336
Edper Investments Ltd: 69, 134, 265, 269-
270, 279. See also: Bronfmans (family)
Efford, Ian: 351
Electrorail: 336
Elican Development Co.: 336
Ellmenreich, Rico: 57
Emard, Mrs France: 25
Empain, baron Edouard-Jean: 180,
335-336, 340-342
Empain-Schneider (groupe): 334-336,
340-342, 352, 362, 365. See also: Schneider
S.A.
Engelstein, Alex: 315
Engineered Homes: 206
English Property: 63, 67-74, 83, 85-86,
89-90, 92, 97, 101, 112-113, 152
ENI: 55
Espresso (paper): 310
Establishment: 38, 281. See also: Agnellis
(family); Bronfmans (family); Sinclair

James; Spino, Mario; Rothschild (family)
*Europrogramme Management Consul-
tants of Canada Ltd:* 59
Expos (baseball team): 268-269
Exxon Oil: 139

F

Fabre, Francis: 254, 281, 283
«Fabrique»: see Parishes
Fabrique Notre-Dame: 297
Facci, Hugo: 308
Fairview Corp. of Canada Ltd: 276
See also: *Cadillac-Fairview*
Famous Players Ltd: 354
Fauconval, baron de: 180-181
Fellmeth, Robert C.: 14
Ferrari: 223. See also: Agnellis
Feru Investments Ltd: 23
Fiat S.p.A.: 223, 225, 228, 230, 232-234,
236. See also: Agnellis
Fiat-Allis: 230. See also: *Allis-Chalmers*
Fidinam Group: 43, 49-53, 161
Fiducan Trust: 22
Field, Kenneth: 74
Finabank: 352
Financial Post: 124
First Boston Corp.: 374
First National Bank of Chicago: 319
First National Bank of New York: 306
First Quebec Corporation: 60
Five Arrows: 132, 139, 142, 145, 153
Flintkote Co.: 249
Float Glass: 117
Floreal Corp.: 56
Flying Diamond Oil Corp.: 355
Flynn, Sen. Jacques: 251
Fobin, Joan: 55
Forbes (magazine): 84, 91, 137, 139
Foreign Investment Review Act: 70, 74,
92, 184, 196, 320, 387
Foreign Investment Review Agency: 23-24,
45, 50, 126, 164, 199, 249
Fortune, magazine: 84, 184
Forum: 269. See also: Canadian Arena
Foundation Co. of Canada: 251-252
Framatome: 335, 365
Francana Oil and Gas Ltd: 85, 140, 357
Francheschini, Léonard: 329, 361
Franck, August: 198-199, 207-208
Francon: 247, 329, 361

Frese, Bernard Guenther: 174
Fromming, Mrs Joannes: 174

G

G&W Realty Corp.: 355
Galeries d'Anjou: 354
Galvin, Edward: 356
Gardner Mountain: 77
Gasse-Finanz Anstalt: 55
Gautrin, Henri-François: 255-261
Gaz Métropolitain: 356
Gazette (the): 256, 261, 291, 293-304, 368, 381-382
Gazocéan: 281
Gélinas, Sen. L.-P.: 251
General Atomic Co.: 365
General Electric: 306
General Mining and Finance Corp. Ltd: 91-93
General Motors: 139, 305, 320, 362
Générale (La): see Société Générale de Belgique
Générale Occidentale-Cavenham: 214
Geneva Investment Establishment: 34
Genstar Ltd: 93, 114, 189, 192-211, 226, 243-247, 284, 320, 342, 359, 362, 385, 387
Gerstner, Harold: 175
Gillies, James: 53
Glaverbel-Mécaniver: 184
Glorieux, J.: 180
Goblet, Marcel: 214
Goldberger, Paul: 116
Goldbloom, Victor: 337
Goldsmith, Sir James: 214
Gort, Mrs Julein: 177
Goston, Don: 309
Gotthard Realty Investments Québec Inc.: 58
Gotthard Secondo S.A.: 59
Gougeon, Brother Pierre-Paul: 295
Grands Travaux de Marseille: 253-254, 257-258
Gray Nuns: 31, 290-291, 297
Greater York Group: 171, 319
Green, Aaron: 316, 331
Greichgaver, Wolfgang: 174
Grieg, I.T.: 368
Gross, Horst Dieter: 176
Grovewood Securities Ltd: 80
Groueff, Stéphane: 217, 221

Guardian Royal Exchange Assurance Ltd: 125, 151
Gulf Oil Corp.: 52, 192, 306, 315, 337, 363-365, 367-368
Gulf & Western Industries Inc.: 309, 316, 354, 366
Gunther, Gottfried: 175
de Gunzberg, baron Alain: 265, 281, 283
de Gunzberg, baronne Minda: 281
Gutstein, Donald: 14, 16, 65, 205, 207

H

de Habsbourg, archiduc Charles: see de Bar, Charles
von Haeften, Jan: 166
Hahto, Eric: 32
Hambro (family): 149-154, 306, 309, 320, 362-363
Hambro Canada Ltd: 107, 150, 363
Hambro, Charles E.A.: 151
Hambro, Jocelyn Olaf: 150, 152, 310
Hambro, R. Nicholas: 363
Hambros Ltd: 146, 167
Hambros Bank: 132, 151
Hammerson Property: 107, 111
Hamoir (family): 209
Hansa Financial & Corporate Management Inc.: 161
Habsbourg, Charles de: See de Bar, Charles
Harvie-Watt, Sir George: 90
Heitman Group Co.: 356
Hétu, Jean: 188
Hill Samuel Bank: 80, 82, 90, 132
Hilti A.G.: 29
Hilti, Josef: 24, 28-30, 36, 38-39, 53, 86, 385
Hilton Hotels: 370
Hiroshima: 220, 366
Holderbank Financière Glaris A.G.: 244, 247, 249, 251
Holiday Inns Inc.: 317
Holywart, Gerhard-Ludwig: 177
Hoolie S.A.: 55
Horne, Paul: 307
Housing and Urban Development Association: 107
Huband, Rolf: 107
Hudson Bay Co.: 107, 355-356

Hudson Bay Mining and Smelting Ltd: 85-86, 131, 140, 143
Hudson, Matthew: 60, 171-173
Huntington, Ron: 189
Hyatt International: 308, 380
Hydroelectric Power: 135-137. See also: Hydro-Québec; James Bay.
Hydro-Québec: 135, 374-375. See also: James Bay

Janin, Alban: 257, 385
A. Janin Cie Ltée: 136, 251-259
Jeunont-Schneider: 335
Jiskoot, Allard: 132, 145
Jones, Father Barry A.: 299-305
de Jonghe (family): 209
Joseph Elie Ltée: 202

I

IBM: 300
IFI (Istituto Finanziario Industriale S.p.A.): 234, 237. See also: Vatican
Imetal: 143, 214
Impala Platinum Ltd: 90, 357, 368
Imperial Chemical Industries (ICI): 108
Imperial Oil Ltd: 139, 241, 362. See also: Exxon Oil
Impregilo S.p.A.: 227-228, 234, 237
Impregilo & Spino Ltd: 227, 231, 237. See also: Spino Construction
Impresit: 228, 237, 253-254
Inchcape, Earl of: 123-125, 151, 360
Inchcape & Co. Ltd: 124, 360
Indal Ltd: 142
Index Holdings & Management Ltd: 255
Inland Cement Industries: 189, 206
«Institutions»: 108-111
Insurance Industry: 76-77, 108-111, 124-125
Intercontinental General Trading Co.: 52-53
Interlocking directorate: 97
Investissements Montfin Ltée: 55
Isis, Herman: 316
Istituto Farmacologico Serono: 306-307
Istituto Finanziario Industriale: See IFI
Italimpianti: 52
ITT: 182, 315-317, 331, 358
IWF Canada Corp.: 170

J

James Bay: 124, 226-227, 230, 234, 247, 335, 367, 375
James Walker Hardware (1955) Ltd: 263-

K

Kaufman & Broad Inc.: 308, 315-317, 361
Kaussen, Guenther: 158, 162, 175-177
Keith, Sir Kenneth: 80-82
Kelly, Brian: 350
Kertz, Friedrich-Wilheim: 177
Kirchstrasse 236 (Liechtenstein): 21-22, 24-25, 27, 29-32, 34, 38
Kirwin-Taylor, Peter: 96
Kowaluk, Lucia: 320

L

Lafarge: See Ciment Lafarge S.A. and Canada Cement Lafarge Ltd
Lafleur, Claude: 60
Lake Ontario Cement Ltd: 249
Lalonde, Jacques et Fernand: 317
Lambert, Allen: 373
Lambert, baron Léon: 132, 140, 145, 180, 184
Lambert, Phyllis (Bronfman): 275-278
Langensiepen, Mrs Heinrich: 176
Langer, Mrs Ferdinand: 177
Langevin, Jacques: 191
Lapointe, Louis-A.: 190, 199
Laprairie Shopping Center Ltd: 316
Layher, Mrs Ulrich: 174
Lazard Frères: 254
Leacock, Stephen: 277
Lebeuf, Gérard: 35-36
Lecerf, Olivier: 250
Lehndorff Group: 165, 320, 360
Von Lehndorff, Nona: 166
Les Associés Sierra Ltée: 171
Les Mir Construction: 247
Lévesque, René: 375-376
Levitt Canada Ltd: 317, 331, 358
Liberals: 17, 46
Liechtensteinische Landesbank: 24, 29
Linlithgow, Maquess of: 79

Lippens (family): 209
Llewellyn, David: 68-71
Lloyd's: 76-77
Lloyd, Edward: 77
Louis-Napoléon (Prince): 198
Luft, Achim and Charlotte: 160, 164
Lumon Consultants Canadian Construction Ltd: 57

M

Mac Namara, Harold S.: 124
Mac Naughton, Angus: 114, 193-197, 199, 209-210
Madsen, Jurgen: 174
Magna International Inc.: 362
Magnum Fund Ltd: 137
Maltais, Pierre: 244
Manchester, William: 335
Manhattan Project: 217-218
Marathon Realty Ltd: 146, 352
Marcil Mortgage Corp.: 109
Marier, Jean: 187
Markborough Properties Ltd: 107, 356
Marler, Dennis: 90
Marois, Pierre: 372
Marsh, Laurie: 71, 83-84
Marshall, Alexander: 123, 125
Martineau, Jean: 146
Martschitz, Kurt: 39-41
Mary Queen of the World (Basilica): 300
Mashaal (brothers): 111
Massey-Ferguson Ltd: 197
Matukas, Louis: 165-166
Maute, Gerhard: 175
Mc Allister Towing & Salvage Ltd: 205
Mc Cutcheon, John: 276, 278
S.B. McLaughlin Associates Ltd: 265
McLaughlin, W. Earle: 197, 242, 336, 362
McNamara, Harold S.: 124
McNamara Corp.: 124, 360
McNeil, Fred: 281
Mehnart, Volker: 160, 162
MEPC Ltd: 74, 107, 110, 118-120, 131, 151, 320
Métallurgie-Hoboken Overpelt: 184
Metrinvest Development: 55
Metropolitan Life Insurance Co.: 319, 375
Metropolitan Structures Inc.: 315
Metternich (family): 168
Meyer, John: 68

Midland Bank: 82, 90
Milanowski, Gisbert: 176
Mirabel International Airport: 226, 247
Miron (brothers): 185
Miron Co. Ltd: 185, 187-192, 205,206, 226, 229, 243, 359, 378, 387
Mobutu, Joseph: 201
Mocatta & Goldsmid Ltd: 149
Moeller-Soenke, Johann: 174
Mokta Group: 138, 143, 151, 367
Monarch Investments Ltd: 107, 111, 150
Moncus & Co.: 336
Monsadel Inc.: 331
Montedison: 55, 310
Montreal Dept. of Public Works: 190
Montreal Home Builders Association: 333
Montreal Life Assurance Co.: 125
Montreal subway system: 190, 230, 247, 335, 349, 378
Montreal Urban Community (MUC): 187-190, 228, 296, 378
Moog, Gerhard: 350
Moore, Henry: 82
Moores, Frank: 135
Morgan Bank: 306
Morgan Guaranty Trust: 319
Morgan Trust: 332, 336
Morton, Frederic: 134
Mostert, Noel: 121
Mount Royal Paving and Supplies Ltd: 247
Mountain (family): 73, 75, 78, 95-98
Mountain, Sir Brian: 71-75, 77, 80, 83, 85, 89, 96-97
Mountain, Denis: 68, 77, 96
Mountain, George: 95
Mountain, Jacob: 95
Mountain, Nicholas: 80, 96
Mountain Place Ltd: 164, 166, 380
Mountain, Rex: 77
Mueller, Dr Kurt: 176
Mulhall, Ken S.C.: 202, 221
Müller, Ronald E.: 209
Multiple Access Ltd: 270-278
Multiple Real Estate Ltd: 51
Murray, Guy: 261

N

Nadeau, P.-A.: 207
Namur Equipements Ltée: 251

Nerenberg, Norman: 317
New Jersey Zinc Co.: 354
Newman, Peter C.: 16, 386
Niagara Realty of Canada Ltd: 265
Nichols, Colonel: 218-219
Nokin, Max: 198, 342
Nootka Investments Ltd: 255, 257
Norcen Gas Ltd: 356
Norwich Union: 90
Nuclear Power: 135, 137-139, 142, 217-238, 335, 365-367. See also: Atomic Energy of Canada Ltd; Belgonucléaire; Candu; Framatome; General Atomic Co.; Gulf Oil; Hiroshima; Manhattan Project; Oppenheimer, Harry; Société Générale de Belgique; Uranium; James Bay; Union Minière
Nutrite: 206

O

Obront, Willie: 279
Ocean Construction Supplies Ltd: 206, 246
Ocean Cement Ltd: 189
Oceanis Investments Establishment: 25
Odeon (cinemas, theatres): 74
Office of Energy Conservation: 350-351
Ogilvy, Angus: 118, 151
Oil Industry: 139-140, 355-356
Olympia & York Development Ltd: 319-320
Olympic facilities: 226, 247, 251, 377-379
Ombudsman: 388
295514 Ontario Ltd: 337
Ontario Trust: 150
Oppenheimer (family): 140
Oppenheimer, Sir Ernest: 86
Oppenheimer, Harry: 87, 91, 143
Osservatore Romano: 299
Oxford Development Group Ltd: 319

P

Pace, Eric: 358
Pallenberg, Corrado: 306-307, 309
Pan Arctic Oils Ltd: 352
Pan Canadian Petroleum Ltd: 352
Panorama (magazine): 48

Paramer S.A.: 336
Paribas: 282-283, 309, 357, 379
Parishes: 297, 300-301
Parizeau, Jacques: 370, 379
Parti Québécois: 22, 44, 59, 120, 370
Paul VI (pope): 307
Pavitt, Edward: 91
Pax Construction Inc.: 251
Peel-Elder Development Ltd: 150
Penarroya (and Penarroya Canada Ltd): 143, 151
Peninsular & Oriental Steam Navigation Co. (P&O): 120-126, 360
Pères Capucins du Québec: 297
Petites Soeurs des Pauvres: 297
Petrofina S.A. (and Petrofina Canada Ltd): 131, 140, 145, 184, 188, 202, 207, 214, 359
Phillips, Ivan E.: 336
Phillips, Lazarus: 258, 330-331
Phillips, Neil: 336
Phillips & Vineberg: 270, 330, 336
Pierce, Robert L.: 362
Pierson, Heldring & Pierson: 132, 145, 153, 214
Pilkington, Sir Alastair: 117, 119, 126, 361
Pilkington Brothers Ltd: 117, 119, 184, 244
Pindar, A.-G.: 34, 331
Pirk, Josef: 174
Place du Canada: 252, 352
Place Portobello: 331
Place Victoria-St.Jacques Co. Ltd: 308
Place Ville-Marie: 64-65, 72-73, 82-83, 94, 98, 193, 202, 252
Placements Camillus Inc.: 47-48
PLM Hotels: 141
Plozig, Franz-Herbert: 176
«Pluvius»: 74, 78
Polaris Realty (Western) Ltd: 166
Port-Royal (apartments): 307-308, 380
Post Office Staff Superannuation Fund: 102, 106, 109, 112-113, 120, 316
Power Corp. of Canada Ltd: 181, 281, 361
Prager, Fritz: 176
PRB: 207
Progressive Conservative Party: 53-54, 75. See also: Clark, Joe and Sinclair, James
Promirad Inc.: 22, 61
Prudential Life Insurance Co. of America: 319

Q

QAN Investments Ltd: 164
Quarries: 185-188, 191, 228, 243. See also: Concrete
Quebec Real Estate Association: 51
Quebec Rent Control Board: 23, 25, 36, 50
Quebec Urban Community: 378

R

Racehorse Owners Association: 96
Ranger Oil: 269, 354
Rank City Wall: 74, 107
Rank Organization: 74, 107
Redi-Mix: 206
Refco-Montreal Inc.: 308
Regional Asphalt Ltd: 251
Religieuses Hospitalières de St-Joseph: 297
Relly, Gavin W.H.: 85
Reston (Virginia, U.S.A.): 338, 363-364
Richard Costain (Canada) Ltd: 107
Richards Group: 355
Rickli, Georges: 163
Riel, Maurice: 47
Riel, Vermette, Ryan, Dunton & Ciaccia: 47
Rio Algom Ltd: 131, 138, 142, 145, 190, 367
Rio Tinto-Zinc Corp. Ltd (RTZ): 86, 88, 124, 136-139, 142-143, 213-214, 361
Rixner, Peter: 175-176
Robiliart, Herman: 182
Rockefeller (family): 213, 235, 375-376
Rockview Corp.: 336
Rolando, Cesare: 254
Roman Catholic Church: See Vatican
Rosen, Herschel: 161
Rothschild (family): Chap. 5 (129-155), 63, 80, 85-86, 91, 110, 180, 190, 213-214, 216, 235, 254, 306
de Rothschild, Anthony: 86
de Rothschild, Edmond: 132, 145, 282-283
de Rothschild, Edmund: 71, 129
de Rothschild, Elie: 141
de Rothschild, Evelyn: 80,81
de Rothschild, Guy: 132-133, 137-138, 143, 254
Rothschild, Jacob: 120, 144, 153
de Rothschild, baron James: 216
de Rothschild, Leopold: 80
Rothschild, Mayor Amschel: 132, 150
Rothschild, Nathan M.: 145, 150
Rothschild International Bank: 80
N.M. Rothschild & Sons Ltd: 71, 80, 83, 86, 88, 90, 113, 120, 130-132, 135, 137, 144, 148-149, 152-153
Rouse Co.: 316
Rowan, Carl: 182
Royal Bank: 24, 98, 197, 202, 209, 259, 328, 336, 362, 372, 385
Royal Commission on Corporate Concentration: 147, 205, 207
Royal Dutch/Shell: 131, 139-140
Royal Insurance Co.: 76
Royal Mint Refinery: 131
RTZ: See Rio Tinto-Zinc Corp.
Rudner's: 164
Rusca, Fausto: 51-52, 161
RWI Holdings Ltd: 166, 175, 379

S

Sack, Joan Abbey: 334, 339
St. Joseph Oratory: 297
St. Lawrence Cement Co.: 244-245, 247, 249, 379
Salbaing, Pierre A.: 255
Sampson, Anthony: 27-28, 109, 232
Samuel Montagu & Co.: 90, 113, 132, 149
Santarelli, Mario: 329
Saskin, Ben: 161
Save Montreal: 32, 278, 320
Scanti Investments Ltd: 160
Scarteen Management Corp. Ltd: 34
Schaan (Liechtenstein): 21, 23, 25, 29, 36-37
Scheibler, Elisa: 48
Schiele, Irmgarde: 176
Schmidheiny (family): 251
Schneider, Adolph and Eugène: 334
Schneider S.A.: 334, 336, 342
Schniewind, Volkmar: 175
Schöller, André: 210
Schreyer, H.: 174
Van de Schueren, Jacques: 190
Seagram Building (New York): 277
Seagram Co. Ltd: 264, 268, 353
Seaspan International Ltd: 205-206
Second Covent Garden Property Co. Ltd: 83

Seltzer Organization: 316, 331
Sengier, Sir Edgar: 218-219, 221
Servoparc Inc.: 292, 295
Sgherri, Umberto: 57
Shackleton, Lord: 138
Shelbourne, Philip: 68, 112-113, 149, 151
Shell Canada Ltd: 139, 306. See also:
Royal Dutch
Shercon Plaza: 321
Sherdell, Samuel P.: 315
Shield Factors Ltd: 80
Shoner, Edmund: 176
Sidmar: 184
Siebens Oil & Gas Ltd: 355, 360
Simkin, Saul: 199
Simon, Robert: 338
Sindona, Michele: 150, 309-311
Sinclair, Ian D.: 145, 147, 281
Sinclair, James: 246
Sinclair, Margaret: 246
Sintlon Bank (Banca del Sempione): 328-329
Sisters of the Holy Names of Jesus and
Mary: 295-298, 385
Slough Estates (Canada) Ltd: 107, 120
Smallwood, Joey: 135, 235
Smith, Clair D.: 114
Società Generale Immobiliàre: 54, 150,
305-309, 380
Société de Banque Suisse: 36
Société Générale de Banque: 180-181, 190
Société Générale de Belgique: Chap. 7
(180-222), 342, 350, 365, 378
Société Générale (France): 60
Société des Grands Travaux de Marseille
(GTM): See Grands Travaux de Marseille
Société Internationale de Finance: 331
Société de Traction et d'Électricité: 190,
365
Soden, James: 68
Soeurs de la Congrégation Notre-Dame:
298
Soeurs Franciscaines: 297
Soeurs de la Providence: 298
Soeurs de Ste-Anne: 297
Soginvest Banca S.A.: 31-33
Solvays (family): 209-210
Soquem: 201
South African Eagle Insurance Co.: 85
Sparmont Corp.: 332, 334, 336
Spie-Batignolles: 335
Spino Construction Co. Ltée: 228-231,
254, 385

Spino, Mario: 231-233, 237
Spino, Pascal: 237
Standard Life Assurance Ltd of Edin-
burgh: 90, 110-111
Star (Great Britain) Holdings Ltd: 83. See
also: English Property Corp. Ltd.
Steger, Gregor: 39-40
Steinberg's Ltd: 331, 336
Stevens, Sinclair: 75
Stikeman, Elliott, Tamaki, Mercier &
Robb: 47
Stock Exchange Tower: 54, 252, 305, 308,
310, 380
Stough, Charles: 111
Strauss, Franz-Josef: 168-169
Strauss, Mrs Franz Josef: 168, 175
Stronach, Frank: 362
Strong, Sir Kenneth: 81
Sulpician Fathers: 294, 297
Sun Alliance & London Insurance Group:
145
Swiss Bank Corp.: 36, 251
Swiss Credit Bank: 36, 251, 379
Sylvite: 143
Szaz, John: 331

T

Tana, Roberto: 310
Tanganyika Concessions: 211-214
Taylor Woodrow Holdings Ltd: 150
Tempglass Ltd: 142
Les Terrasses: 265, 316-317
Tétrault, Jean-Louis: 48
Tettamanti, Tettamanti, Tito: 52-53
Texas Pacific Oil Co.: 353
Thierry, Jacques: 180
Thompson, Sir Richard Hilton Marler:
89
Von Thurn und Taxis, Johannes: 167
Tidal power: 140-141
Tipmobil Anstalt: 23, 36
Tittley, John: 245
Tomlinson, Alexander C.: 374
Tories: 53, 189. See also: Progressive
Conservative Party and Clark, Joe
Toronto-Dominion Bank: 98, 114-115,
142, 197, 209, 373
Total Petroleum (North America) Ltd:
358
Tozzi, Gian Carlo: 25

Trading Fund Establishment: 25-26, 28, 31, 33
Trans Canada Pipeline: 360
Trend Explorations Ltd: 140, 357
Trizec Corp.: Chap. 3 (63-98), 101, 110-113, 119, 134, 190, 196, 199, 265, 320, 330, 354, 360-361, 367, 370, 385, 387
Trudeau, Pierre E.: 47, 138, 246
Truroc Supplies: 206
Tschombé, Moïse: 182
Turner, Sir Mark: 137-138, 142
Turner, Ross: 193-196, 199, 210
Turnkey Development Engineering & Contract Management Ltd: 251
Tuxana A.G.: 34
TWA: 306

U

UIC (Italy): 48
Union Corp.: 90-93, 150, 310, 357, 367
Union Bank: 251, 379
Union de Remorquage et de Sauvetage: 207
Union Minière: 182, 184, 201-202, 212-214, 218-219
Union des Transports Aériens: 253-254
United Dominions Trust Ltd: 74
United North American Holdings Ltd: 334, 336
United Racecourses Ltd: 80
Unsworth, A. James: 199
Upson, Sally: 68
Uranium: 137-139, 217-218, 335, 365-367, See also: Nuclear power
Usinages Industriels Ltée: 251

V

Vachon, Bernard: 332, 339
Vadeboncoeur, André: 56, 327-330
Vaduz (Liechtenstein): 24, 37, 39
Vagnozzi, Egidio (Cardinal): 307
Valorinvest (Canada) Ltd: 31-32, 36, 49
Valver Real Estate Inc.: 163
Van Horne (mansion): 156-159
Vancouver Shipyards Co. Ltd: 205
Vatican: 54, 150, Chap. 11, 385

Venicana Investments Ltd: 47
S.A. des Verreries de Mariemont: 214
Vertical integration: 191, 249
Viebig, Alfred: 175
Vieille-Montagne: 184
Vineberg, Philip: 270-276
Virgint, Ernest: 132
VK Estates Ltd: 316
Volberg, Rolf-Dieter: 177

W

Wankie Colliery: 213
Warburg Bank: 132
Webb & Knapp (Canada) Ltd: 82
Websters (family): 319
Wechsburg, Joseph: 134, 151
Weiss, Hortense: 176
Wells Fargo: 319
Von Wersebe, Karsten: 166
Westdeutsche Landesbank Girozentrale: 379
Western Decalta Petroleum Ltd: 85, 140
White Pass & Yukon Corp.: 363
Whitehorse Copper Mines Ltd: 85
Wimpey Homes Ltd: 107, 116
Wolfe, Jeanne: 324, 338-339

Y

York Establishment: 34
YUL Associates: 316, 319, 356

Z

Zeckendorf, William, Jr.: 82
Zeckendorf, William, Sr.: 72, 82-83, 98, 316-318
Zentner, Max: 161, 362
Zilch, Ingeborg: 332
Zunenshine (family): 362